尾田栄一郎

Hello and thank you for taking our bus tour. We're heading toward the 100th chapter of *One Piece*. On your right, you can see the thumbs held up high. There's plenty more action and adventure ahead!

-Eiichiro Oda, 1999

Eiichiro Oda began his manga career at the age of 17, when his one-shot cowboy manga **Wanted!** won second place in the coveted Tezuka manga awards. Oda went on to work as an assistant to some of the biggest manga artists in the industry, including Nobuhiro Watsuki, before winning the Hop Step Award for new artists. His pirate adventure **One Piece**, which debuted in **Weekly Shonen Jump** in 1997, quickly became one of the most popular manga in Japan.

ONE PIECE VOL. 11
EAST BLUE PART 11

SHONEN JUMP Manga Edition

This graphic novel contains material that was originally
published in English in **SHONEN JUMP** #39–41.

STORY AND ART BY EIICHIRO ODA

English Adaptation/Lance Caselman
Translation/JN Productions & Michie Yamakawa
Touch-up Art & Lettering/Mark McMurray, Vanessa Satone
Additional Touch-up/Josh Simpson
Design/Sean Lee
Editor/Yuki Takagaki

ONE PIECE © 1997 by Eiichiro Oda. All rights reserved.
First published in Japan in 1997 by SHUEISHA Inc., Tokyo.
English translation rights arranged by SHUEISHA Inc.

The stories, characters and incidents mentioned in this
publication are entirely fictional.

No portion of this book may be reproduced or transmitted in
any form or by any means without written permission from
the copyright holders.

Printed in the U.S.A.

Published by VIZ Media, LLC
P.O. Box 77010
San Francisco, CA 94107

20
First printing, July 2006
Twentieth printing, November 2023

viz.com

PARENTAL ADVISORY
ONE PIECE is rated T for Teen and is recommended
for ages 13 and up. This volume contains fantasy
violence and tobacco usage.

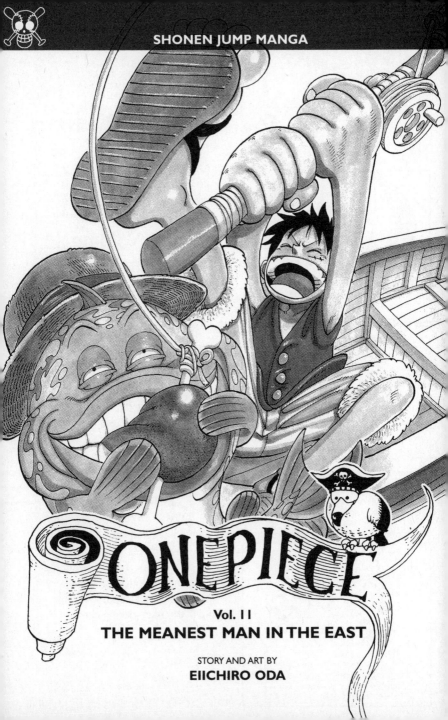

ONEPIECE

Vol. 11
THE MEANEST MAN IN THE EAST

STORY AND ART BY
EIICHIRO ODA

Arlong

Nami
A thief who once specialized in robbing pirates. Although she hates pirates, Luffy convinced her to be his navigator.

Monkey D. Luffy
Boundlessly optimistic and able to stretch like rubber, he is determined to become King of the Pirates.

Usopp
His penchant for tall tales is matched by his accuracy with a slingshot. His father, Yasopp, is a member of "Red-Haired" Shanks's crew.

THE STORY OF ONE PIECE

Volume 11

Monkey D. Luffy started out as just a kid with a dream—and that dream was to become the greatest pirate in history! Stirred by the tales of pirate "Red-Haired" Shanks, Luffy vowed to become a pirate himself. That was before the enchanted Devil Fruit gave Luffy the power to stretch like rubber, at the cost of being unable to swim—a serious handicap for an aspiring sea dog. Undeterred, Luffy set out to sea and recruited some crewmates: master swordsman Zolo, treasure-hunting thief Nami, lying sharpshooter Usopp, and Sanji, the high-kicking chef.

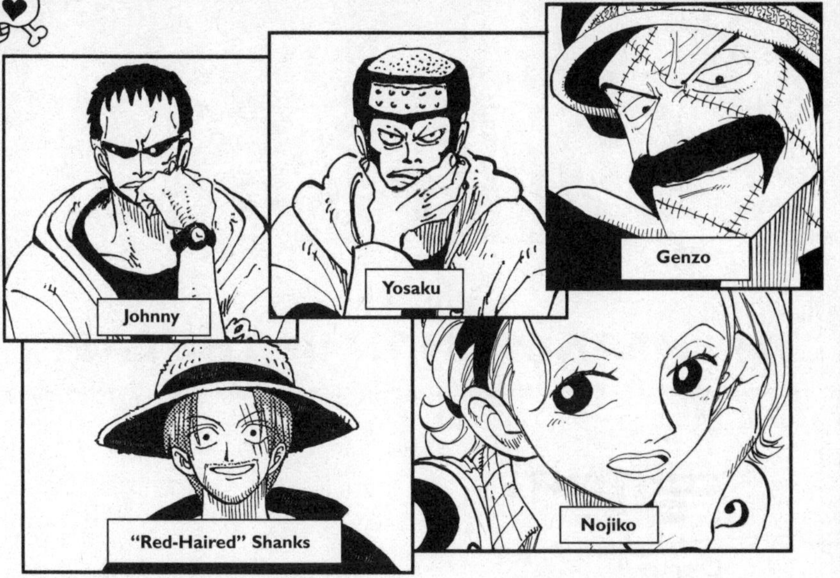
Genzo
Yosaku
Johnny
Nojiko
"Red-Haired" Shanks

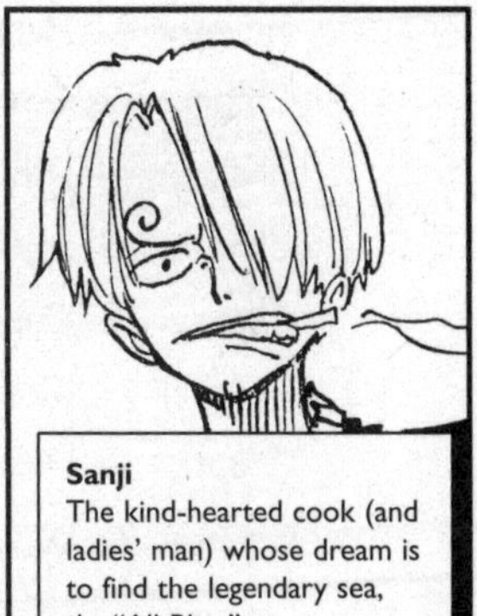

Sanji
The kind-hearted cook (and ladies' man) whose dream is to find the legendary sea, the "All Blue."

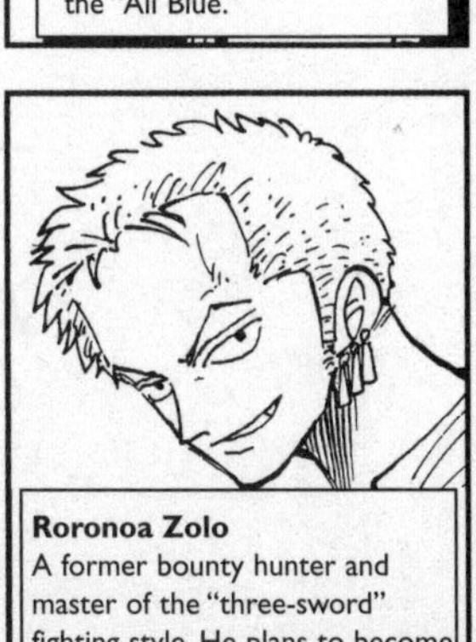

Roronoa Zolo
A former bounty hunter and master of the "three-sword" fighting style. He plans to become the world's greatest swordsman!

Searching for Nami, Luffy and his crew head to Arlong Park, stronghold of the ferocious Fish-Man Pirates, only to discover that Nami herself is one of them! They learn the story of Belle Mère and the origin of Nami's hatred of pirates from Nami's stepsister, Nojiko, who also explains how Nami swallowed her hatred and went to work for Arlong, gathering loot to buy her village's freedom.

Moved by Nami's secret suffering, Luffy goes toe to toe with Arlong, but is hurled into the ocean! Sanji and the others fight and defeat Arlong's men and rescue Luffy. But they still have to contend with the most terrible foe of all—Arlong himself!

Vol. 11
THE MEANEST MAN IN THE EAST

CONTENTS

Chapter 91: DARTS

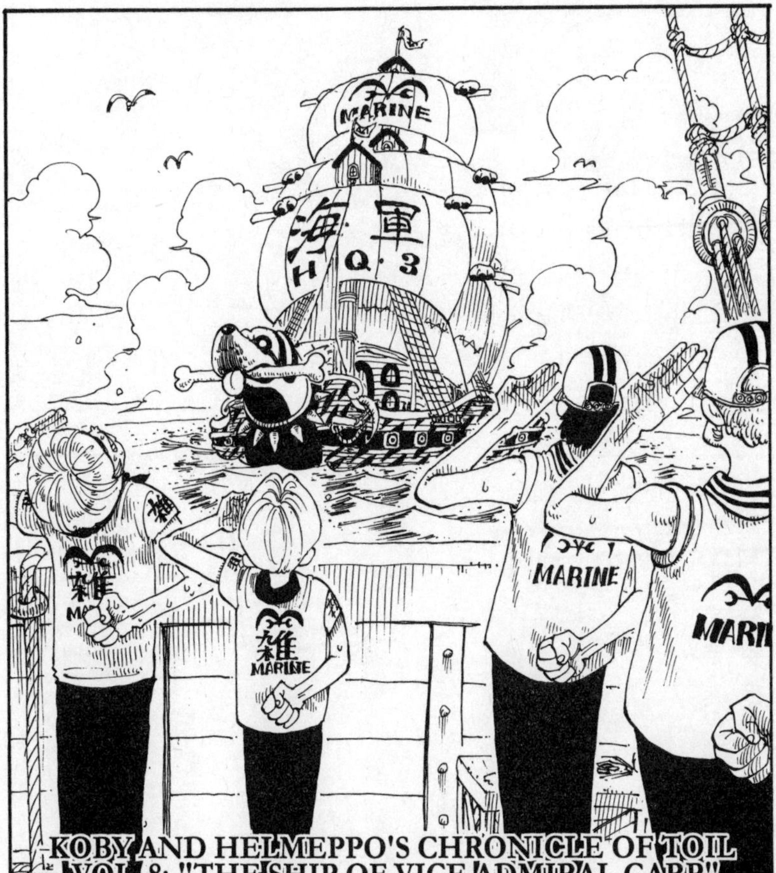
MARINE
海軍
H Q 3
MARINE
MARINE
MARINE
MARI
KOBY AND HELMEPPO'S CHRONICLE OF TOIL
VOL. 8: "THE SHIP OF VICE-ADMIRAL GARP"

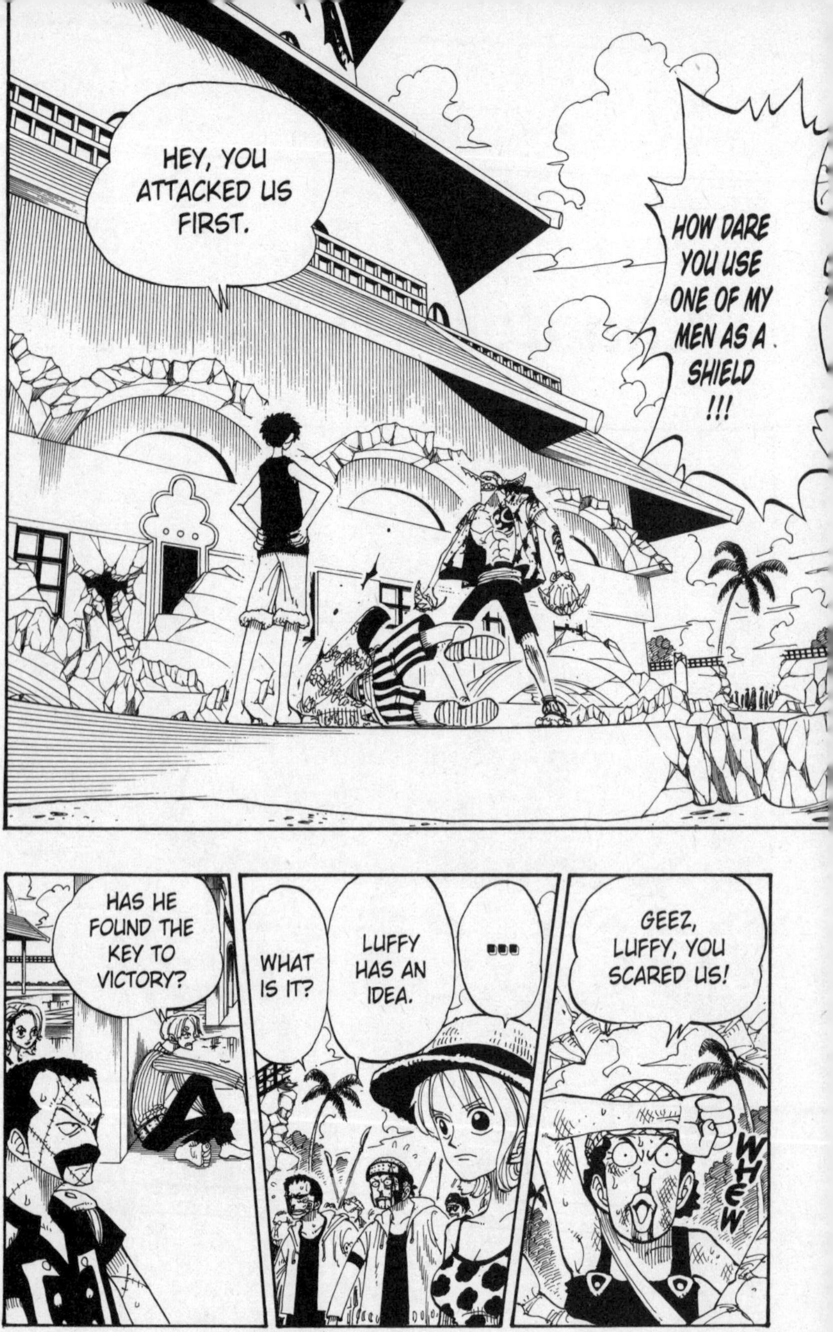
HOW DARE YOU USE ONE OF MY MEN AS A SHIELD !!!
HEY, YOU ATTACKED US FIRST.
GEEZ, LUFFY, YOU SCARED US!
WHEW
...
LUFFY HAS AN IDEA.
WHAT IS IT?
HAS HE FOUND THE KEY TO VICTORY?

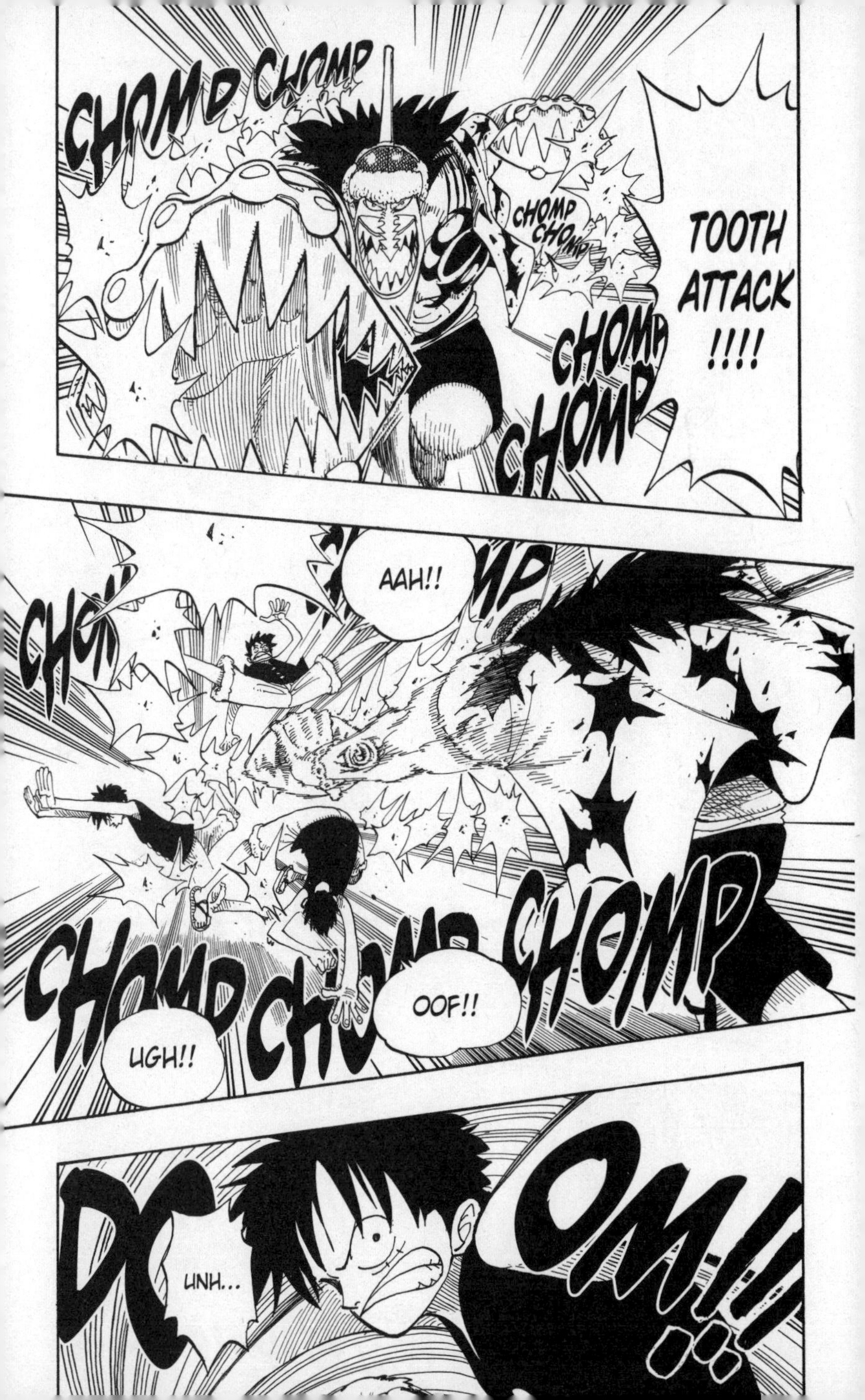

TOOTH ATTACK!!!!
CHOMP CHOMP
CHOMP CHOMP
CHOMP CHOMP
AAH!!
OOF!!
UGH!!
CHOMP CHOMP CHOMP
UNH...

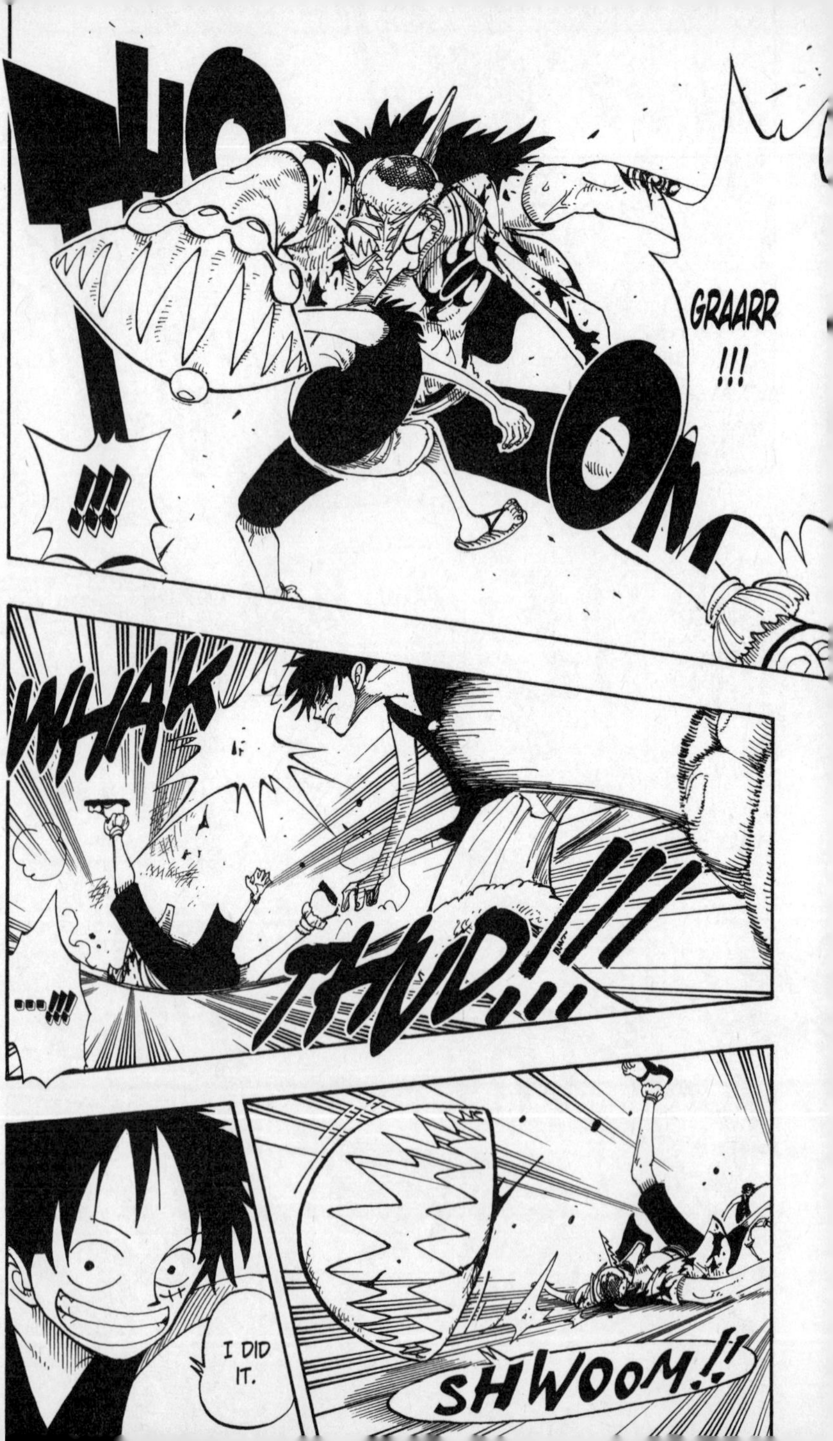
GRAARR !!!
THO
OM
!!!
WHAK
THUD!!!
...!!!
SHWOOM!!
I DID IT.

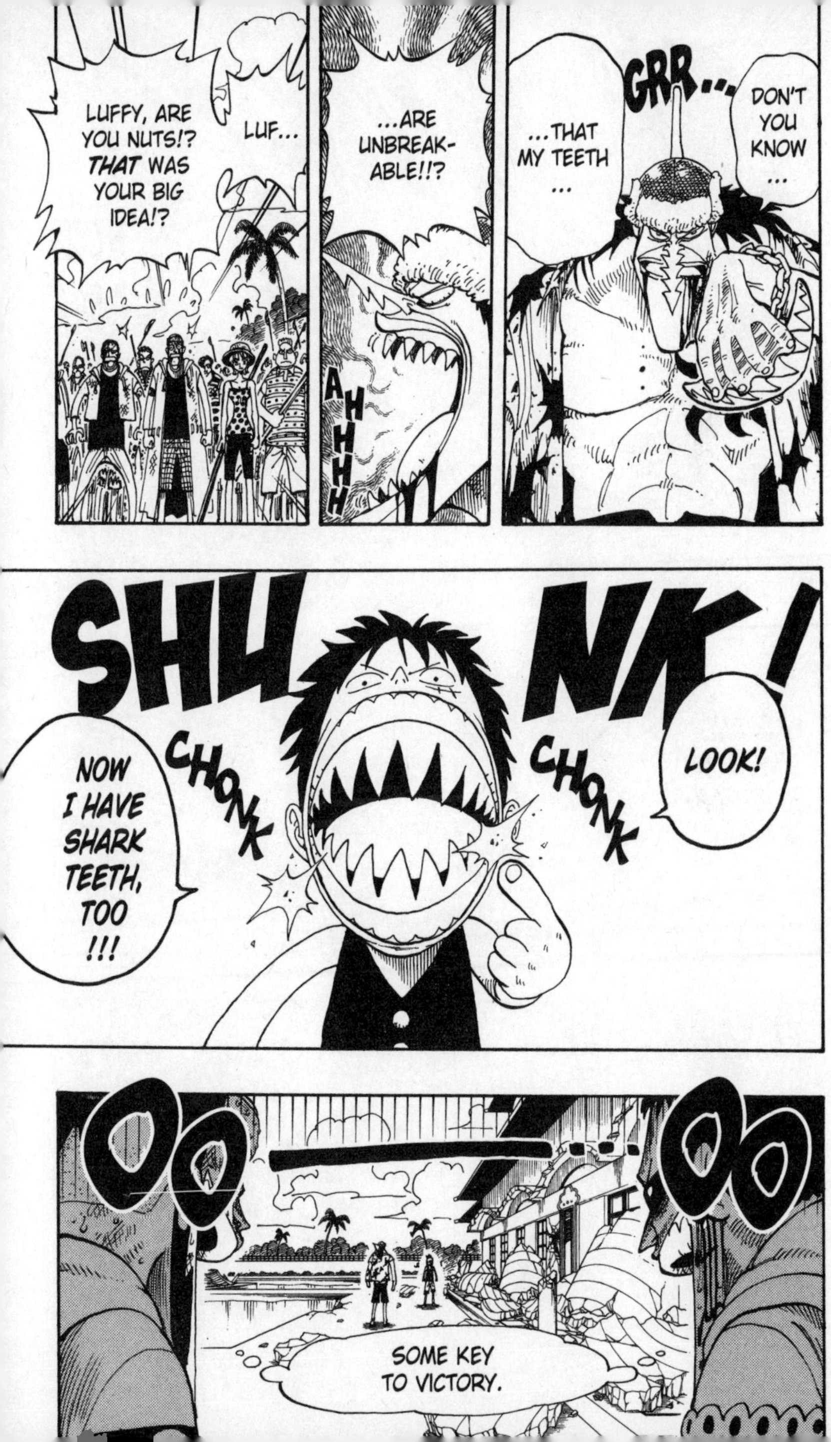

GRR...
DON'T YOU KNOW ...
...THAT MY TEETH ...
...ARE UNBREAKABLE!!?
AHHHH
LUF...
LUFFY, ARE YOU NUTS!? THAT WAS YOUR BIG IDEA!?
SHUNK!
LOOK!
CHONK
CHONK
NOW I HAVE SHARK TEETH, TOO !!!
OOO—...OO
SOME KEY TO VICTORY.

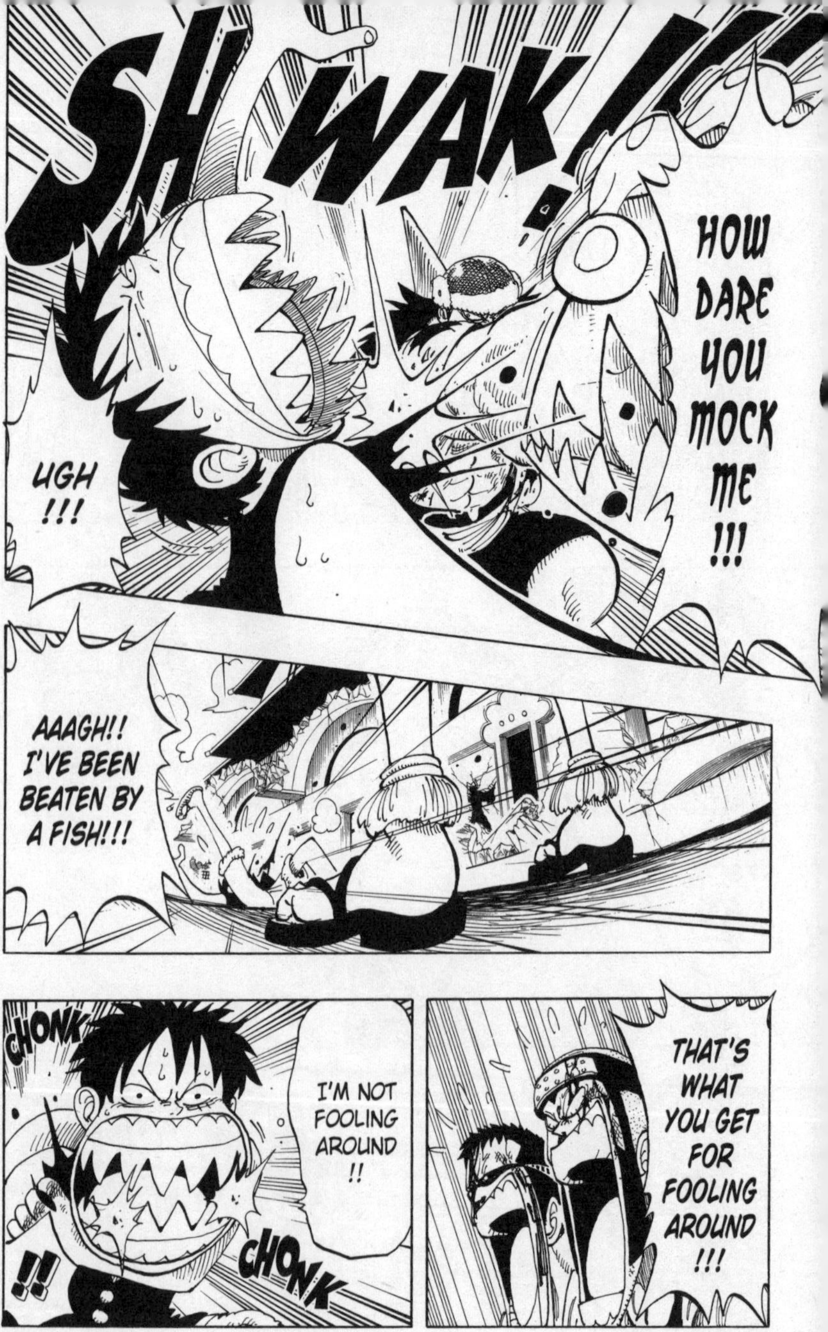
SHWAK!!
HOW DARE YOU MOCK ME!!!
UGH!!!
AAAGH!! I'VE BEEN BEATEN BY A FISH!!!
THAT'S WHAT YOU GET FOR FOOLING AROUND!!!
CHONK
I'M NOT FOOLING AROUND!!
CHONK

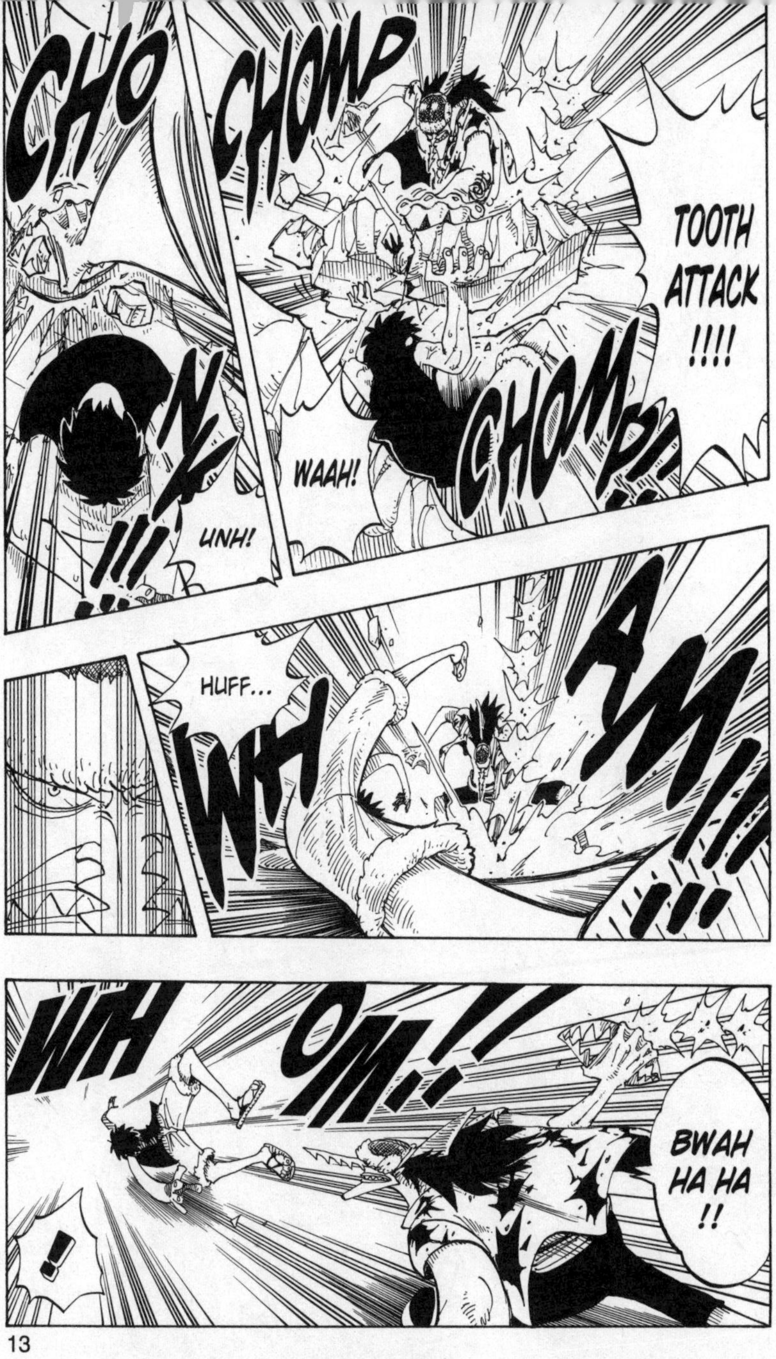
CHOMP
TOOTH ATTACK !!!!
CHOMP!!
WAAH!
CHO
NK!!!
UNH!
AM!!!!
HUFF...
WH
WH OM!!
BWAH HA HA !!
!

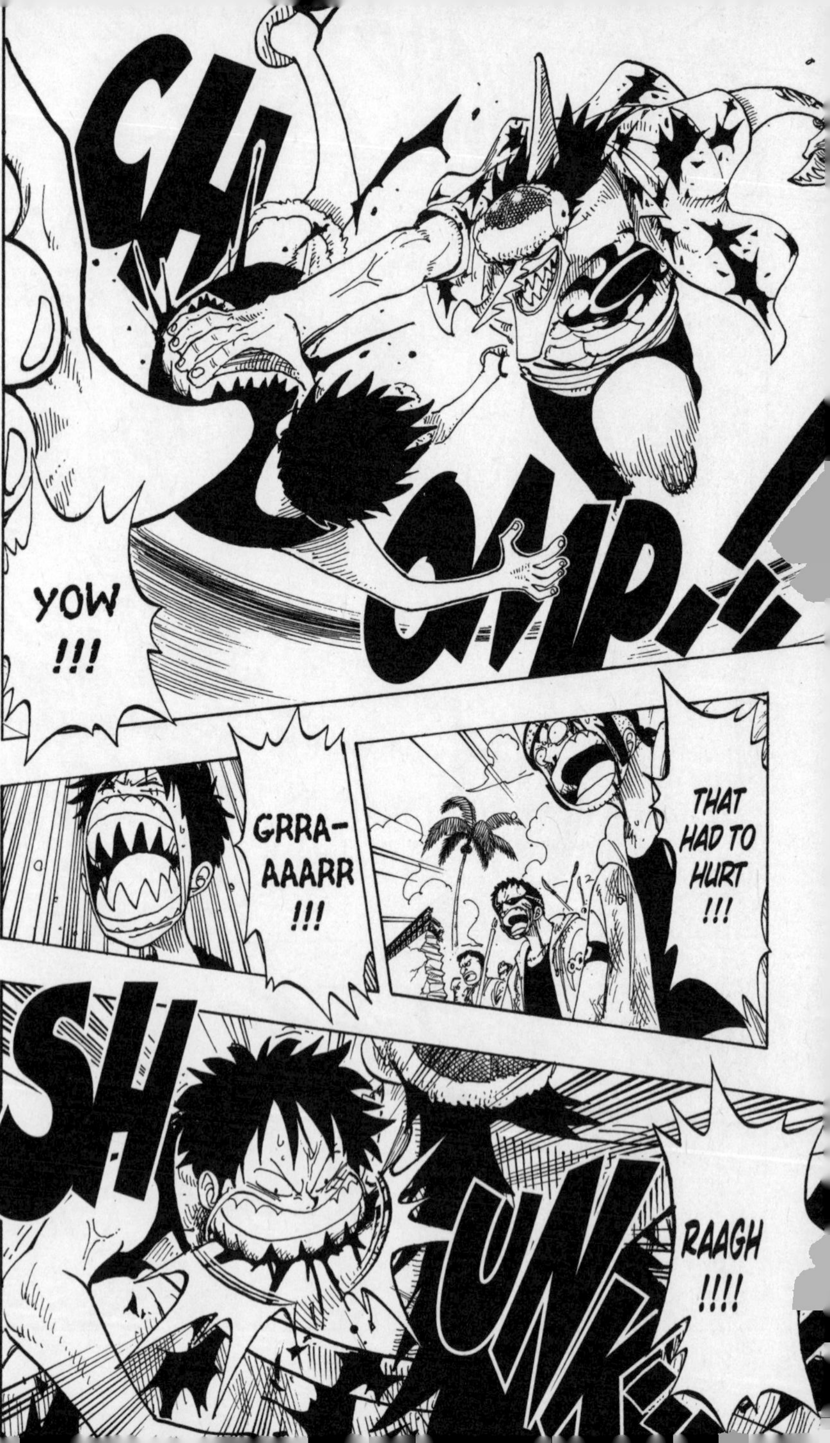
CH
OMP!!
YOW !!!
THAT HAD TO HURT !!!
GRRA-AAARR !!!
SH
UNK
RAAGH !!!!

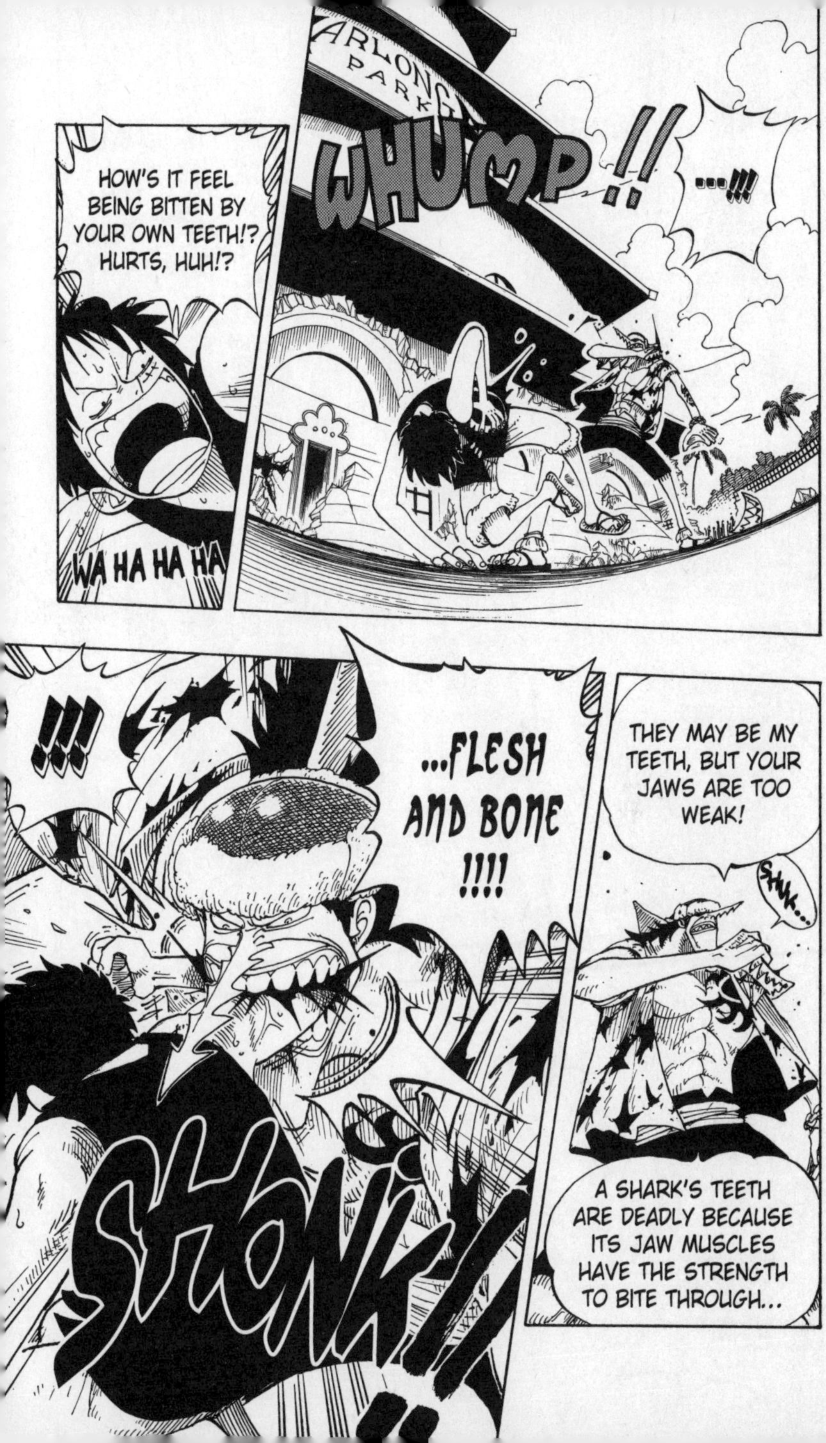
ARLONG PARK
WHUMP!!
...!!!
HOW'S IT FEEL BEING BITTEN BY YOUR OWN TEETH!? HURTS, HUH!?
WA HA HA HA
THEY MAY BE MY TEETH, BUT YOUR JAWS ARE TOO WEAK!
SHUK...
A SHARK'S TEETH ARE DEADLY BECAUSE ITS JAW MUSCLES HAVE THE STRENGTH TO BITE THROUGH...
...FLESH AND BONE!!!!
!!!
STONK!!

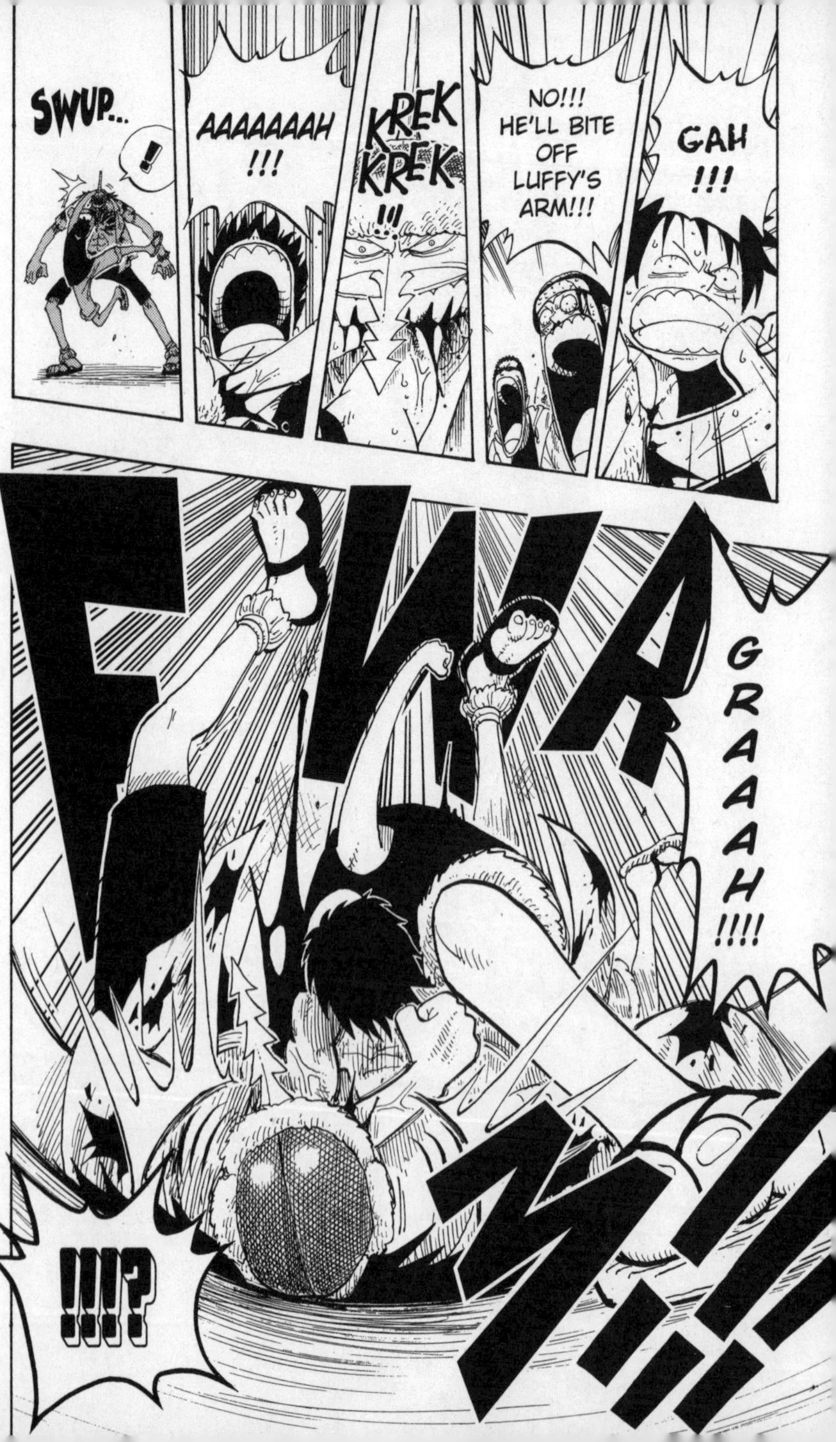
GAH !!!
NO!!! HE'LL BITE OFF LUFFY'S ARM!!!
KREK KREK !!!
AAAAAAAH !!!
SWUP...
!
GRAAAAH!!!!
FWA
!!!?

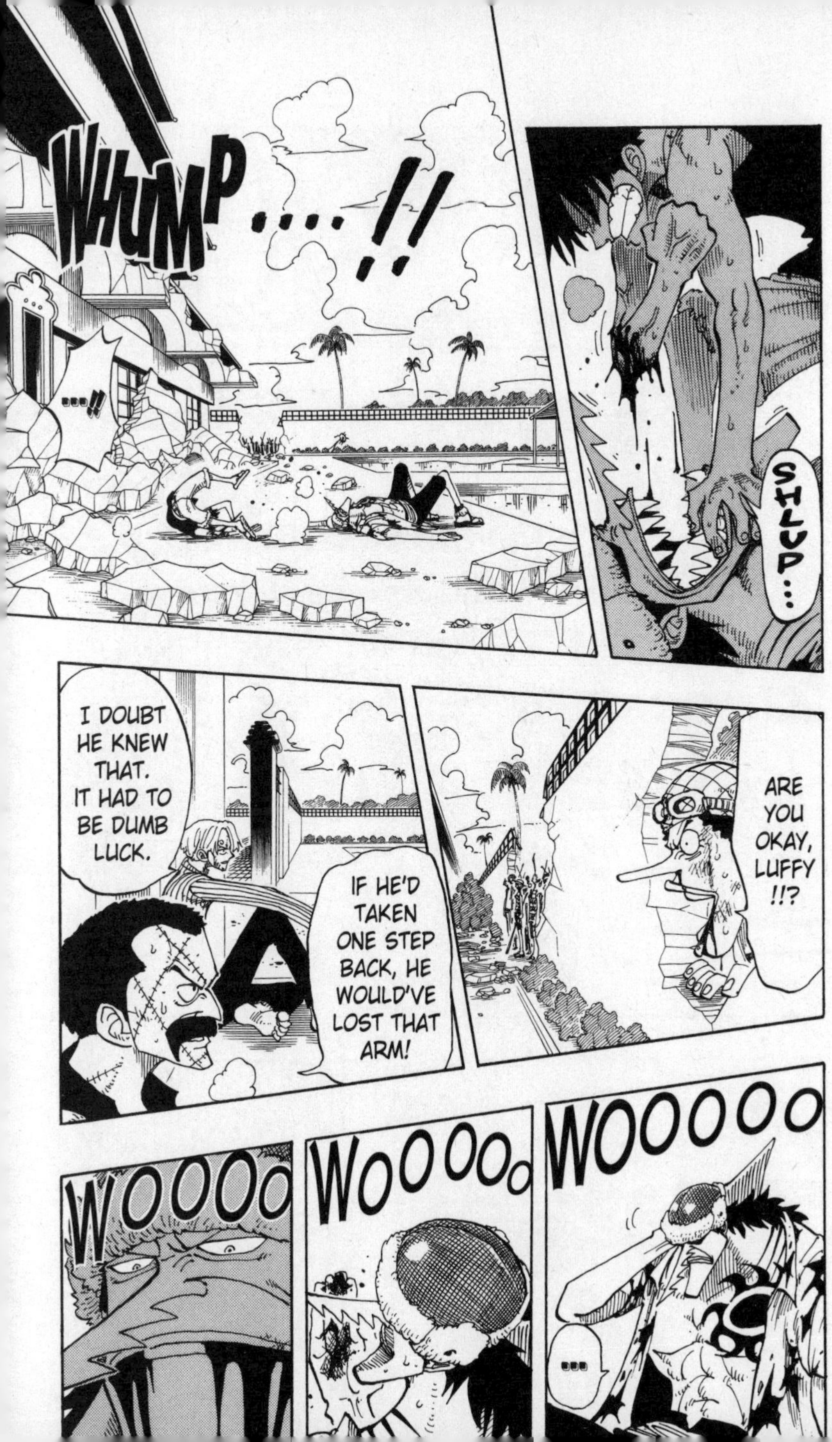
SHLUP...
WHUMP....!!
...!!
ARE YOU OKAY, LUFFY!!?
IF HE'D TAKEN ONE STEP BACK, HE WOULD'VE LOST THAT ARM!
I DOUBT HE KNEW THAT. IT HAD TO BE DUMB LUCK.
WOOOOO
...
WOOOOo
WOOOOo

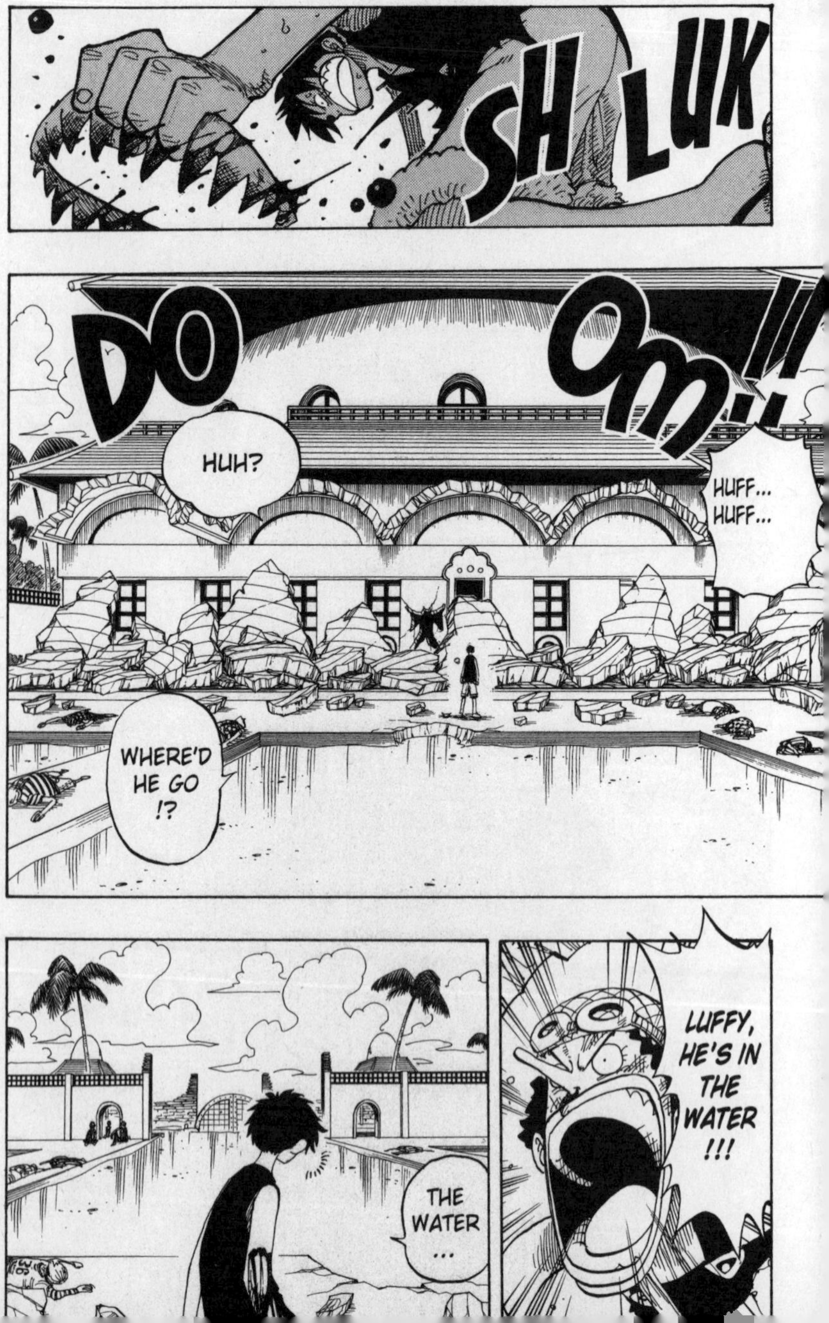
SHLUK
DOOM!!
HUFF... HUFF...
HUH?
WHERE'D HE GO !?
LUFFY, HE'S IN THE WATER !!!
THE WATER ...

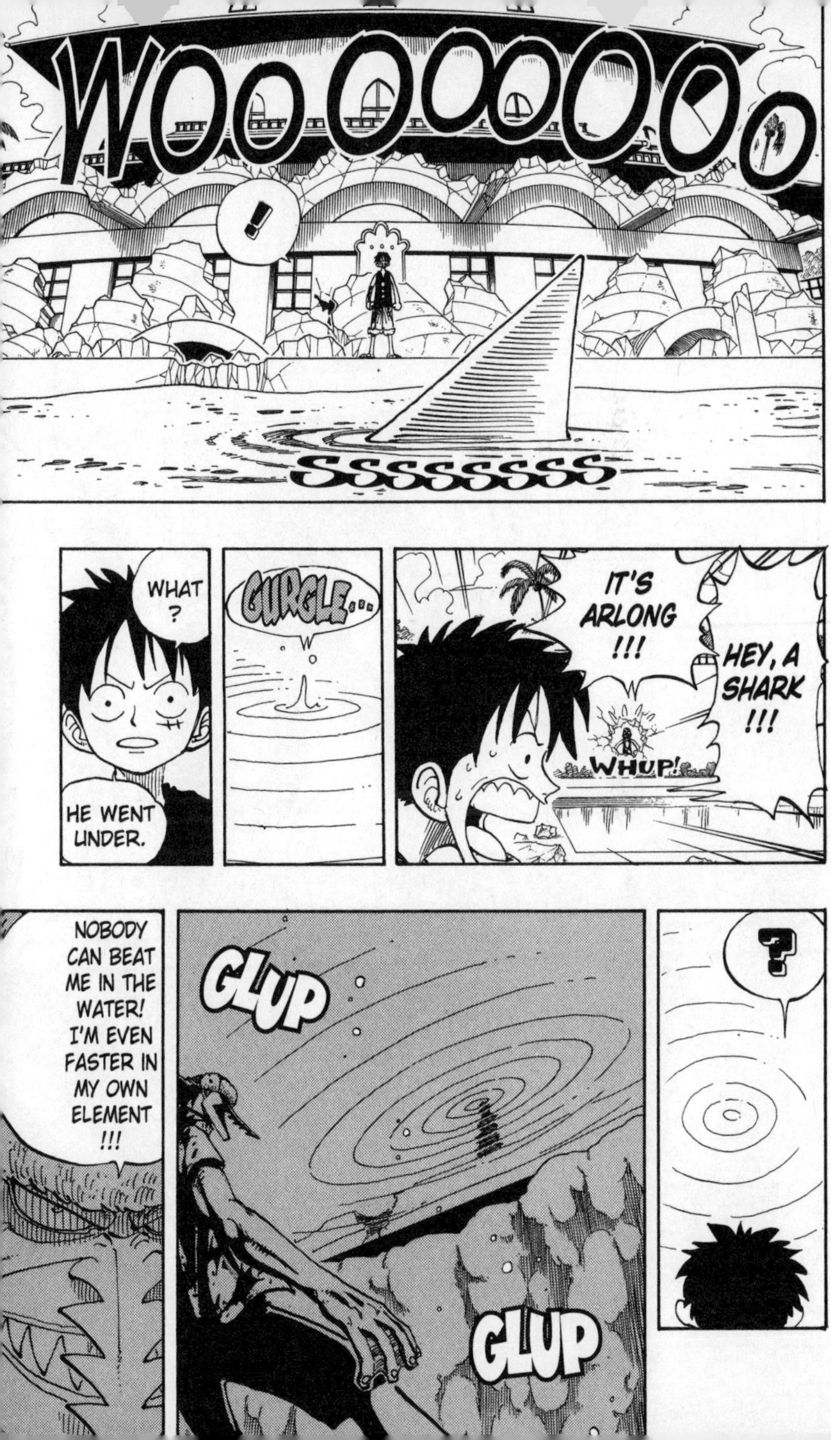
WOOOOOOOOO
!
SSSSSSSS
HEY, A SHARK !!!
IT'S ARLONG !!!
WHUP!
GURGLE...
WHAT ?
HE WENT UNDER.
?
GLUP
GLUP
NOBODY CAN BEAT ME IN THE WATER! I'M EVEN FASTER IN MY OWN ELEMENT !!!

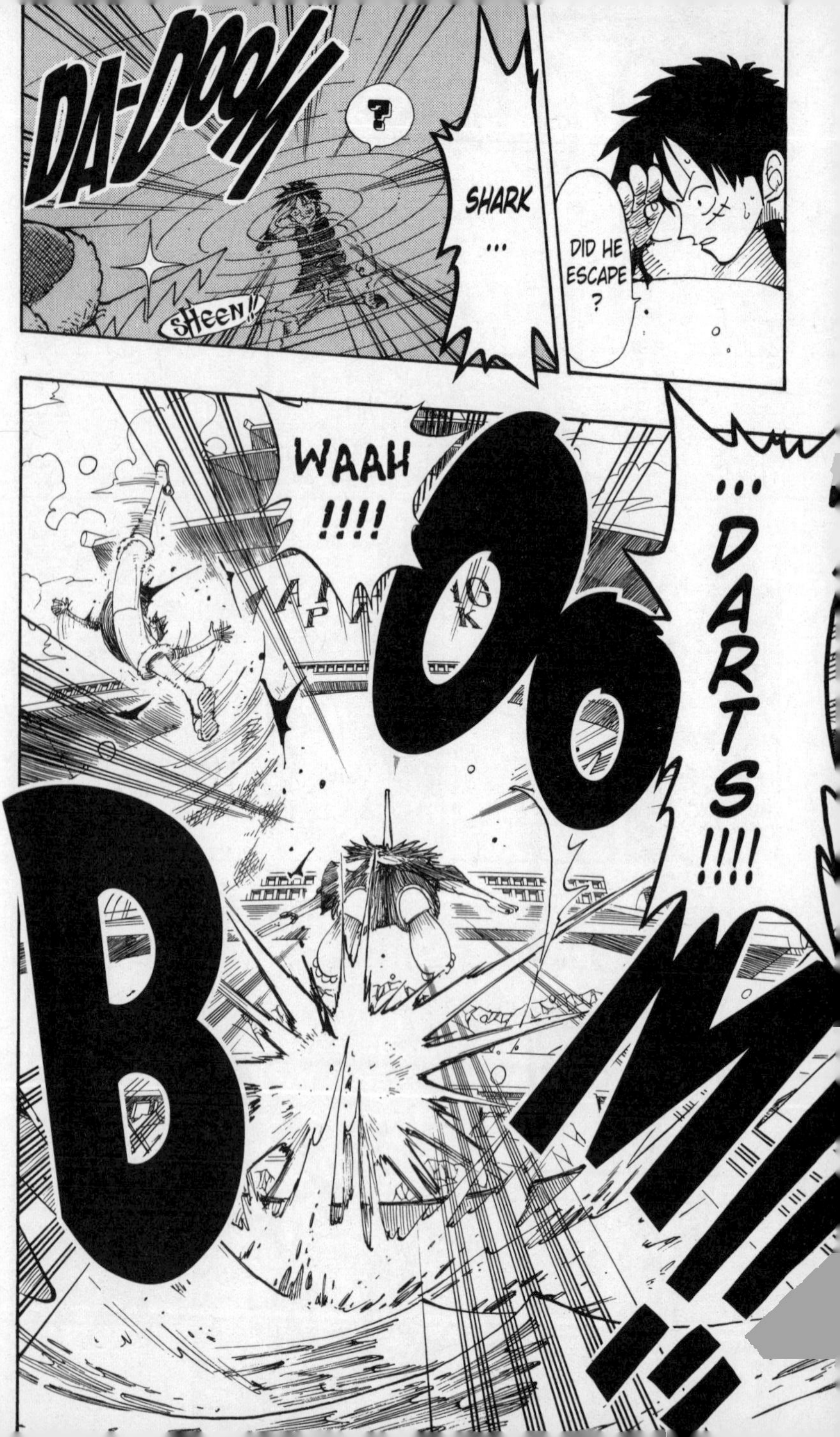
DID HE ESCAPE?
SHARK ...
?
DA-DOOM
SHEEN!!
...DARTS!!!!
WAAH!!!!
BOOM!!!

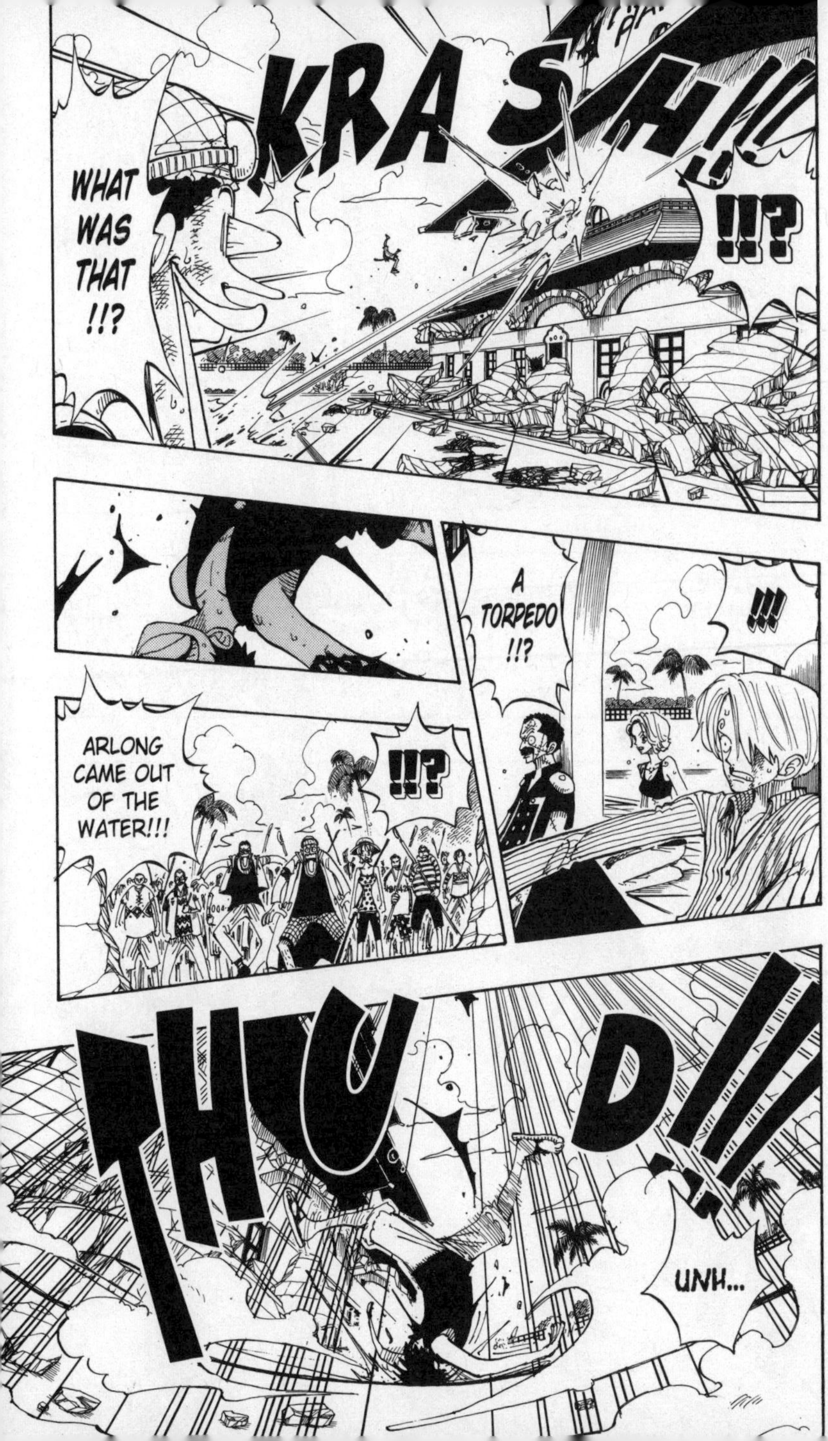
KRASH!!!
!!?
WHAT WAS THAT !!?
!!!
A TORPEDO !!?
!!?
ARLONG CAME OUT OF THE WATER!!!
THUD!!
UNH...

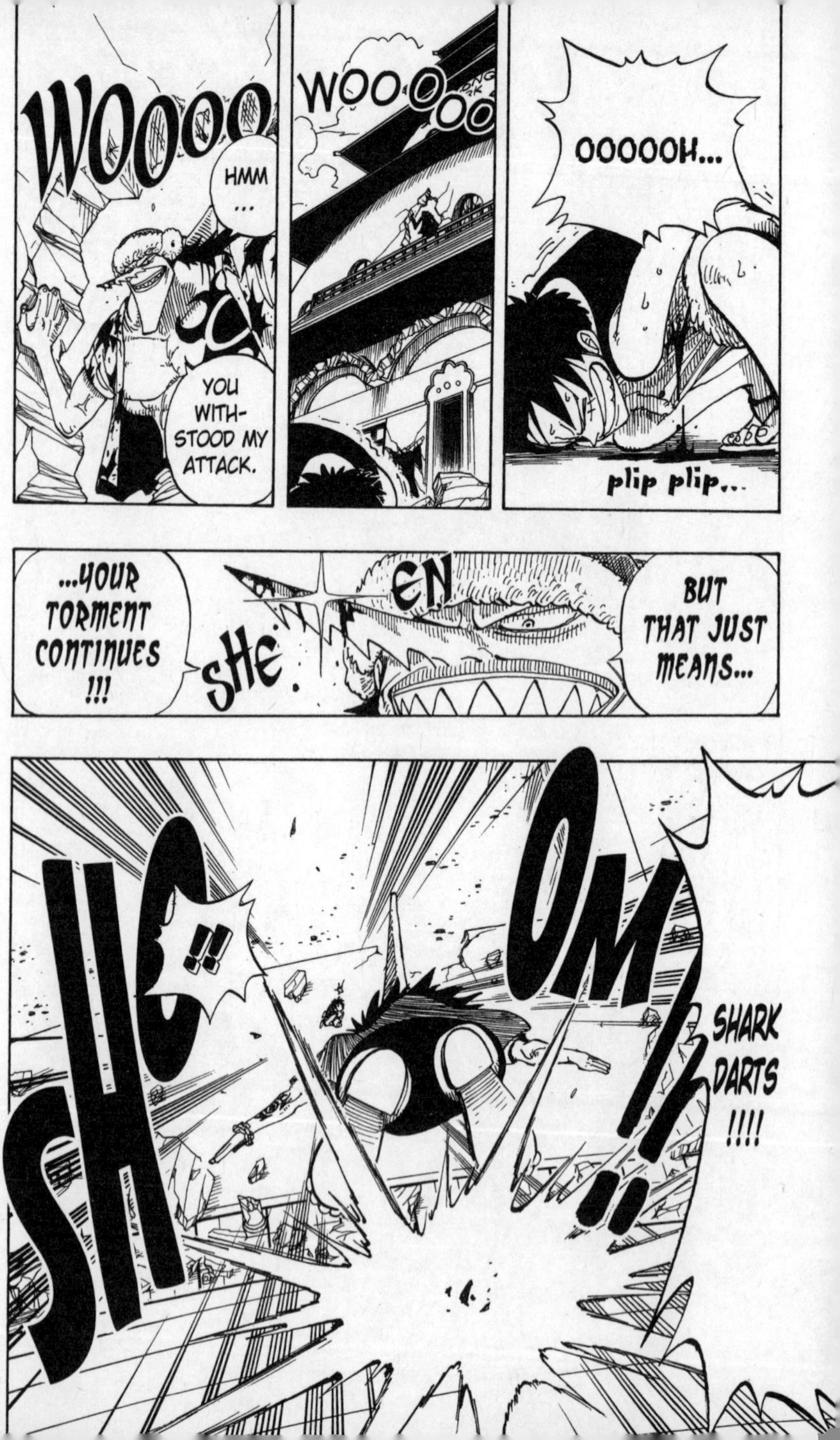
OOOOOH...
plip plip...
WOOOOOO
WOOOO
HMM ...
YOU WITH-STOOD MY ATTACK.
BUT THAT JUST MEANS...
SHE EN
...YOUR TORMENT CONTINUES !!!
SHARK DARTS !!!!
OM!!
SHO!!

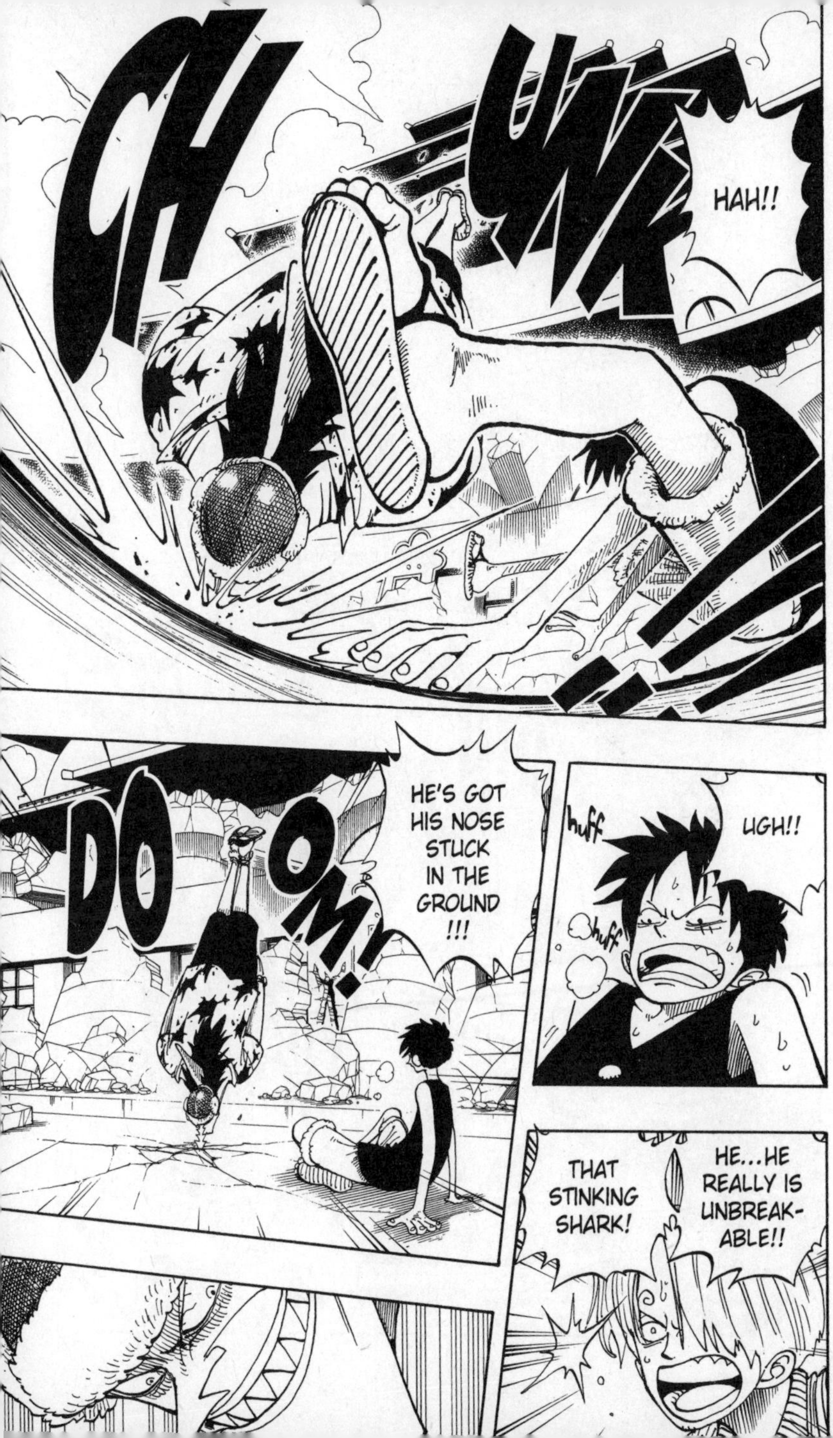
HAH!!
CH-UNK
HE'S GOT HIS NOSE STUCK IN THE GROUND !!!
DOOM!
UGH!!
huff
huff
HE...HE REALLY IS UNBREAK-ABLE!!
THAT STINKING SHARK!

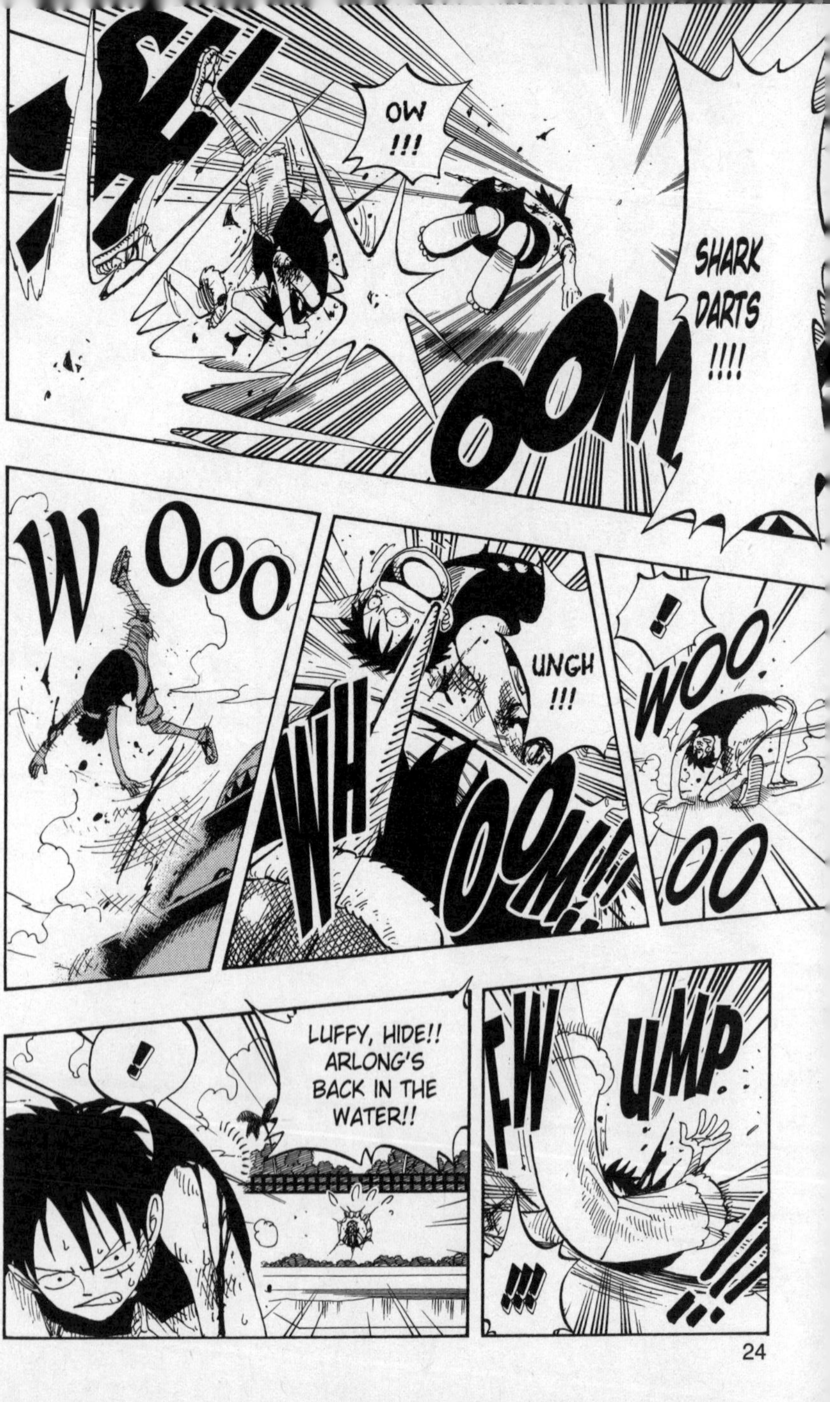
SHARK DARTS !!!!
OW !!!
SH
OOM
!
WOO
OO
UNGH !!!
WH
OOM!!
W OOO
FW
UMP
!!!
!!!
!
LUFFY, HIDE!! ARLONG'S BACK IN THE WATER!!

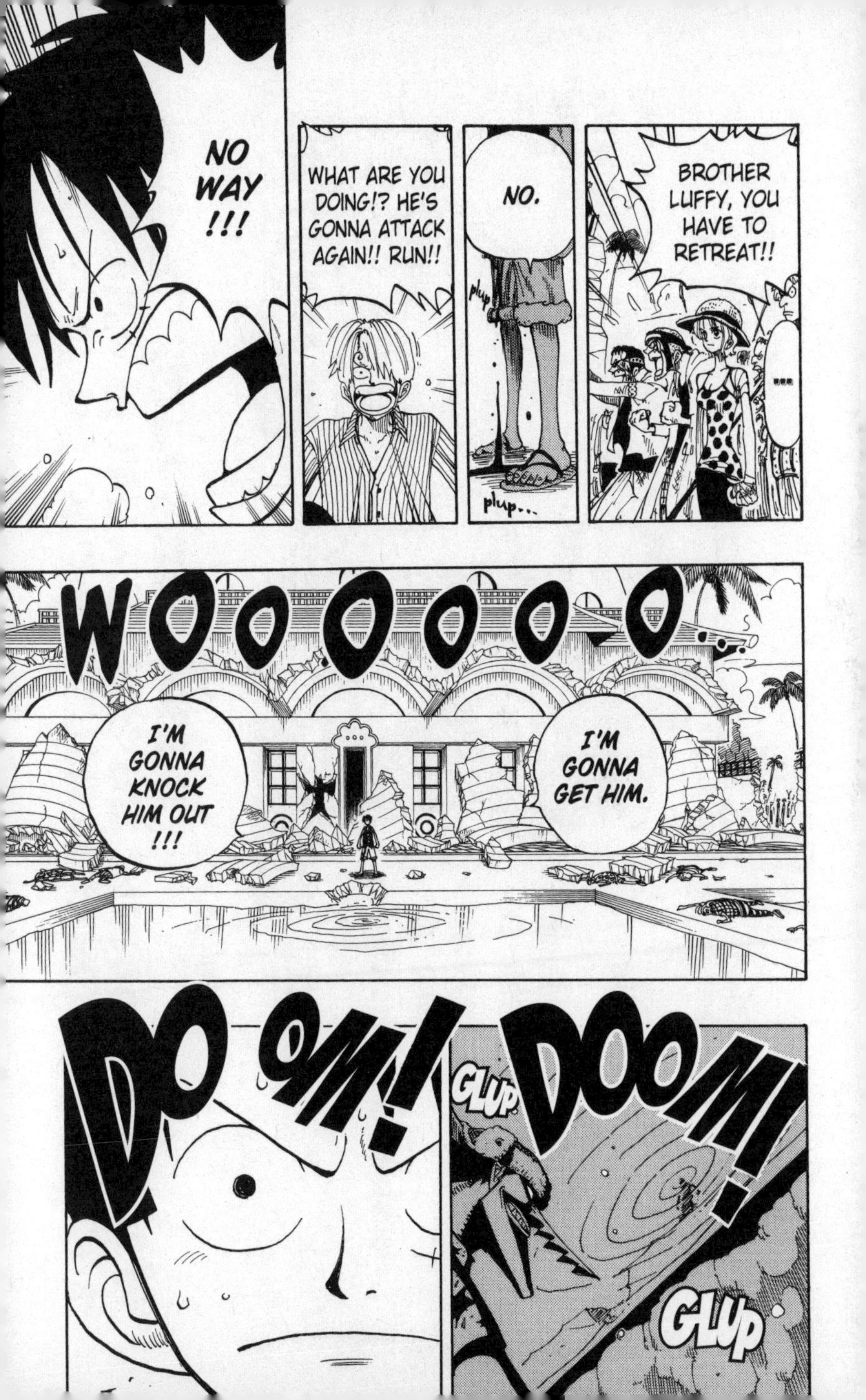
BROTHER LUFFY, YOU HAVE TO RETREAT!!
...
NO.
plup
plup...
WHAT ARE YOU DOING!? HE'S GONNA ATTACK AGAIN!! RUN!!
NO WAY!!!
WOOOOOO
I'M GONNA GET HIM.
I'M GONNA KNOCK HIM OUT!!!
GLUP
DOOM!
GLUP
DOOM!

INSTEAD OF THE SBS QUESTION CORNER, HERE'S A CUT-AWAY VIEW OF LUFFY'S SHIP, THE *MERRY GO*. A LOT OF READERS HAVE ASKED ABOUT IT.

THE MERRY GO
8. (p164) Nami's Tangerine Grove
1. (p46) Conference Room, Galley, and Bridge
3. (p84) Storeroom and Battery Deck
6 (p144) Bathroom
7. (p164) Luffy's Cabin
5. (p124) Gun Deck and Anchor Rope Storage
2. (p66) Men's Quarters
4. (p104) Women's Quarters

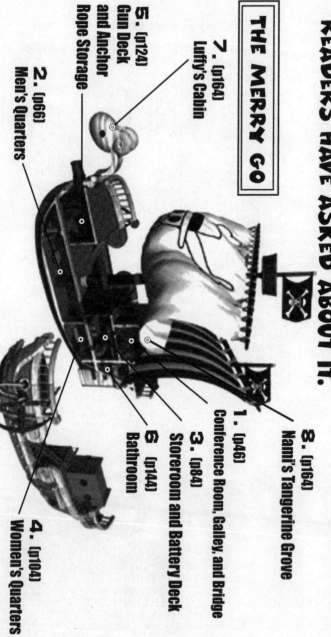

Chapter 92: HAPPINESS

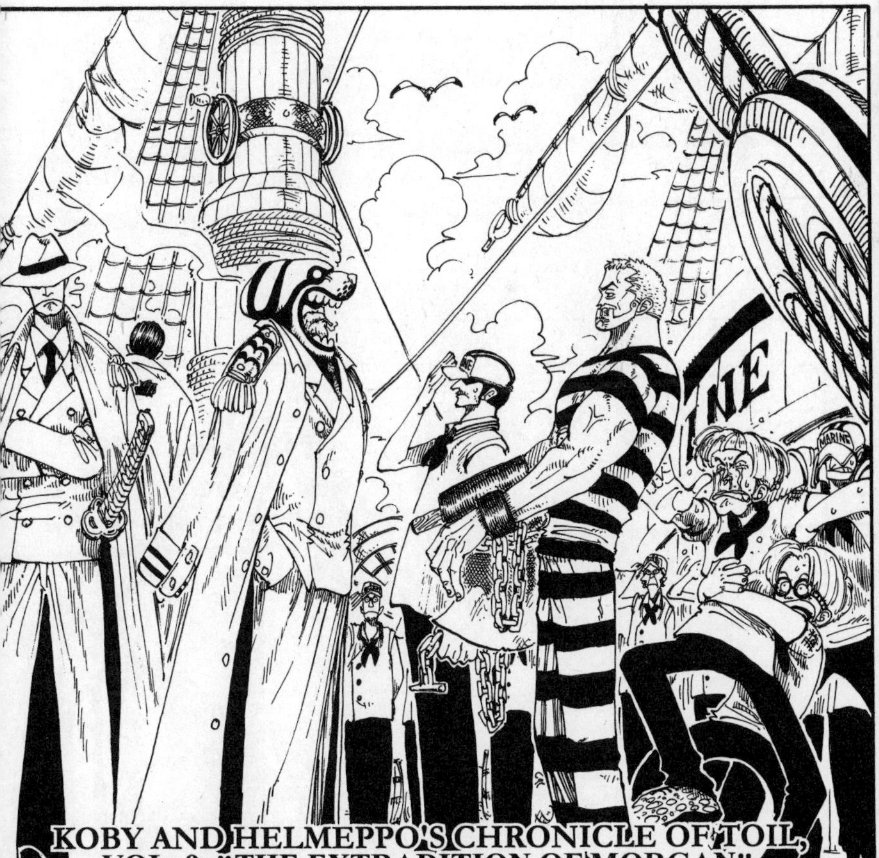

MARINE
MARINE

KOBY AND HELMEPPO'S CHRONICLE OF TOIL, VOL. 9: "THE EXTRADITION OF MORGAN"

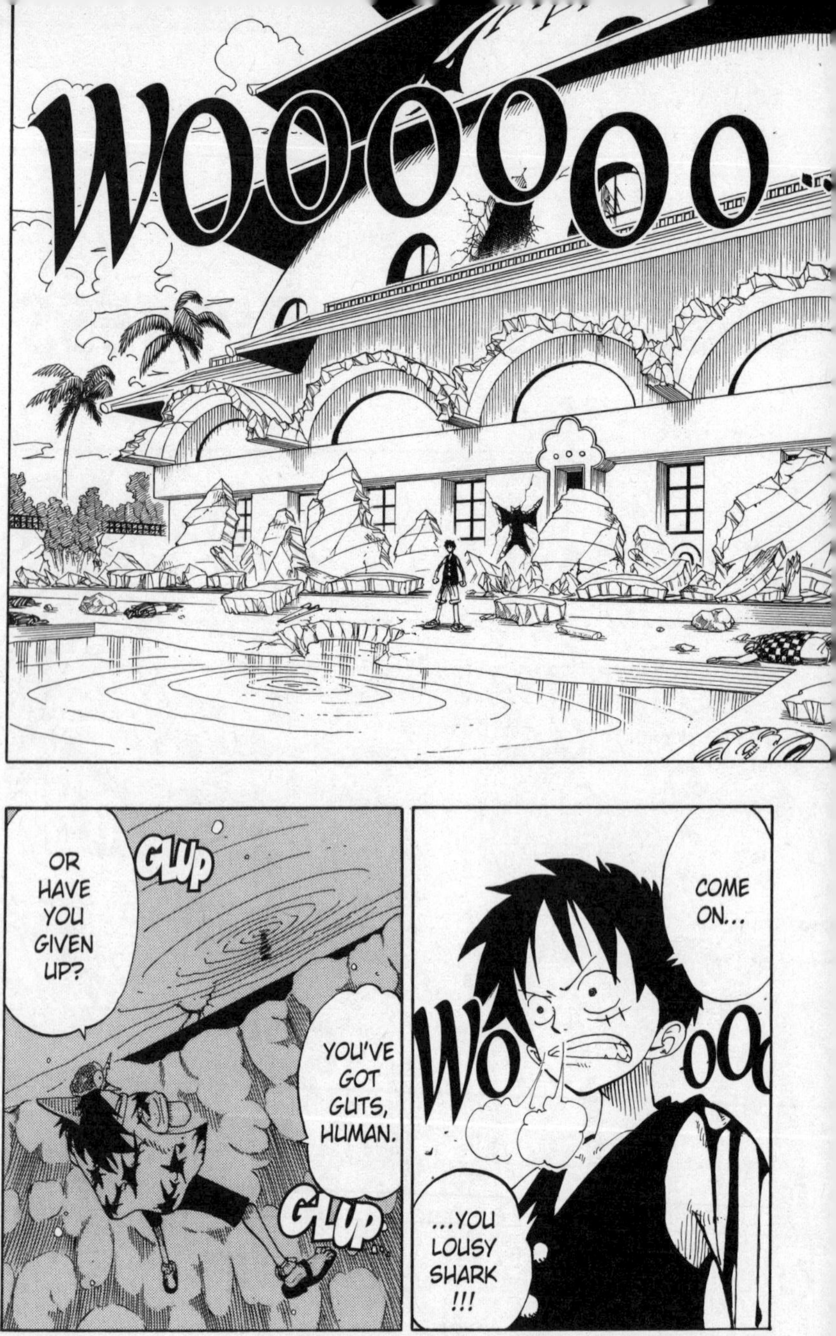
WOOOOOO...
COME ON...
WO OOO
...YOU LOUSY SHARK!!!
GLUP
YOU'VE GOT GUTS, HUMAN.
OR HAVE YOU GIVEN UP?
GLUP

READ THIS WAY

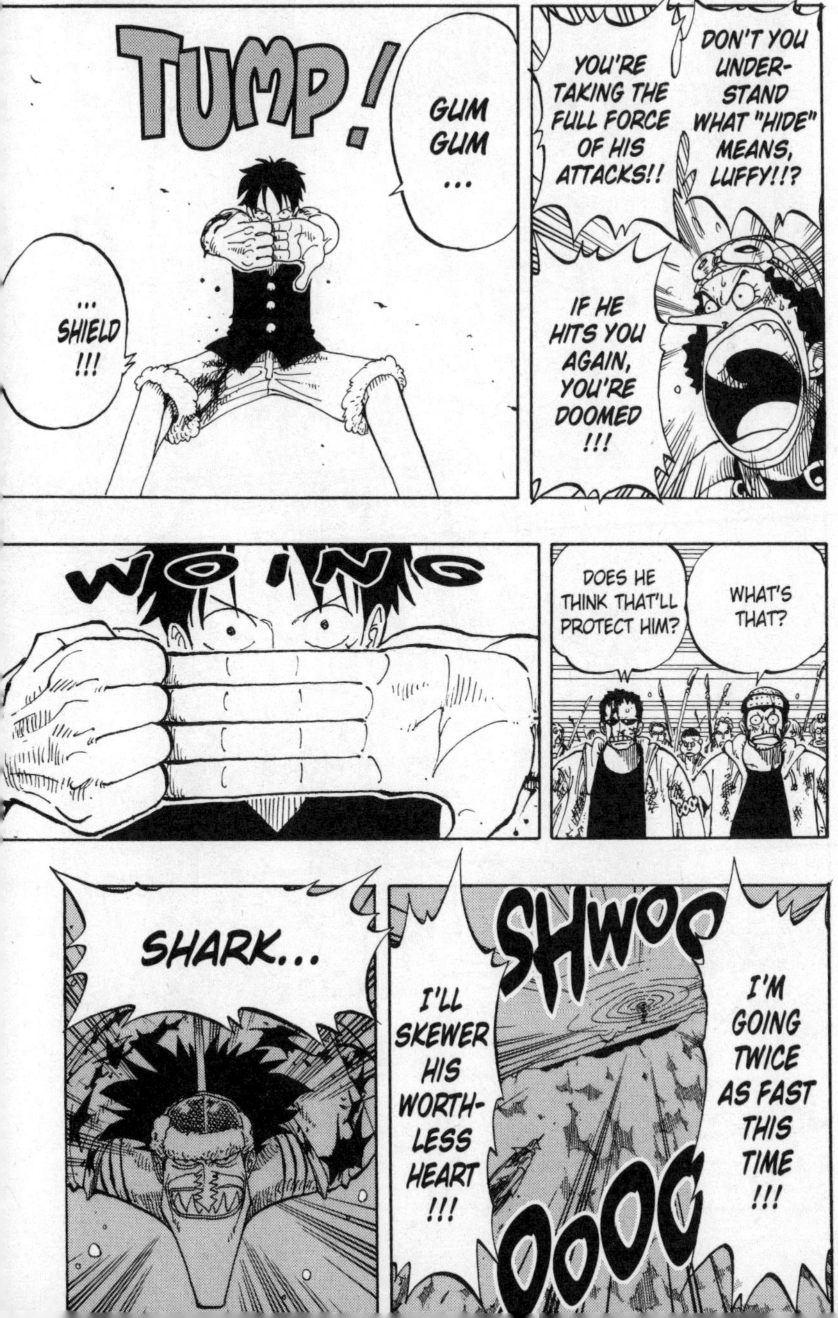
DON'T YOU UNDER-STAND WHAT "HIDE" MEANS, LUFFY!!?
YOU'RE TAKING THE FULL FORCE OF HIS ATTACKS!!
IF HE HITS YOU AGAIN, YOU'RE DOOMED!!!
TUMP!
GUM GUM ...
... SHIELD!!!
WHAT'S THAT?
DOES HE THINK THAT'LL PROTECT HIM?
WOING
SHWOO
OOOC
I'M GOING TWICE AS FAST THIS TIME!!!
I'LL SKEWER HIS WORTH-LESS HEART!!!
SHARK...

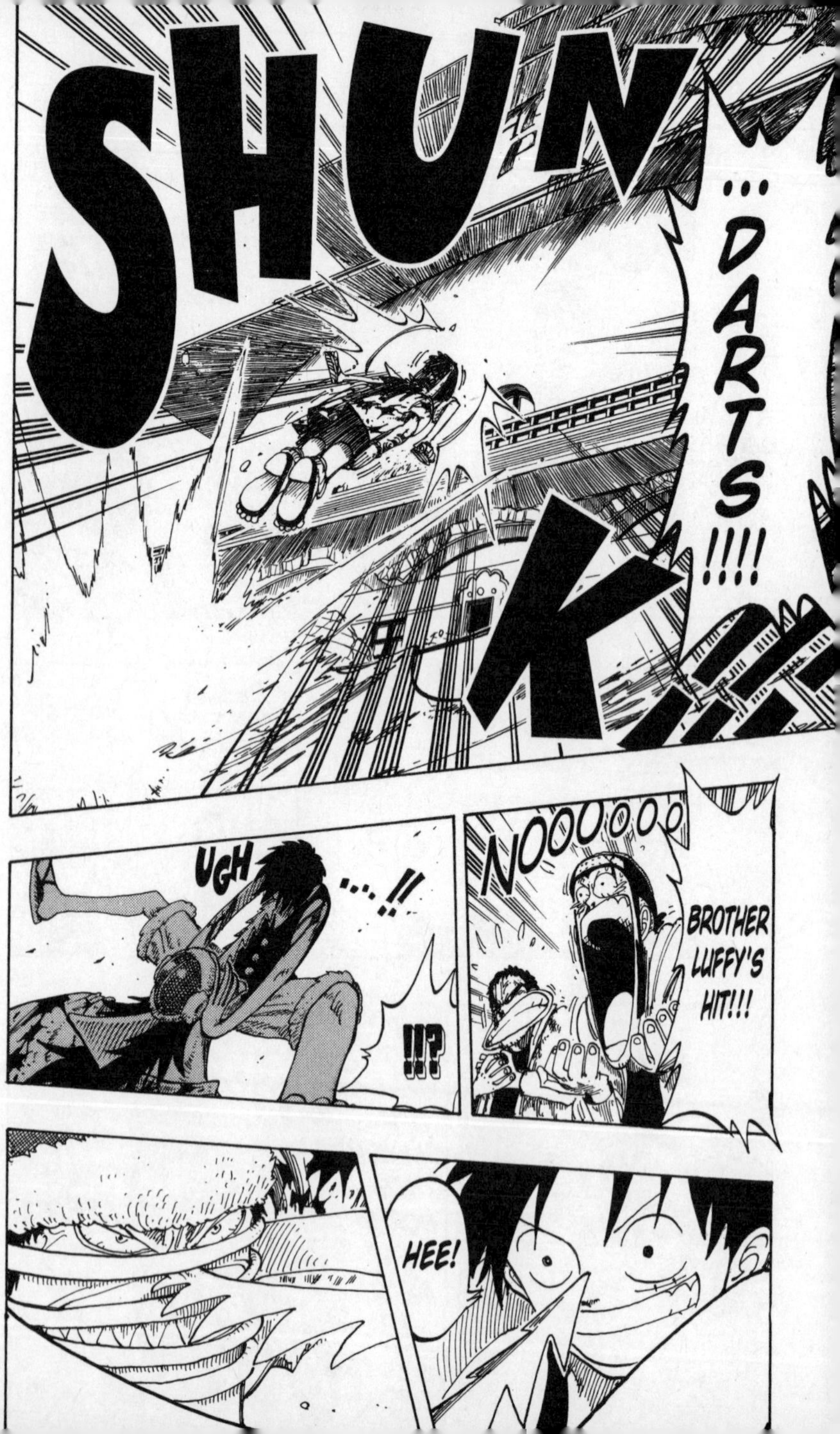
SHUN
...DARTS!!!!
NOOOOOOO
BROTHER LUFFY'S HIT!!!
UGH
...!!
!!?
HEE!

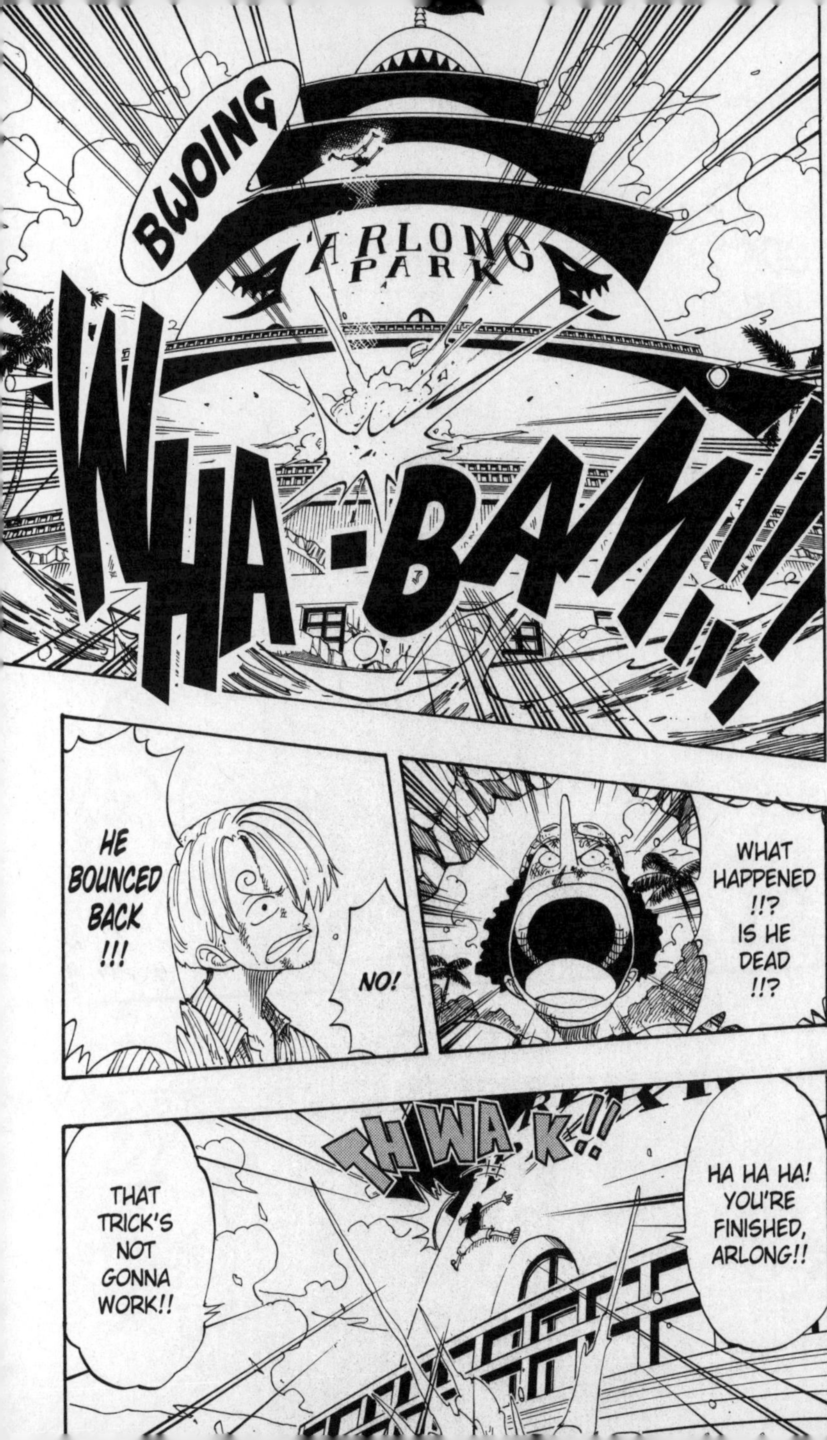
BWOING
ARLONG PARK
WHA-BAM!!!
WHAT HAPPENED!!? IS HE DEAD!!?
HE BOUNCED BACK!!!
NO!
HA HA HA! YOU'RE FINISHED, ARLONG!!
THWAK!!
THAT TRICK'S NOT GONNA WORK!!

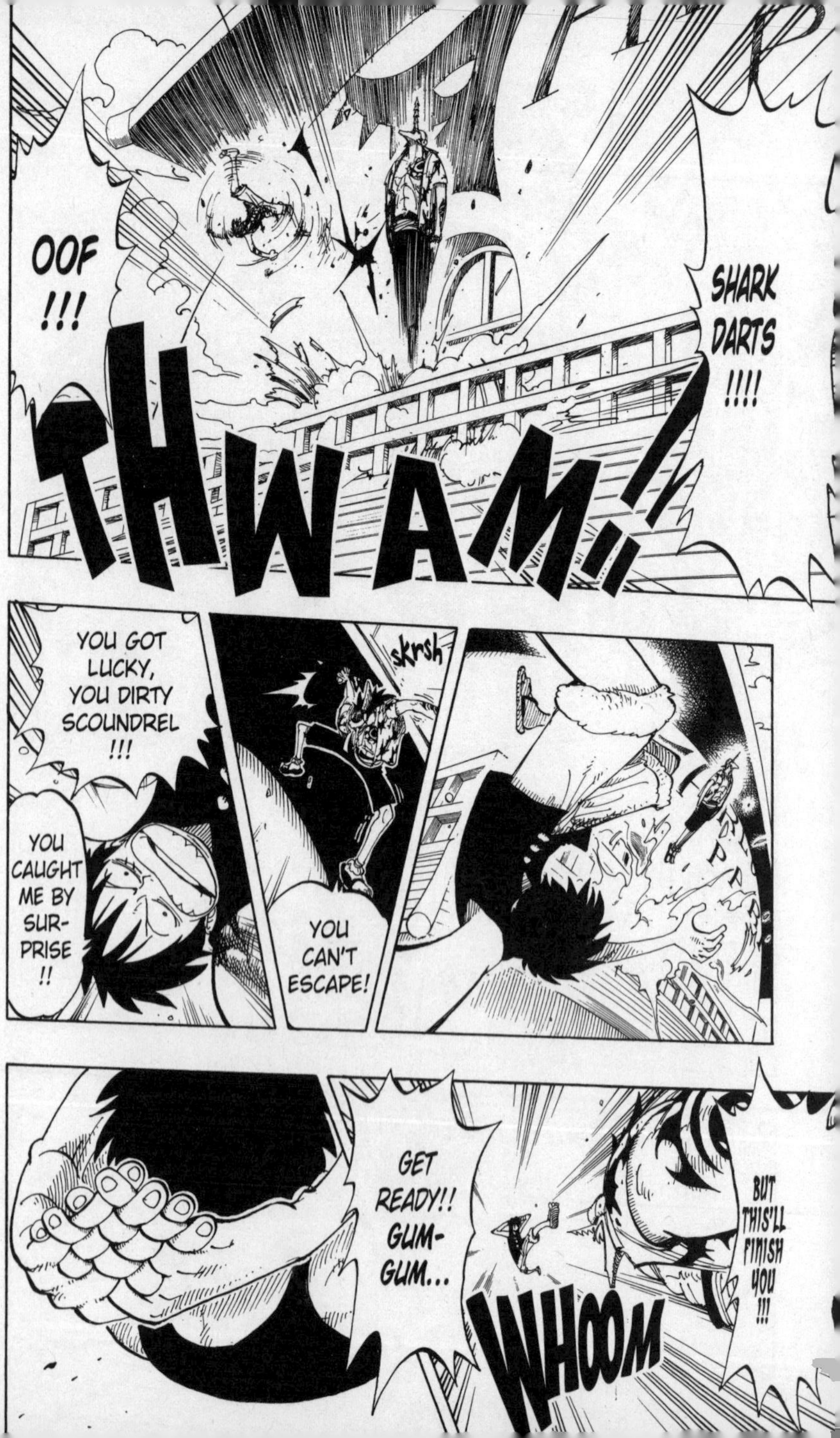
SHARK DARTS !!!!
OOF !!!
THWAM!!
skrsh
YOU CAN'T ESCAPE!
YOU GOT LUCKY, YOU DIRTY SCOUNDREL !!!
YOU CAUGHT ME BY SUR-PRISE !!
BUT THIS'LL FINISH YOU !!!
GET READY!! GUM-GUM...
WHOOM

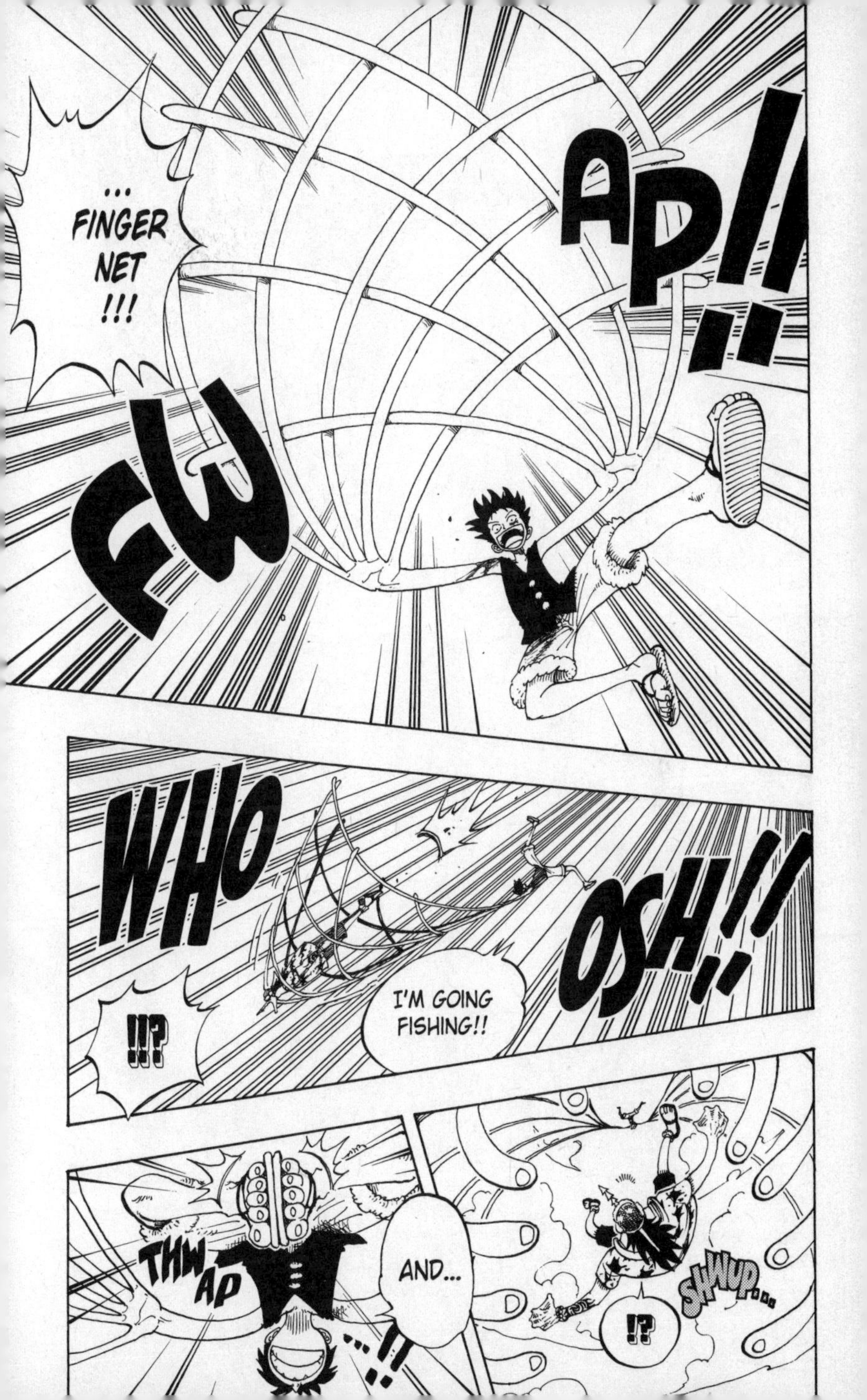
FWAP!!
... FINGER NET !!!
WHOOSH!!
I'M GOING FISHING!!
!!?
SHWUP...
!?
AND...
THWAP
...!!

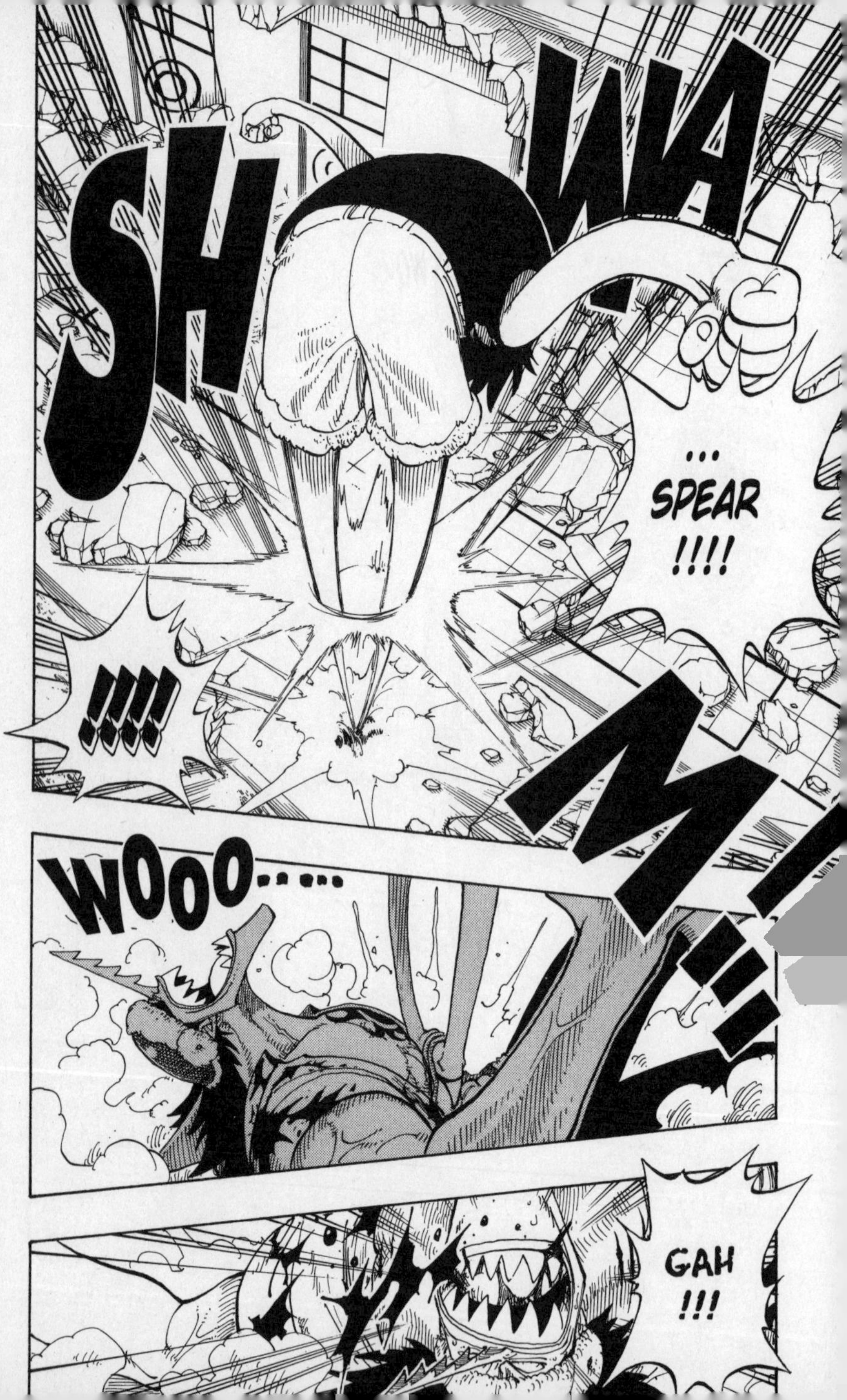
SH
WA
... SPEAR !!!!
!!!!!
WOOO...
M!!
GAH !!!

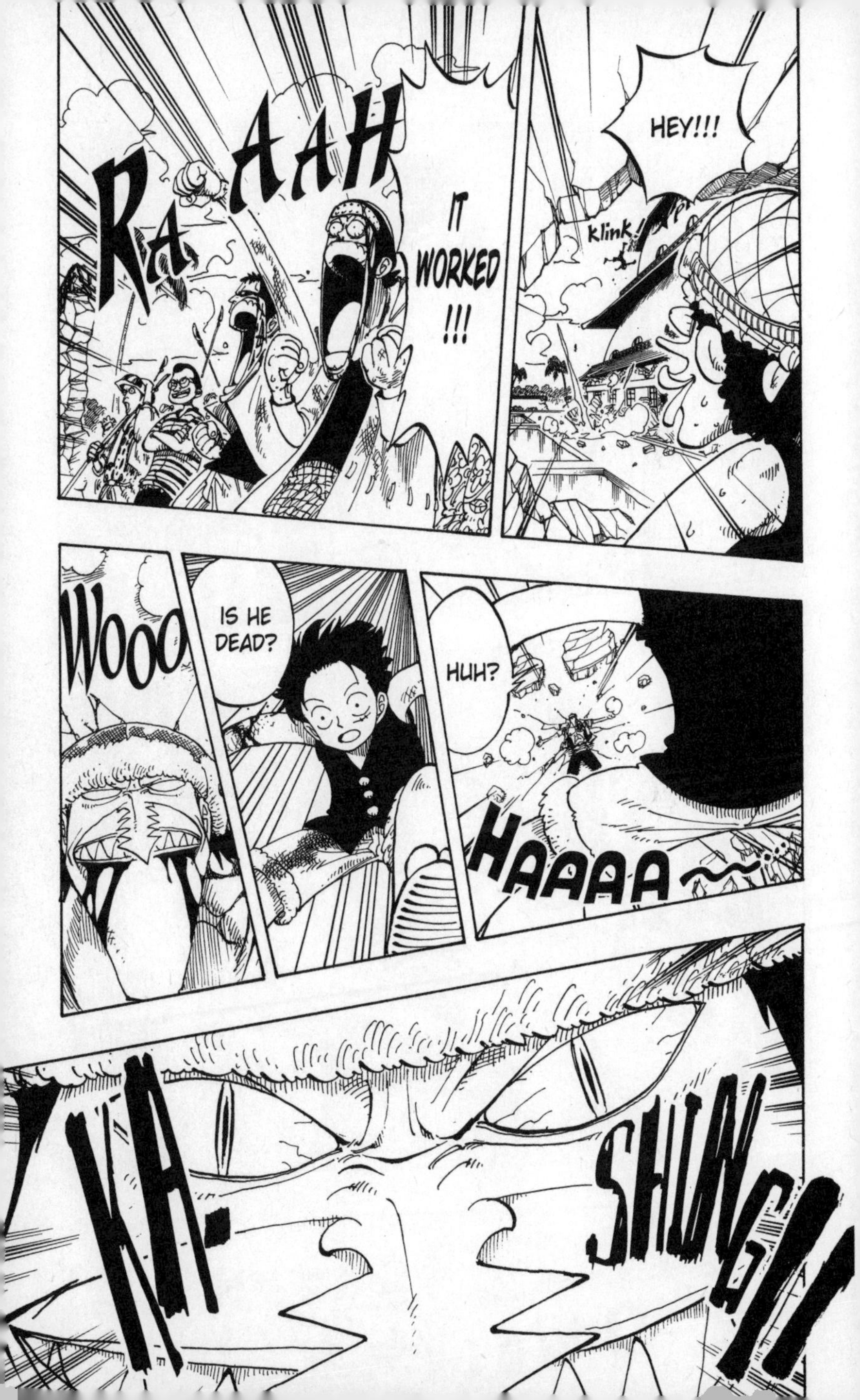
HEY!!!
klink!
IT WORKED !!!
RA AAH
HUH?
HAAAA~~
IS HE DEAD?
WOOO
KA-
SHUNG!!

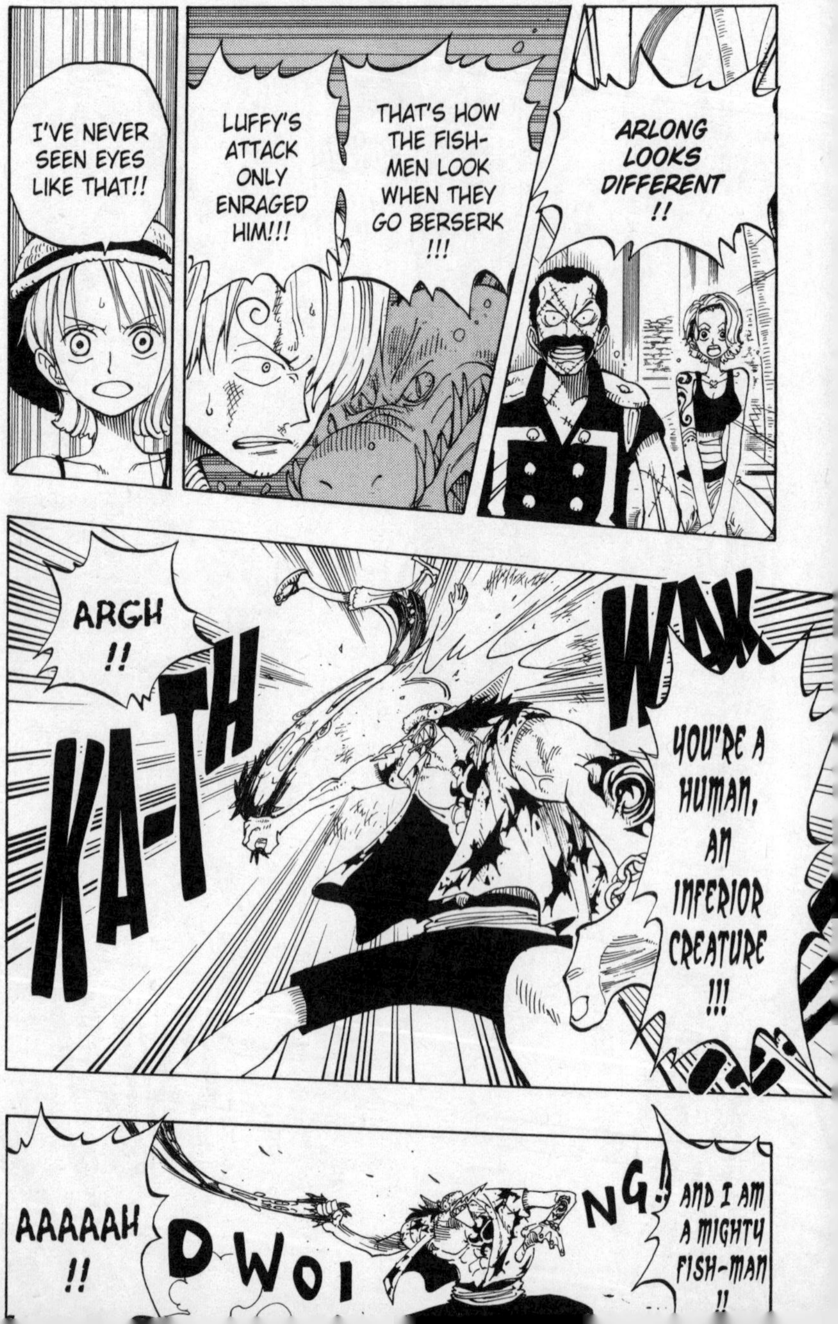
ARLONG LOOKS DIFFERENT !!
THAT'S HOW THE FISH-MEN LOOK WHEN THEY GO BERSERK !!!
LUFFY'S ATTACK ONLY ENRAGED HIM!!!
I'VE NEVER SEEN EYES LIKE THAT!!
WAK
YOU'RE A HUMAN, AN INFERIOR CREATURE !!!
KA-TH
ARGH !!
AND I AM A MIGHTY FISH-MAN !!
DWOING!!
AAAAAH !!

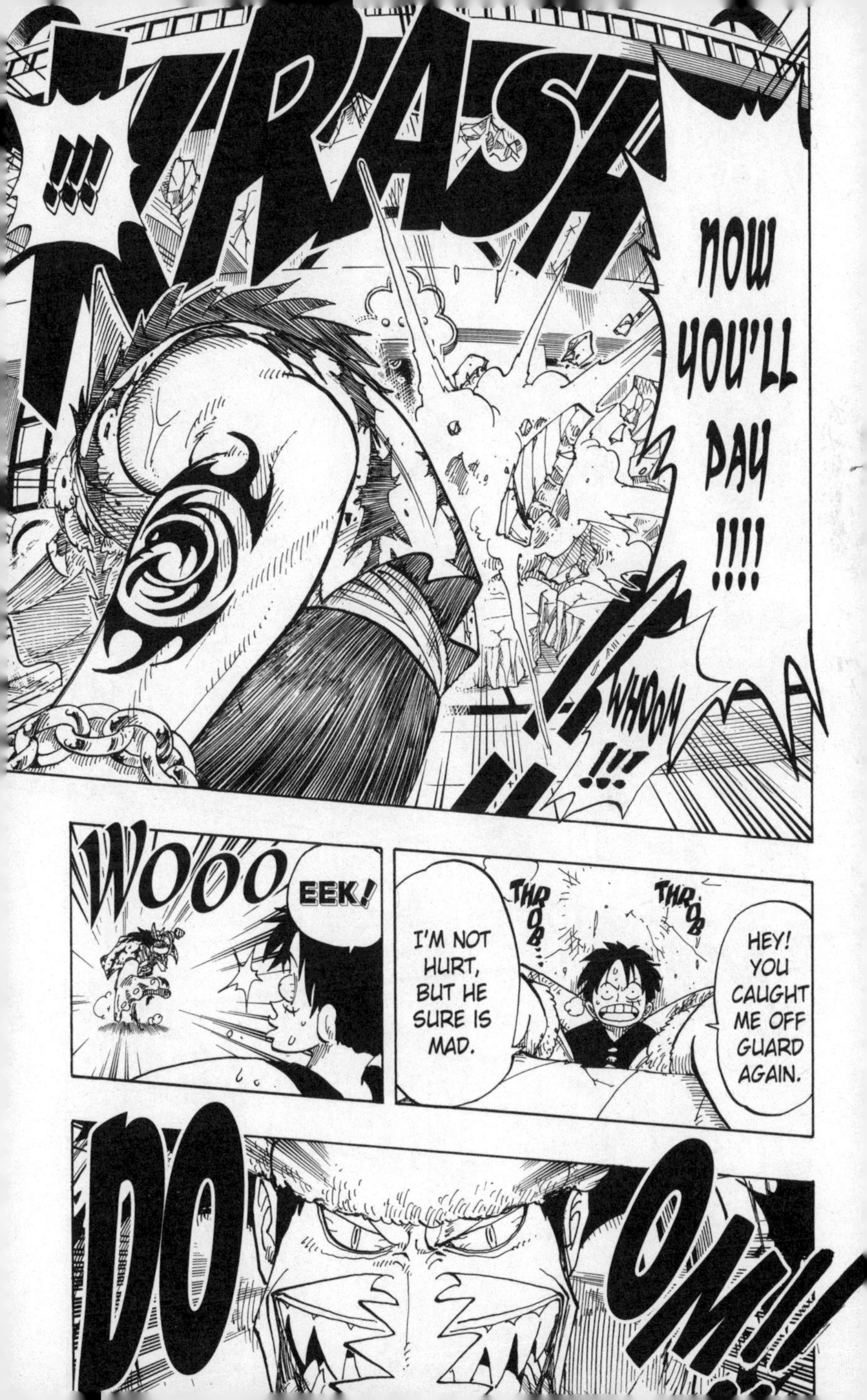
CRASH!!!
NOW YOU'LL PAY!!!!
WHOOM!!!
HEY! YOU CAUGHT ME OFF GUARD AGAIN.
THROB THROB
I'M NOT HURT, BUT HE SURE IS MAD.
WOOO
EEK!
DOOM!!

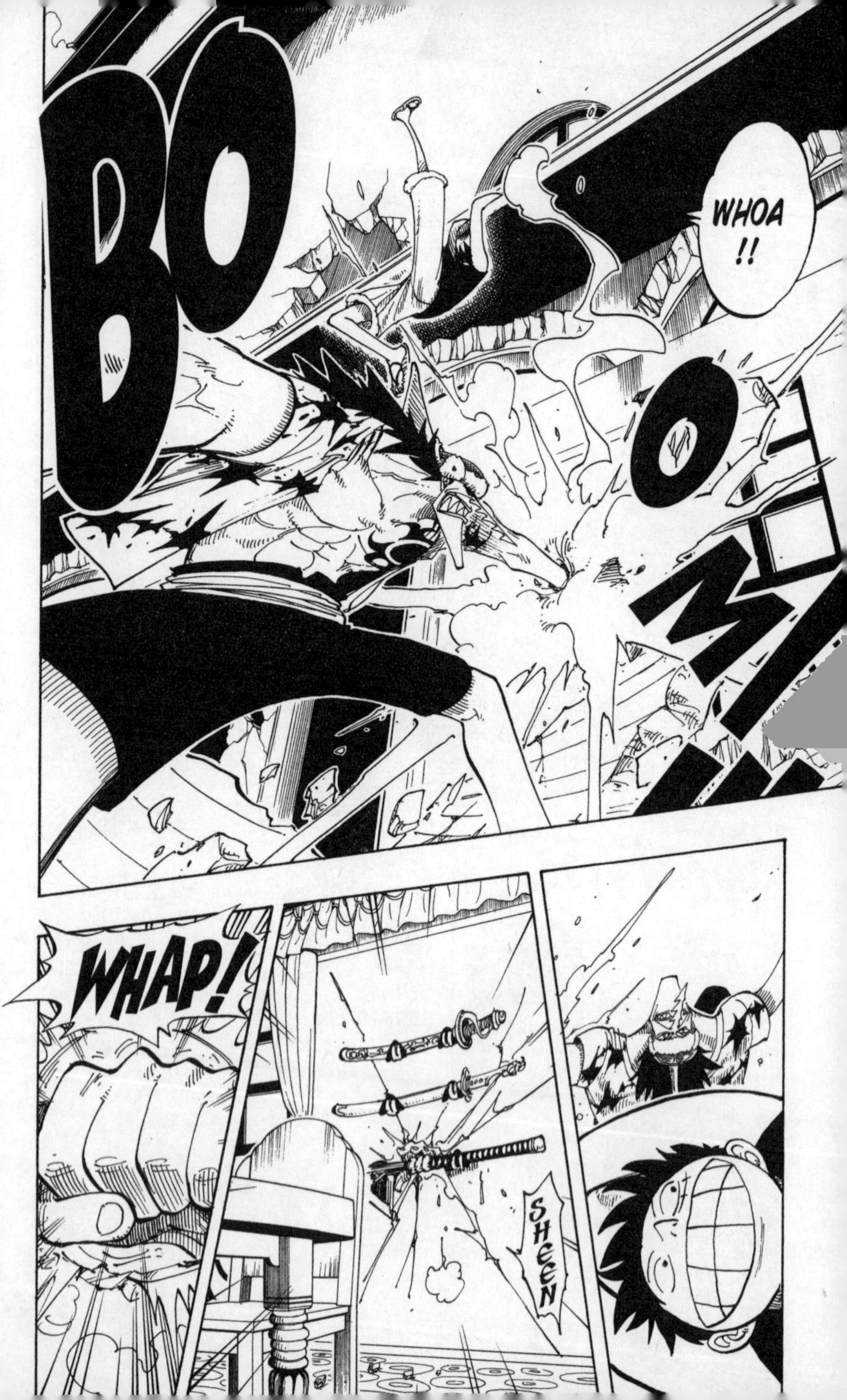
WHOA !!
BOOM
SHEEN
WHAP!

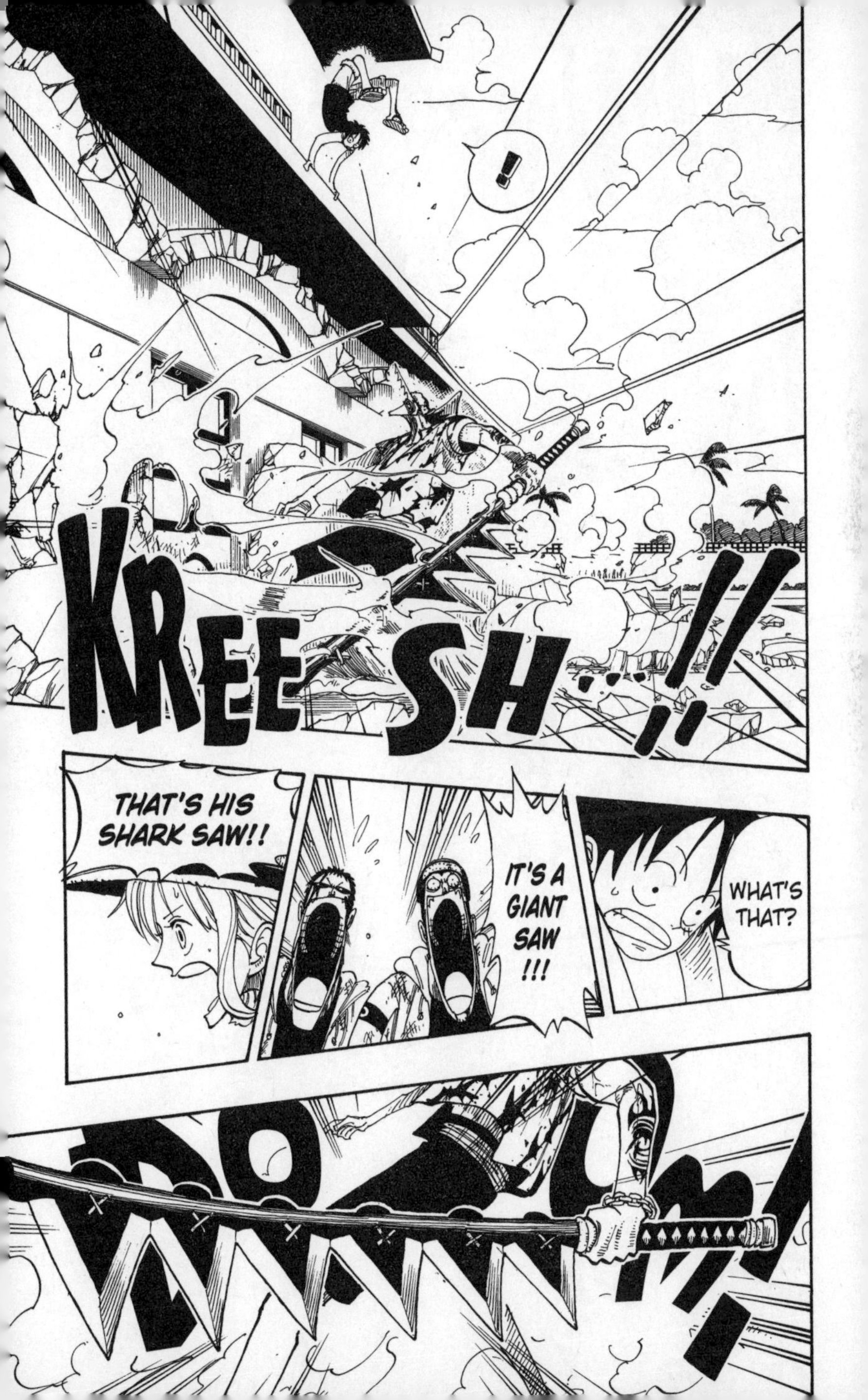
!
KREESH..!!
WHAT'S THAT?
IT'S A GIANT SAW!!!
THAT'S HIS SHARK SAW!!

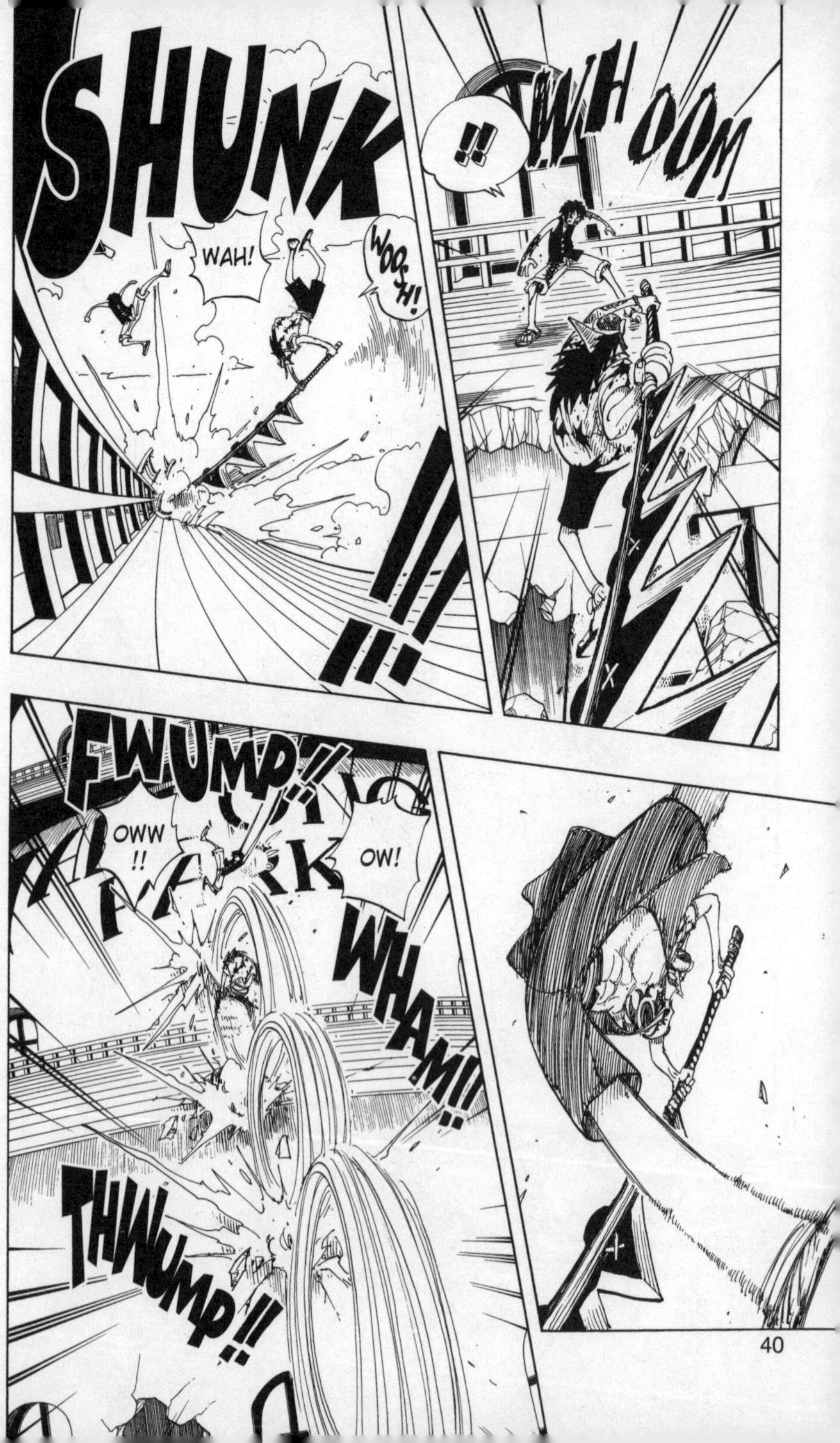
!!
TWHOOM
SHUNK
WOOSH!
WAH!
!!
!!
FWUMP!!
OW!
OWW !!
WHAM!!
THWUMP!!

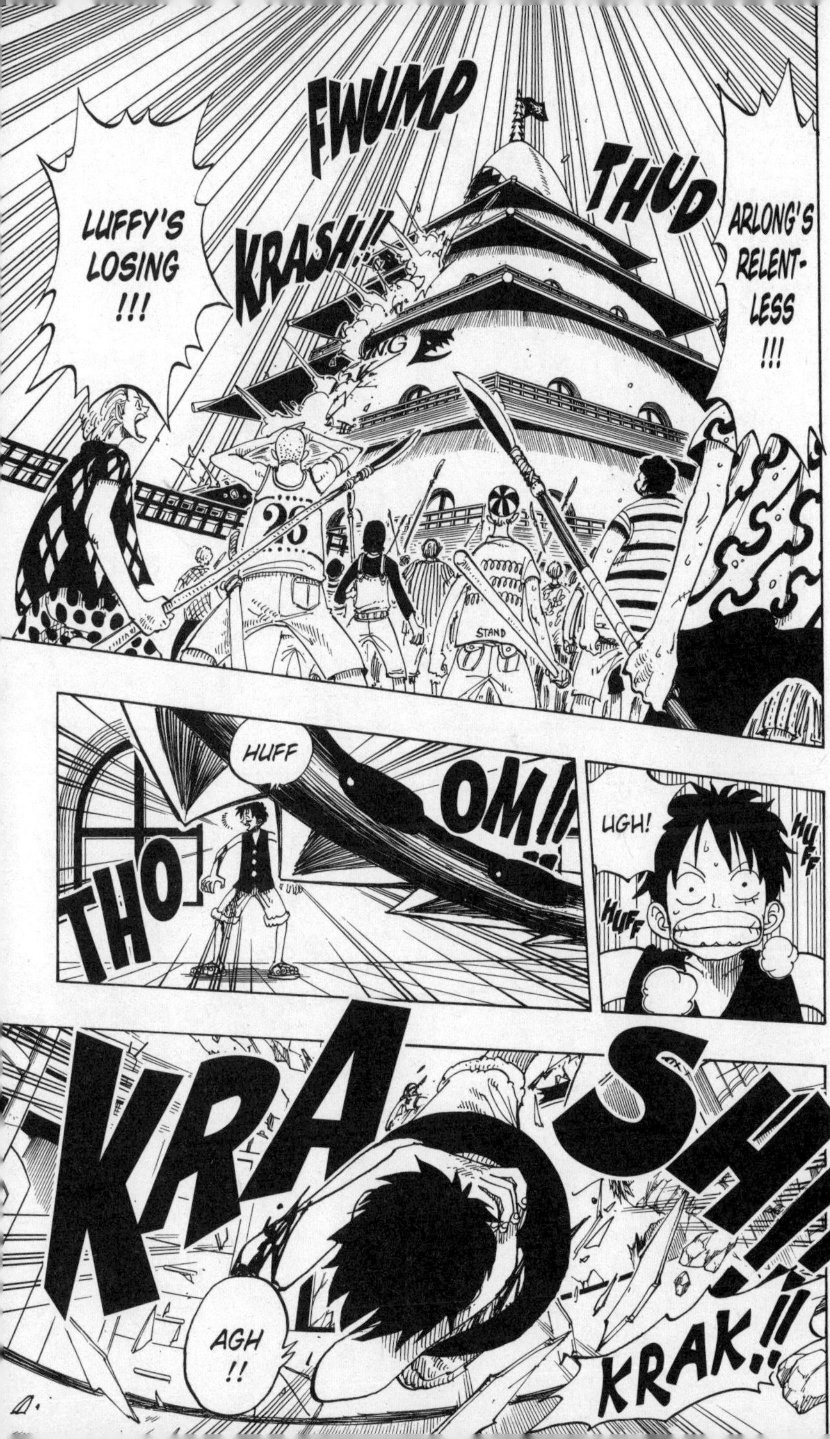
ARLONG'S RELENT-LESS!!!
THUD
FWUMP
KRASH!!
LUFFY'S LOSING!!!
UGH!
HUFF
HUFF
HUFF
THO OM!!
KRA SH!!
KRAK!!
AGH!!

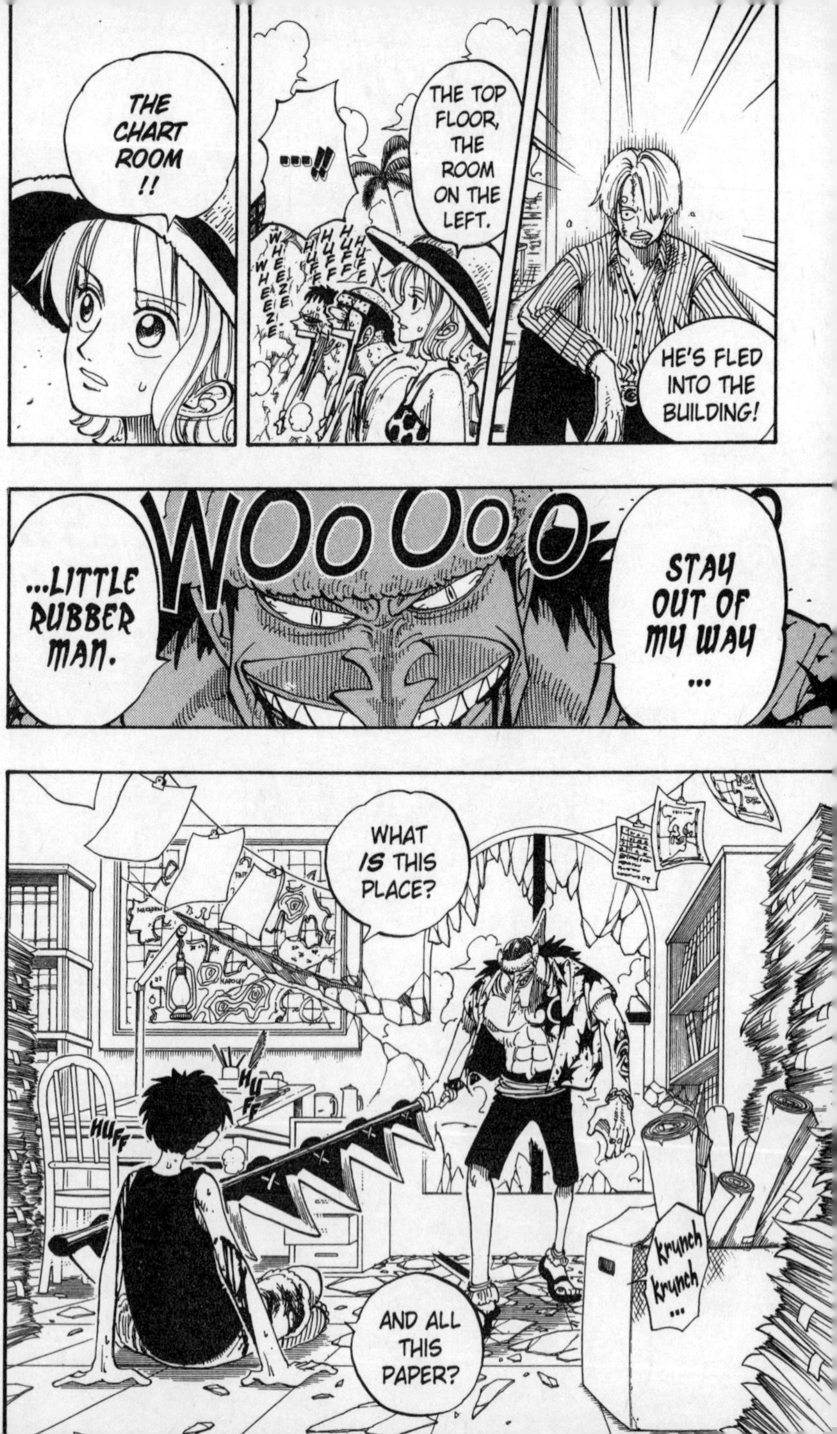
HE'S FLED INTO THE BUILDING!
THE TOP FLOOR, THE ROOM ON THE LEFT.
...!!
HUFF HUFF
WHEEZE WHEEZE
THE CHART ROOM !!
STAY OUT OF MY WAY ...
WOOOOO
...LITTLE RUBBER MAN.
WHAT *IS* THIS PLACE?
krunch krunch ...
HUFF
HUFF
AND ALL THIS PAPER?

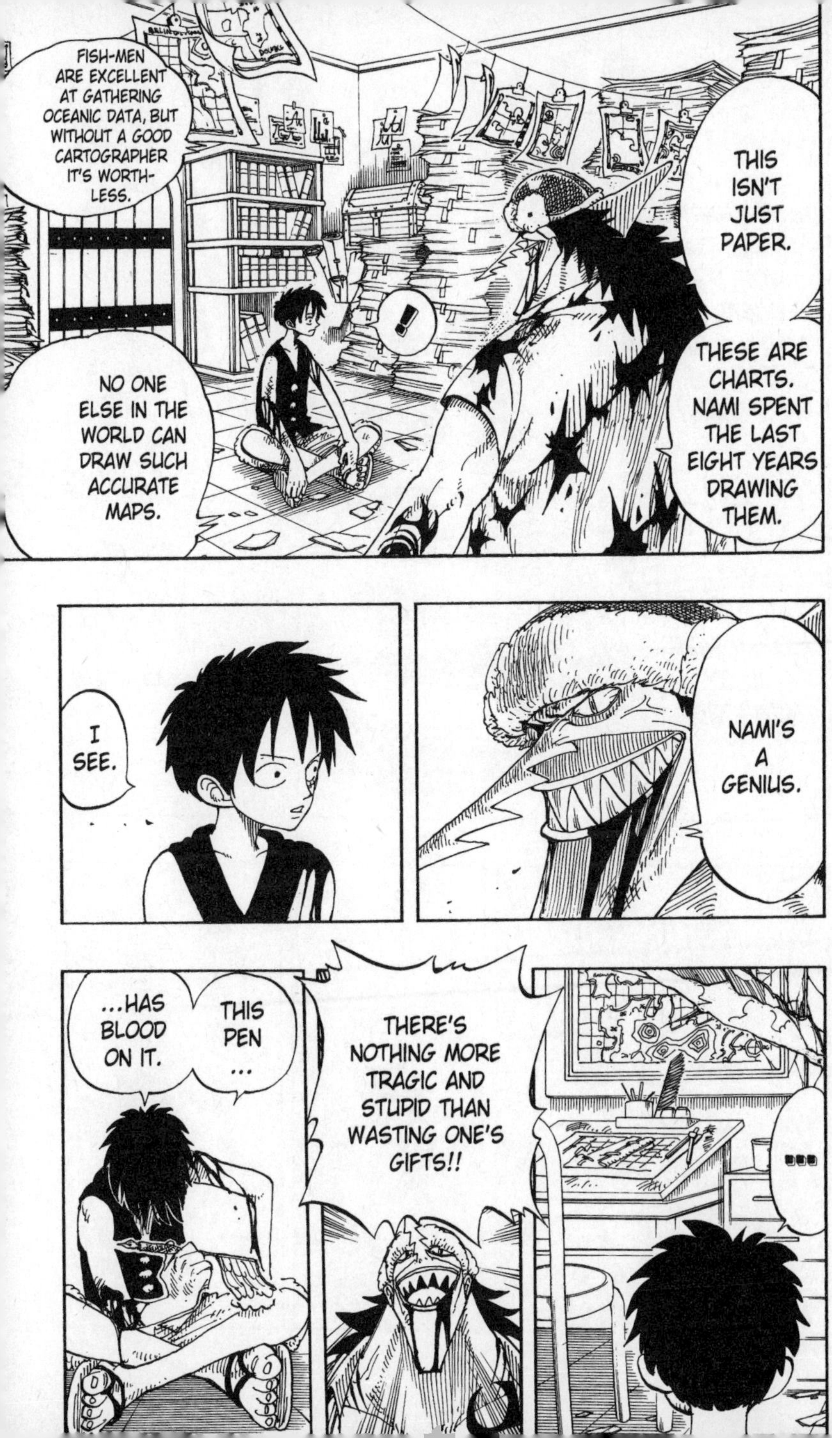
THIS ISN'T JUST PAPER.
THESE ARE CHARTS. NAMI SPENT THE LAST EIGHT YEARS DRAWING THEM.
!
FISH-MEN ARE EXCELLENT AT GATHERING OCEANIC DATA, BUT WITHOUT A GOOD CARTOGRAPHER IT'S WORTH-LESS.
NO ONE ELSE IN THE WORLD CAN DRAW SUCH ACCURATE MAPS.
NAMI'S A GENIUS.
I SEE.
...
THERE'S NOTHING MORE TRAGIC AND STUPID THAN WASTING ONE'S GIFTS!!
THIS PEN ...
...HAS BLOOD ON IT.

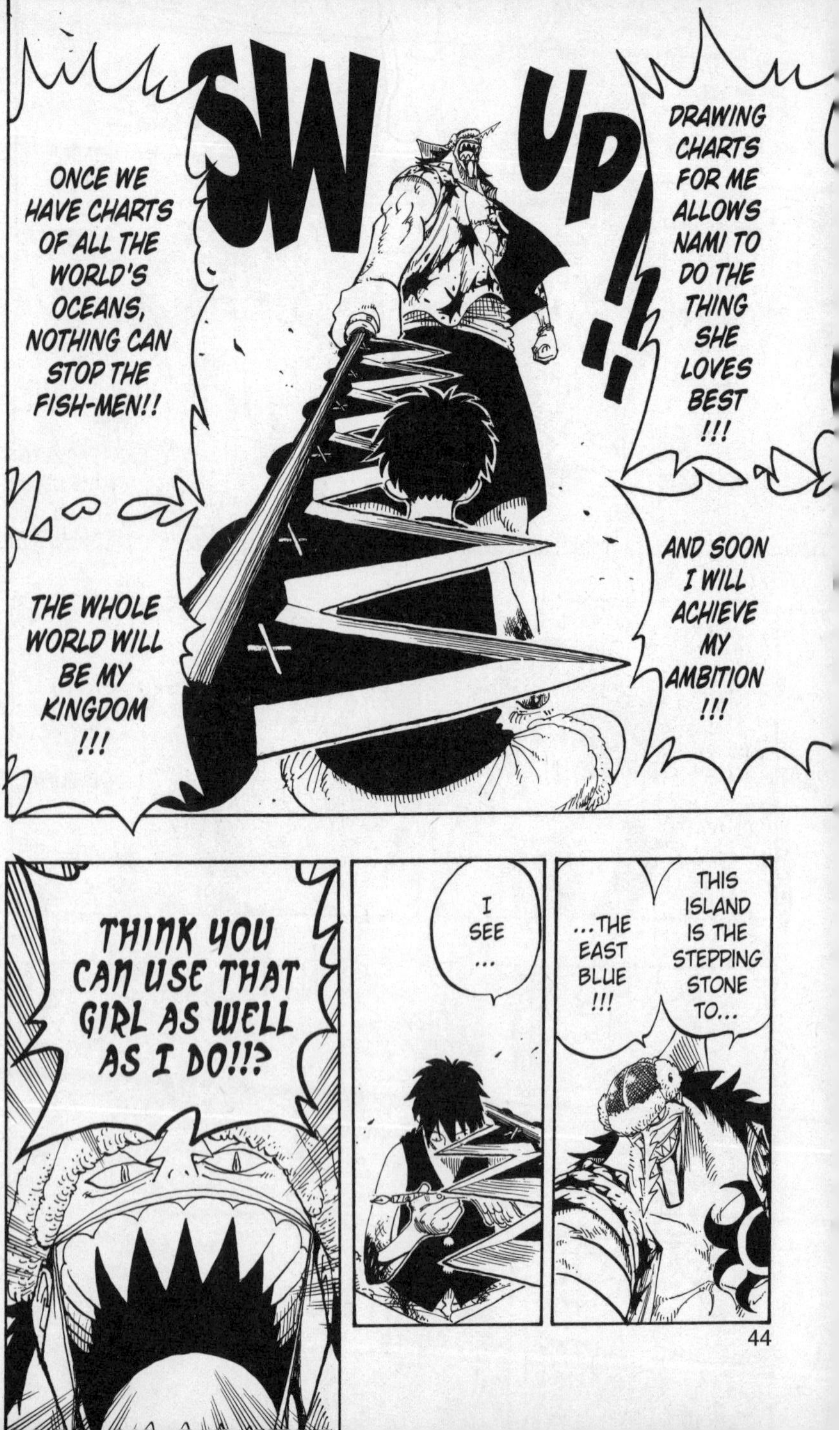
DRAWING CHARTS FOR ME ALLOWS NAMI TO DO THE THING SHE LOVES BEST!!!
SWUP!!
ONCE WE HAVE CHARTS OF ALL THE WORLD'S OCEANS, NOTHING CAN STOP THE FISH-MEN!!
AND SOON I WILL ACHIEVE MY AMBITION!!!
THE WHOLE WORLD WILL BE MY KINGDOM!!!
THIS ISLAND IS THE STEPPING STONE TO...
...THE EAST BLUE!!!
I SEE...
THINK YOU CAN USE THAT GIRL AS WELL AS I DO!!?

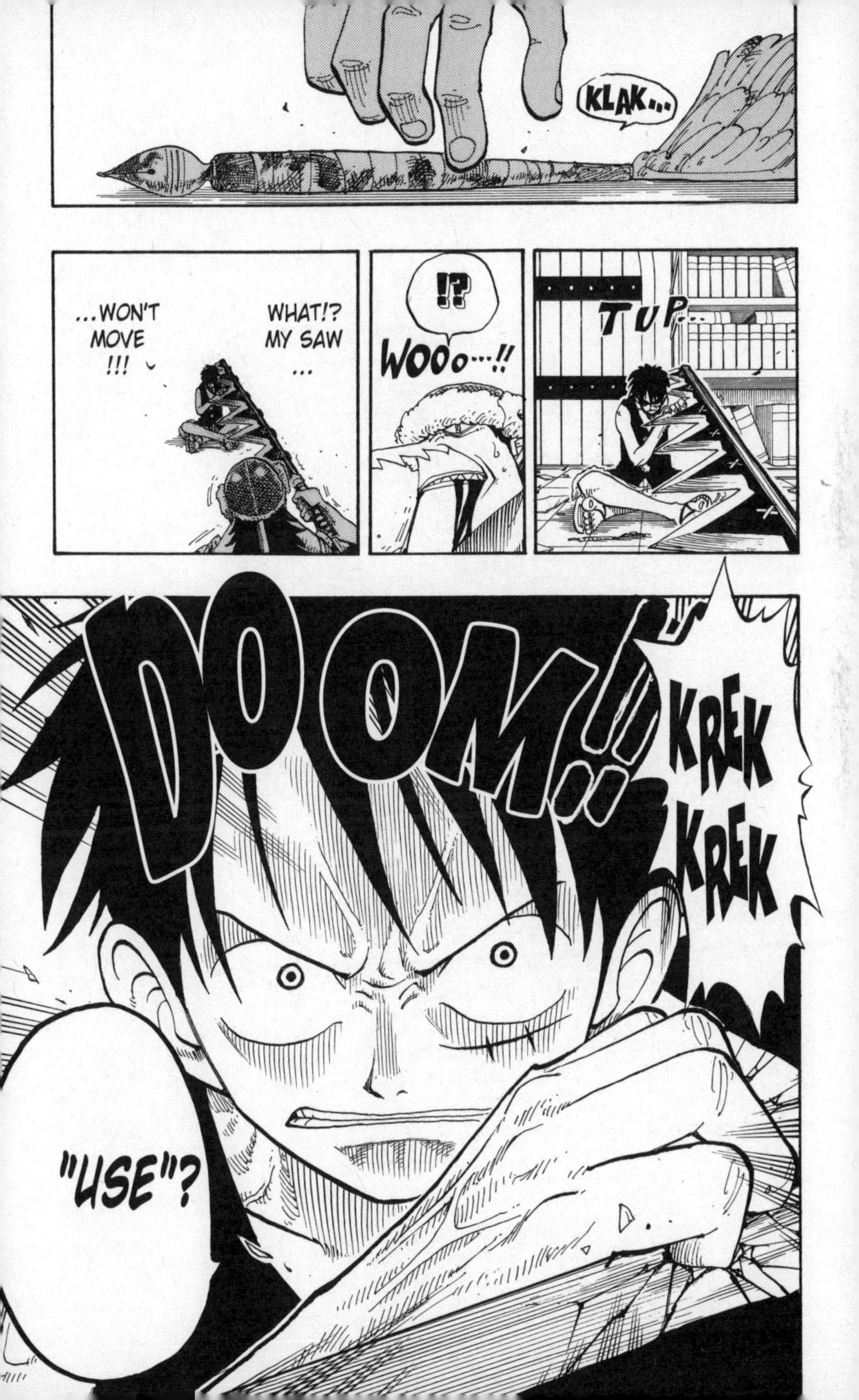
KLAK...
TUP...
!?
WOOo...!!
WHAT!? MY SAW ...
...WON'T MOVE !!!
KREK KREK
DOOM!!
"USE"?

1. Lounge

Conference Room, Galley, and Bridge

@ Room for meetings and discussions

@ The crew gathers here for meals and breaks.

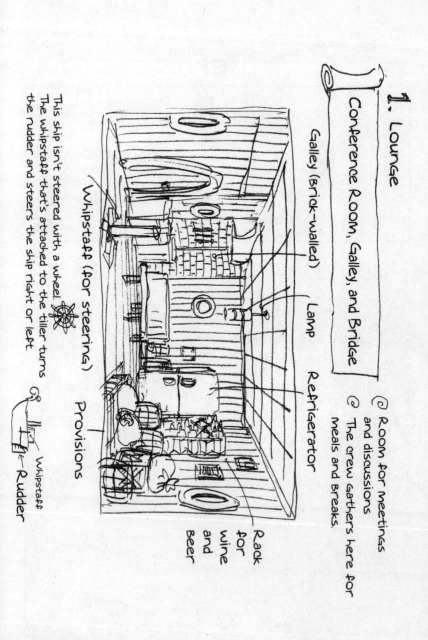

Galley (Brick-walled)
Lamp
Refrigerator
Rack for wine and Beer
Whipstaff (for steering)
Provisions

This ship isn't steered with a wheel.
The whipstaff that's attached to the tiller turns the rudder and steers the ship right or left.

Whipstaff
Rudder

Chapter 93: GOING DOWN

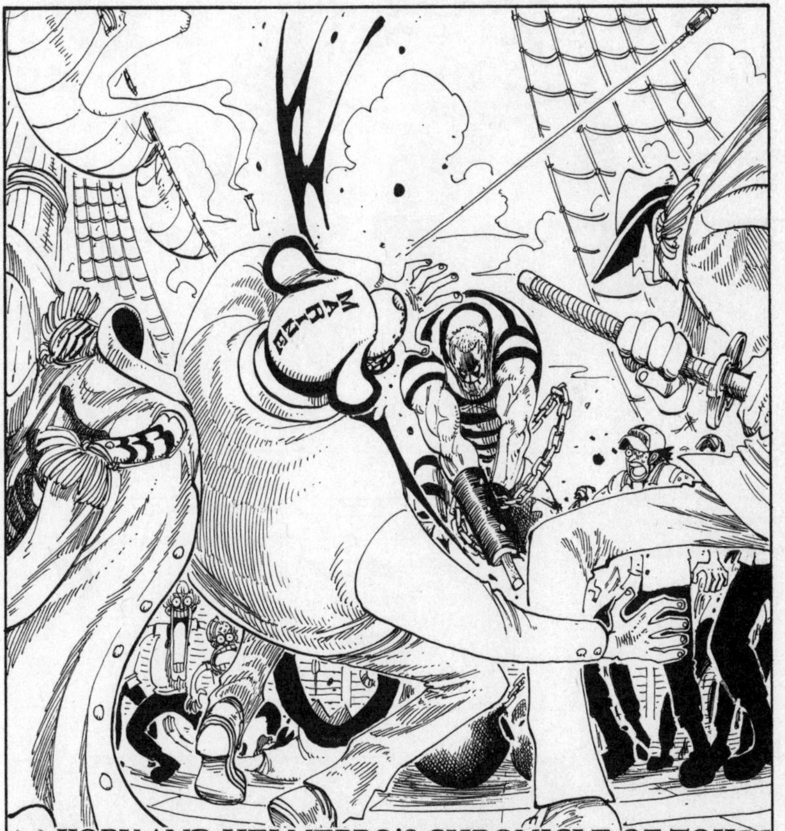
MARINE

KOBY AND HELMEPPO'S CHRONICLE OF TOIL
VOL. 10: "VICE ADMIRAL GARP LETS DOWN HIS GUARD"

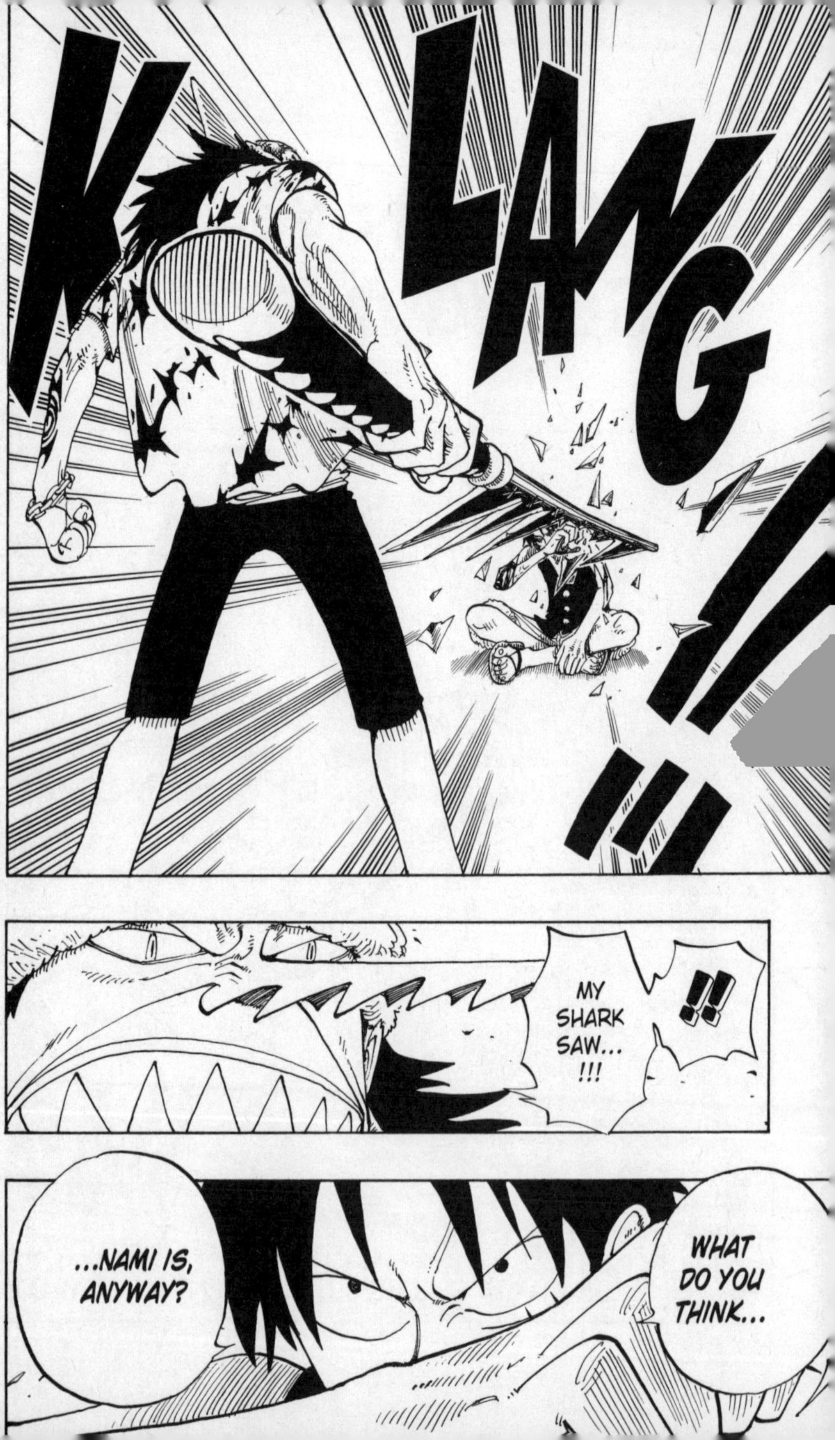
KLANG!!
!!
MY SHARK SAW... !!!
WHAT DO YOU THINK...
...NAMI IS, ANYWAY?

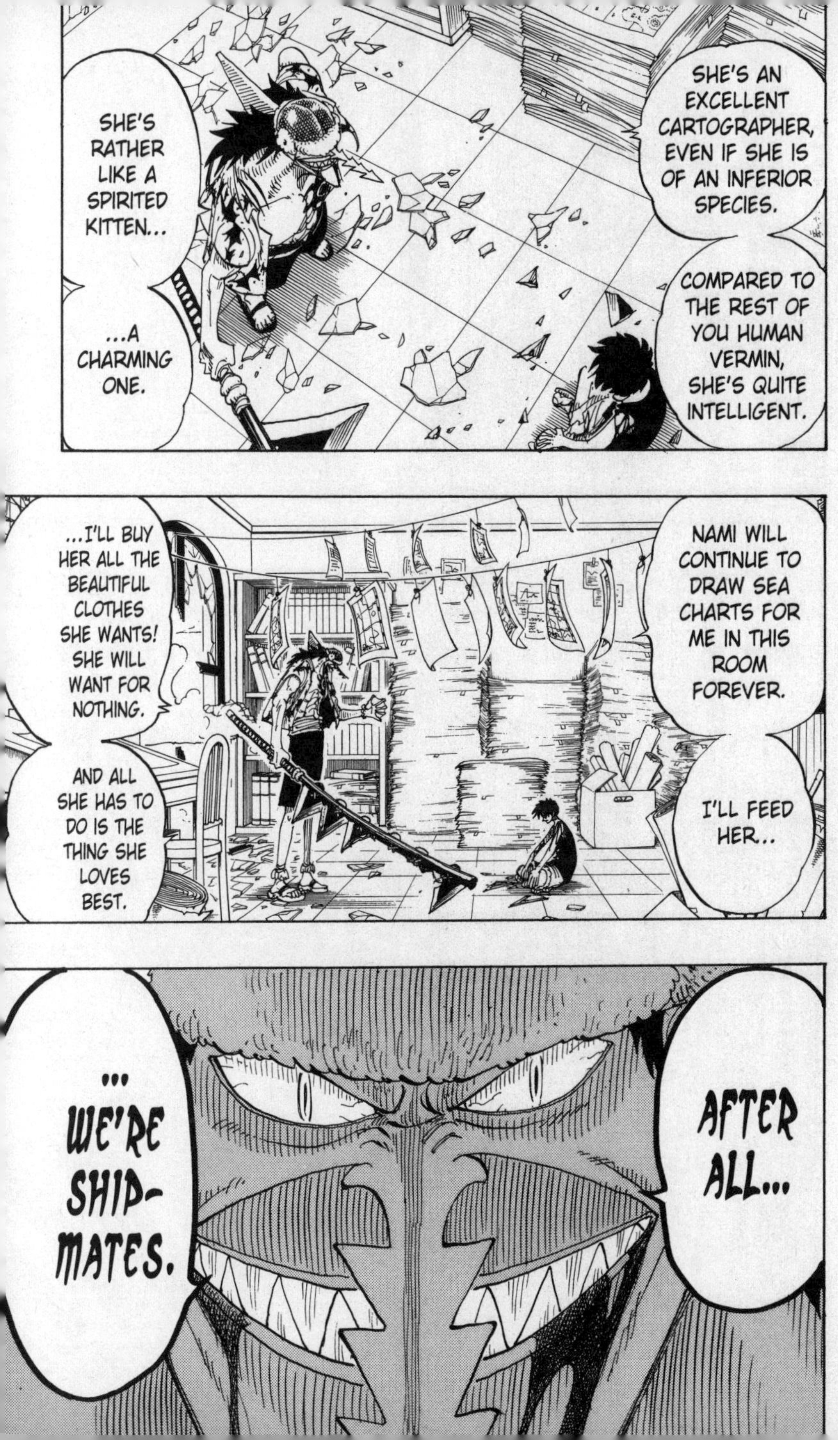
SHE'S AN EXCELLENT CARTOGRAPHER, EVEN IF SHE IS OF AN INFERIOR SPECIES.
COMPARED TO THE REST OF YOU HUMAN VERMIN, SHE'S QUITE INTELLIGENT.
SHE'S RATHER LIKE A SPIRITED KITTEN...
...A CHARMING ONE.
NAMI WILL CONTINUE TO DRAW SEA CHARTS FOR ME IN THIS ROOM FOREVER.
I'LL FEED HER...
...I'LL BUY HER ALL THE BEAUTIFUL CLOTHES SHE WANTS! SHE WILL WANT FOR NOTHING.
AND ALL SHE HAS TO DO IS THE THING SHE LOVES BEST.
AFTER ALL...
...WE'RE SHIP-MATES.

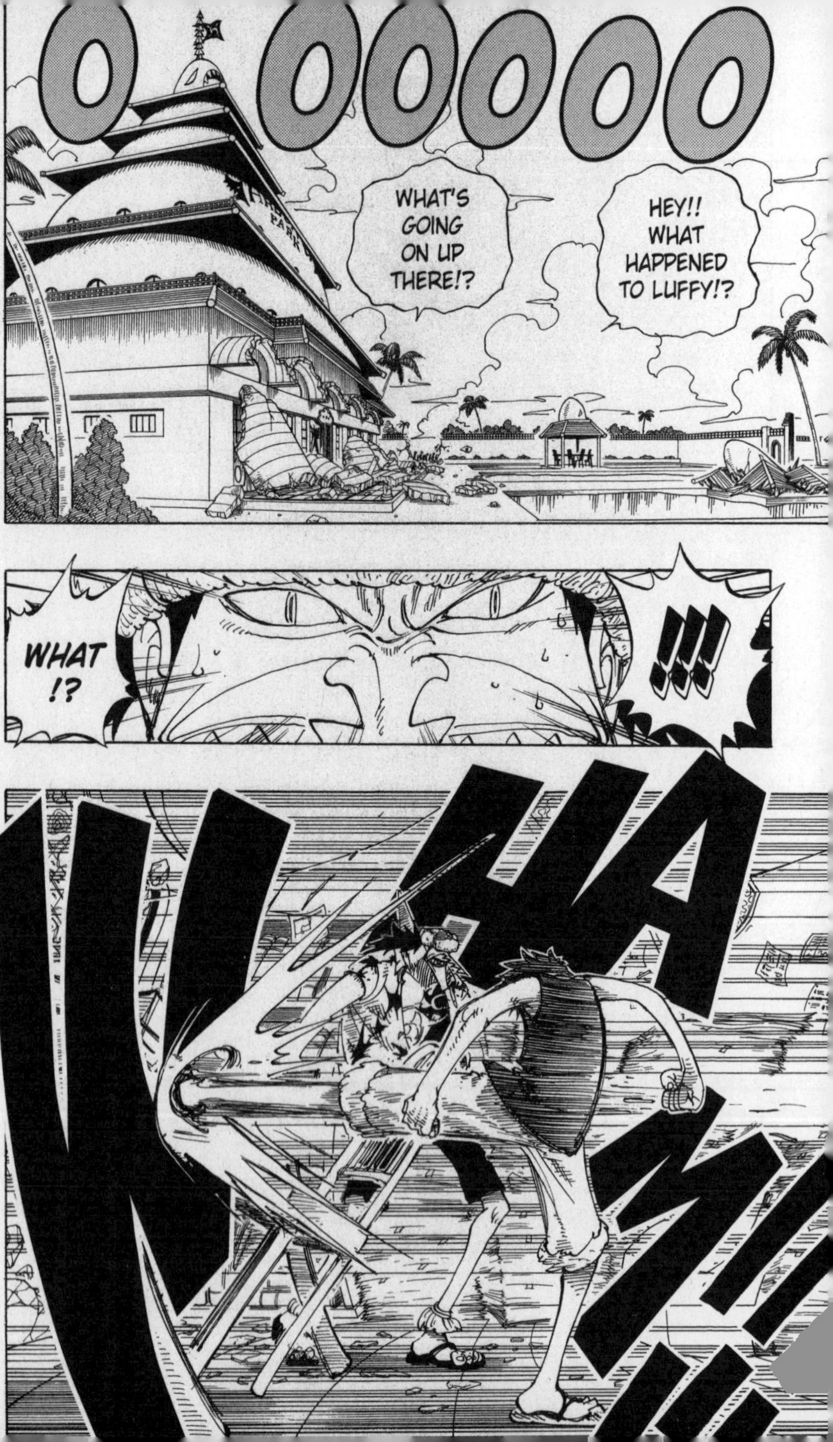
O OOOOO
HEY!! WHAT HAPPENED TO LUFFY!?
WHAT'S GOING ON UP THERE!?
!!!
WHAT !?

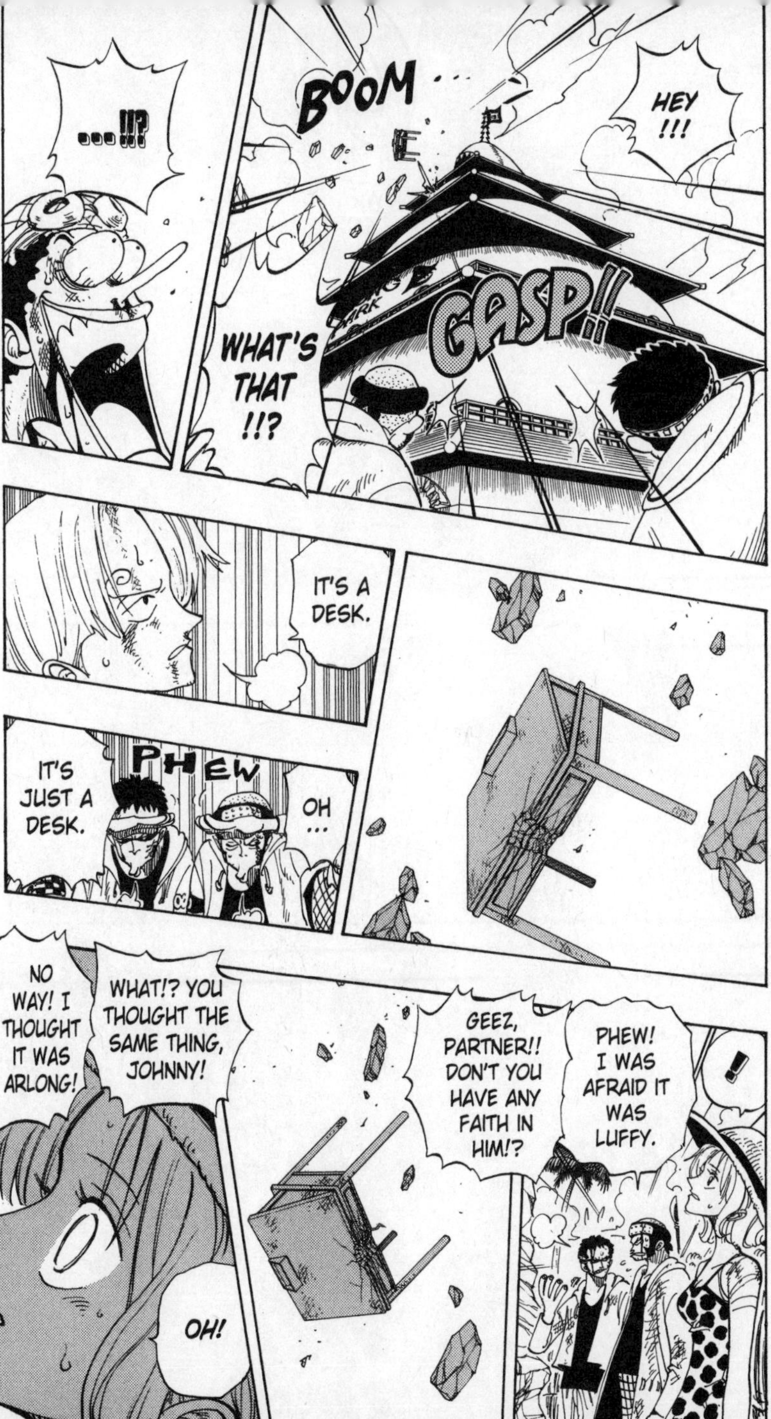
HEY !!!
BOOM...
GASP!!
WHAT'S THAT !!?
...!!?
IT'S A DESK.
OH ...
PHEW
IT'S JUST A DESK.
!
PHEW! I WAS AFRAID IT WAS LUFFY.
GEEZ, PARTNER!! DON'T YOU HAVE ANY FAITH IN HIM!?
WHAT!? YOU THOUGHT THE SAME THING, JOHNNY!
NO WAY! I THOUGHT IT WAS ARLONG!
OH!

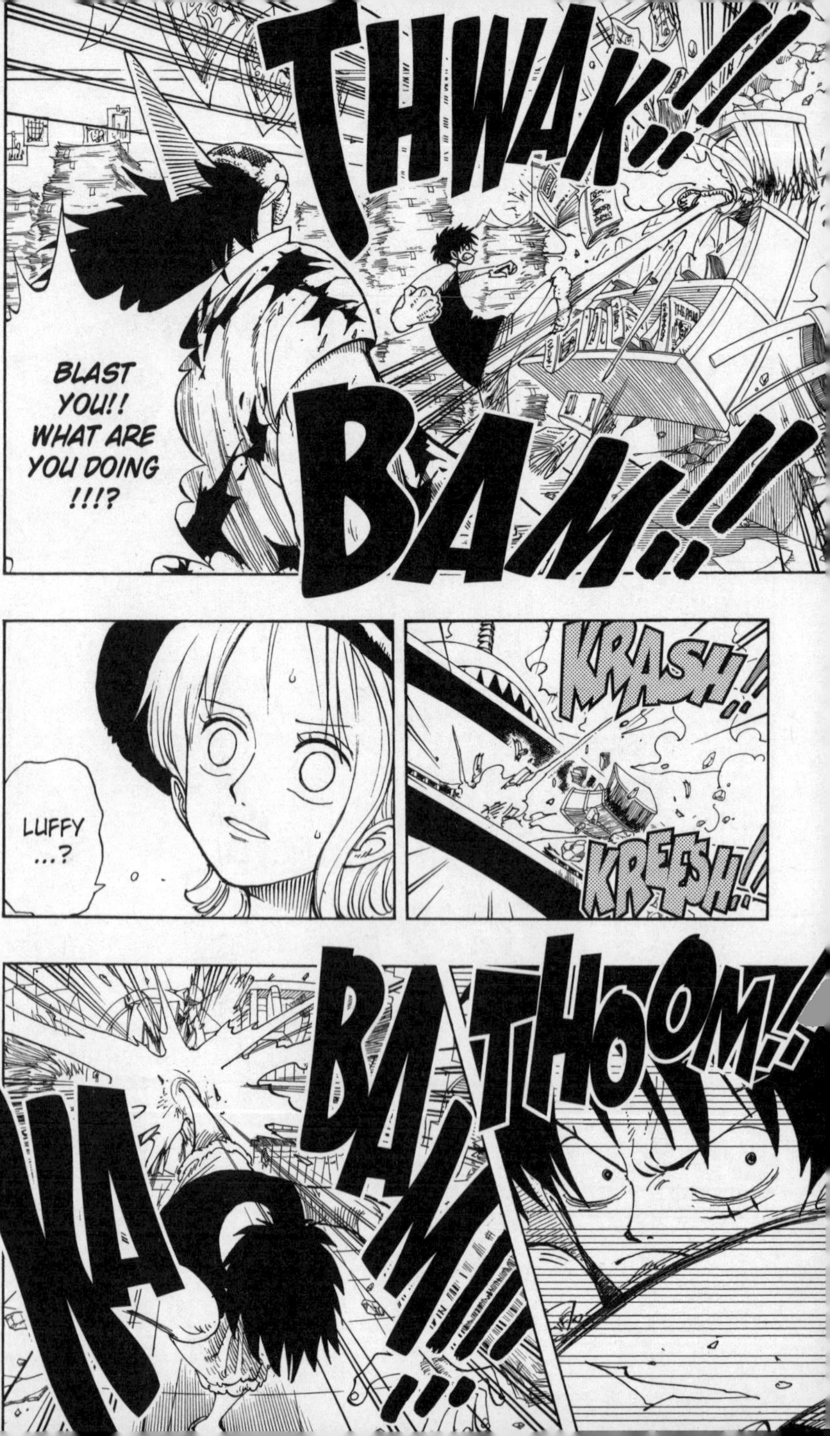
THWAK!!
BAM!!
BLAST YOU!! WHAT ARE YOU DOING!!!?
KRASH!!
KREESH!!
LUFFY ...?
BATHOOM!!
BAM!!
KA

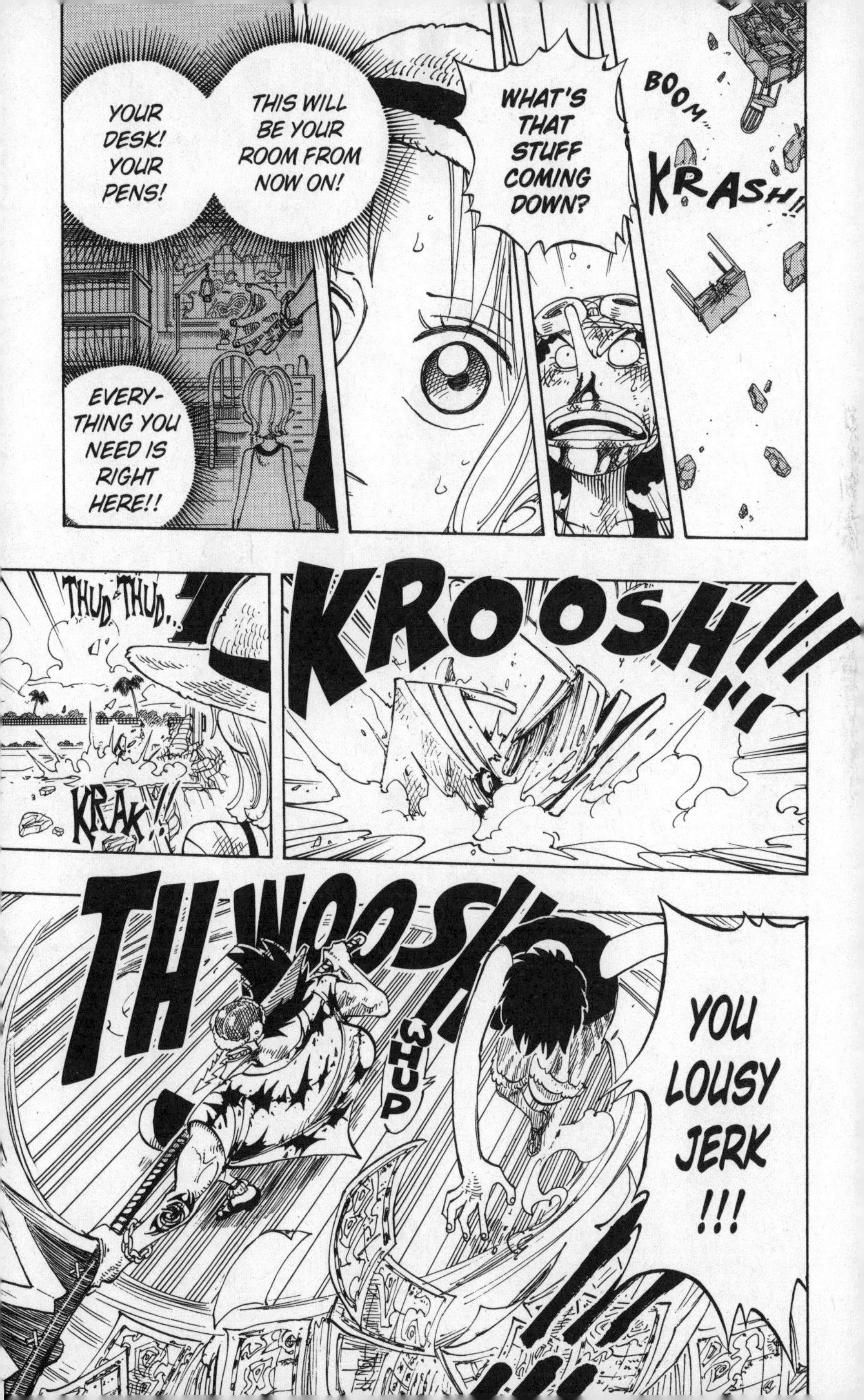
BOOM...
KRASH!!
WHAT'S THAT STUFF COMING DOWN?
THIS WILL BE YOUR ROOM FROM NOW ON!
YOUR DESK! YOUR PENS!
EVERY-THING YOU NEED IS RIGHT HERE!!
KROOSH!!!
THUD THUD...
KRAK!!
YOU LOUSY JERK!!!
SHUP
THWOOSH

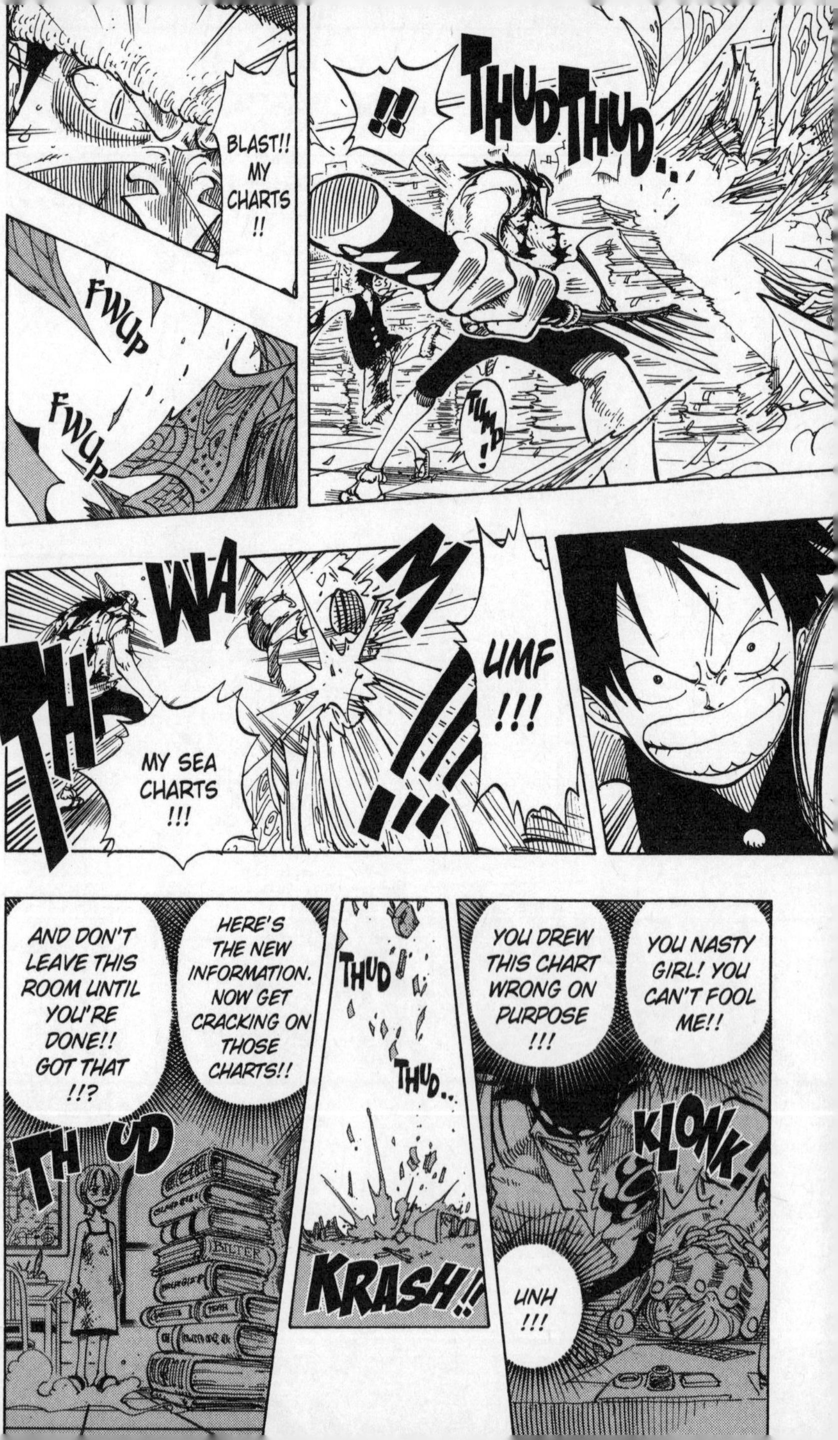

!!
THUD THUD..
TUMP!
BLAST!! MY CHARTS!!
FWUP
FWUP
UMF!!!
THWAM!!!
MY SEA CHARTS!!!
YOU NASTY GIRL! YOU CAN'T FOOL ME!!
YOU DREW THIS CHART WRONG ON PURPOSE!!!
KLONK!
UNH!!!
THUD
THUD..
KRASH!!
HERE'S THE NEW INFORMATION. NOW GET CRACKING ON THOSE CHARTS!!
AND DON'T LEAVE THIS ROOM UNTIL YOU'RE DONE!! GOT THAT!!?
THUD

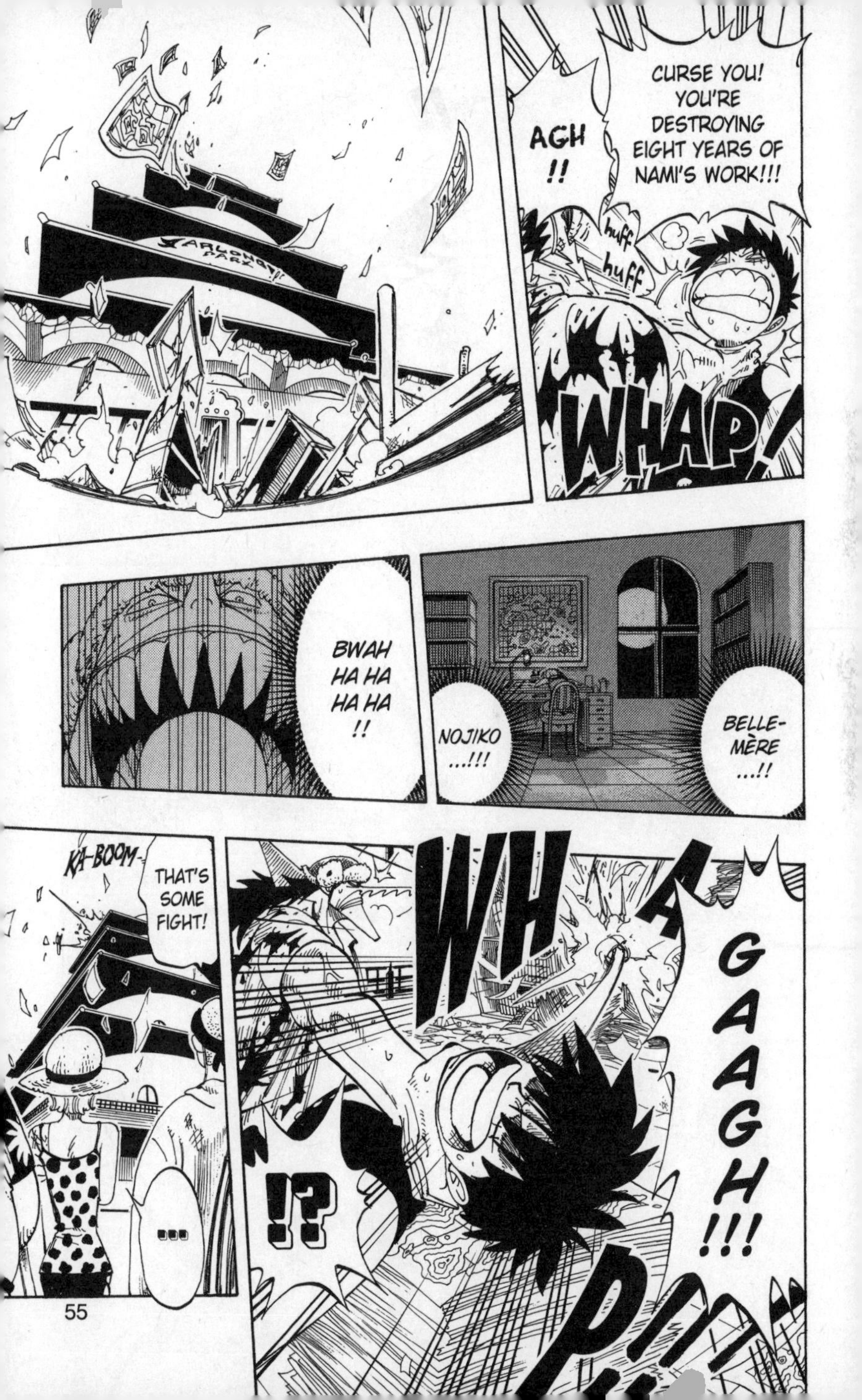
CURSE YOU! YOU'RE DESTROYING EIGHT YEARS OF NAMI'S WORK!!!
AGH !!
huff huff
WHAP!
BELLE-MÈRE ...!!
NOJIKO ...!!!
BWAH HA HA HA HA !!
WHAAGAAGH!!!
!?
KA-BOOM
THAT'S SOME FIGHT!
...

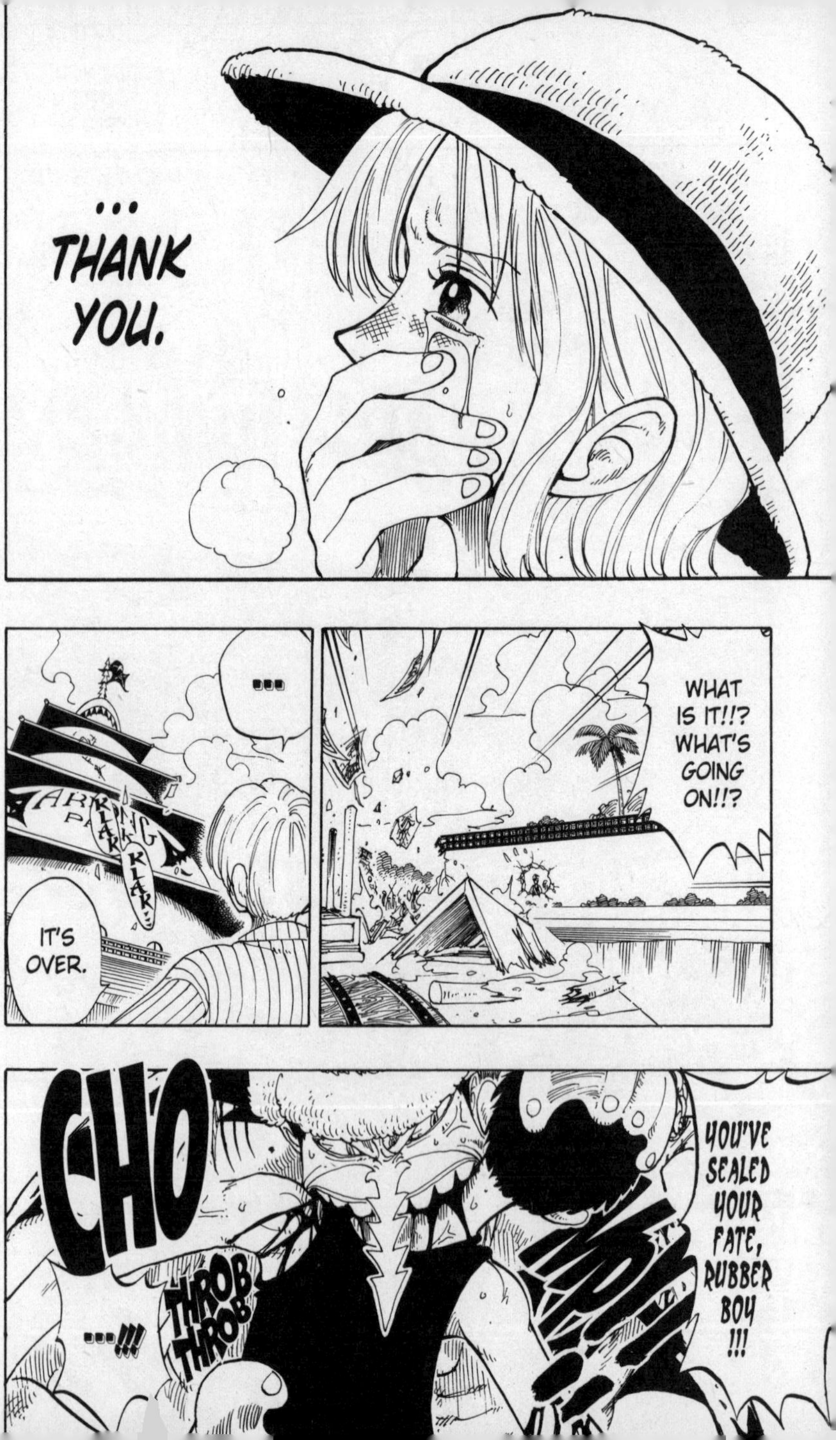
...THANK YOU.
WHAT IS IT!!? WHAT'S GOING ON!!?
...
IT'S OVER.
KLAK KLAK KLAK
YOU'VE SEALED YOUR FATE, RUBBER BOY!!!
CHO
THROB THROB
...!!!

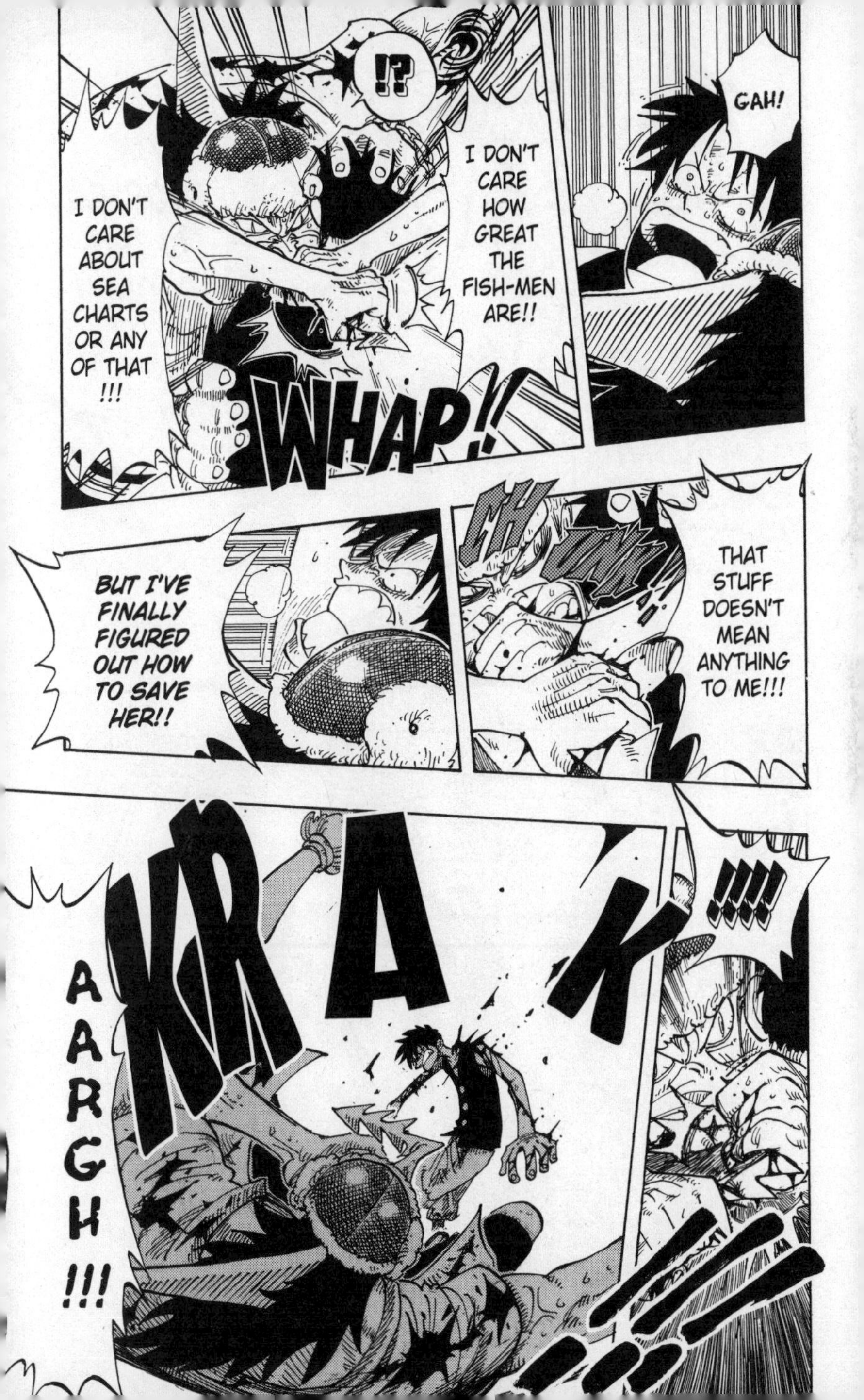
GAH!
!?
I DON'T CARE HOW GREAT THE FISH-MEN ARE!!
I DON'T CARE ABOUT SEA CHARTS OR ANY OF THAT !!!
WHAP!!
THAT STUFF DOESN'T MEAN ANYTHING TO ME!!!
BUT I'VE FINALLY FIGURED OUT HOW TO SAVE HER!!
KRAK!!!!
AARGH!!!

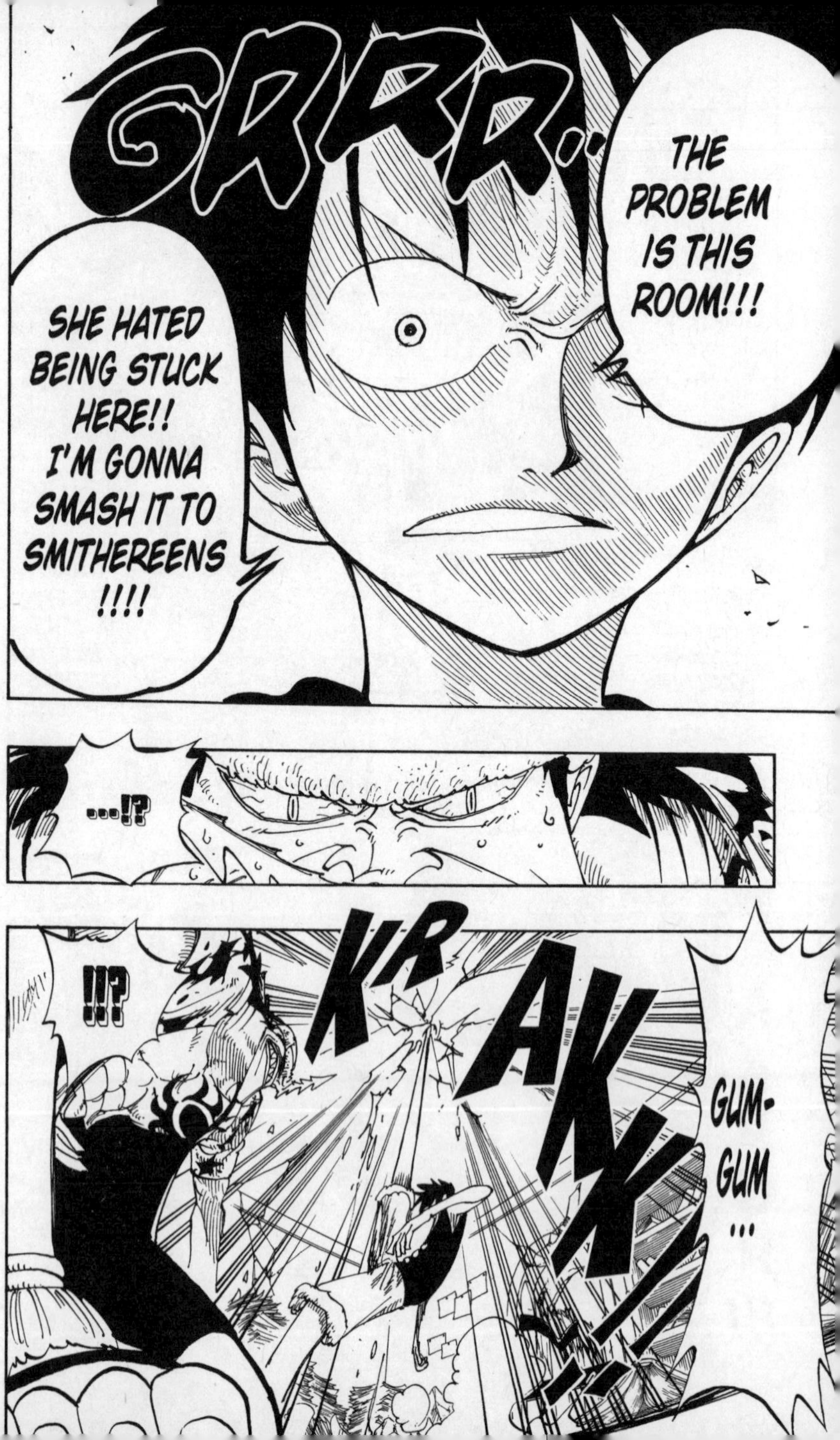
GRRR..
THE PROBLEM IS THIS ROOM!!!
SHE HATED BEING STUCK HERE!! I'M GONNA SMASH IT TO SMITHEREENS !!!!
...!?
GUM-GUM ...
KRAK
!!?

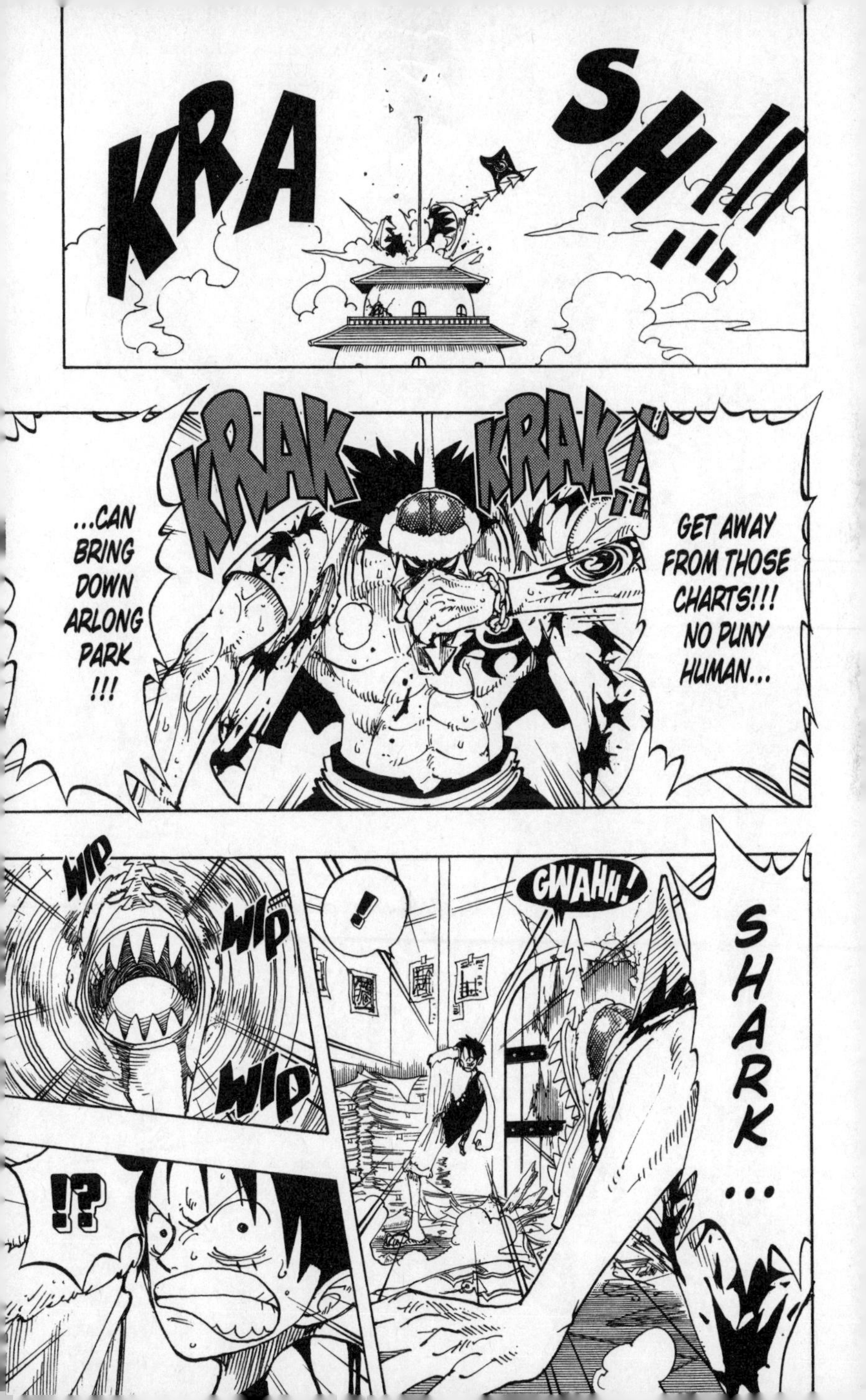
KRA
SH!!!!!
KRAK KRAK!!
GET AWAY FROM THOSE CHARTS!!! NO PUNY HUMAN...
...CAN BRING DOWN ARLONG PARK!!!
SHARK...
GWAHH!
!
WIP
WIP
WIP
!?

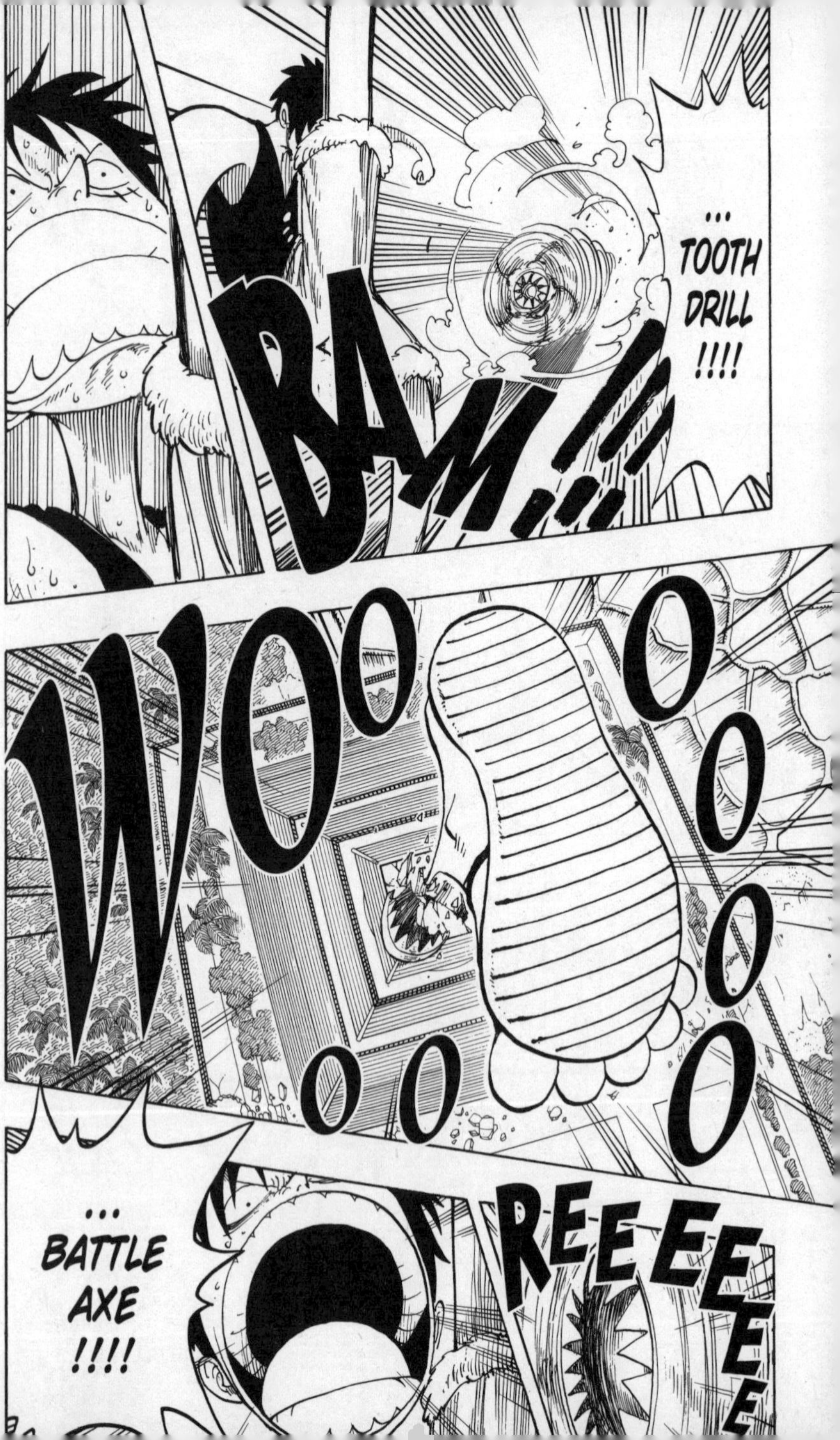
... TOOTH DRILL !!!!
BAM!!!!
WOOOOOOOOOO
... BATTLE AXE !!!!
REEEEEEE

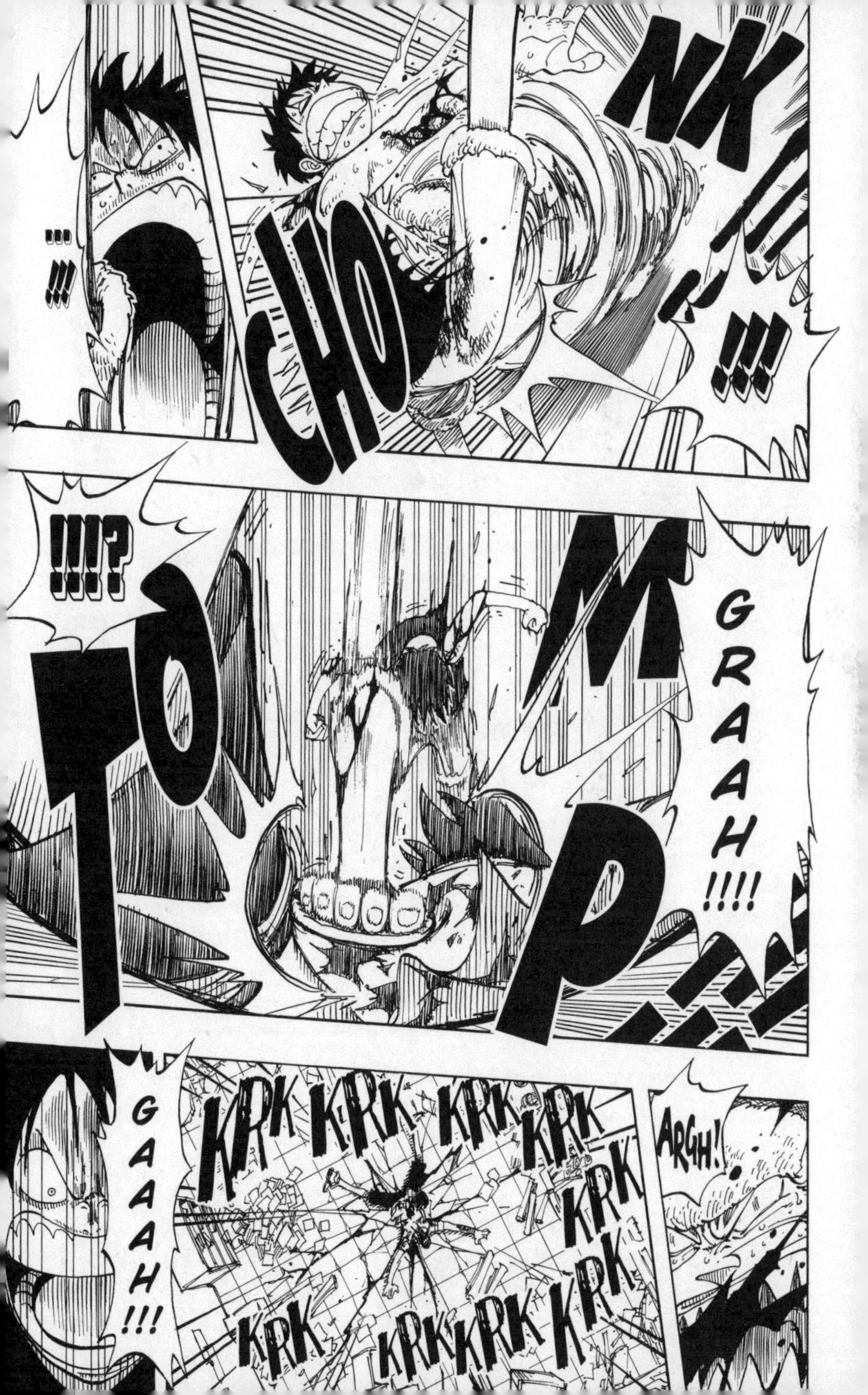
CHO
NK!!!
...!!!
GRAAH!!!!
TOMP
!!!?
ARGH!
KRK KRK KRK KRK KRK KRK KRK KRK KRK KRK KRK
GAAAAH!!!

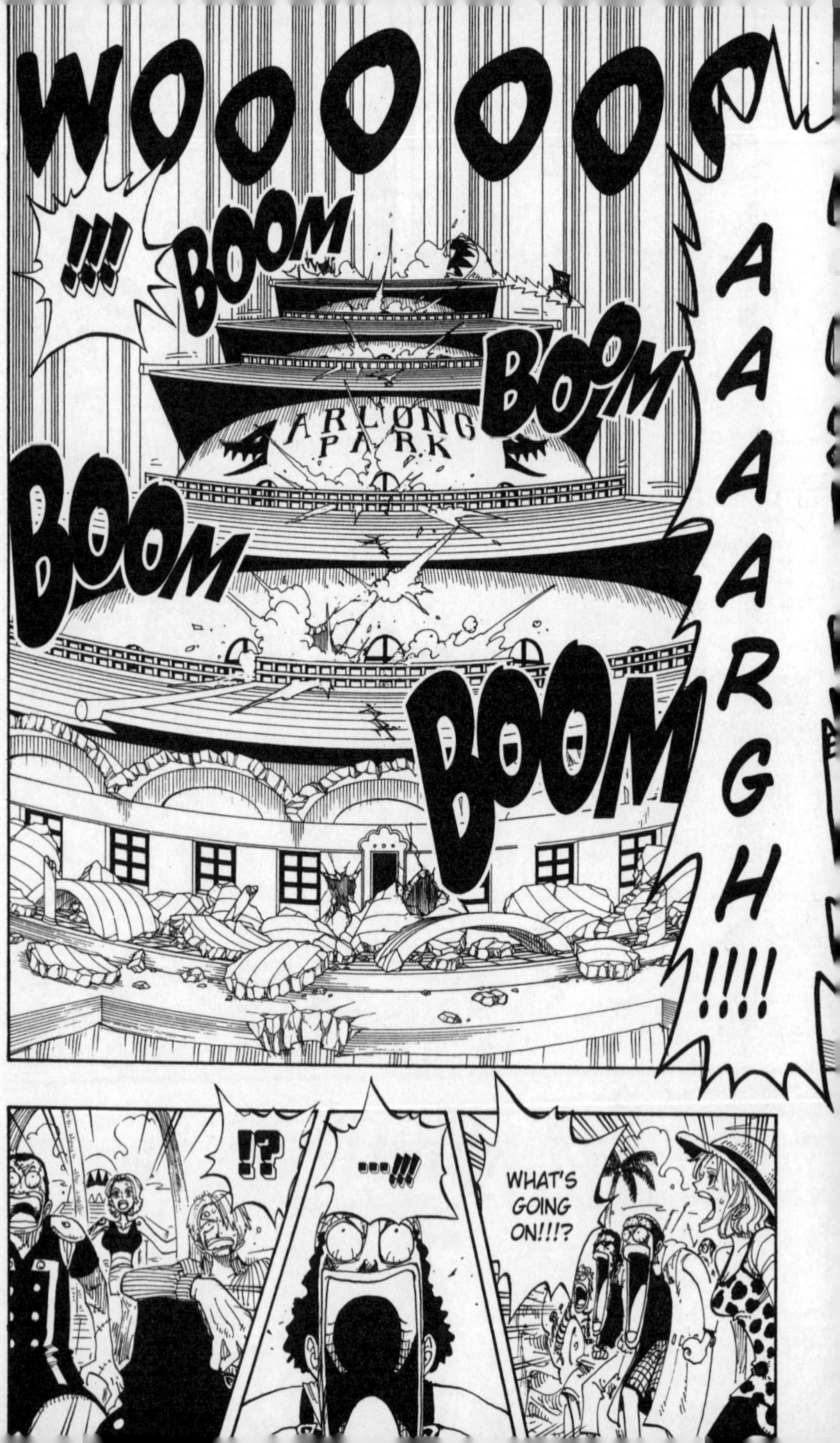
WOOOOOO
AAAARGH!!!!
!!!
BOOM
BOOM
ARLONG PARK
BOOM
BOOM
WHAT'S GOING ON!!!?
...!!!
!?

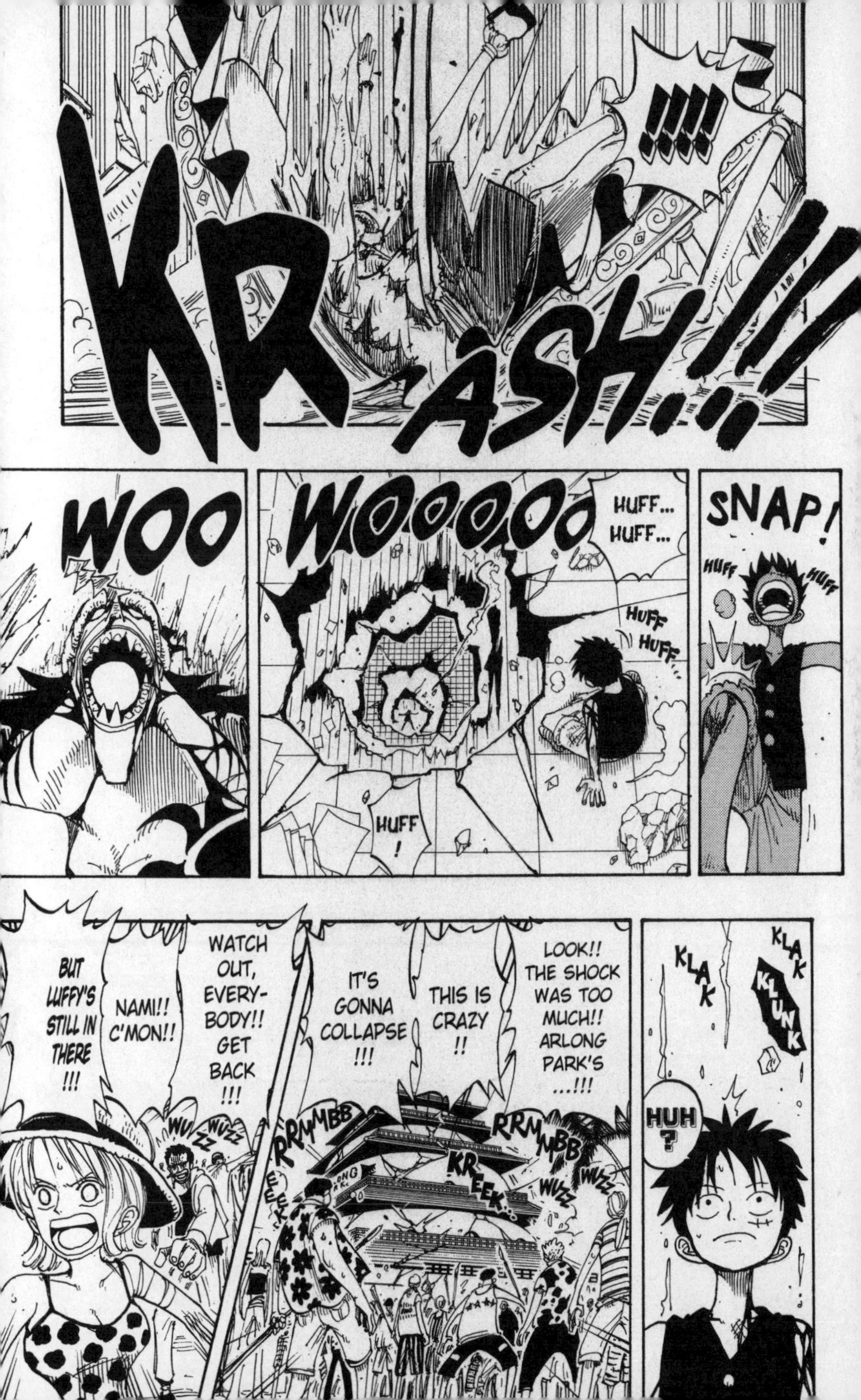
!!!!
KRASH!!!
SNAP!
HUFF
HUFF
HUFF... HUFF...
HUFF
HUFF
HUFF!
WOOOOO
WOO
KLAK
KLAK
KLUNK
HUH?
LOOK!! THE SHOCK WAS TOO MUCH!! ARLONG PARK'S ...!!!
THIS IS CRAZY!!
IT'S GONNA COLLAPSE!!!
RRRMMBB
KREEEK
RRRMMBB
WUZZ
WATCH OUT, EVERYBODY!! GET BACK!!!
NAMI!! C'MON!!
BUT LUFFY'S STILL IN THERE!!!
WUZZ
WUZZ

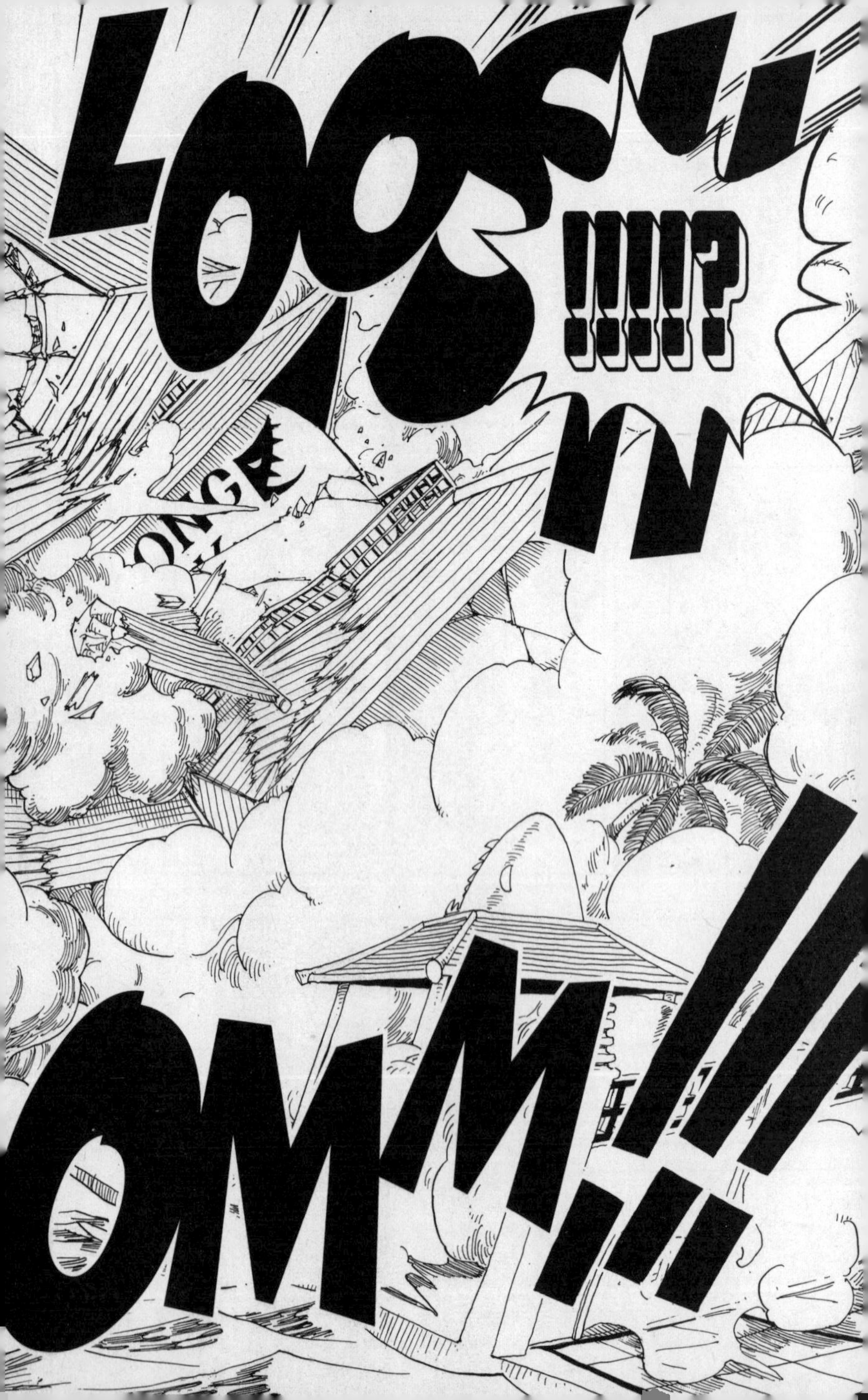
!!!!?

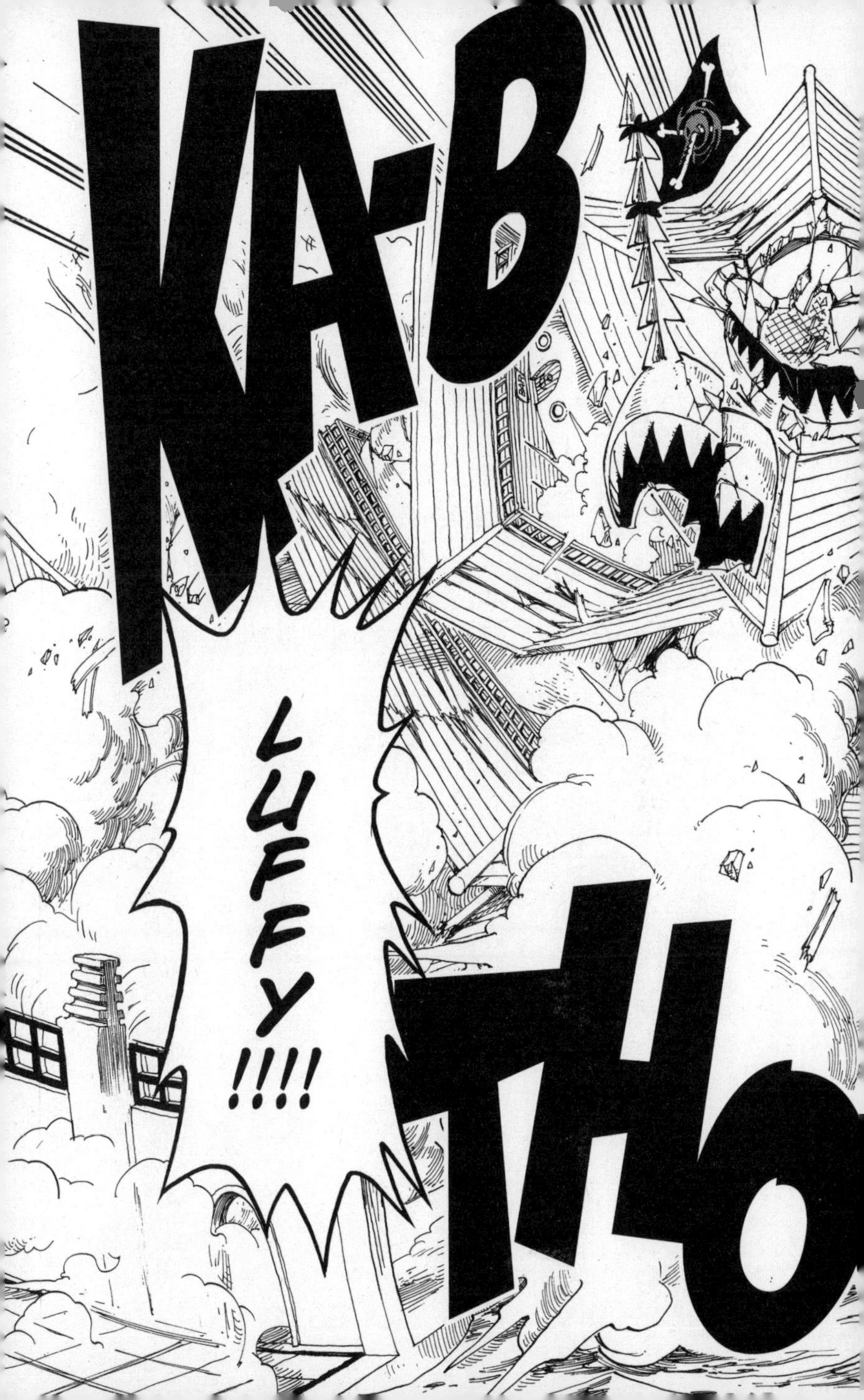
KA-B
LUFFY!!!!
THO

2. Men's Quarters

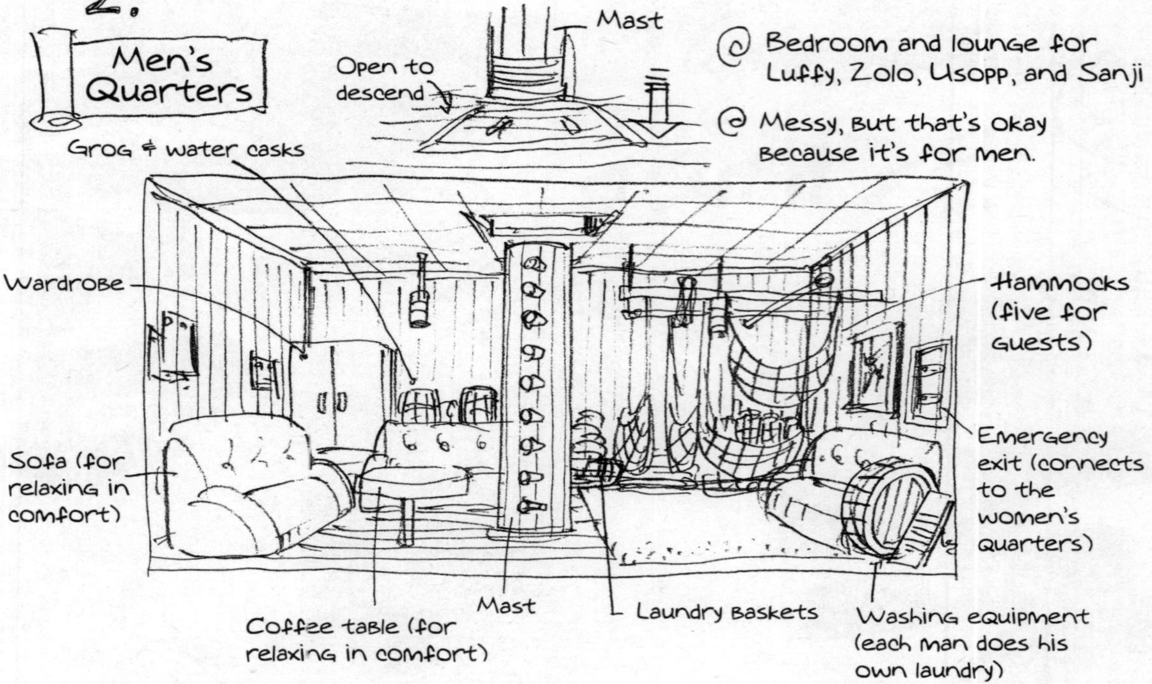
Mast
Open to descend
@ Bedroom and lounge for Luffy, Zolo, Usopp, and Sanji
@ Messy, but that's okay because it's for men.
Grog & water casks
Wardrobe
Hammocks (five for guests)
Emergency exit (connects to the women's quarters)
Sofa (for relaxing in comfort)
Mast
Laundry baskets
Coffee table (for relaxing in comfort)
Washing equipment (each man does his own laundry)

Chapter 94:
THE OTHER VILLAIN

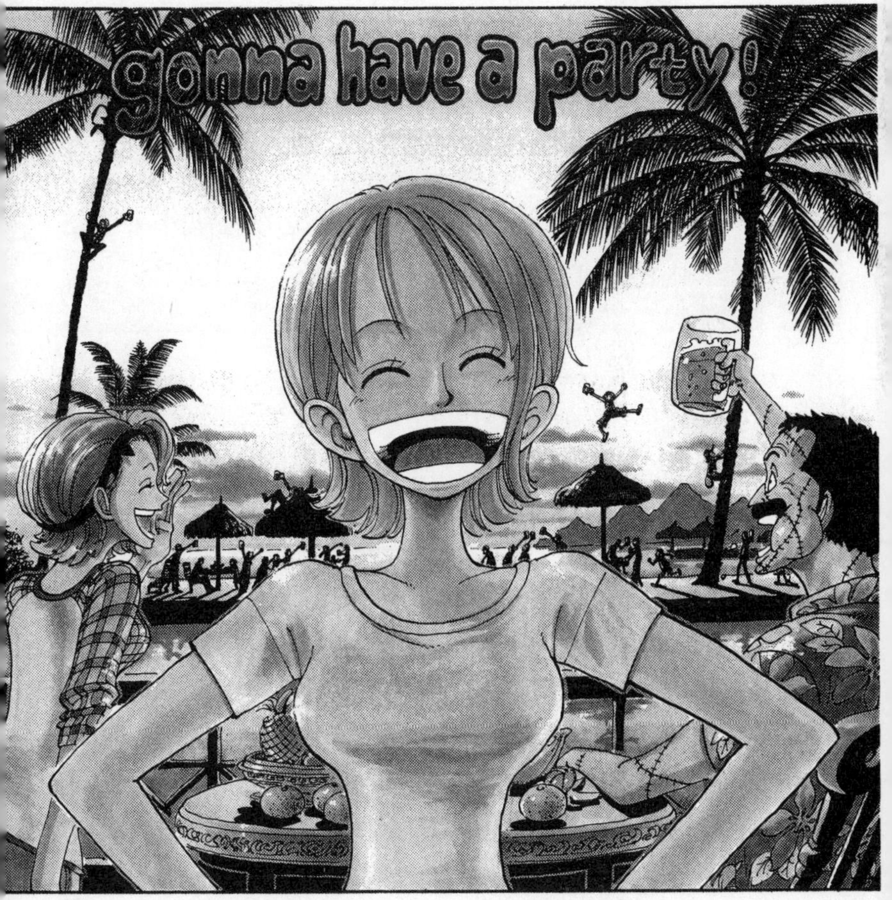
gonna have a party!

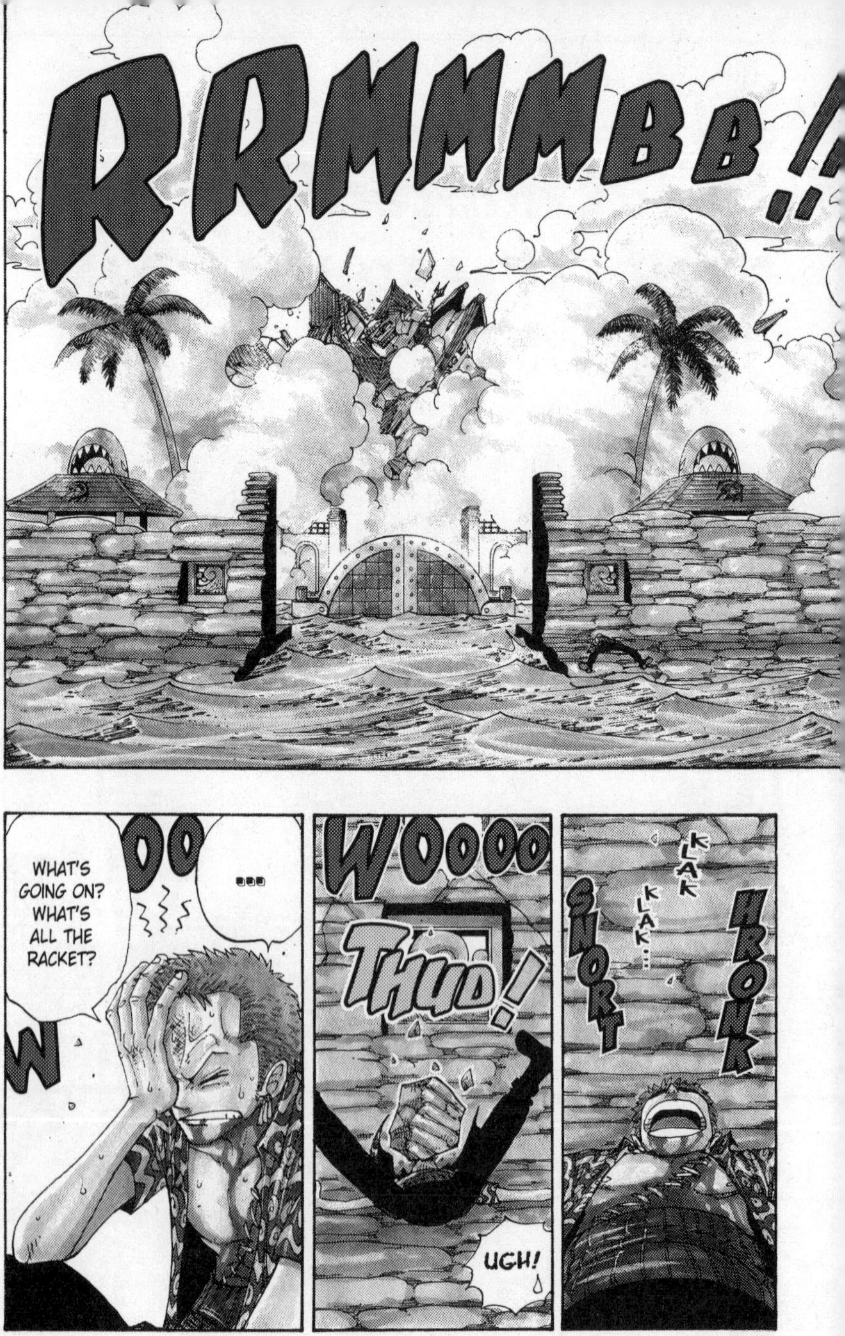
RRMMMMBB!!
HRONK
KLAK
KLAK...
SNORT
WOOOO
THUD!
UGH!
OO
...
WHAT'S GOING ON? WHAT'S ALL THE RACKET?
W

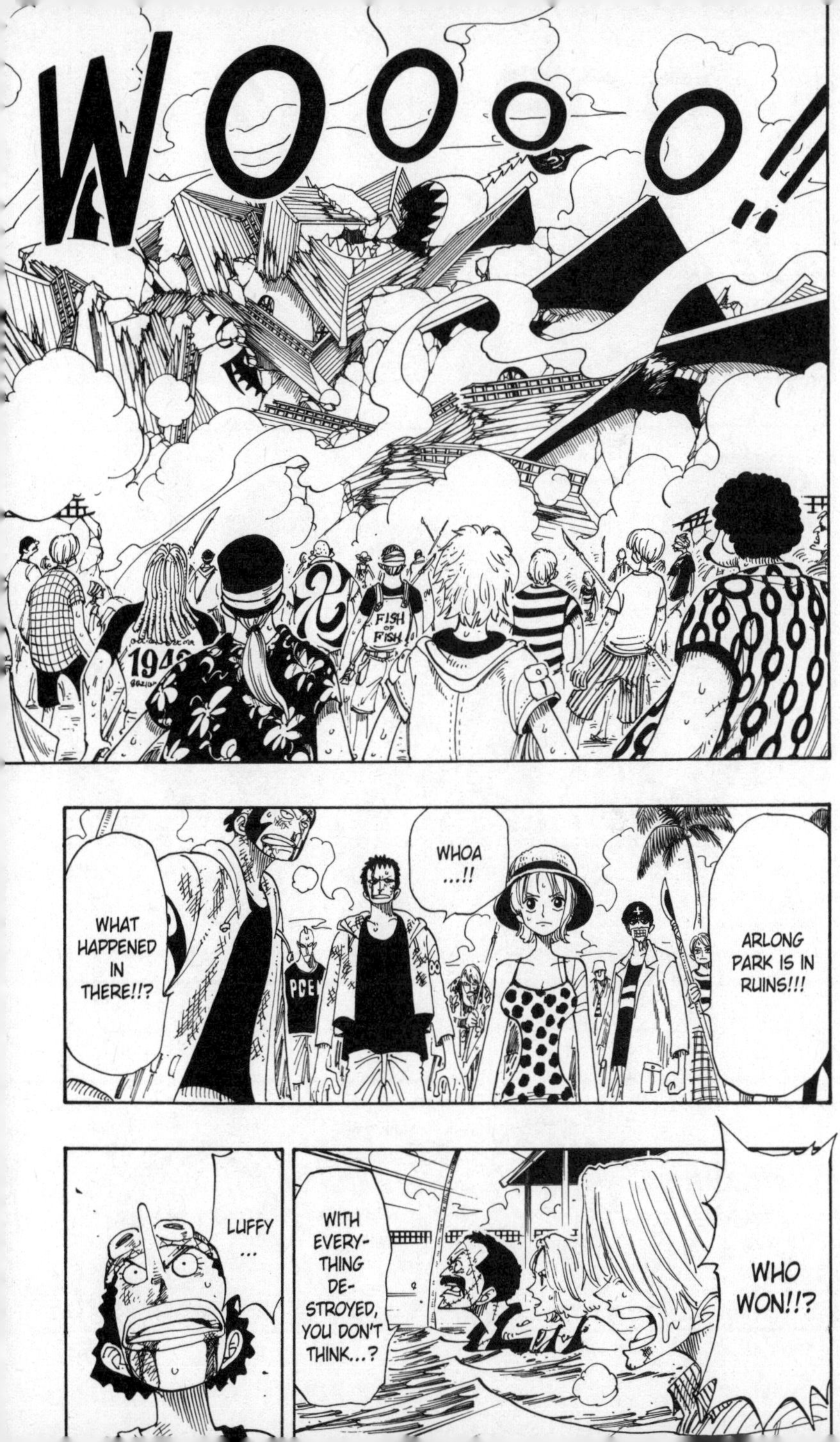
WOOOOO!!
ARLONG PARK IS IN RUINS!!!
WHOA ...!!
WHAT HAPPENED IN THERE!!?
WHO WON!!?
WITH EVERY-THING DE-STROYED, YOU DON'T THINK...?
LUFFY ...

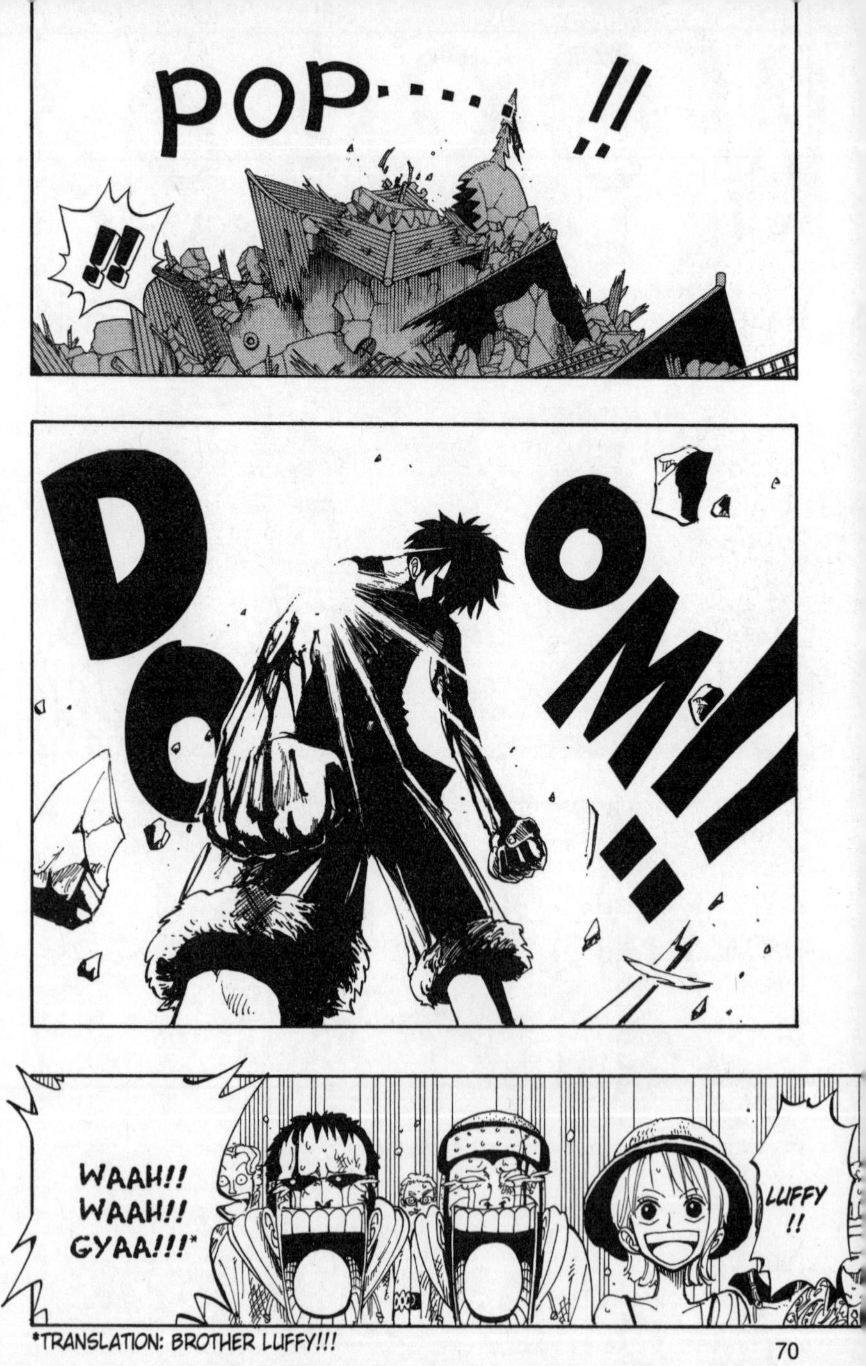
POP....!!
!!
DOOM!!
LUFFY!!
WAAH!! WAAH!! GYAA!!!*

*TRANSLATION: BROTHER LUFFY!!!

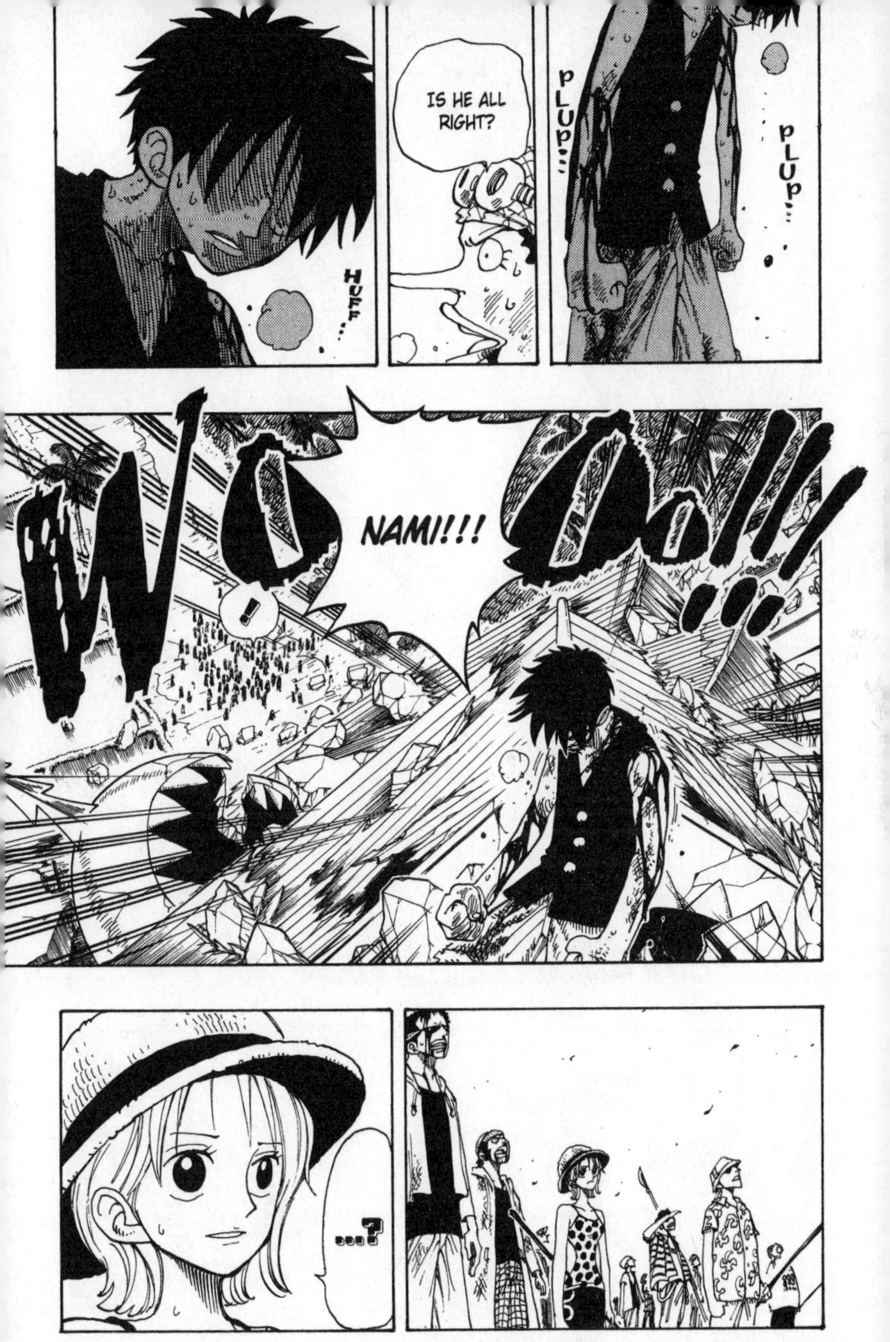
PLUP...
PLUP...
IS HE ALL RIGHT?
HUFF...
NAMI!!!
!
...?

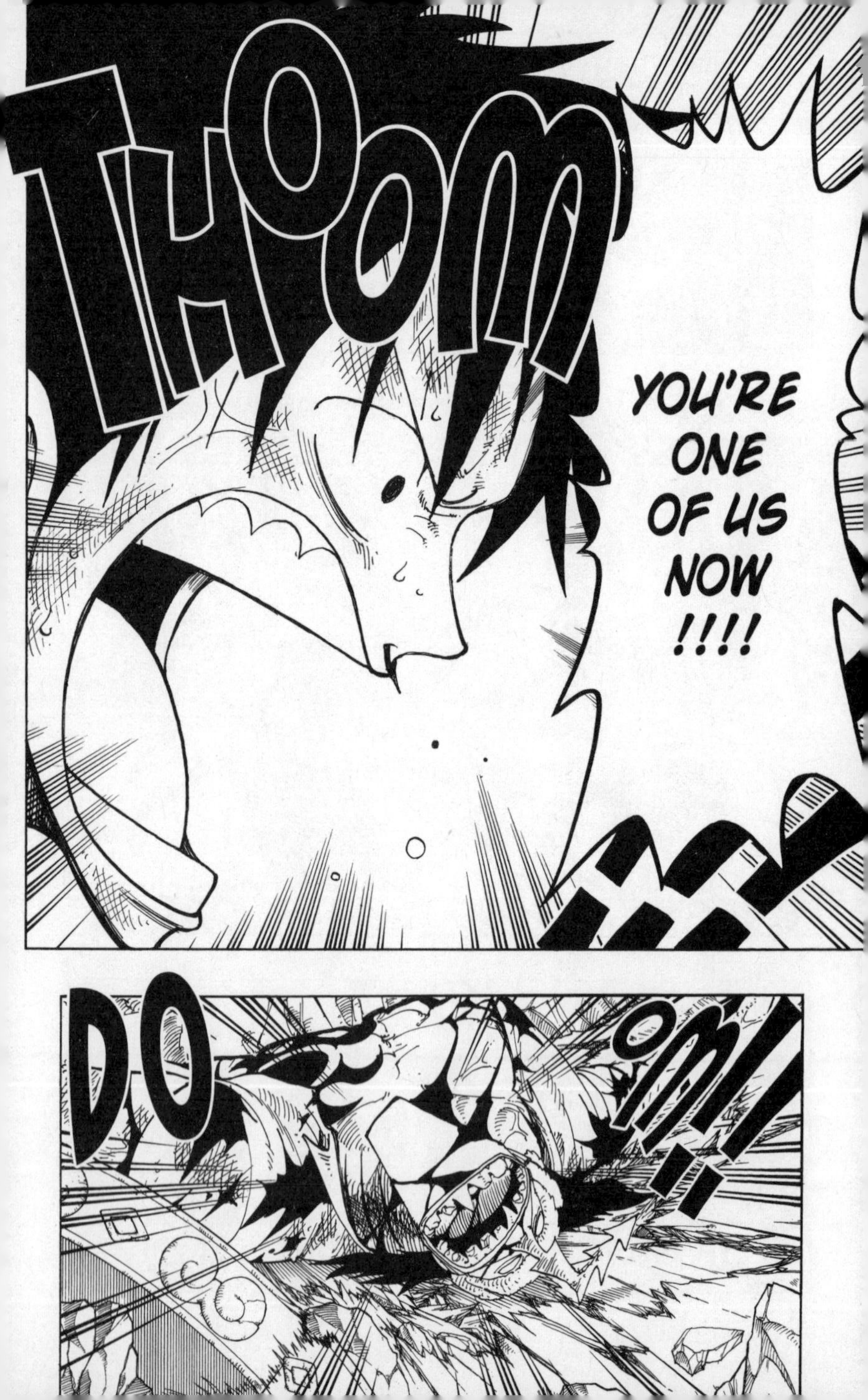
THOOM
YOU'RE ONE OF US NOW!!!!
DOOM!!

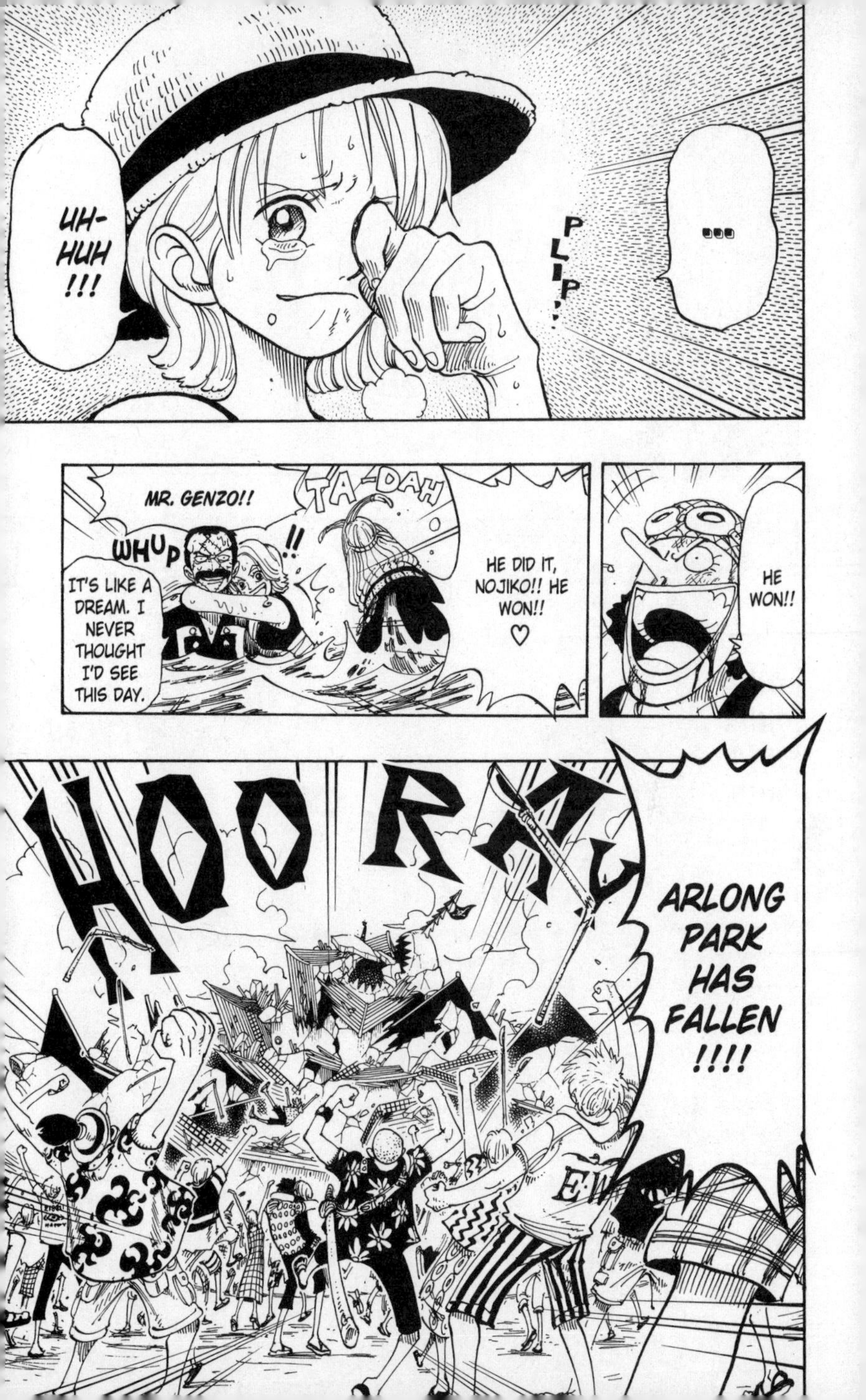
...
PLIP
UH-HUH!!!
HE WON!!
TA-DAH
HE DID IT, NOJIKO!! HE WON!! ♡
MR. GENZO!!
!!
WHUP
IT'S LIKE A DREAM. I NEVER THOUGHT I'D SEE THIS DAY.
ARLONG PARK HAS FALLEN!!!!
HOORAY

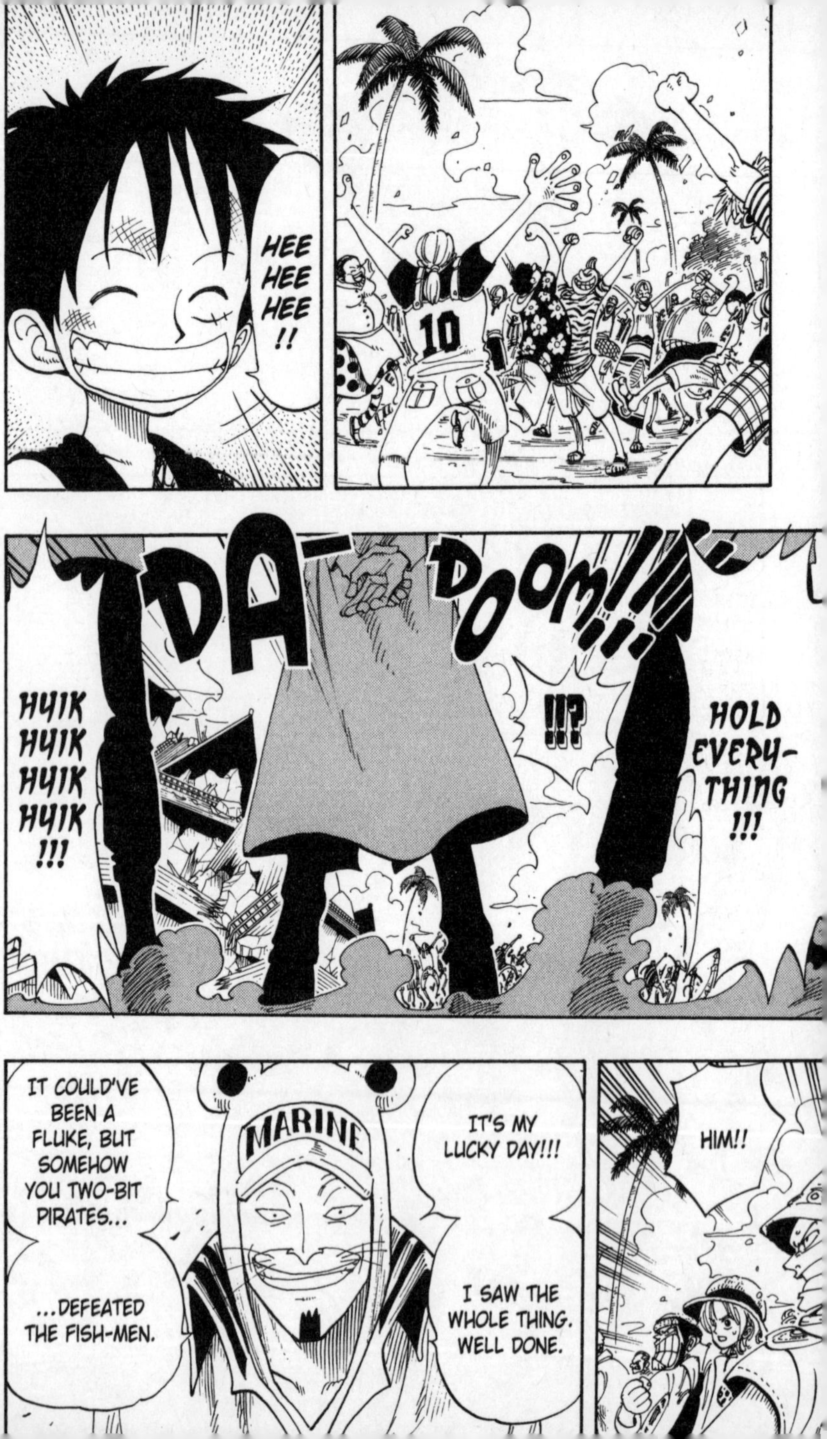
HEE HEE HEE!!
HOLD EVERY-THING!!!
!!?
DA-DOOM!!!
HYIK HYIK HYIK HYIK!!!
HIM!!
IT'S MY LUCKY DAY!!!
I SAW THE WHOLE THING. WELL DONE.
IT COULD'VE BEEN A FLUKE, BUT SOMEHOW YOU TWO-BIT PIRATES...
...DEFEATED THE FISH-MEN.

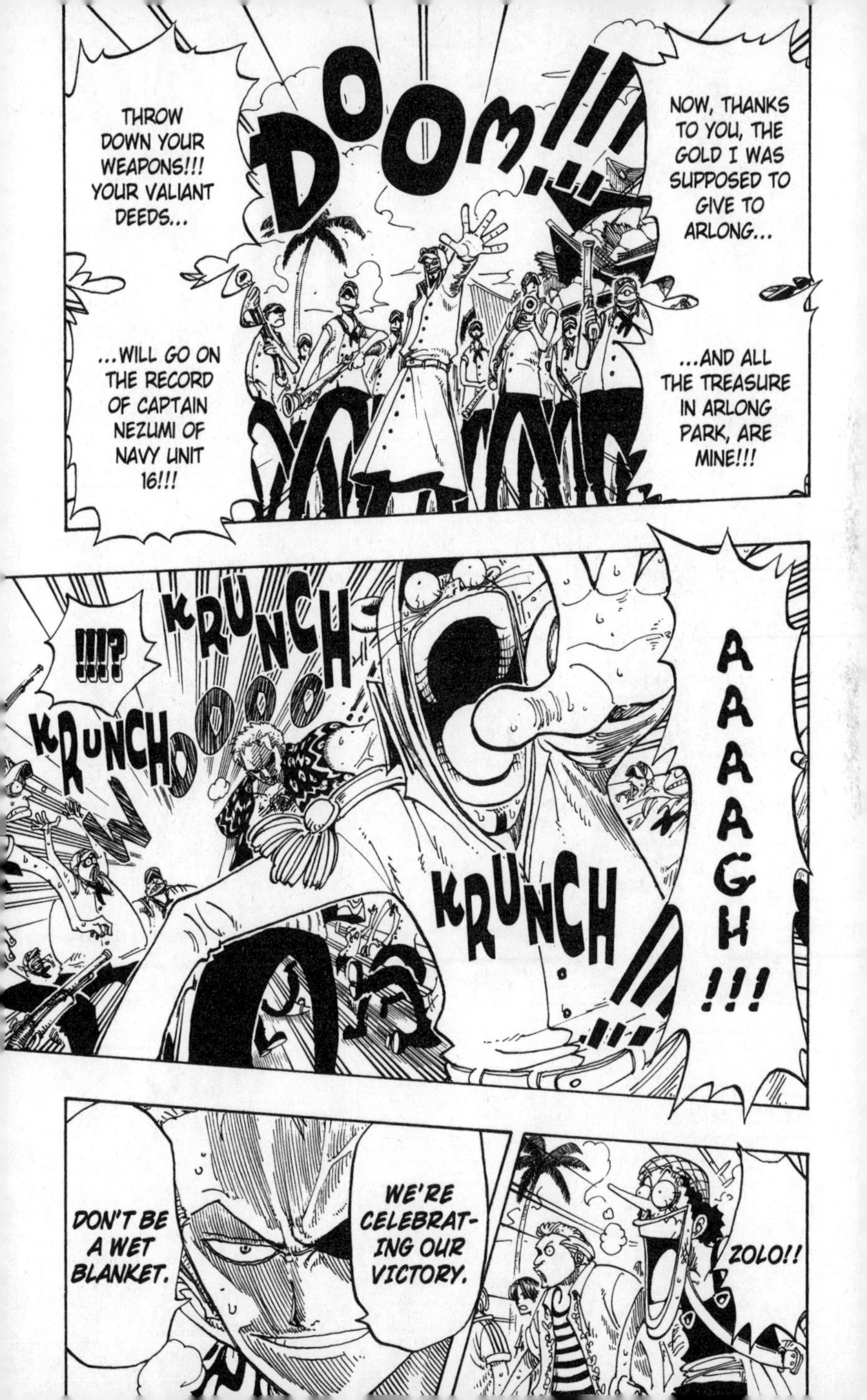
NOW, THANKS TO YOU, THE GOLD I WAS SUPPOSED TO GIVE TO ARLONG...
DOOM!!!
THROW DOWN YOUR WEAPONS!!! YOUR VALIANT DEEDS...
...AND ALL THE TREASURE IN ARLONG PARK, ARE MINE!!!
...WILL GO ON THE RECORD OF CAPTAIN NEZUMI OF NAVY UNIT 16!!!
AAAAGH!!!
KRUNCH
!!!?
KRUNCH
KRUNCH
ZOLO!!
WE'RE CELEBRAT-ING OUR VICTORY.
DON'T BE A WET BLANKET.

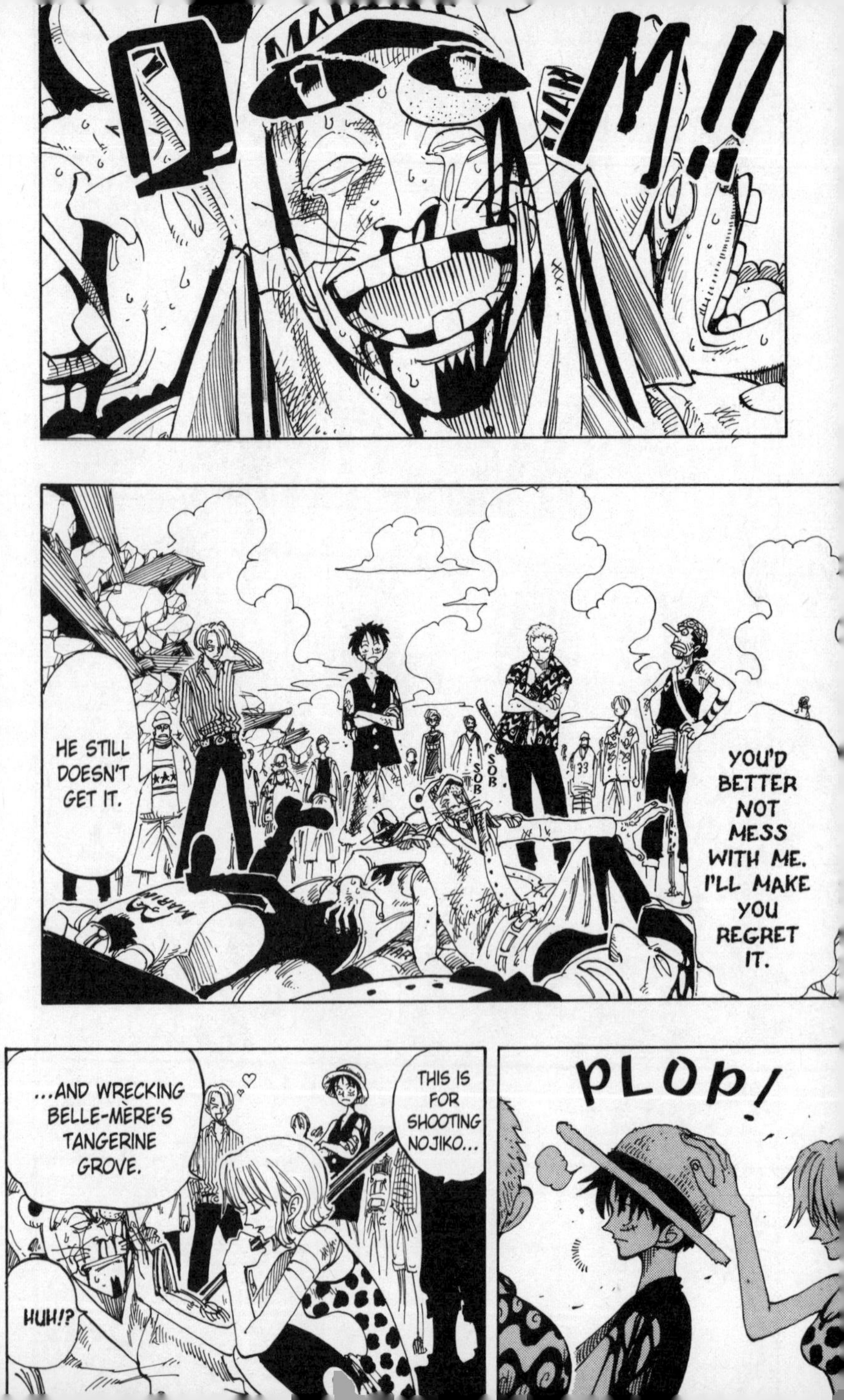
YOU'D BETTER NOT MESS WITH ME. I'LL MAKE YOU REGRET IT.
SOB SOB
HE STILL DOESN'T GET IT.
PLOP!
THIS IS FOR SHOOTING NOJIKO...
...AND WRECKING BELLE-MÈRE'S TANGERINE GROVE.
HUH!?

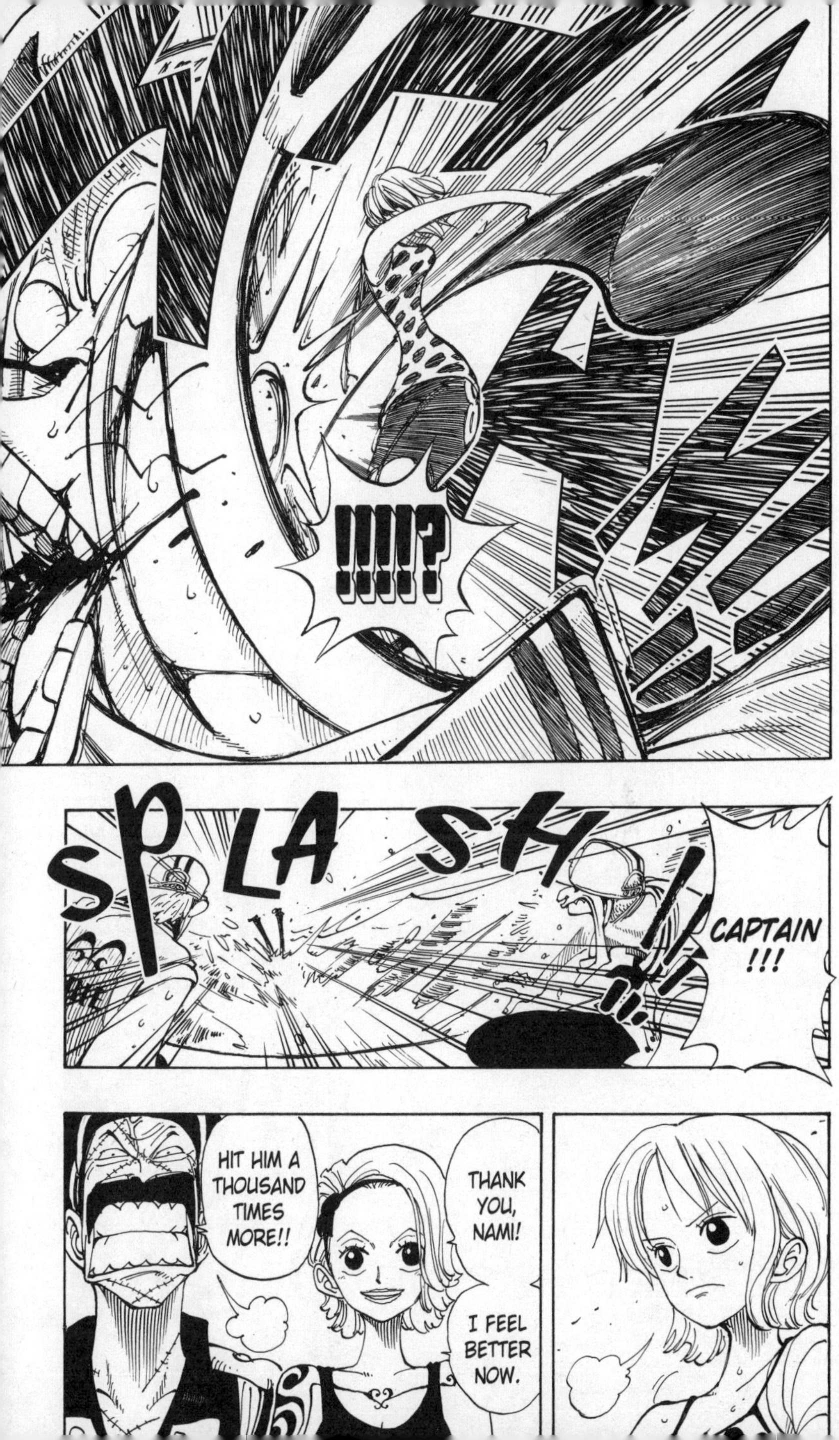
!!!!?
SPLASH!!
CAPTAIN!!!
THANK YOU, NAMI!
I FEEL BETTER NOW.
HIT HIM A THOUSAND TIMES MORE!!

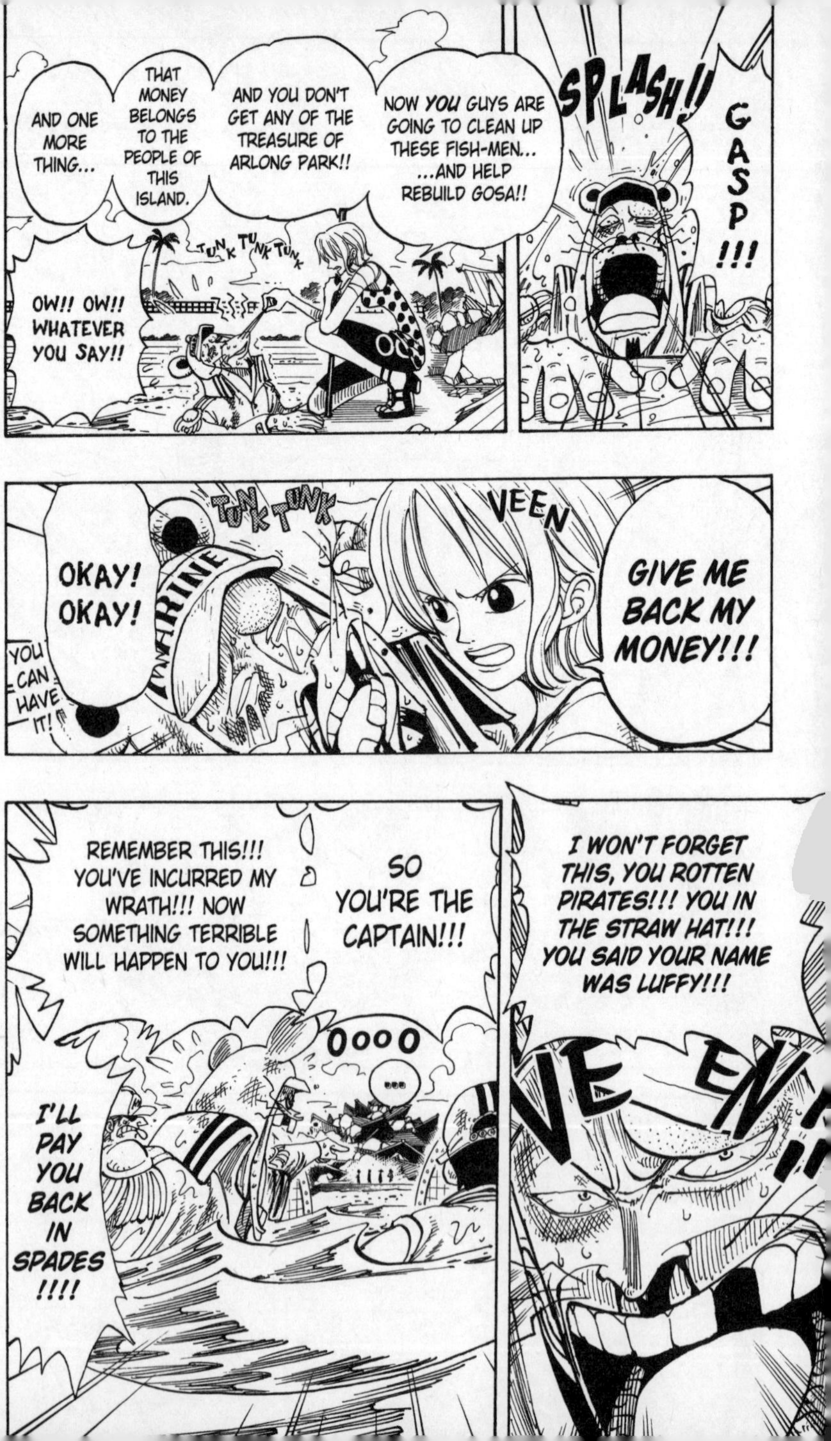
SPLASH!!
GASP!!!
NOW YOU GUYS ARE GOING TO CLEAN UP THESE FISH-MEN... ...AND HELP REBUILD GOSA!!
AND YOU DON'T GET ANY OF THE TREASURE OF ARLONG PARK!!
THAT MONEY BELONGS TO THE PEOPLE OF THIS ISLAND.
AND ONE MORE THING...
TUNK TUNK TUNK
OW!! OW!! WHATEVER YOU SAY!!
GIVE ME BACK MY MONEY!!!
VEEN
TUNK TUNK
OKAY! OKAY!
YOU CAN HAVE IT!
I WON'T FORGET THIS, YOU ROTTEN PIRATES!!! YOU IN THE STRAW HAT!!! YOU SAID YOUR NAME WAS LUFFY!!!
VEEN!!
SO YOU'RE THE CAPTAIN!!!
REMEMBER THIS!!! YOU'VE INCURRED MY WRATH!!! NOW SOMETHING TERRIBLE WILL HAPPEN TO YOU!!!
OOOO
I'LL PAY YOU BACK IN SPADES!!!!

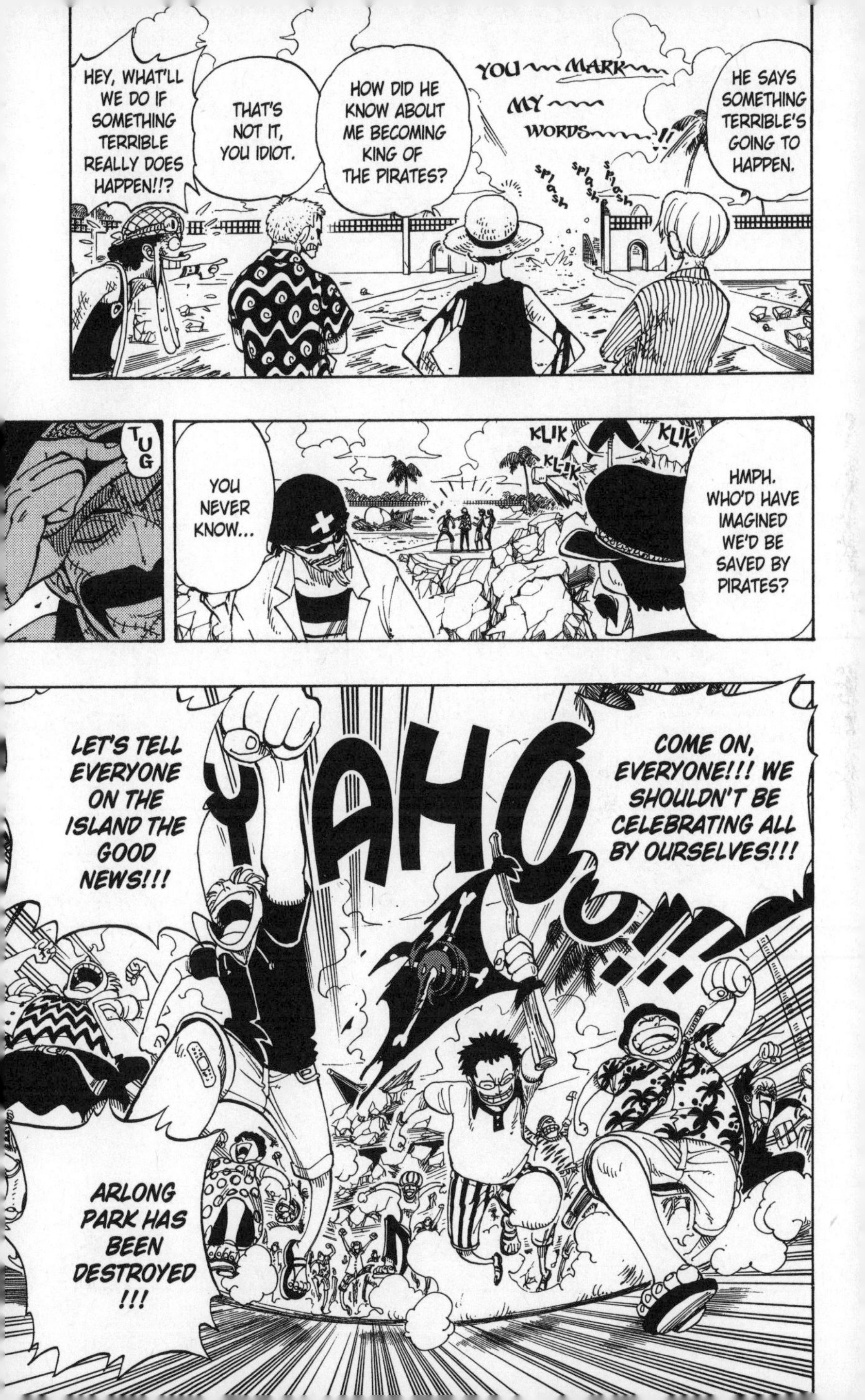
HE SAYS SOMETHING TERRIBLE'S GOING TO HAPPEN.
YOU~~ MARK~~ MY~~ WORDS~~!!
SPLASH SPLASH SPLASH
HOW DID HE KNOW ABOUT ME BECOMING KING OF THE PIRATES?
THAT'S NOT IT, YOU IDIOT.
HEY, WHAT'LL WE DO IF SOMETHING TERRIBLE REALLY DOES HAPPEN!!?
HMPH. WHO'D HAVE IMAGINED WE'D BE SAVED BY PIRATES?
KLIK KLIK KLIK
YOU NEVER KNOW...
TUG
COME ON, EVERYONE!!! WE SHOULDN'T BE CELEBRATING ALL BY OURSELVES!!!
YAHOO!!!
LET'S TELL EVERYONE ON THE ISLAND THE GOOD NEWS!!!
ARLONG PARK HAS BEEN DESTROYED!!!

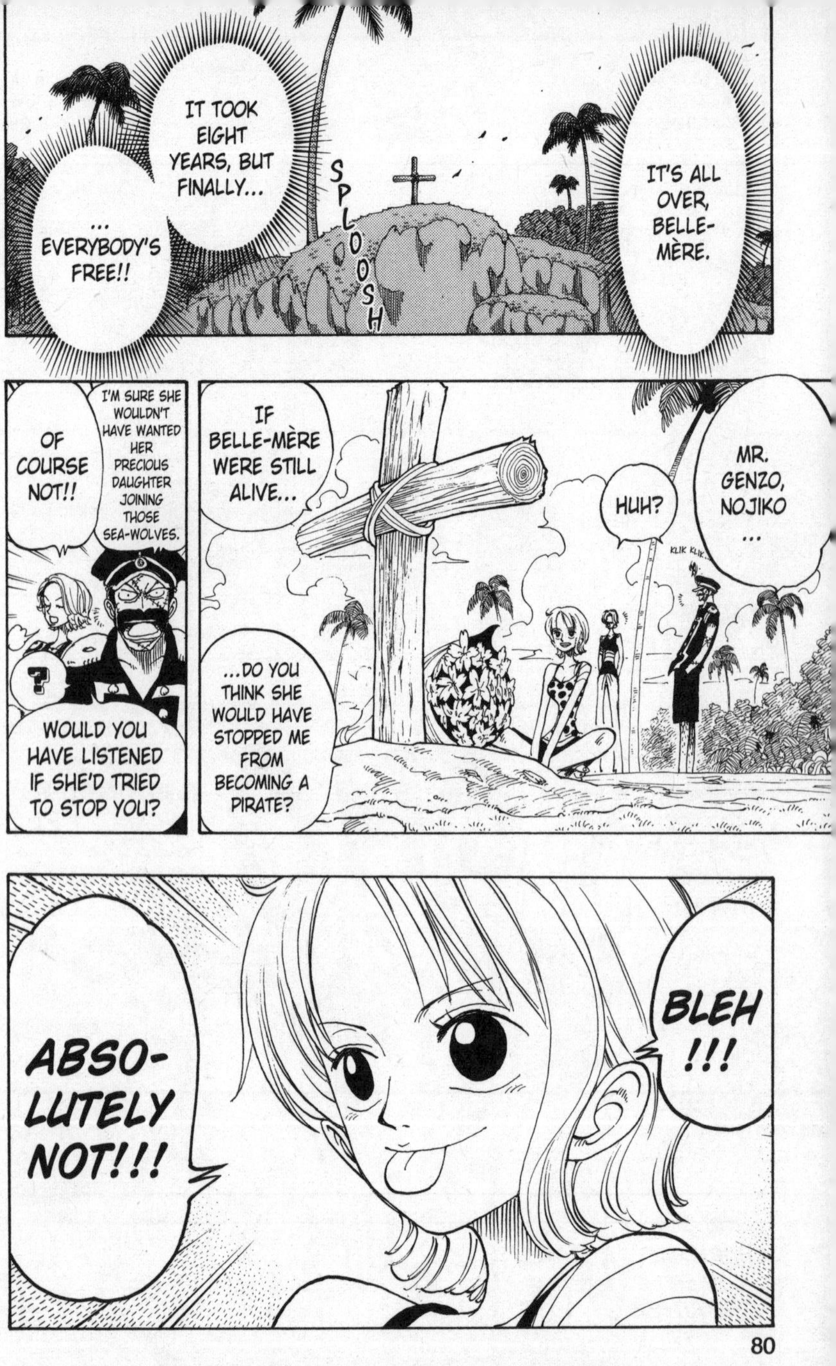
IT'S ALL OVER, BELLE-MÈRE.
IT TOOK EIGHT YEARS, BUT FINALLY...
SPLOOSH
...EVERYBODY'S FREE!!
MR. GENZO, NOJIKO...
KLIK KLIK...
HUH?
IF BELLE-MÈRE WERE STILL ALIVE...
...DO YOU THINK SHE WOULD HAVE STOPPED ME FROM BECOMING A PIRATE?
I'M SURE SHE WOULDN'T HAVE WANTED HER PRECIOUS DAUGHTER JOINING THOSE SEA-WOLVES.
OF COURSE NOT!!
?
WOULD YOU HAVE LISTENED IF SHE'D TRIED TO STOP YOU?
BLEH!!!
ABSO-LUTELY NOT!!!

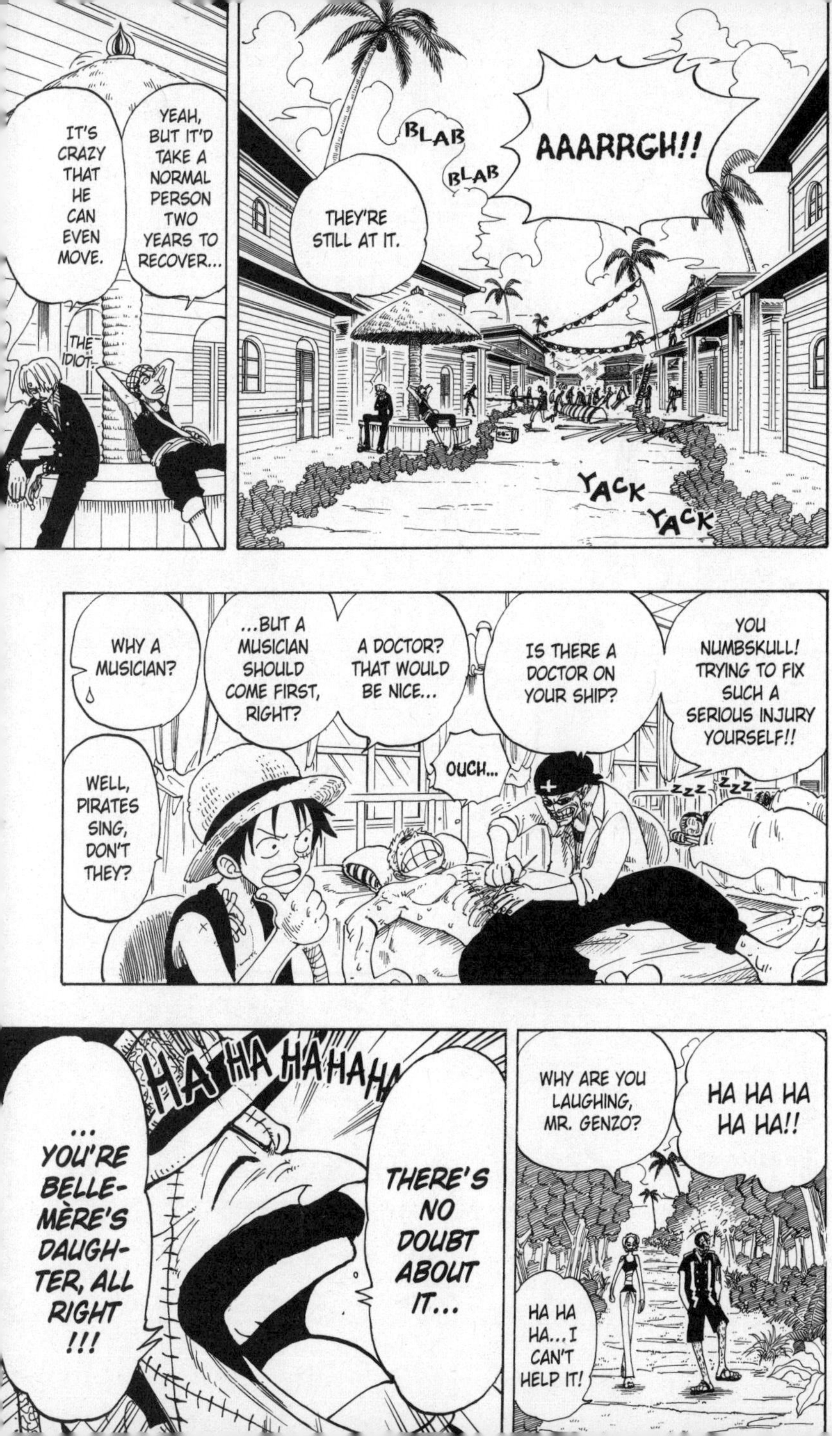
AAARRGH!!
BLAB
BLAB
THEY'RE STILL AT IT.
YACK YACK
YEAH, BUT IT'D TAKE A NORMAL PERSON TWO YEARS TO RECOVER...
IT'S CRAZY THAT HE CAN EVEN MOVE.
THE IDIOT.
YOU NUMBSKULL! TRYING TO FIX SUCH A SERIOUS INJURY YOURSELF!!
IS THERE A DOCTOR ON YOUR SHIP?
A DOCTOR? THAT WOULD BE NICE...
...BUT A MUSICIAN SHOULD COME FIRST, RIGHT?
WHY A MUSICIAN?
OUCH...
ZZZ ZZZ
WELL, PIRATES SING, DON'T THEY?
HA HA HA HA HA!!
WHY ARE YOU LAUGHING, MR. GENZO?
HA HA HA...I CAN'T HELP IT!
HA HA HA HA HA
THERE'S NO DOUBT ABOUT IT...
...YOU'RE BELLE-MÈRE'S DAUGHTER, ALL RIGHT!!!

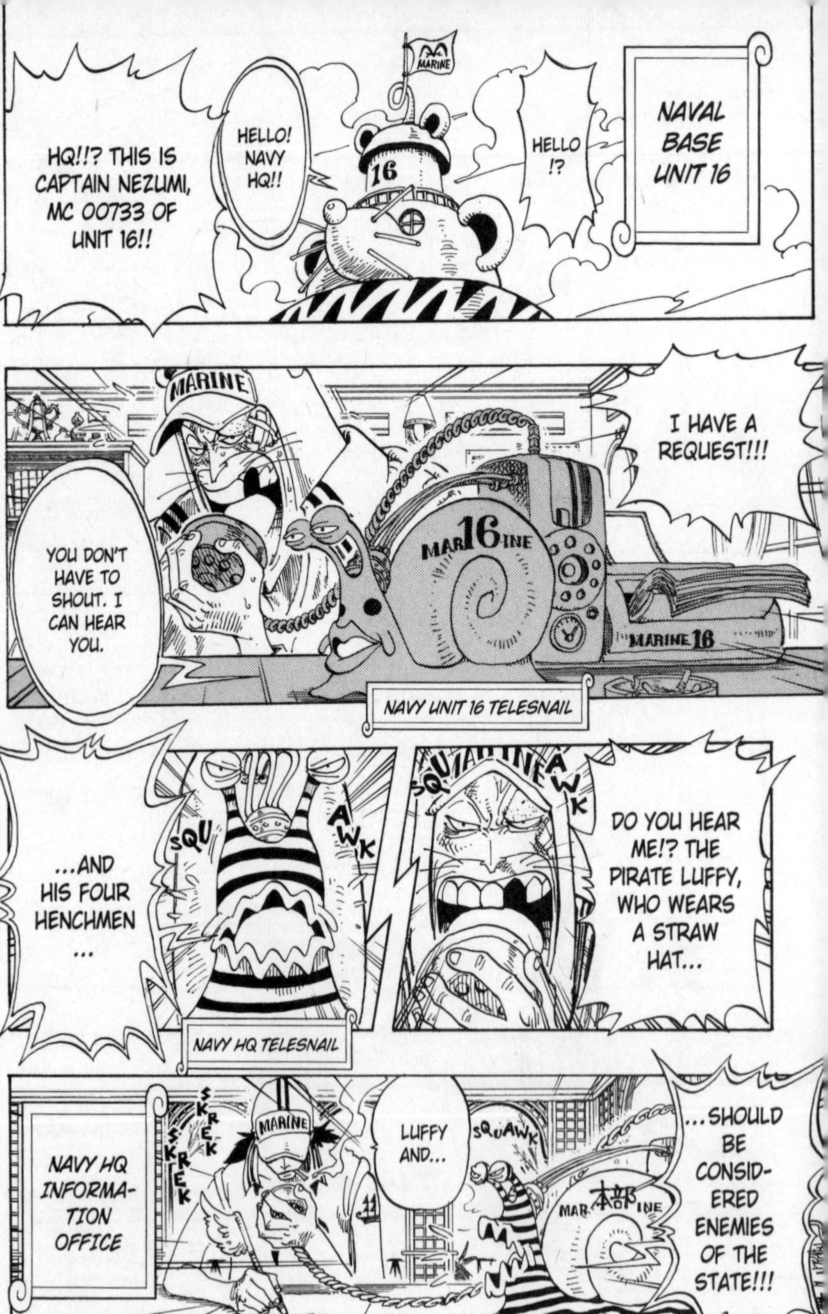
NAVAL BASE UNIT 16
HELLO !?
HELLO! NAVY HQ!!
HQ!!? THIS IS CAPTAIN NEZUMI, MC 00733 OF UNIT 16!!
I HAVE A REQUEST!!!
YOU DON'T HAVE TO SHOUT. I CAN HEAR YOU.
NAVY UNIT 16 TELESNAIL
SQUAWK
DO YOU HEAR ME!? THE PIRATE LUFFY, WHO WEARS A STRAW HAT...
SQUAWK
...AND HIS FOUR HENCHMEN ...
NAVY HQ TELESNAIL
...SHOULD BE CONSID-ERED ENEMIES OF THE STATE!!!
SQUAWK
LUFFY AND...
SKREK
SKREK
NAVY HQ INFORMA-TION OFFICE

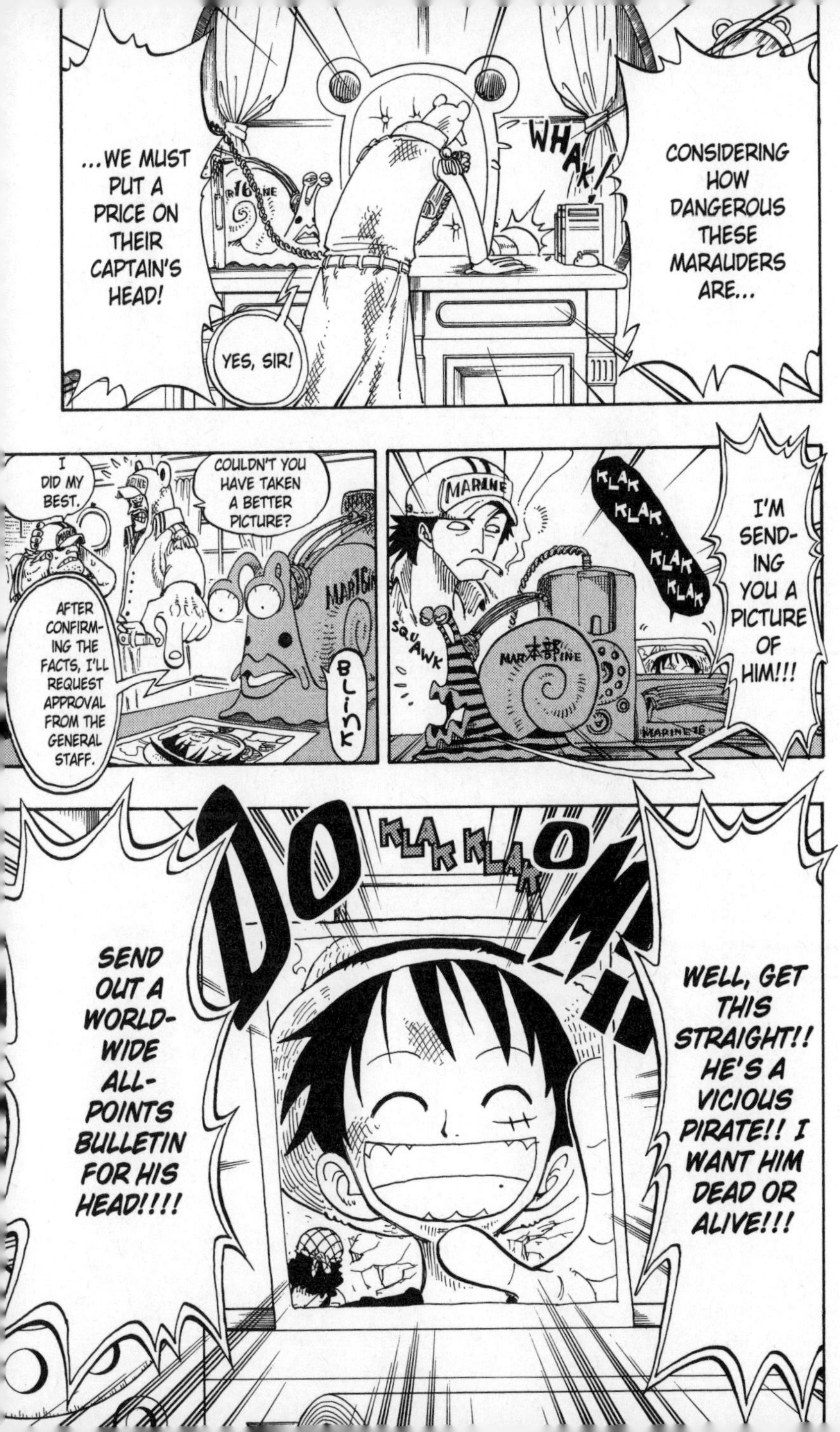
CONSIDERING HOW DANGEROUS THESE MARAUDERS ARE...
WHAK!
...WE MUST PUT A PRICE ON THEIR CAPTAIN'S HEAD!
YES, SIR!
I'M SENDING YOU A PICTURE OF HIM!!!
KLAK KLAK KLAK KLAK
SQUAWK
COULDN'T YOU HAVE TAKEN A BETTER PICTURE?
I DID MY BEST.
BLINK
AFTER CONFIRMING THE FACTS, I'LL REQUEST APPROVAL FROM THE GENERAL STAFF.
WELL, GET THIS STRAIGHT!! HE'S A VICIOUS PIRATE!! I WANT HIM DEAD OR ALIVE!!!
DOOM!!
KLAK KLAK
SEND OUT A WORLD-WIDE ALL-POINTS BULLETIN FOR HIS HEAD!!!!

3.

Storeroom & Battery Deck

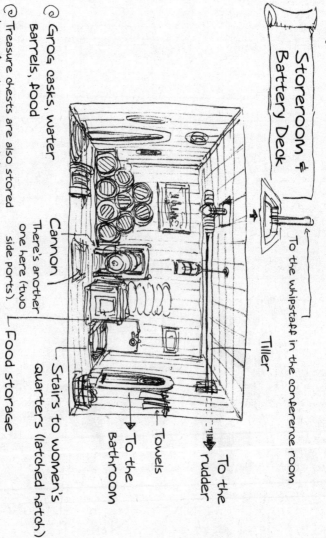

To the whipstaff in the conference room
Tiller
To the rudder
Towels
To the Bathroom
Cannon
There's another one here (two side ports).
Stairs to women's quarters (latched hatch)
Food storage

@ Grog casks, water barrels, food

@ Treasure chests are also stored here. Any treasure not taken by Nami to her room is kept here.

Chapter 95:
SPIN, PINWHEEL

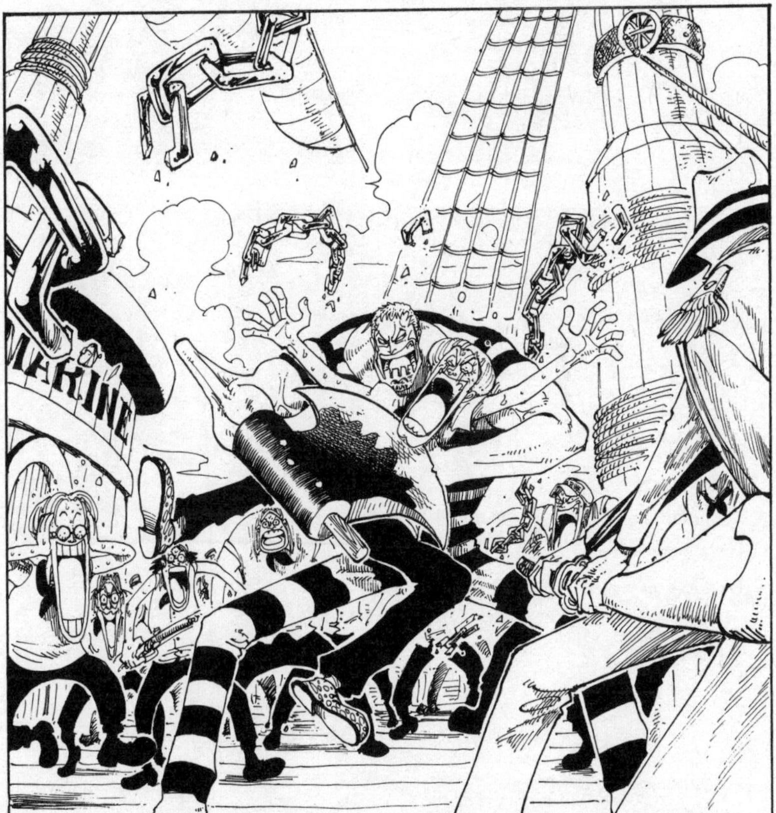
MARINE
KOBY AND HELMEPPO'S CHRONICLE OF TOIL
VOL. 11: "THE IMPROBABLE HOSTAGE"

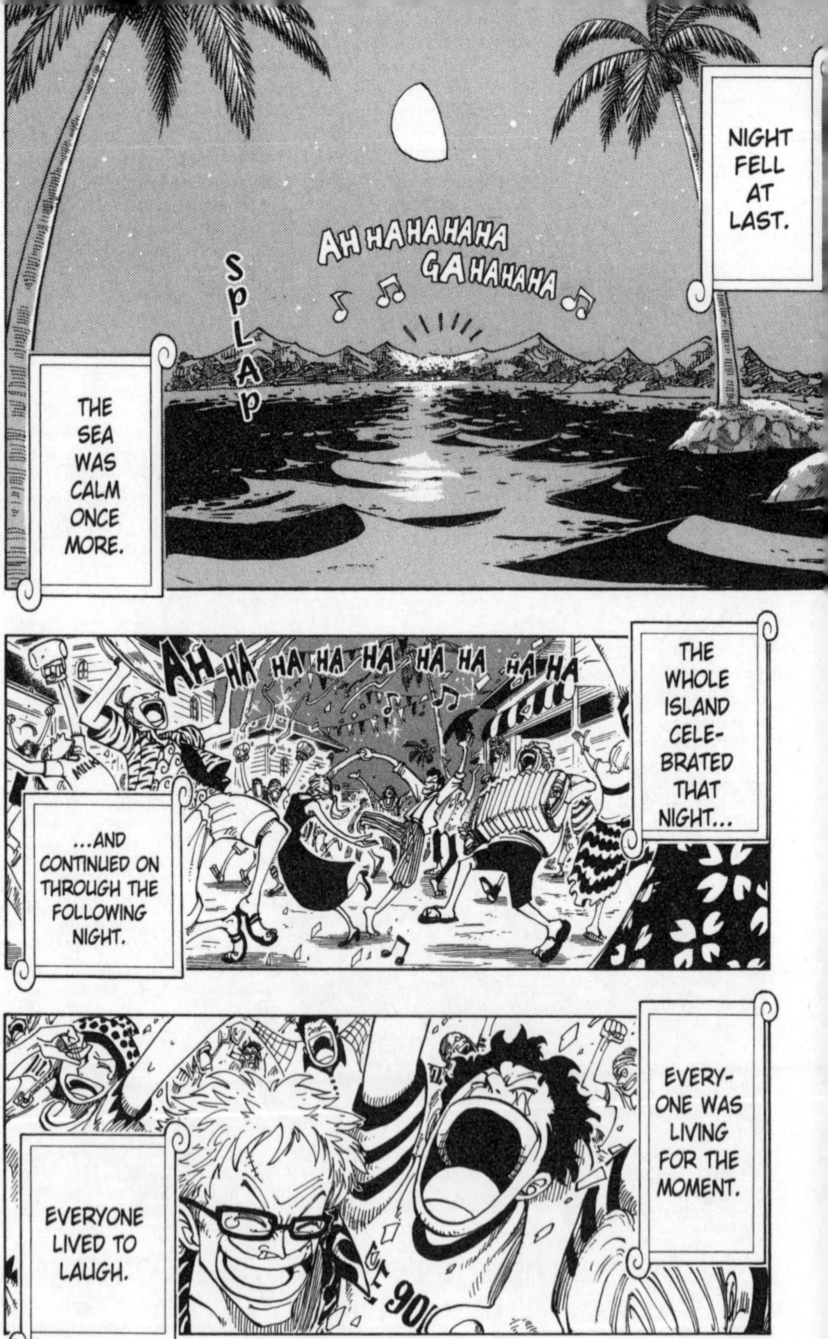
NIGHT FELL AT LAST.
AH HAHAHAHA GAHAHAHA
SPLAP
THE SEA WAS CALM ONCE MORE.
THE WHOLE ISLAND CELE-BRATED THAT NIGHT...
AH HA HA HA HA HA HA HA HA
MILK
...AND CONTINUED ON THROUGH THE FOLLOWING NIGHT.
EVERY-ONE WAS LIVING FOR THE MOMENT.
EVERYONE LIVED TO LAUGH.

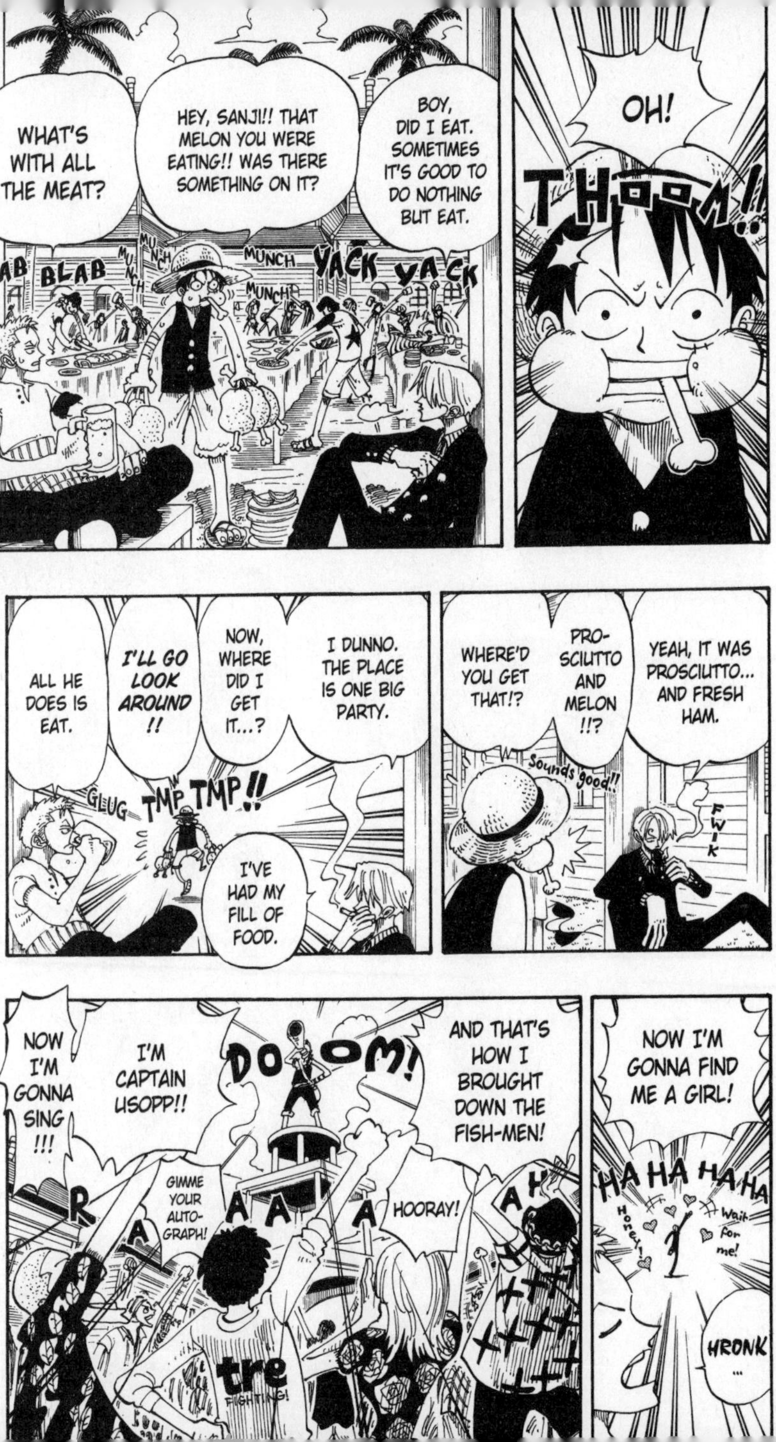
OH!
THOOM!!
BOY, DID I EAT. SOMETIMES IT'S GOOD TO DO NOTHING BUT EAT.
HEY, SANJI!! THAT MELON YOU WERE EATING!! WAS THERE SOMETHING ON IT?
WHAT'S WITH ALL THE MEAT?
YACK YACK
MUNCH
MUNCH
MUNCH MUNCH
BLAB BLAB
YEAH, IT WAS PROSCIUTTO... AND FRESH HAM.
PRO-SCIUTTO AND MELON !!?
WHERE'D YOU GET THAT!?
Sounds good!!
FWIK
I DUNNO. THE PLACE IS ONE BIG PARTY.
NOW, WHERE DID I GET IT...?
I'LL GO LOOK AROUND !!
ALL HE DOES IS EAT.
TMP TMP!!
GLUG
I'VE HAD MY FILL OF FOOD.
NOW I'M GONNA FIND ME A GIRL!
HAHAHAHA
Wait for me!
Honey!!
HRONK ...
AND THAT'S HOW I BROUGHT DOWN THE FISH-MEN!
DOOM!
I'M CAPTAIN USOPP!!
NOW I'M GONNA SING !!!
AH
HOORAY!
GIMME YOUR AUTO-GRAPH!
RAAAA
tre
FIGHTING!

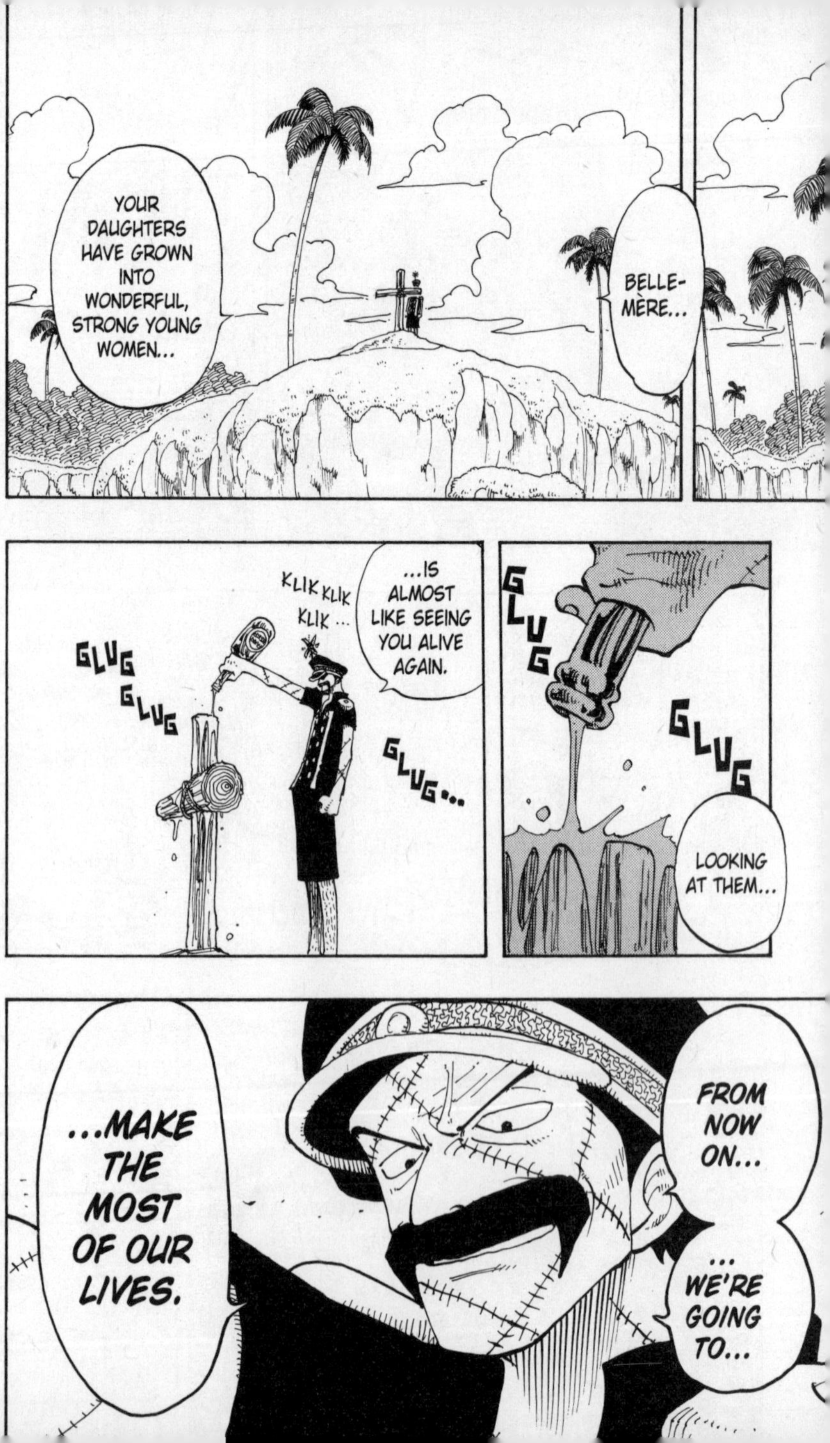
BELLE-MÈRE...
YOUR DAUGHTERS HAVE GROWN INTO WONDERFUL, STRONG YOUNG WOMEN...
GLUG
GLUG
LOOKING AT THEM...
KLIK KLIK KLIK...
...IS ALMOST LIKE SEEING YOU ALIVE AGAIN.
GLUG GLUG
GLUG...
FROM NOW ON...
...WE'RE GOING TO...
...MAKE THE MOST OF OUR LIVES.

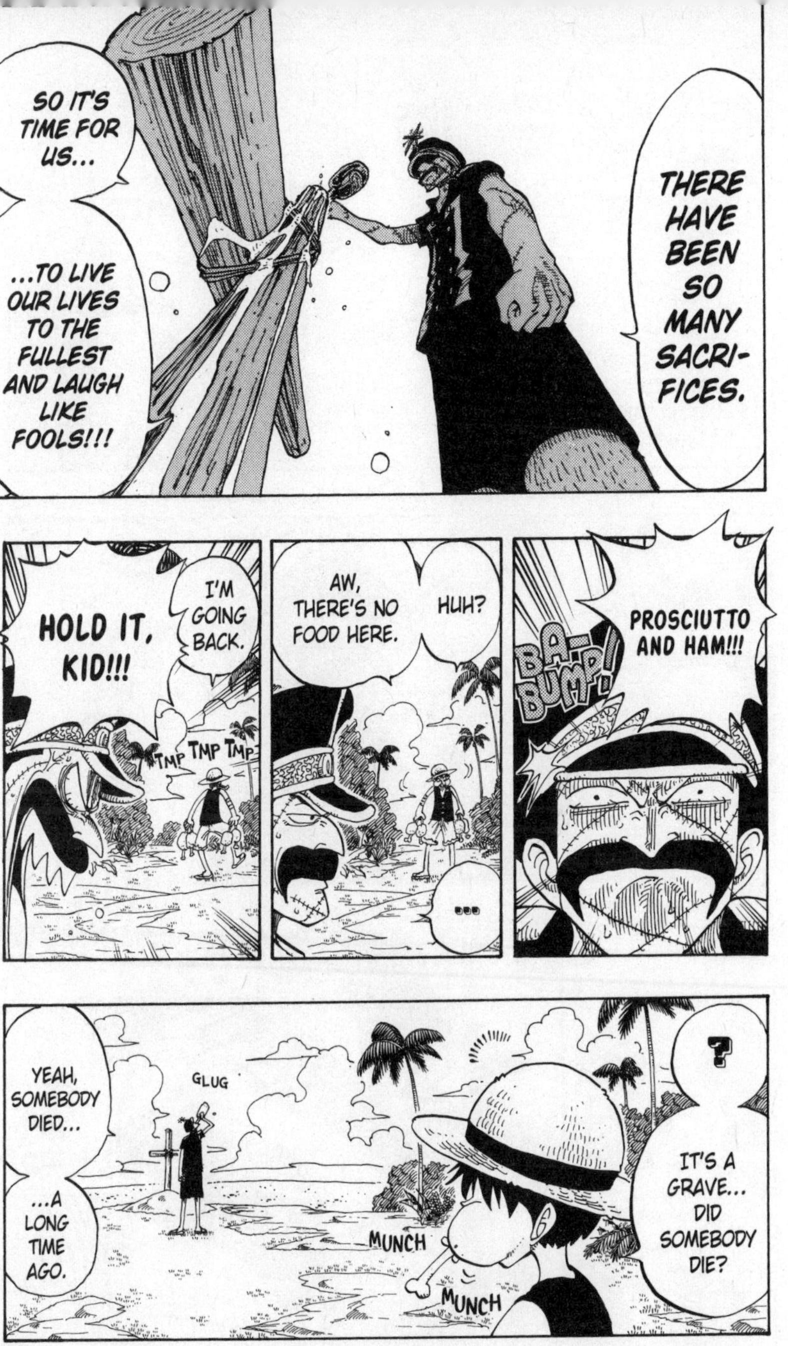
THERE HAVE BEEN SO MANY SACRI-FICES.
SO IT'S TIME FOR US...
...TO LIVE OUR LIVES TO THE FULLEST AND LAUGH LIKE FOOLS!!!
PROSCIUTTO AND HAM!!!
BA-BUMP!
HUH?
AW, THERE'S NO FOOD HERE.
...
I'M GOING BACK.
HOLD IT, KID!!!
TMP TMP TMP
?
IT'S A GRAVE... DID SOMEBODY DIE?
MUNCH
MUNCH
GLUG
YEAH, SOMEBODY DIED...
...A LONG TIME AGO.

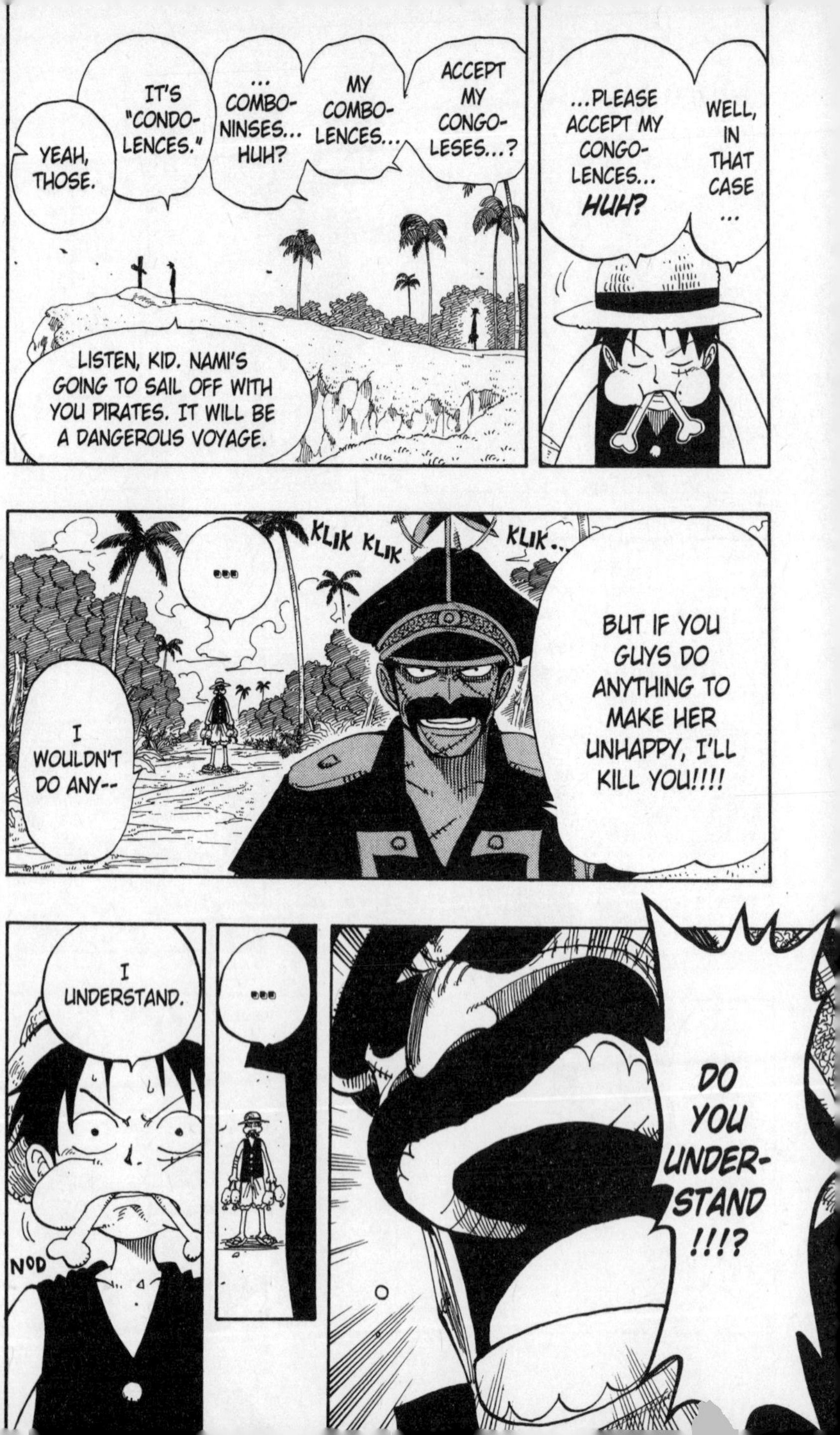
WELL, IN THAT CASE ...
...PLEASE ACCEPT MY CONGO-LENCES... HUH?
ACCEPT MY CONGO-LESES...?
MY COMBO-LENCES...
... COMBO-NINSES... HUH?
IT'S "CONDO-LENCES."
YEAH, THOSE.
LISTEN, KID. NAMI'S GOING TO SAIL OFF WITH YOU PIRATES. IT WILL BE A DANGEROUS VOYAGE.
KLIK KLIK KLIK...
BUT IF YOU GUYS DO ANYTHING TO MAKE HER UNHAPPY, I'LL KILL YOU!!!!
...
I WOULDN'T DO ANY--
DO YOU UNDER-STAND!!!?
...
I UNDERSTAND.
NOD

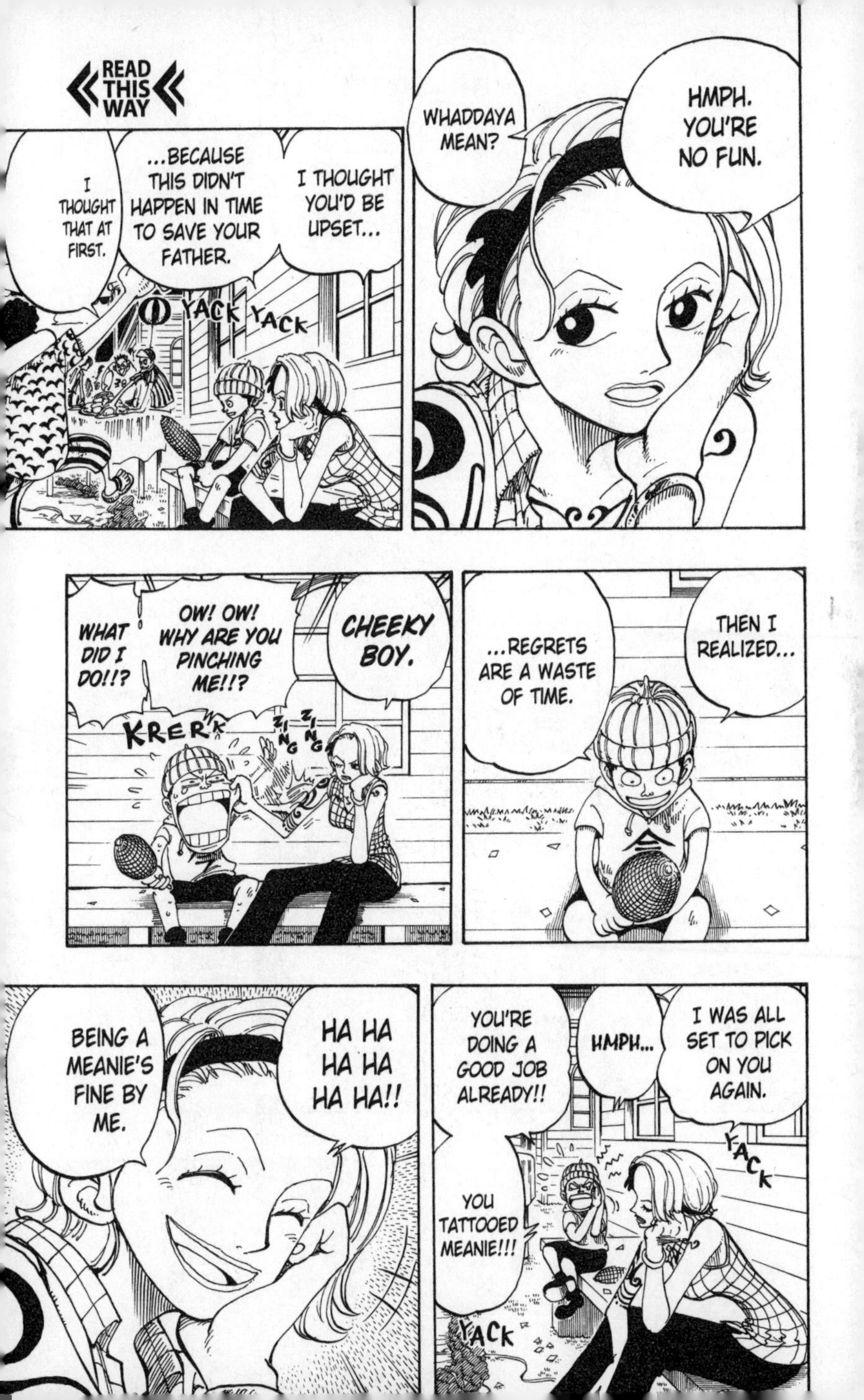
READ THIS WAY
HMPH. YOU'RE NO FUN.
WHADDAYA MEAN?
I THOUGHT YOU'D BE UPSET...
...BECAUSE THIS DIDN'T HAPPEN IN TIME TO SAVE YOUR FATHER.
I THOUGHT THAT AT FIRST.
YACK YACK
THEN I REALIZED...
...REGRETS ARE A WASTE OF TIME.
CHEEKY BOY.
OW! OW! WHY ARE YOU PINCHING ME!!?
WHAT DID I DO!!?
KRERK
ZING ZING
I WAS ALL SET TO PICK ON YOU AGAIN.
HMPH...
YACK
YOU'RE DOING A GOOD JOB ALREADY!!
YOU TATTOOED MEANIE!!!
YACK
HA HA HA HA HA HA!!
BEING A MEANIE'S FINE BY ME.

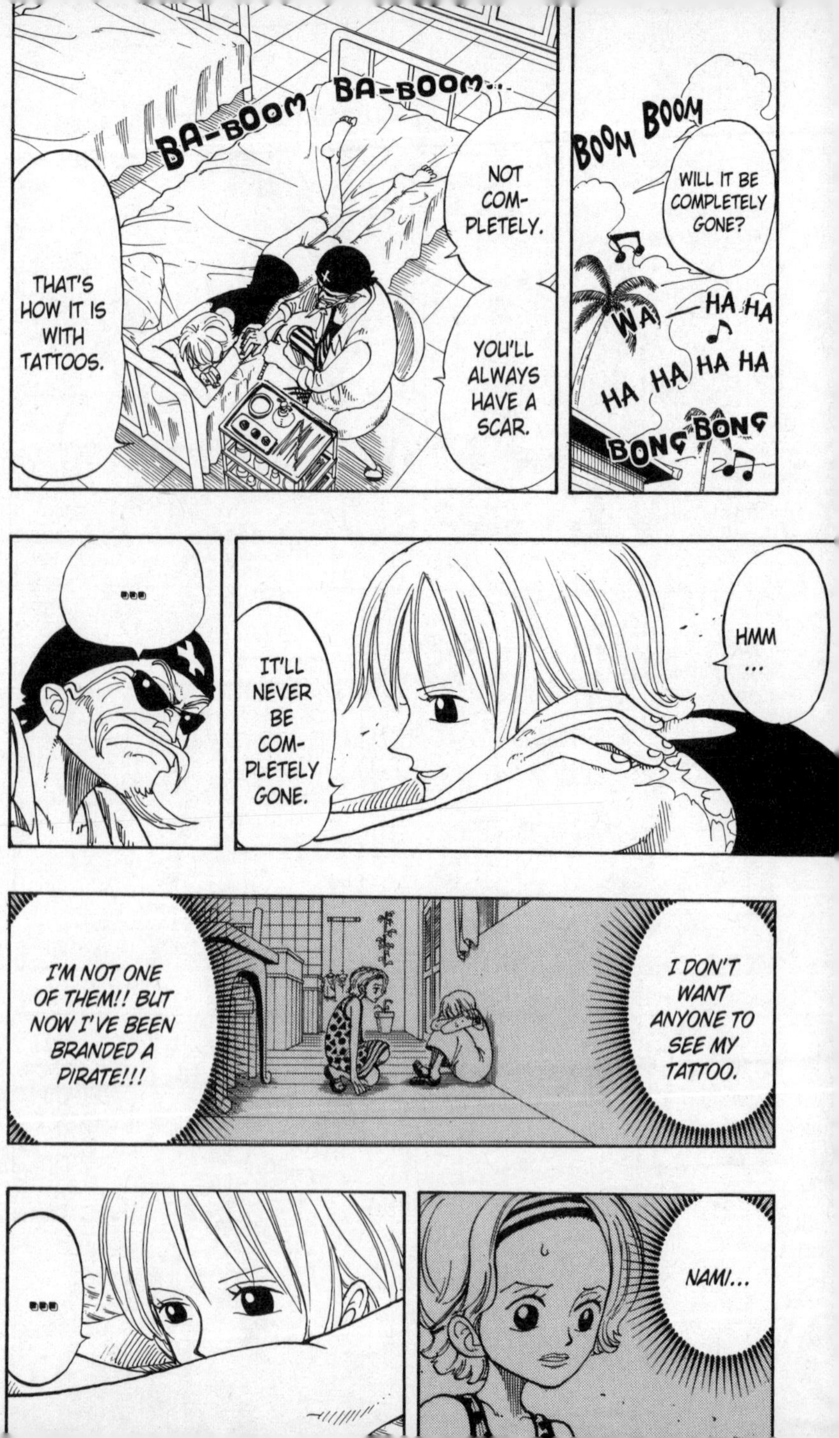
BOOM BOOM
WILL IT BE COMPLETELY GONE?
WA-HA HA
HA HA HA HA
BONG BONG
BA-BOOM BA-BOOM...
NOT COMPLETELY.
YOU'LL ALWAYS HAVE A SCAR.
THAT'S HOW IT IS WITH TATTOOS.
HMM...
IT'LL NEVER BE COMPLETELY GONE.
...
I DON'T WANT ANYONE TO SEE MY TATTOO.
I'M NOT ONE OF THEM!! BUT NOW I'VE BEEN BRANDED A PIRATE!!!
NAMI...
...

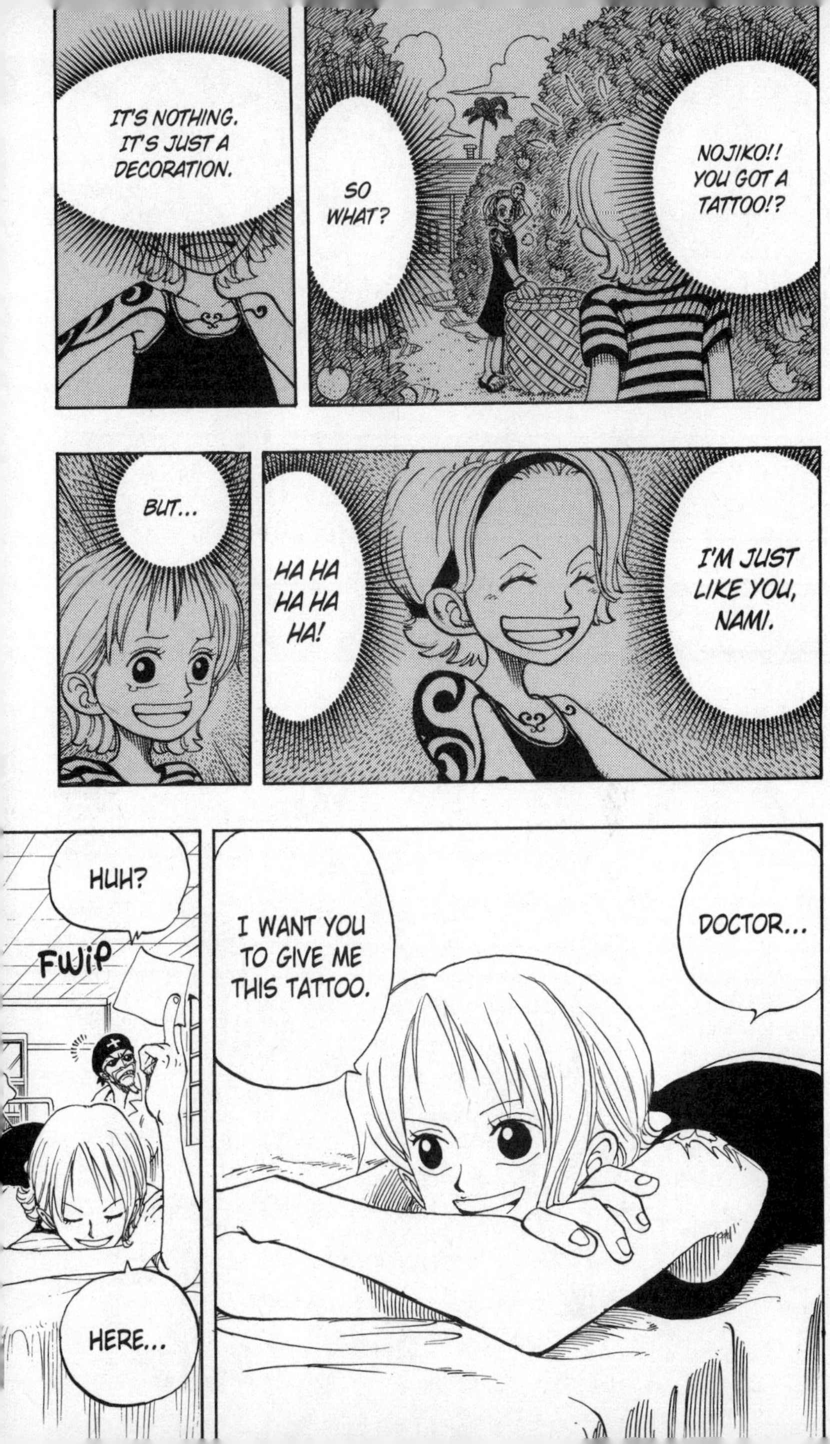
NOJIKO!! YOU GOT A TATTOO!?
SO WHAT?
IT'S NOTHING. IT'S JUST A DECORATION.
I'M JUST LIKE YOU, NAMI.
HA HA HA HA HA!
BUT...
DOCTOR...
I WANT YOU TO GIVE ME THIS TATTOO.
HUH?
FWIP
HERE...

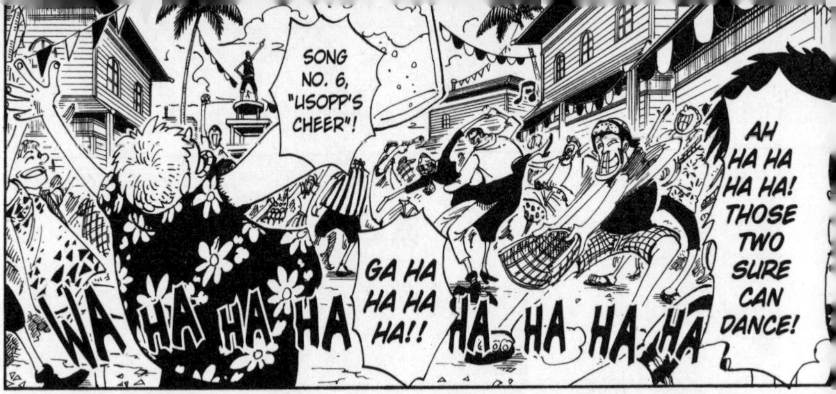
AH HA HA HA HA! THOSE TWO SURE CAN DANCE!
SONG NO. 6, "USOPP'S CHEER"!
GA HA HA HA HA!!
WA HA HA HA HA HA HA HA

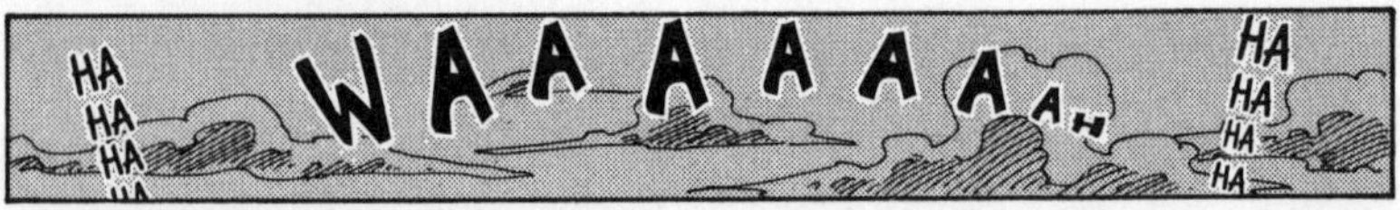
HA HA HA HA
WAAAAAAAH
HA HA HA

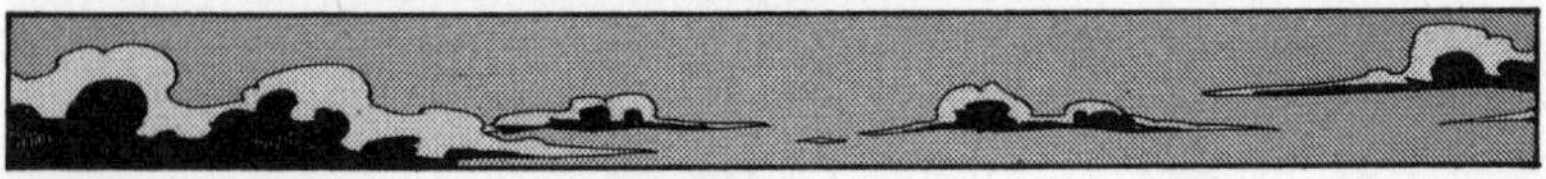

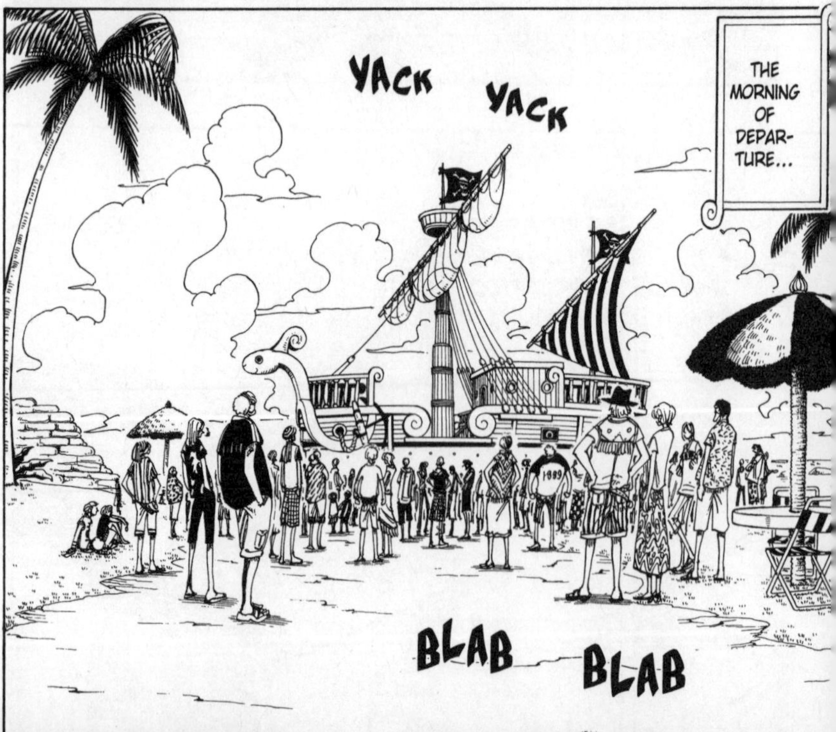
THE MORNING OF DEPARTURE...
YACK YACK
BLAB BLAB

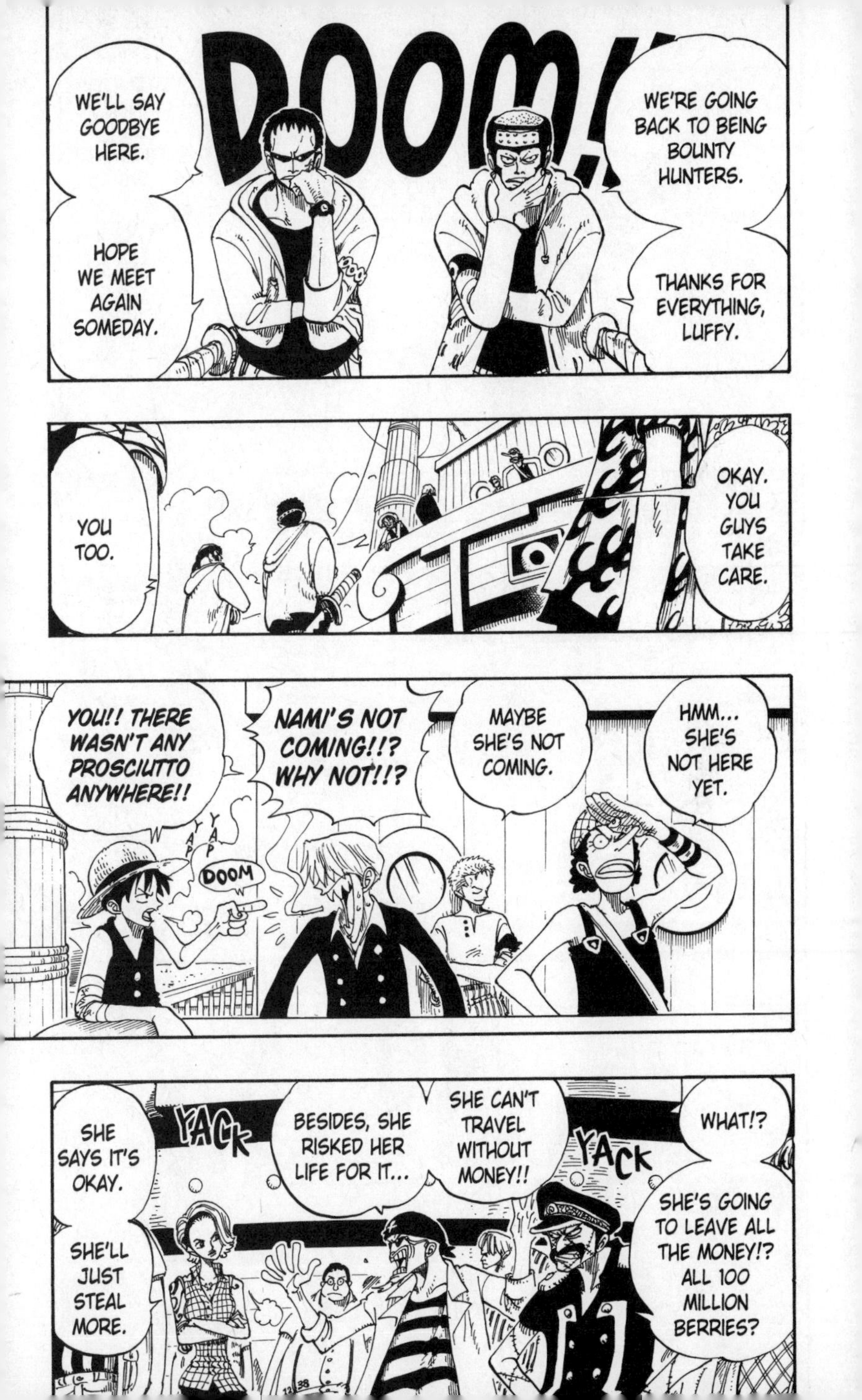
WE'RE GOING BACK TO BEING BOUNTY HUNTERS.
THANKS FOR EVERYTHING, LUFFY.
DOOM!!
WE'LL SAY GOODBYE HERE.
HOPE WE MEET AGAIN SOMEDAY.
OKAY. YOU GUYS TAKE CARE.
YOU TOO.
HMM... SHE'S NOT HERE YET.
MAYBE SHE'S NOT COMING.
NAMI'S NOT COMING!!? WHY NOT!!?
YAP YAP
YOU!! THERE WASN'T ANY PROSCIUTTO ANYWHERE!!
DOOM
WHAT!?
SHE'S GOING TO LEAVE ALL THE MONEY!? ALL 100 MILLION BERRIES?
YACK
SHE CAN'T TRAVEL WITHOUT MONEY!!
BESIDES, SHE RISKED HER LIFE FOR IT...
YACK
SHE SAYS IT'S OKAY.
SHE'LL JUST STEAL MORE.

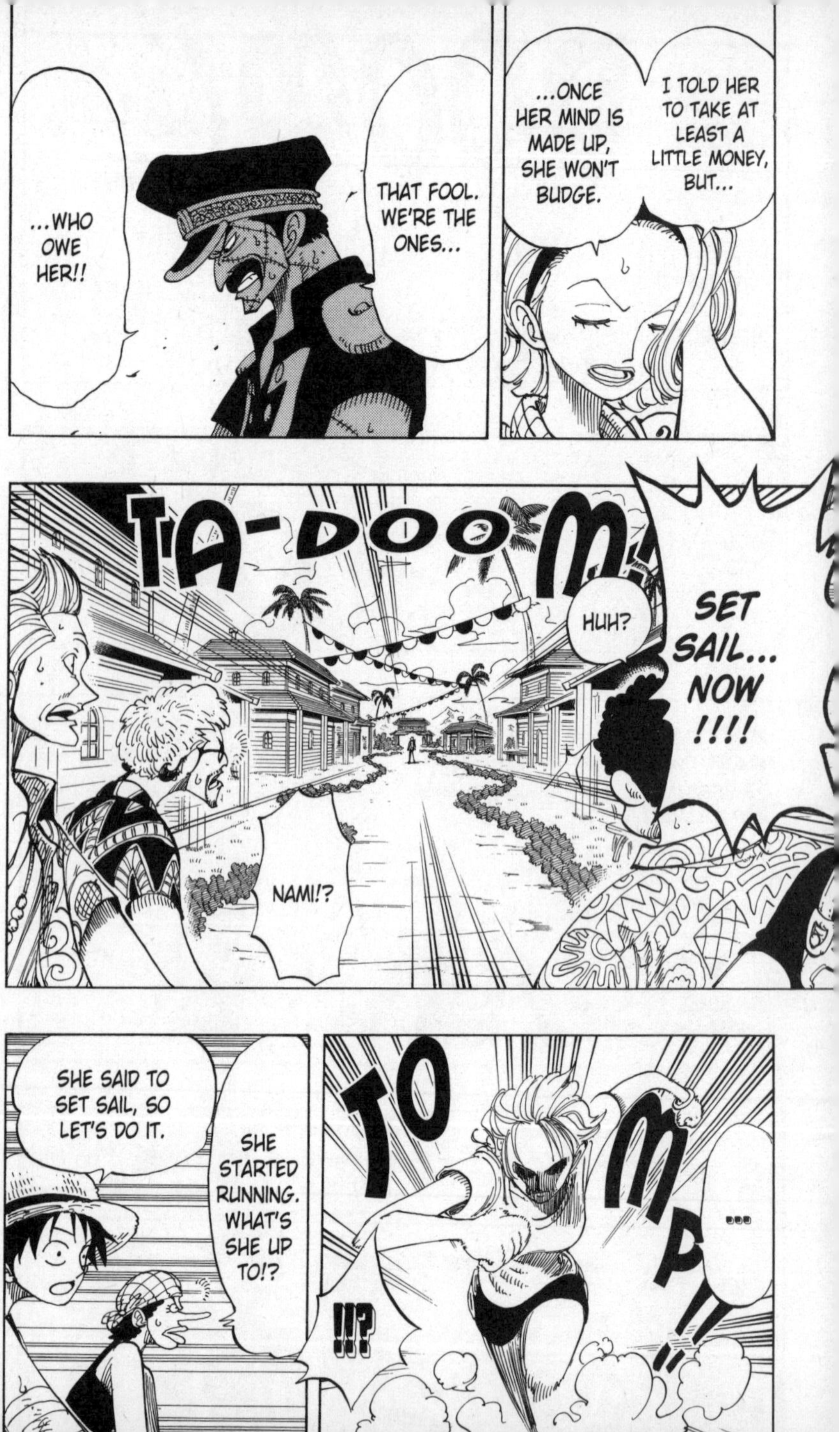
I TOLD HER TO TAKE AT LEAST A LITTLE MONEY, BUT...
...ONCE HER MIND IS MADE UP, SHE WON'T BUDGE.
THAT FOOL. WE'RE THE ONES...
...WHO OWE HER!!
TA-DOOM!
SET SAIL... NOW!!!!
HUH?
NAMI!?
TOMP!!
...
!!?
SHE SAID TO SET SAIL, SO LET'S DO IT.
SHE STARTED RUNNING. WHAT'S SHE UP TO!?

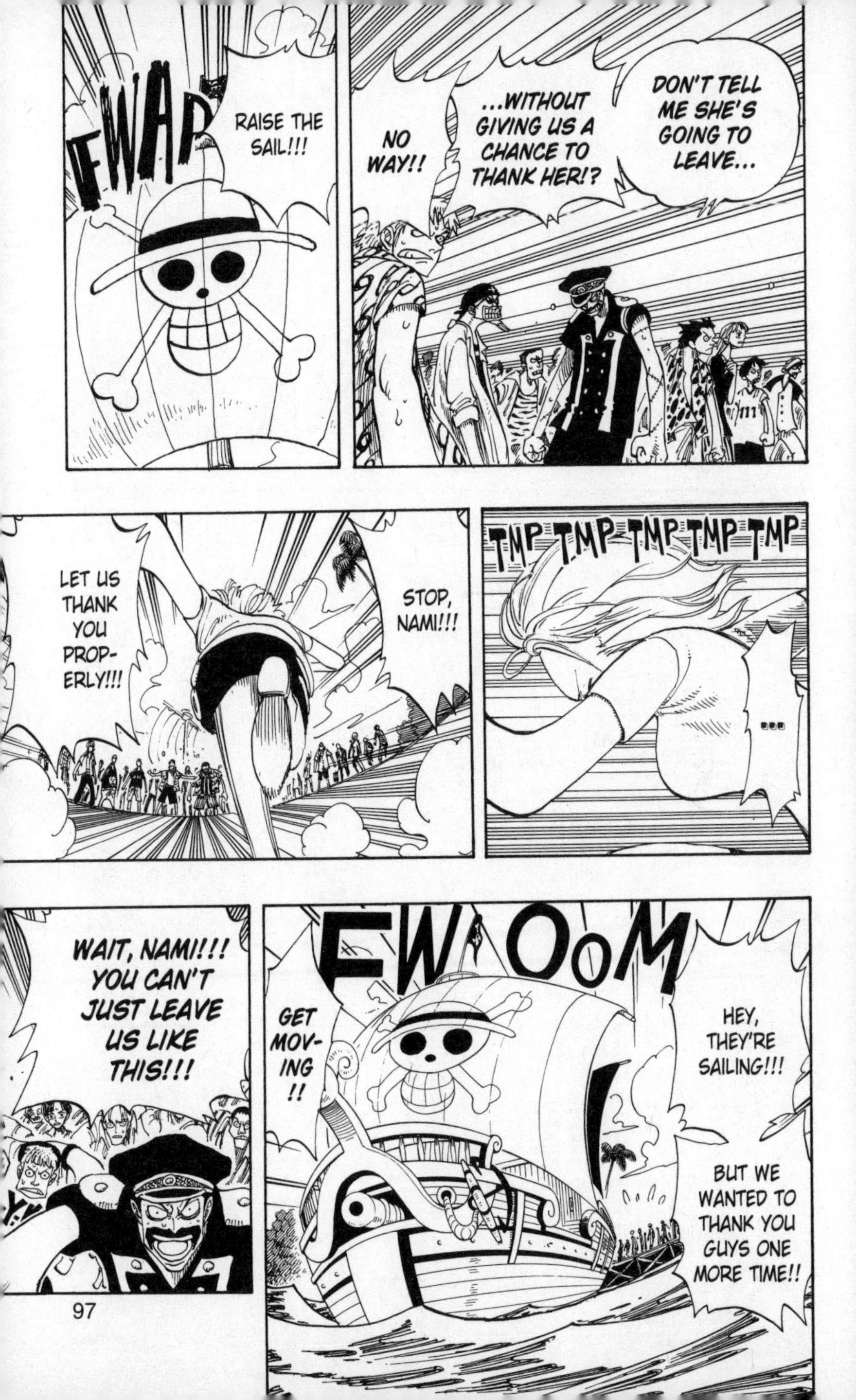
DON'T TELL ME SHE'S GOING TO LEAVE...
...WITHOUT GIVING US A CHANCE TO THANK HER!?
NO WAY!!
FWAP
RAISE THE SAIL!!!
TMP TMP TMP TMP TMP
...
STOP, NAMI!!!
LET US THANK YOU PROPERLY!!!
FWOOM
HEY, THEY'RE SAILING!!!
BUT WE WANTED TO THANK YOU GUYS ONE MORE TIME!!
GET MOVING!!
WAIT, NAMI!!! YOU CAN'T JUST LEAVE US LIKE THIS!!!

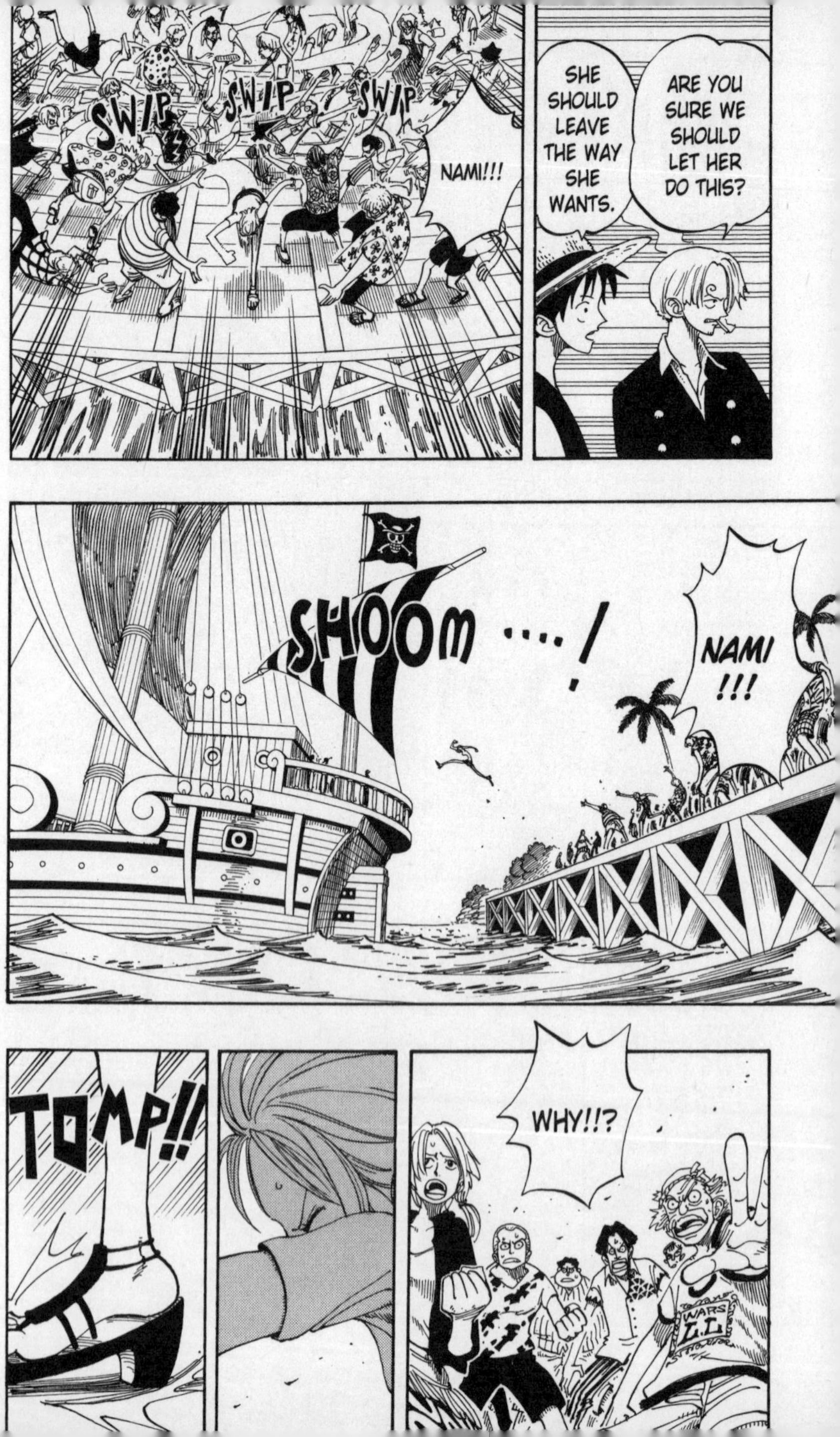
ARE YOU SURE WE SHOULD LET HER DO THIS?
SHE SHOULD LEAVE THE WAY SHE WANTS.
SWIP
SWIP
SWIP
NAMI!!!
NAMI !!!
SHOOM ....!
WHY!!?
TOMP!!

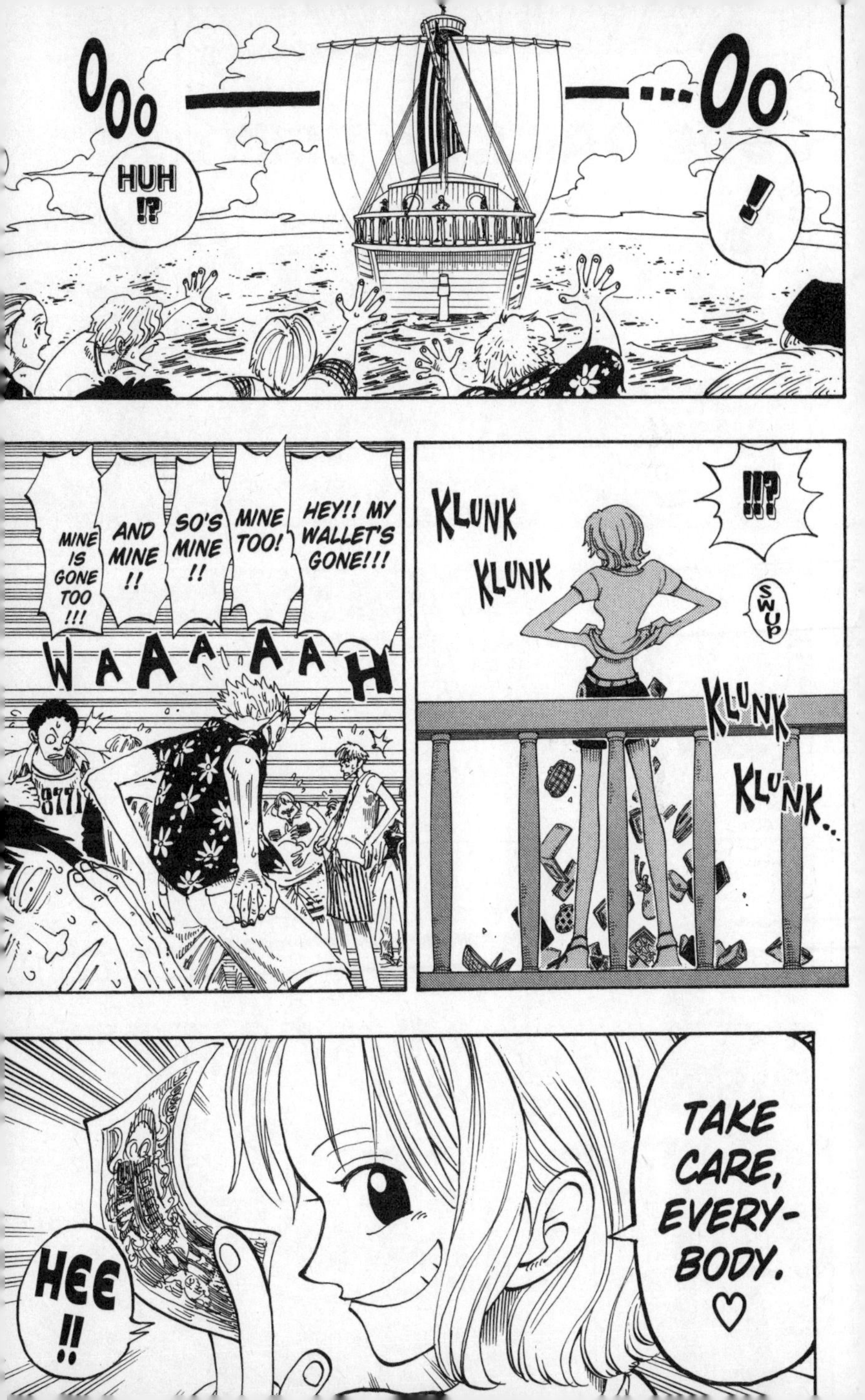
OOO — — — ...OO
!
HUH !?
!!?
KLUNK
KLUNK
SWUP
KLUNK
KLUNK...
HEY!! MY WALLET'S GONE!!!
MINE TOO!
SO'S MINE !!
AND MINE !!
MINE IS GONE TOO !!!
WAAAAAH
TAKE CARE, EVERY-BODY. ♥
HEE !!

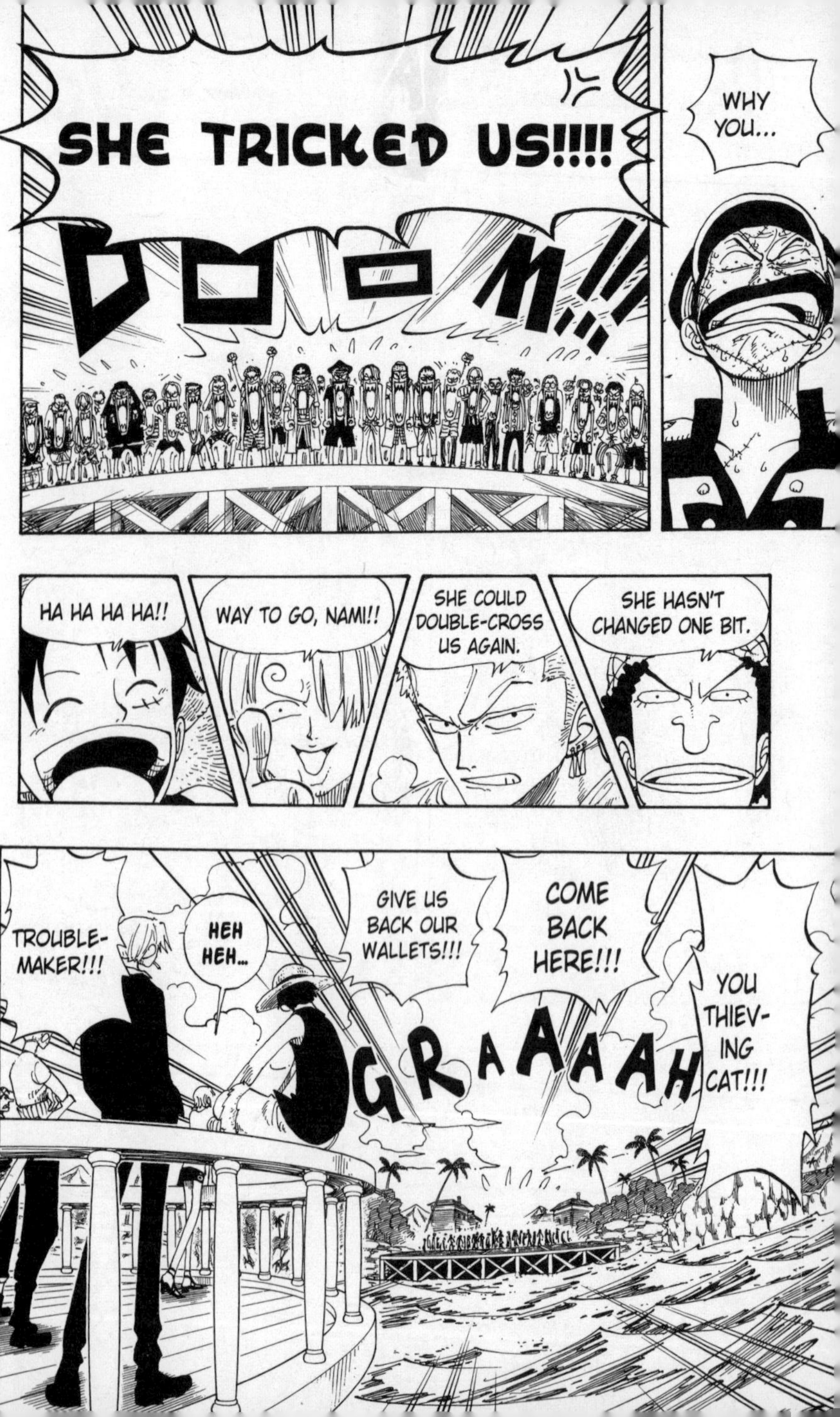
WHY YOU...
SHE TRICKED US!!!!
DOOM!!
SHE HASN'T CHANGED ONE BIT.
SHE COULD DOUBLE-CROSS US AGAIN.
WAY TO GO, NAMI!!
HA HA HA HA!!
YOU THIEV-ING CAT!!!
COME BACK HERE!!!
GIVE US BACK OUR WALLETS!!!
GRAAAAH
HEH HEH...
TROUBLE-MAKER!!!

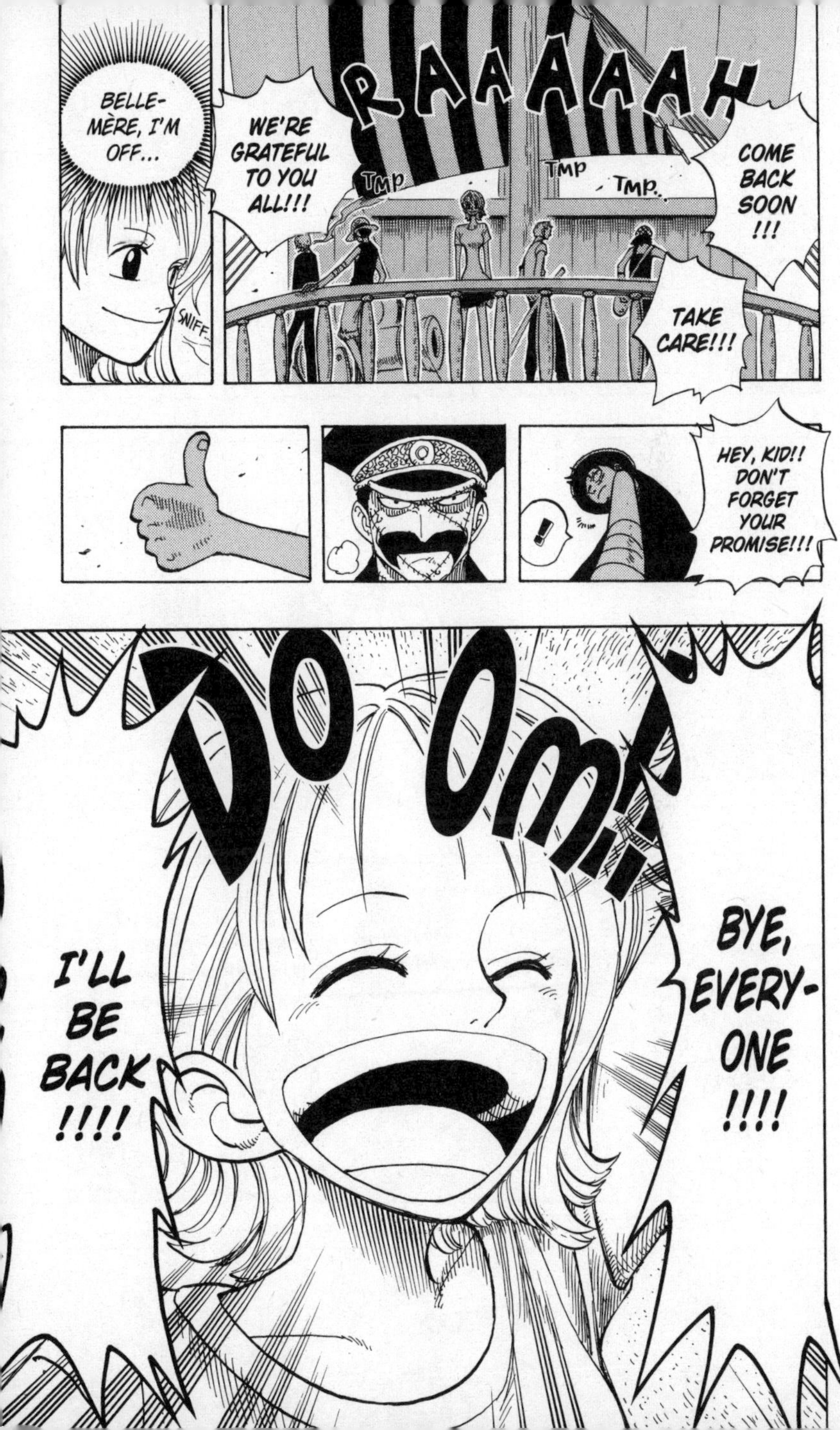
RAAAAAH
COME BACK SOON!!!
TMP TMP TMP...
TAKE CARE!!!
WE'RE GRATEFUL TO YOU ALL!!!
BELLE-MÈRE, I'M OFF...
SNIFF...
HEY, KID!! DON'T FORGET YOUR PROMISE!!!
!
DOOM!!
BYE, EVERY-ONE!!!!
I'LL BE BACK!!!!

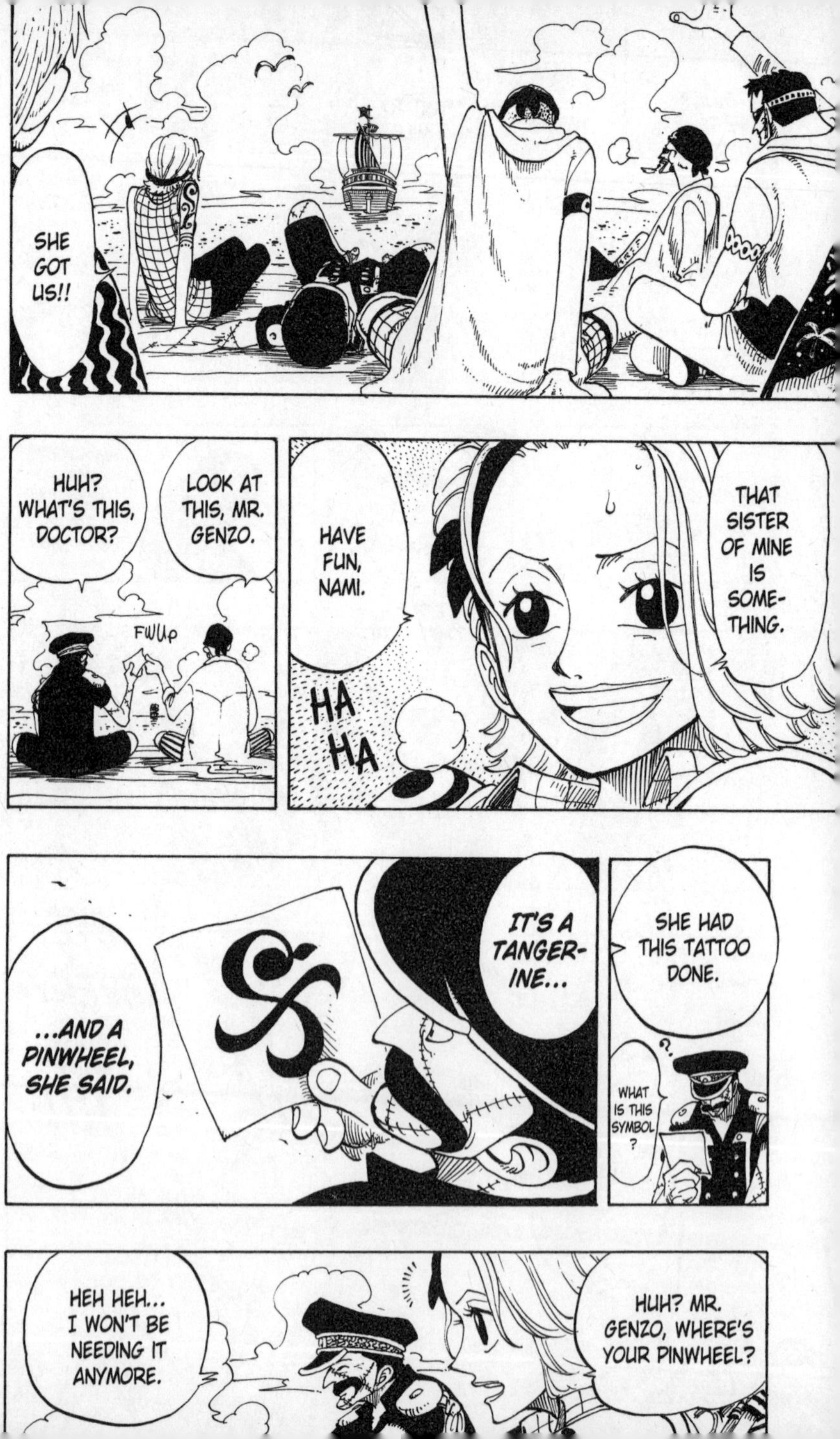
SHE GOT US!!
THAT SISTER OF MINE IS SOME-THING.
HAVE FUN, NAMI.
HA HA
LOOK AT THIS, MR. GENZO.
HUH? WHAT'S THIS, DOCTOR?
FWUP
SHE HAD THIS TATTOO DONE.
WHAT IS THIS SYMBOL ?
IT'S A TANGER-INE...
...AND A PINWHEEL, SHE SAID.
HUH? MR. GENZO, WHERE'S YOUR PINWHEEL?
HEH HEH... I WON'T BE NEEDING IT ANYMORE.

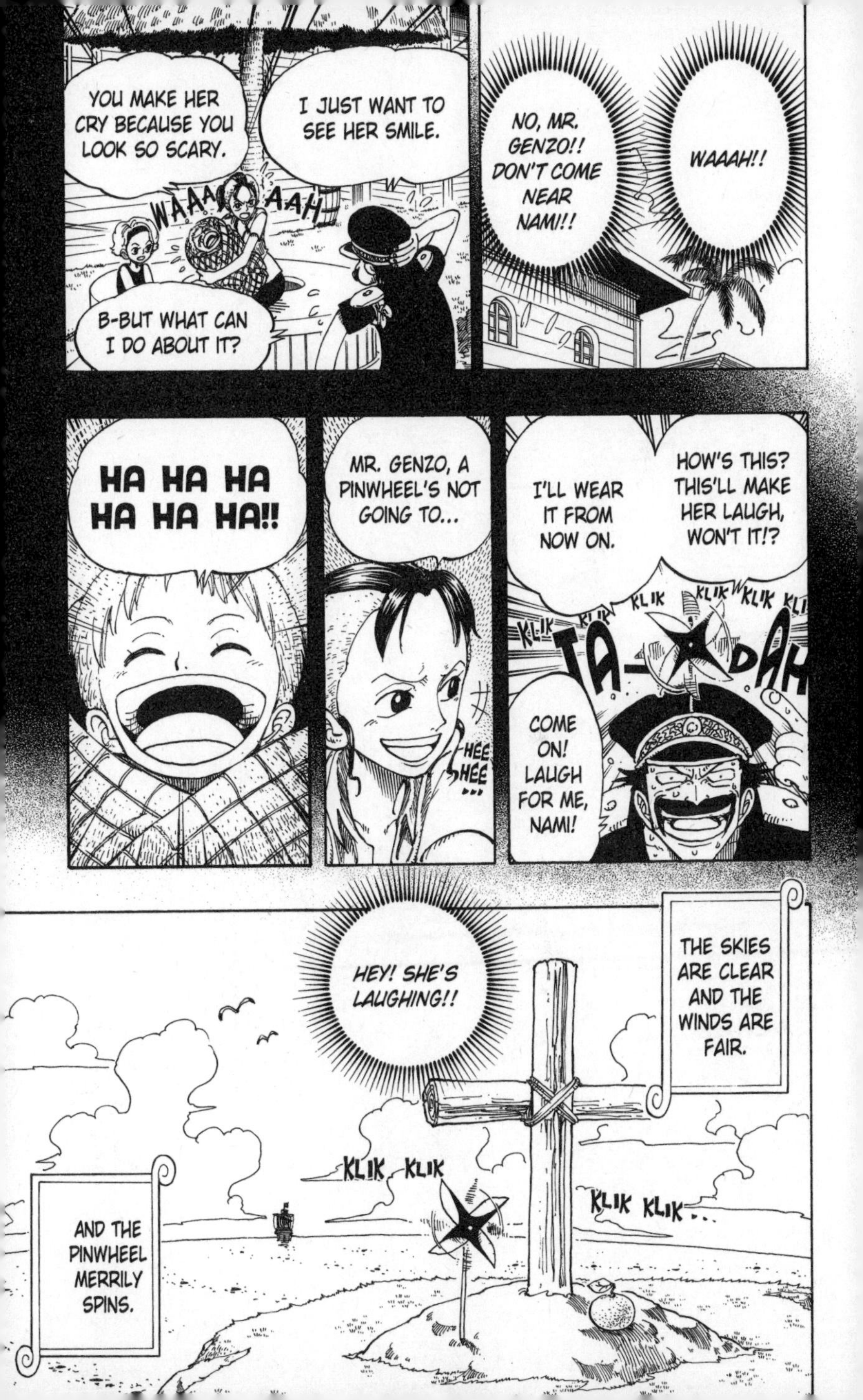
WAAAH!!
NO, MR. GENZO!! DON'T COME NEAR NAMI!!
I JUST WANT TO SEE HER SMILE.
YOU MAKE HER CRY BECAUSE YOU LOOK SO SCARY.
WAAAAAH
B-BUT WHAT CAN I DO ABOUT IT?
HOW'S THIS? THIS'LL MAKE HER LAUGH, WON'T IT!?
I'LL WEAR IT FROM NOW ON.
KLIK KLIK KLIK KLIK KLIK KLIK
TA-DAH
COME ON! LAUGH FOR ME, NAMI!
MR. GENZO, A PINWHEEL'S NOT GOING TO...
HEE HEE...
HA HA HA HA HA HA!!
THE SKIES ARE CLEAR AND THE WINDS ARE FAIR.
HEY! SHE'S LAUGHING!!
KLIK KLIK
KLIK KLIK...
AND THE PINWHEEL MERRILY SPINS.

4.

Women's Quarters

@ Nami's room. It's clean.

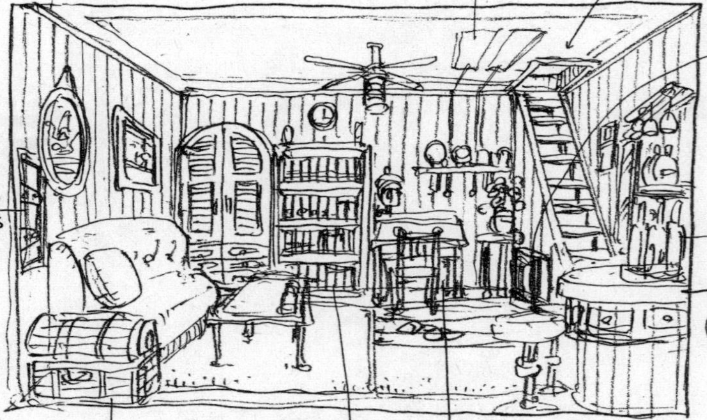

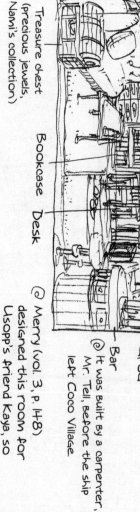

Hammock storage (Pull the rope and a hammock descends.)
Stairs (enter from storeroom)
Storage box for surveying and navigation tools
Emergency exit (connects with the men's quarters, but isn't normally used).
Grog
Bar
@ It was built by a carpenter, Mr. Tell, before the ship left Coco Village.
Treasure chest (precious jewels, Nami's collection)
Bookcase
Desk

@ Merry (vol. 3, p. 148) designed this room for Usopp's friend Kaya, so it's nicely decorated.

Chapter 96:
THE MEANEST MAN IN THE EAST

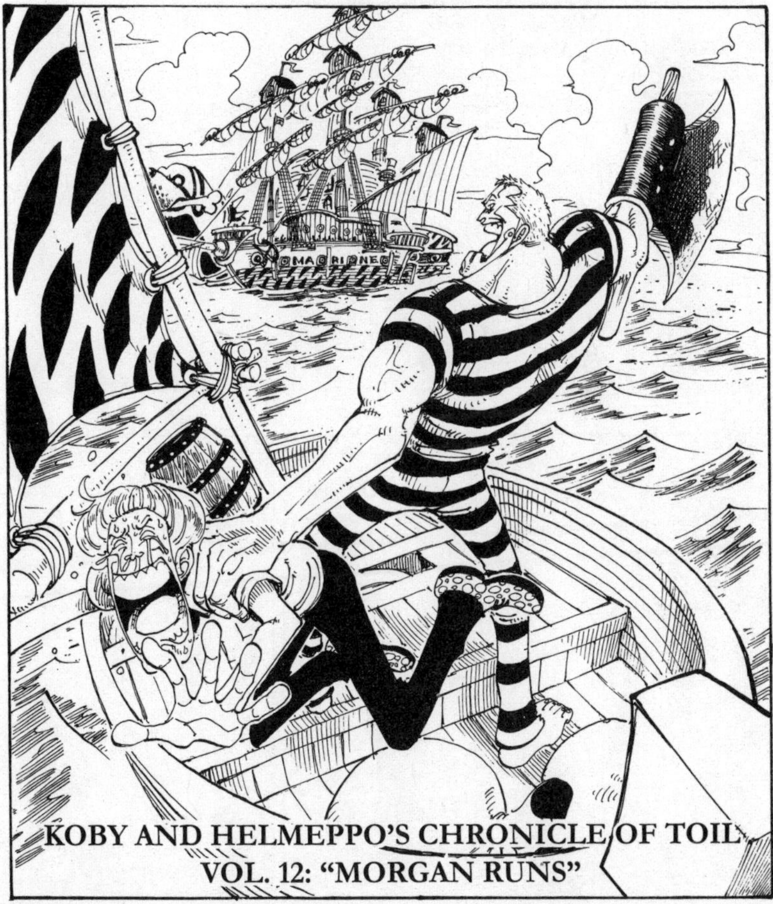
MARINE
KOBY AND HELMEPPO'S CHRONICLE OF TOIL
VOL. 12: "MORGAN RUNS"

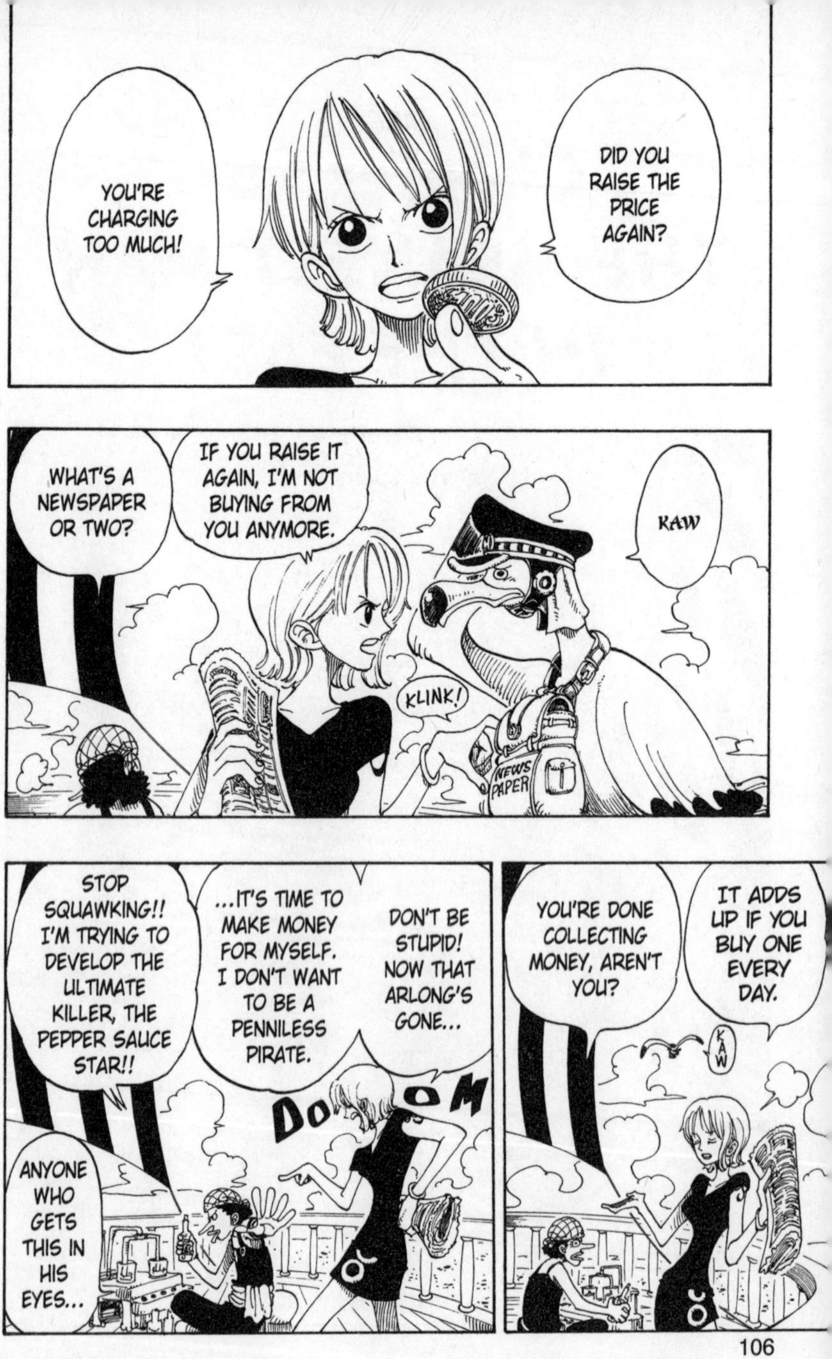
DID YOU RAISE THE PRICE AGAIN?
YOU'RE CHARGING TOO MUCH!
KAW
IF YOU RAISE IT AGAIN, I'M NOT BUYING FROM YOU ANYMORE.
WHAT'S A NEWSPAPER OR TWO?
KLINK!
NEWS PAPER
IT ADDS UP IF YOU BUY ONE EVERY DAY.
YOU'RE DONE COLLECTING MONEY, AREN'T YOU?
KAW
DON'T BE STUPID! NOW THAT ARLONG'S GONE...
...IT'S TIME TO MAKE MONEY FOR MYSELF. I DON'T WANT TO BE A PENNILESS PIRATE.
STOP SQUAWKING!! I'M TRYING TO DEVELOP THE ULTIMATE KILLER, THE PEPPER SAUCE STAR!!
DOOM
ANYONE WHO GETS THIS IN HIS EYES...

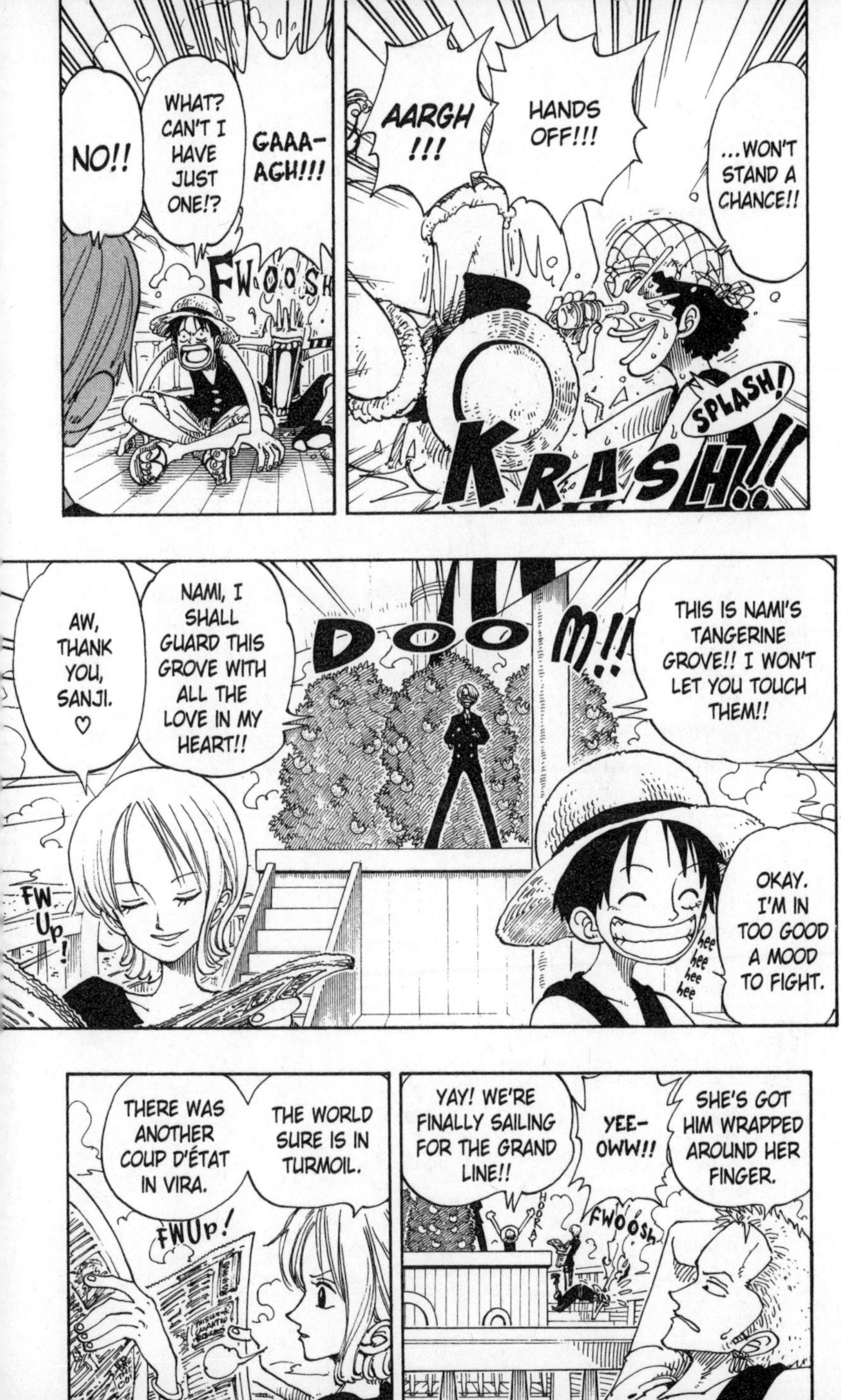
...WON'T STAND A CHANCE!!
HANDS OFF!!!
AARGH!!!
SPLASH!
KRASH!!
GAAA-AGH!!!
WHAT? CAN'T I HAVE JUST ONE!?
NO!!
FWOOSH
THIS IS NAMI'S TANGERINE GROVE!! I WON'T LET YOU TOUCH THEM!!
DOOM!!
OKAY. I'M IN TOO GOOD A MOOD TO FIGHT.
hee hee hee hee
NAMI, I SHALL GUARD THIS GROVE WITH ALL THE LOVE IN MY HEART!!
AW, THANK YOU, SANJI. ♡
FWUp!
SHE'S GOT HIM WRAPPED AROUND HER FINGER.
YEE-OWW!!
YAY! WE'RE FINALLY SAILING FOR THE GRAND LINE!!
HOORAY
FWOOSH
THE WORLD SURE IS IN TURMOIL.
THERE WAS ANOTHER COUP D'ÉTAT IN VIRA.
FWUp!

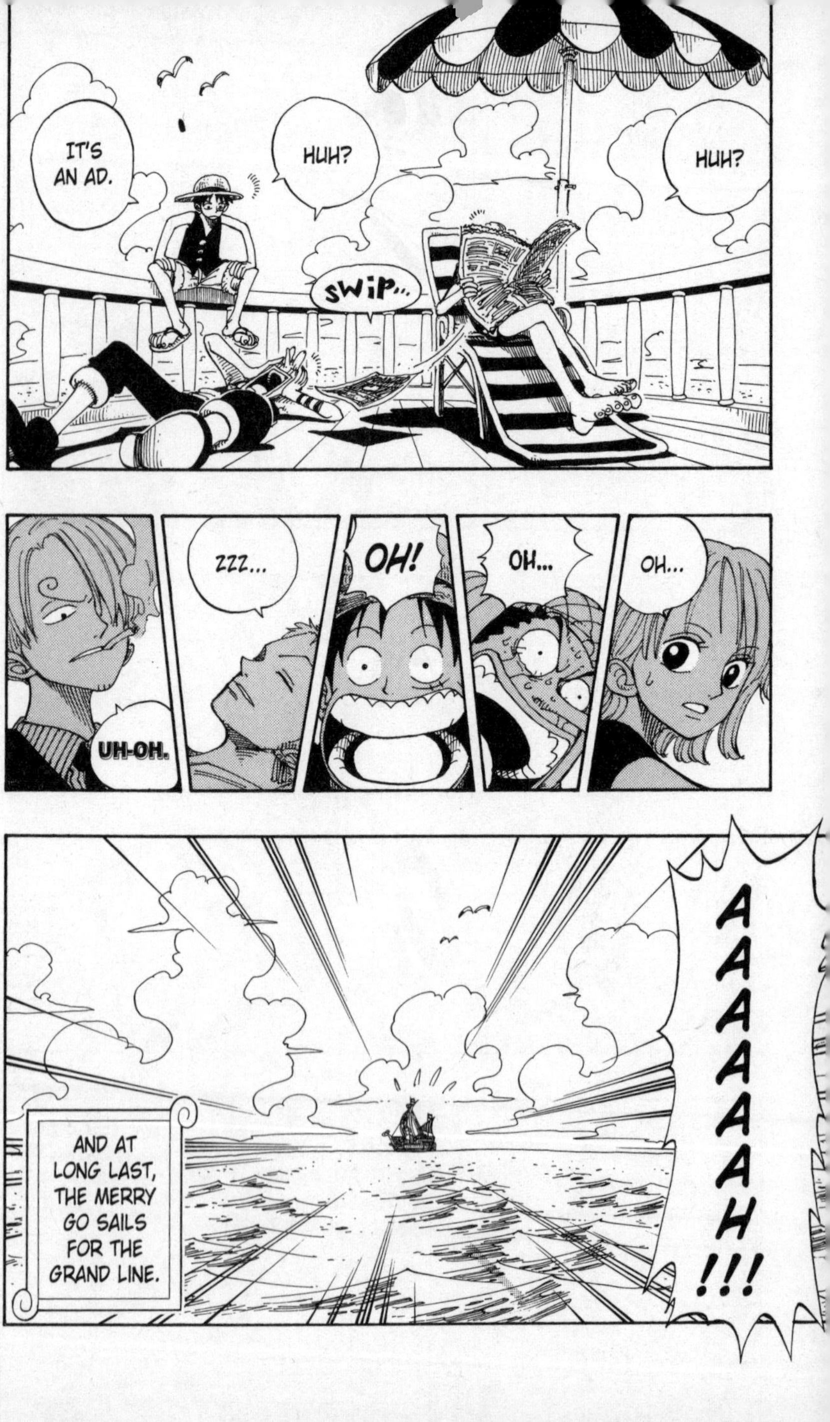
HUH?
HUH?
IT'S AN AD.
SWIP...
OH...
OH...
OH!
ZZZ...
UH-OH.
AAAAAAAH!!!
AND AT LONG LAST, THE MERRY GO SAILS FOR THE GRAND LINE.

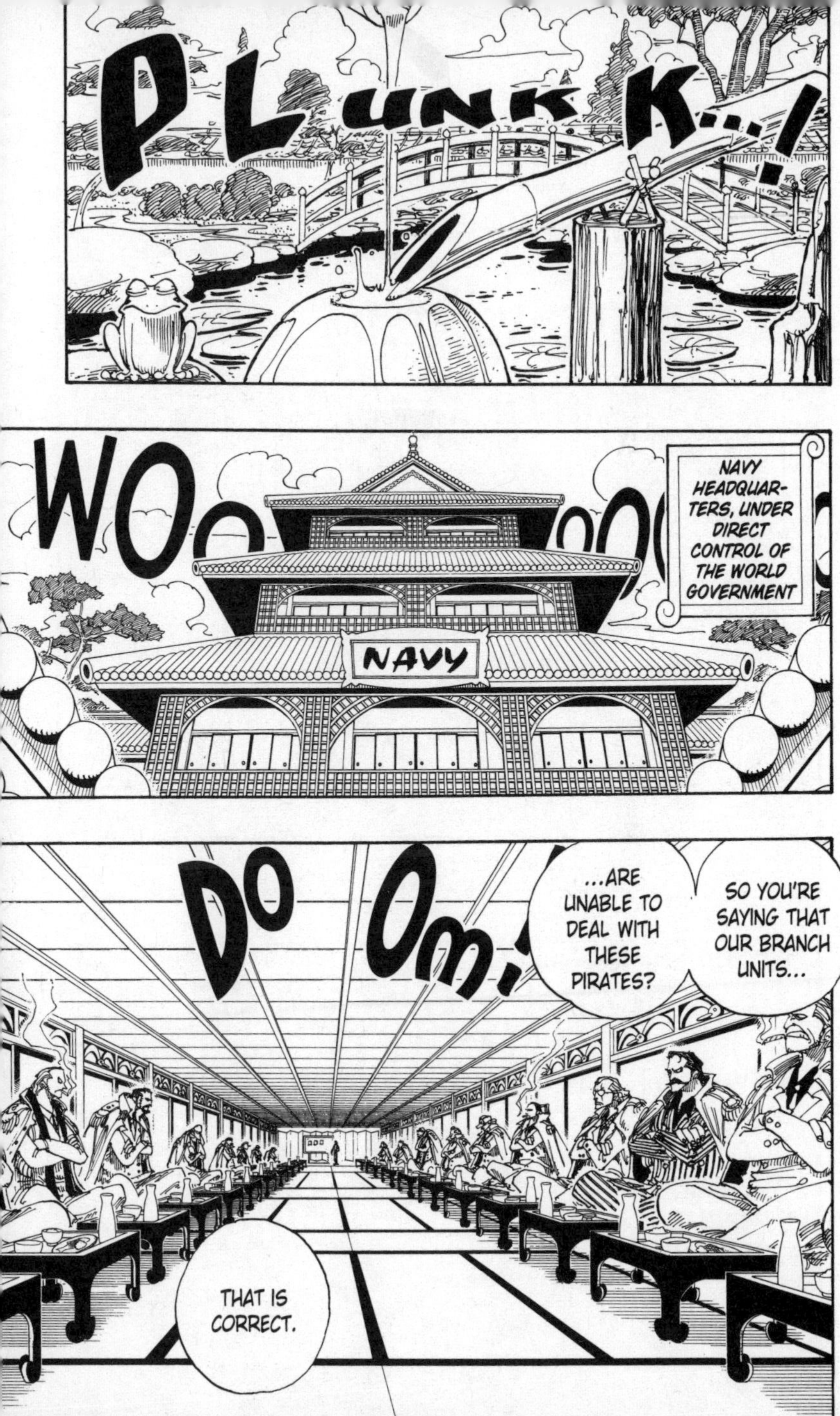
PLUNKK...!
NAVY HEADQUARTERS, UNDER DIRECT CONTROL OF THE WORLD GOVERNMENT
WOOOOOO
NAVY
SO YOU'RE SAYING THAT OUR BRANCH UNITS...
...ARE UNABLE TO DEAL WITH THESE PIRATES?
DOOM!
THAT IS CORRECT.

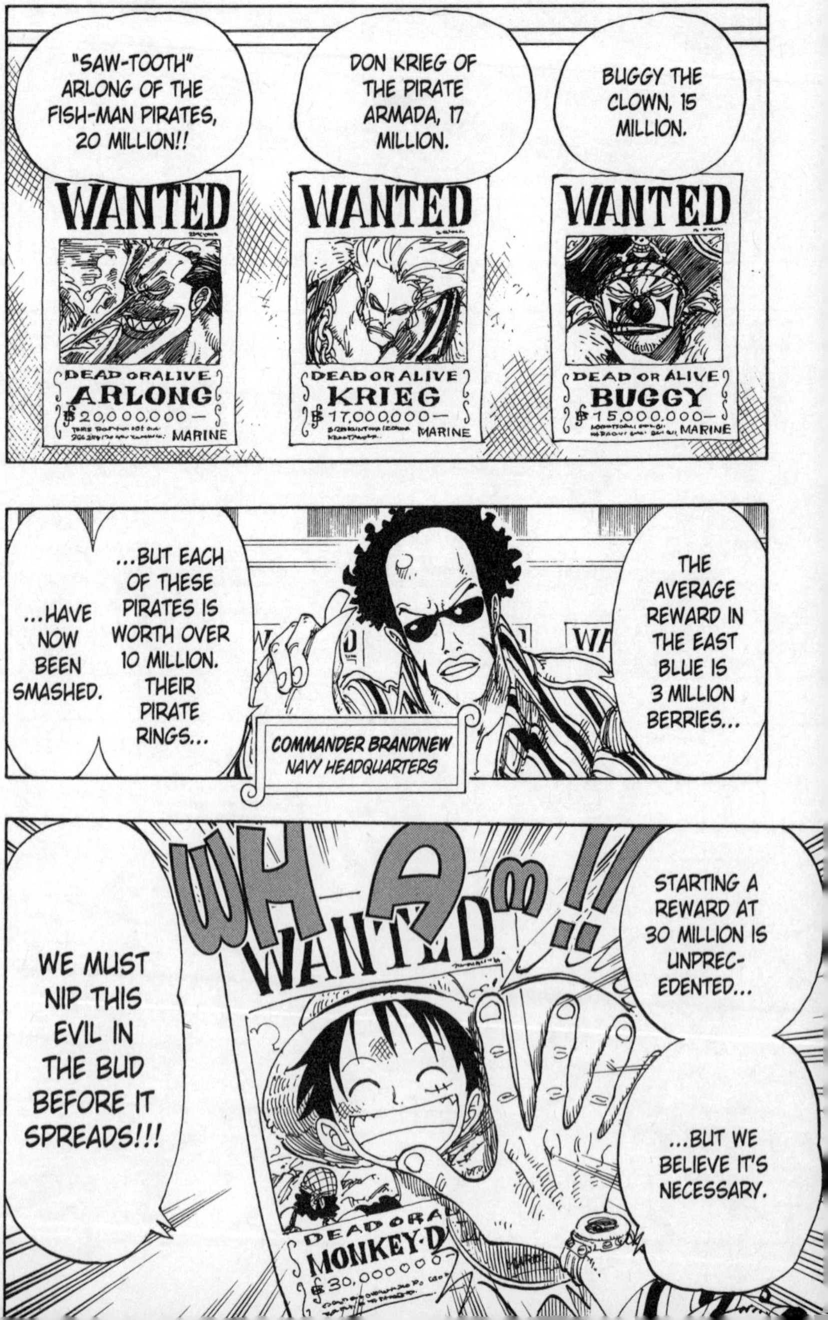
BUGGY THE CLOWN, 15 MILLION.
WANTED
DEAD OR ALIVE
BUGGY
฿15,000,000—
MARINE
DON KRIEG OF THE PIRATE ARMADA, 17 MILLION.
WANTED
DEAD OR ALIVE
KRIEG
฿17,000,000—
MARINE
"SAW-TOOTH" ARLONG OF THE FISH-MAN PIRATES, 20 MILLION!!
WANTED
DEAD OR ALIVE
ARLONG
฿20,000,000—
MARINE
THE AVERAGE REWARD IN THE EAST BLUE IS 3 MILLION BERRIES...
...BUT EACH OF THESE PIRATES IS WORTH OVER 10 MILLION. THEIR PIRATE RINGS...
...HAVE NOW BEEN SMASHED.
COMMANDER BRANDNEW NAVY HEADQUARTERS
STARTING A REWARD AT 30 MILLION IS UNPRECEDENTED...
...BUT WE BELIEVE IT'S NECESSARY.
WHAM!!
WANTED
DEAD OR A
MONKEY·D
฿30,000000
WE MUST NIP THIS EVIL IN THE BUD BEFORE IT SPREADS!!!

READ THIS WAY

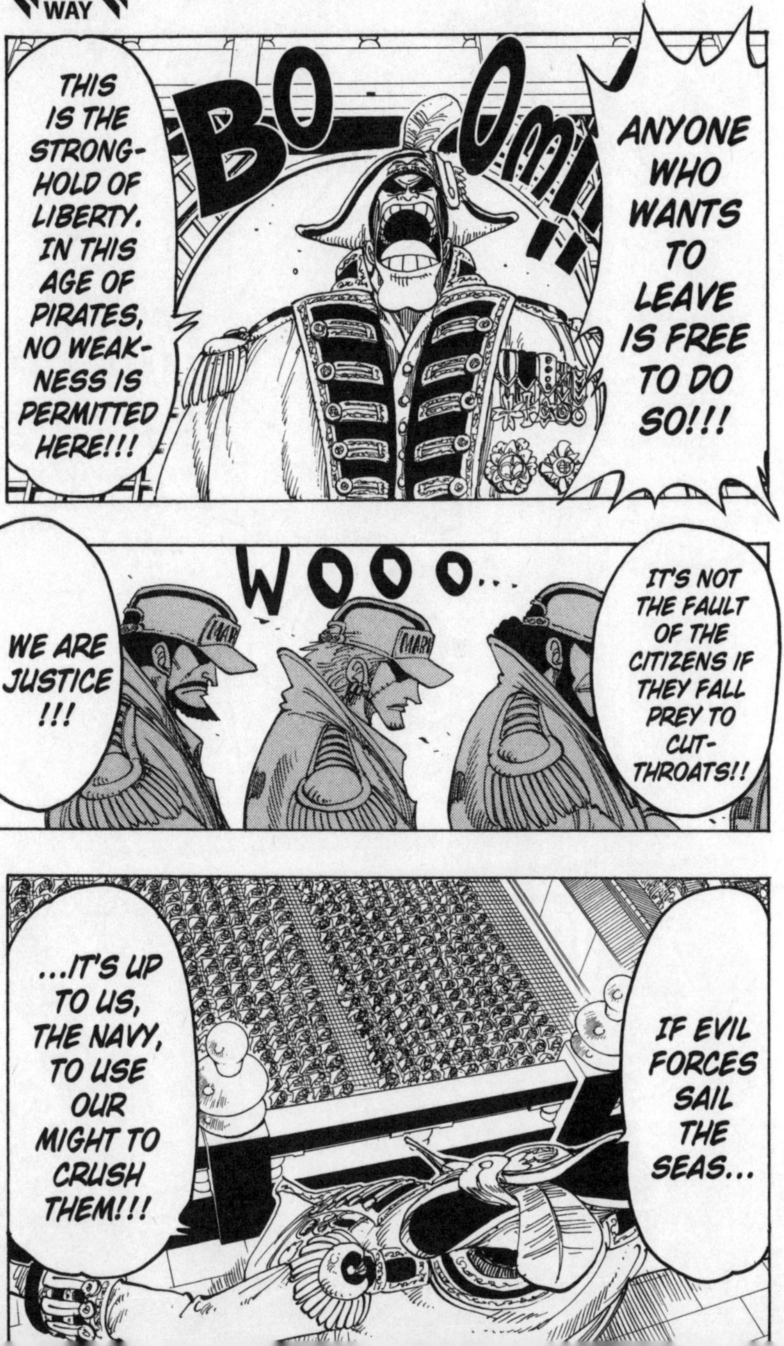
ANYONE WHO WANTS TO LEAVE IS FREE TO DO SO!!!
BOOM!!
THIS IS THE STRONGHOLD OF LIBERTY. IN THIS AGE OF PIRATES, NO WEAKNESS IS PERMITTED HERE!!!
IT'S NOT THE FAULT OF THE CITIZENS IF THEY FALL PREY TO CUT-THROATS!!
WOOO...
WE ARE JUSTICE!!!
IF EVIL FORCES SAIL THE SEAS...
...IT'S UP TO US, THE NAVY, TO USE OUR MIGHT TO CRUSH THEM!!!

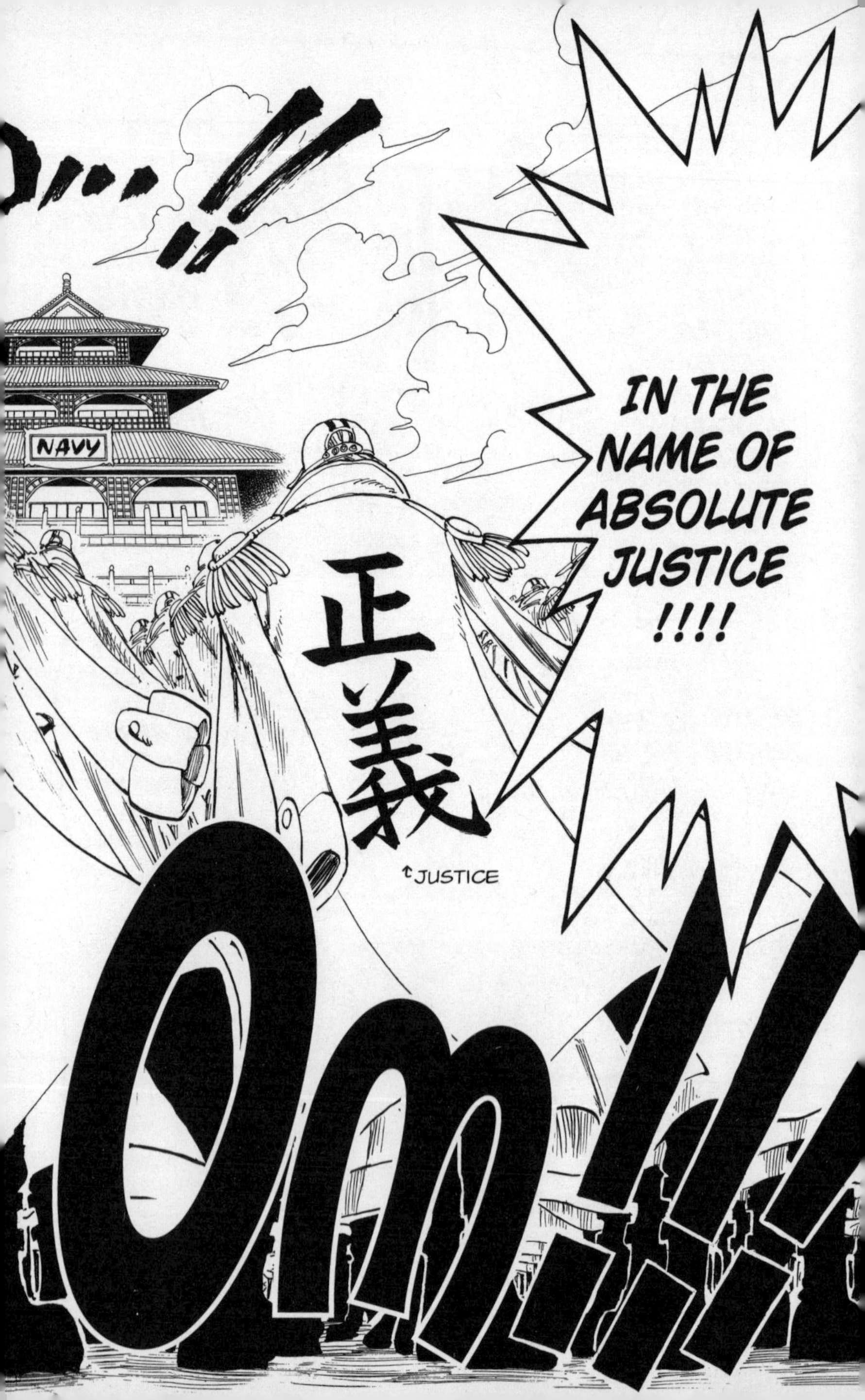
D...!!
NAVY
IN THE NAME OF ABSOLUTE JUSTICE !!!!
正義
JUSTICE
OOH!!!

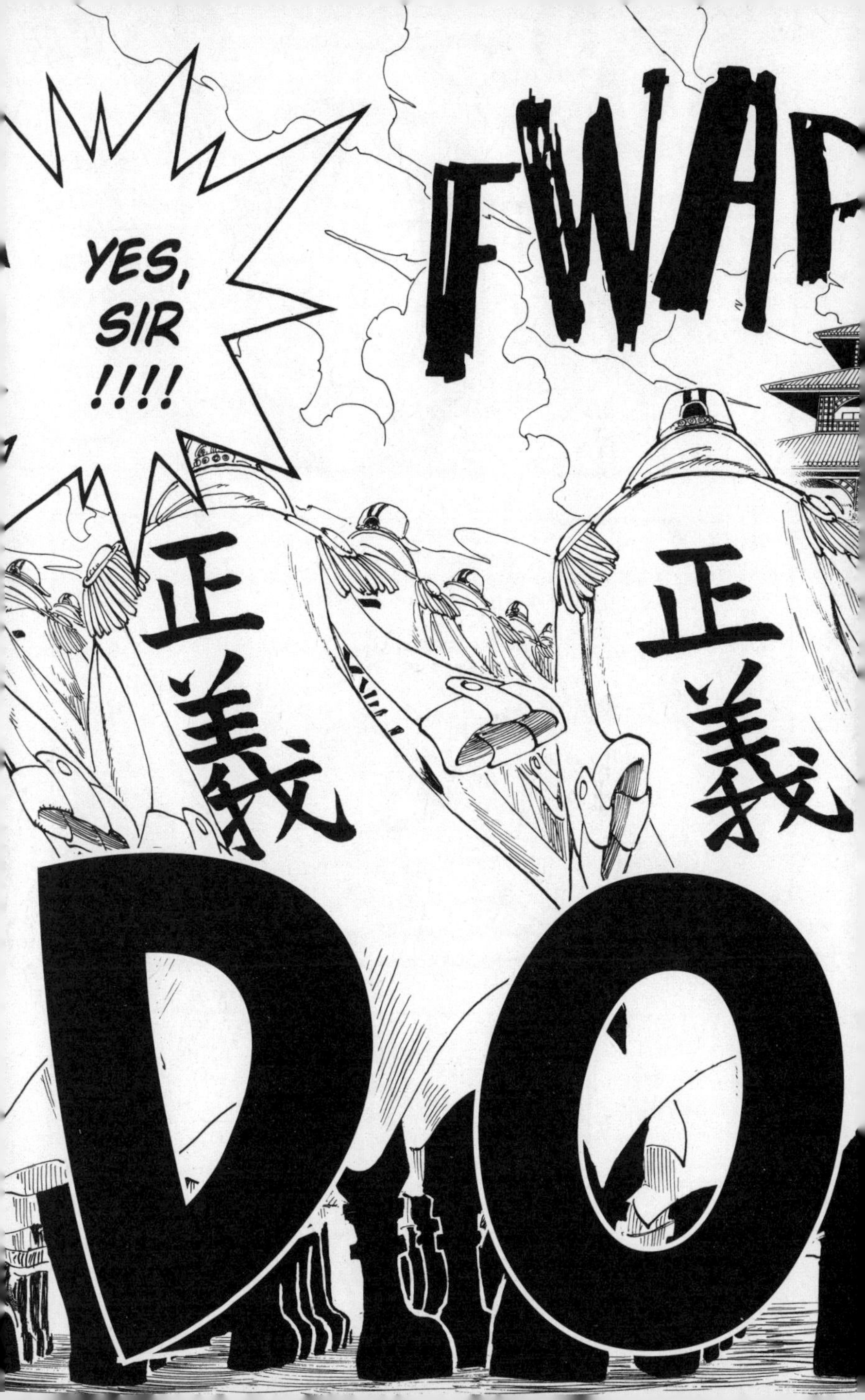
FWAP
YES, SIR !!!!
正義
正義
DO

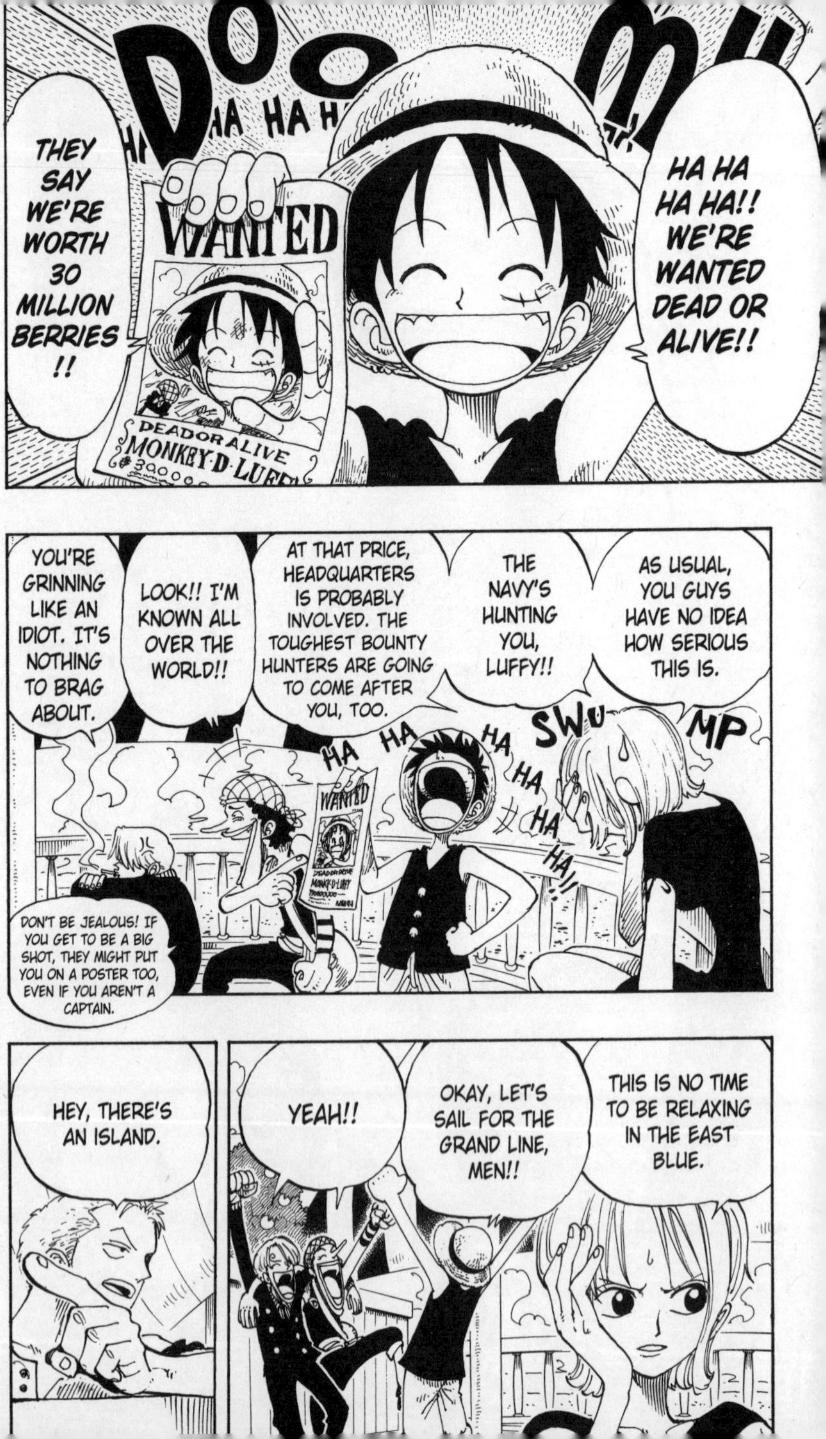
DOOOM!!
HA HA HA H
WANTED
DEAD OR ALIVE
MONKEY D. LUFFY
HA HA HA HA!! WE'RE WANTED DEAD OR ALIVE!!
THEY SAY WE'RE WORTH 30 MILLION BERRIES!!
AS USUAL, YOU GUYS HAVE NO IDEA HOW SERIOUS THIS IS.
THE NAVY'S HUNTING YOU, LUFFY!!
AT THAT PRICE, HEADQUARTERS IS PROBABLY INVOLVED. THE TOUGHEST BOUNTY HUNTERS ARE GOING TO COME AFTER YOU, TOO.
LOOK!! I'M KNOWN ALL OVER THE WORLD!!
YOU'RE GRINNING LIKE AN IDIOT. IT'S NOTHING TO BRAG ABOUT.
SWUMP
HA HA HA HA HA HA HA!!
WANTED
DON'T BE JEALOUS! IF YOU GET TO BE A BIG SHOT, THEY MIGHT PUT YOU ON A POSTER TOO, EVEN IF YOU AREN'T A CAPTAIN.
THIS IS NO TIME TO BE RELAXING IN THE EAST BLUE.
OKAY, LET'S SAIL FOR THE GRAND LINE, MEN!!
YEAH!!
HEY, THERE'S AN ISLAND.

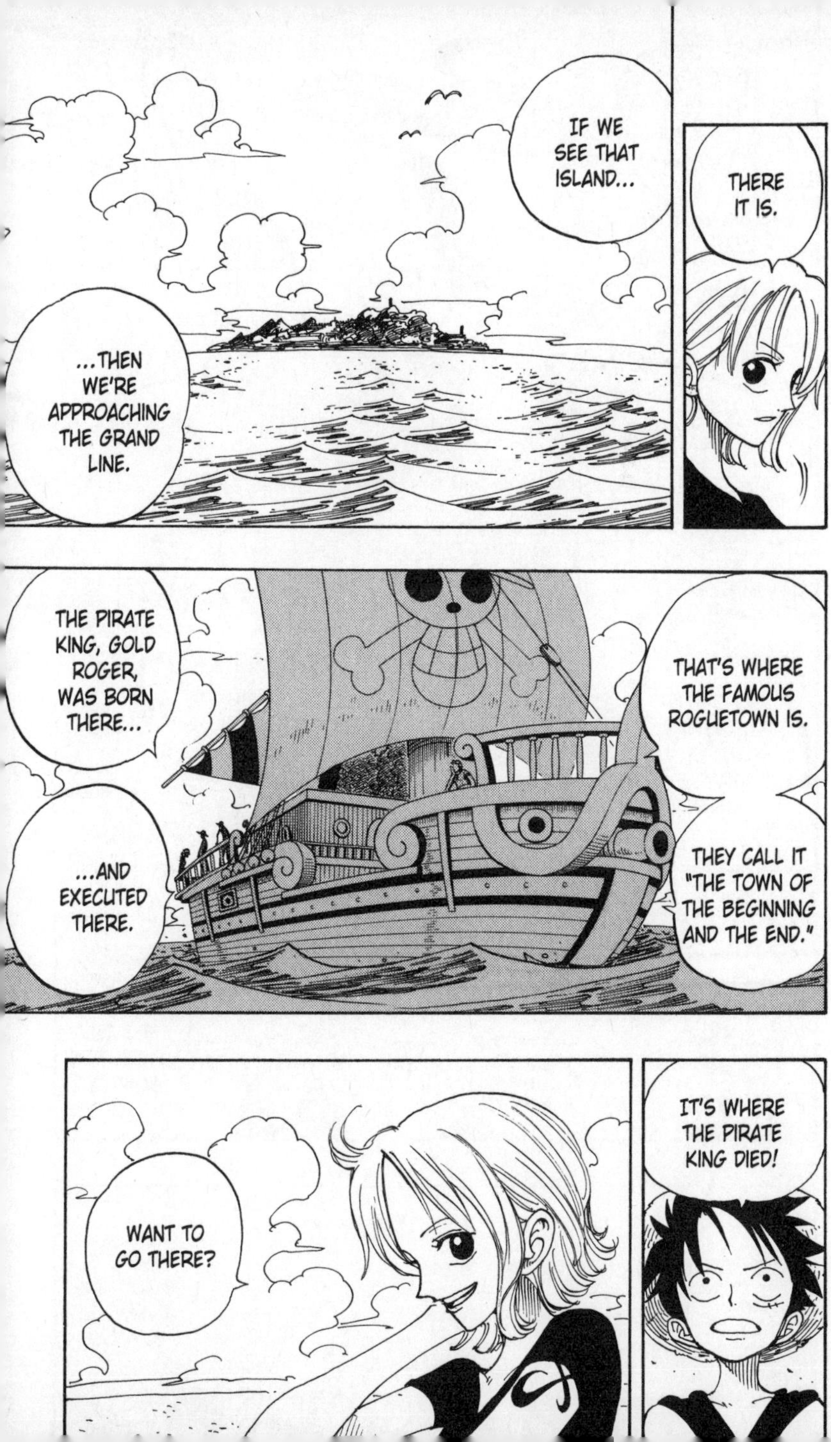
THERE IT IS.
IF WE SEE THAT ISLAND...
...THEN WE'RE APPROACHING THE GRAND LINE.
THAT'S WHERE THE FAMOUS ROGUETOWN IS.
THEY CALL IT "THE TOWN OF THE BEGINNING AND THE END."
THE PIRATE KING, GOLD ROGER, WAS BORN THERE...
...AND EXECUTED THERE.
IT'S WHERE THE PIRATE KING DIED!
WANT TO GO THERE?

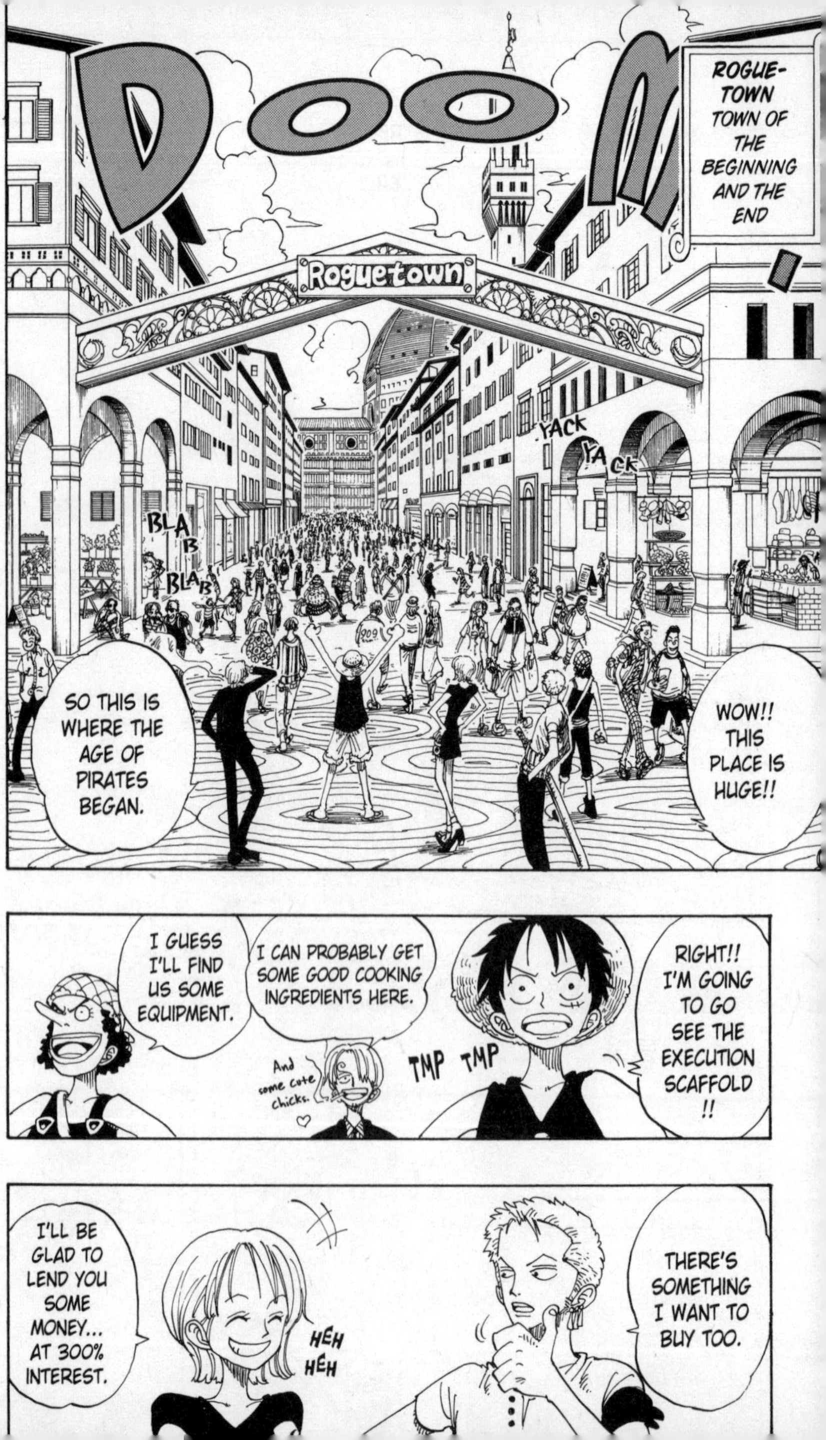
ROGUE-TOWN TOWN OF THE BEGINNING AND THE END
DOOM
Roguetown
YACK YACK
BLAB BLAB
WOW!! THIS PLACE IS HUGE!!
SO THIS IS WHERE THE AGE OF PIRATES BEGAN.
RIGHT!! I'M GOING TO GO SEE THE EXECUTION SCAFFOLD !!
TMP TMP
I CAN PROBABLY GET SOME GOOD COOKING INGREDIENTS HERE.
And some cute chicks. ♡
I GUESS I'LL FIND US SOME EQUIPMENT.
THERE'S SOMETHING I WANT TO BUY TOO.
HEH HEH
I'LL BE GLAD TO LEND YOU SOME MONEY... AT 300% INTEREST.

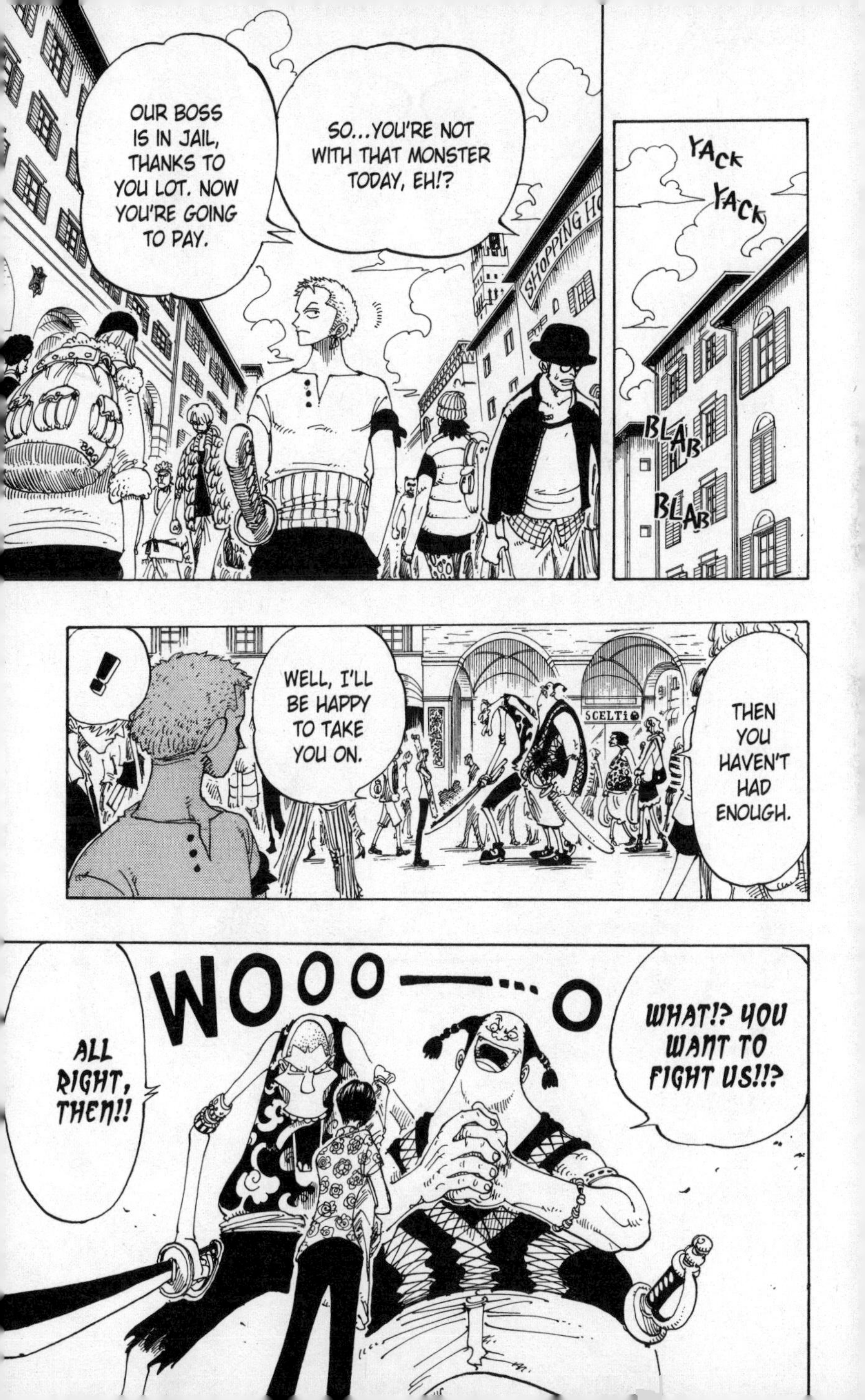
YACK
YACK
BLAB
BLAB
SO...YOU'RE NOT WITH THAT MONSTER TODAY, EH!?
OUR BOSS IS IN JAIL, THANKS TO YOU LOT. NOW YOU'RE GOING TO PAY.
THEN YOU HAVEN'T HAD ENOUGH.
WELL, I'LL BE HAPPY TO TAKE YOU ON.
!
SCELTI
WHAT!? YOU WANT TO FIGHT US!!?
WOOO—...O
ALL RIGHT, THEN!!

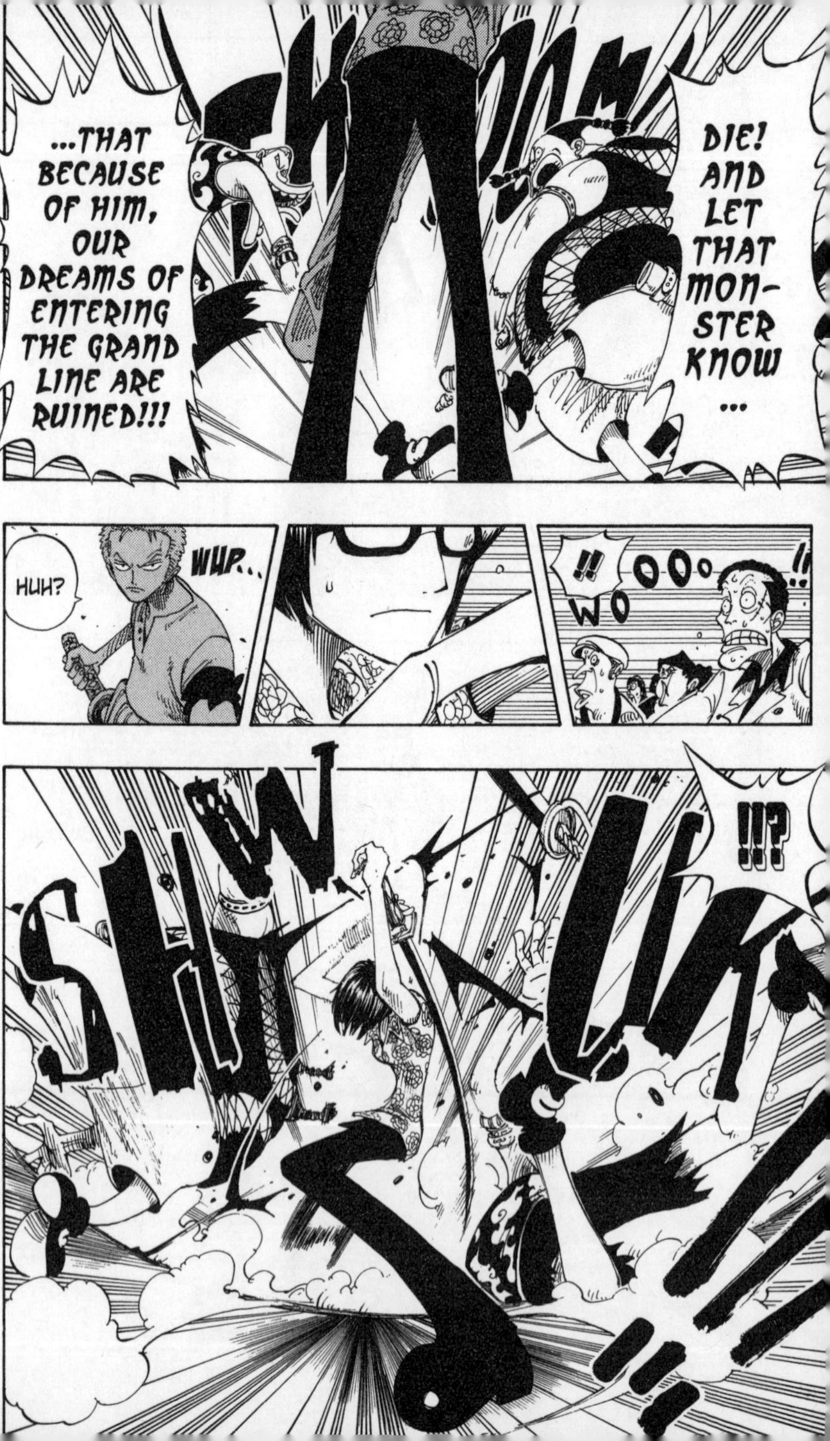
DIE! AND LET THAT MON-STER KNOW ...
...THAT BECAUSE OF HIM, OUR DREAMS OF ENTERING THE GRAND LINE ARE RUINED!!!
!! WOOOo !!
WUP...
HUH?
!!?

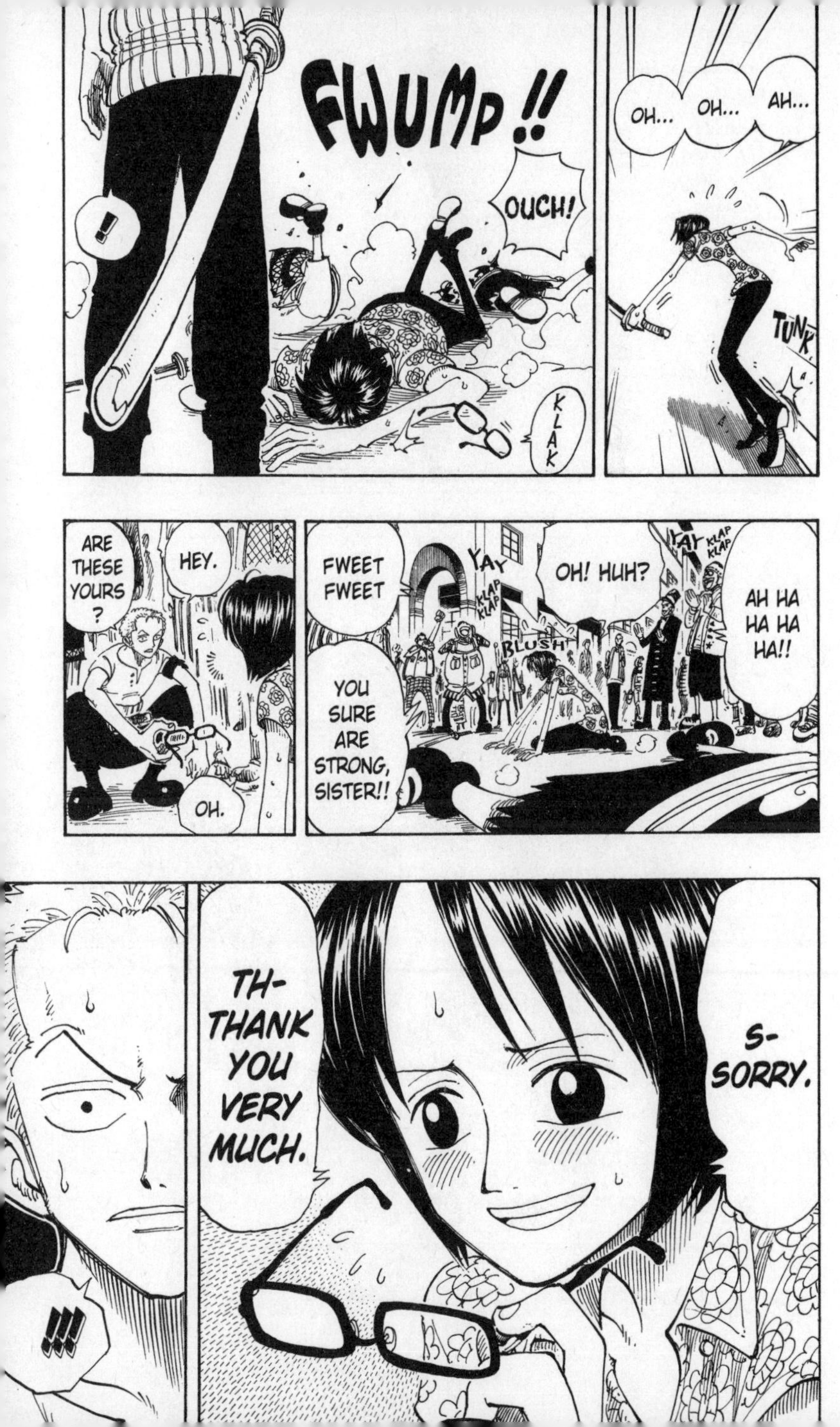
AH...
OH...
OH...
TUNK
FWUMP!!
OUCH!
KLAK
!
AH HA HA HA HA!!
YAY
KLAP KLAP
OH! HUH?
YAY
KLAP KLAP
FWEET FWEET
BLUSH
YOU SURE ARE STRONG, SISTER!!
HEY.
ARE THESE YOURS?
OH.
S-SORRY.
TH-THANK YOU VERY MUCH.
!!!

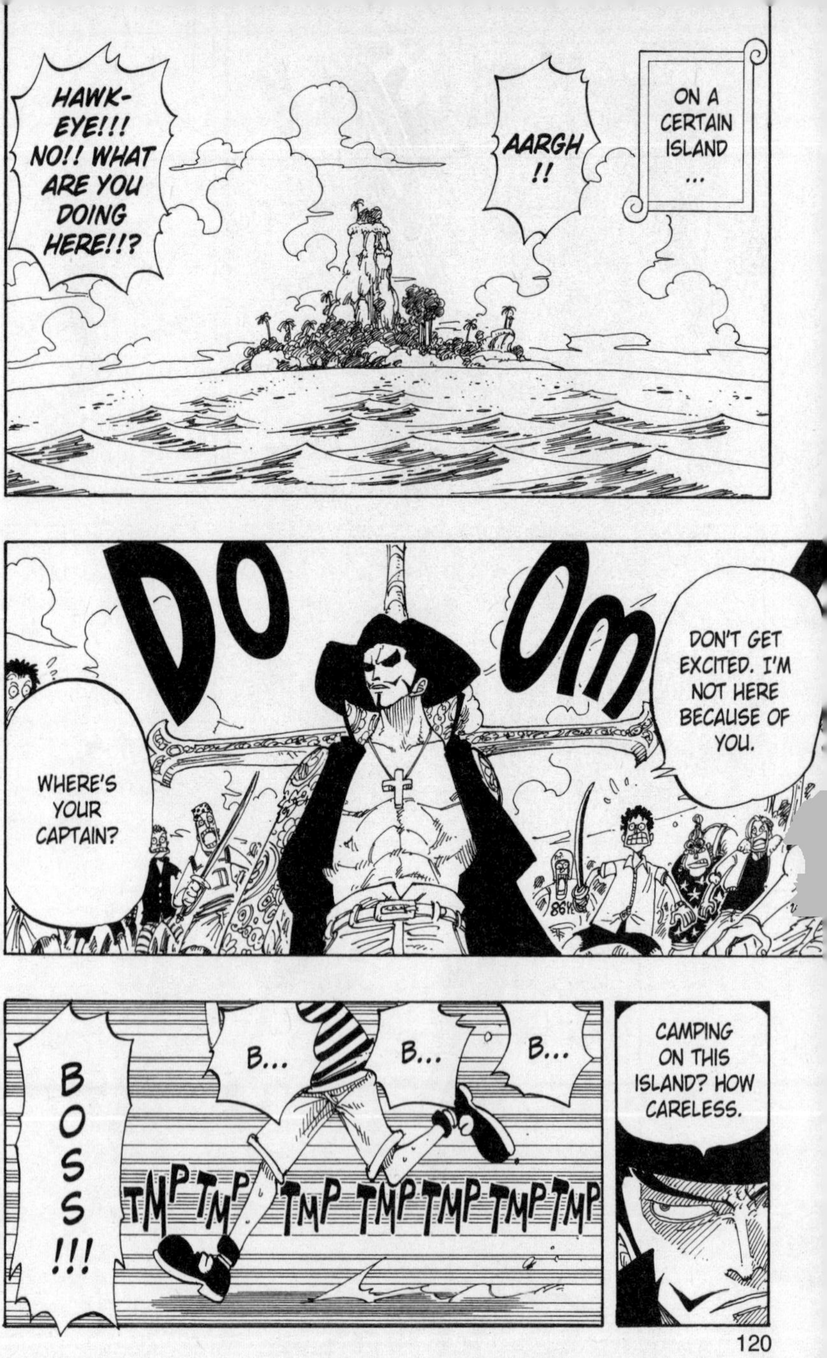
ON A CERTAIN ISLAND ...
AARGH !!
HAWK-EYE!!! NO!! WHAT ARE YOU DOING HERE!!?
DON'T GET EXCITED. I'M NOT HERE BECAUSE OF YOU.
DO OM
WHERE'S YOUR CAPTAIN?
CAMPING ON THIS ISLAND? HOW CARELESS.
B...
B...
B...
BOSS!!!
TMP TMP TMP TMP TMP TMP TMP

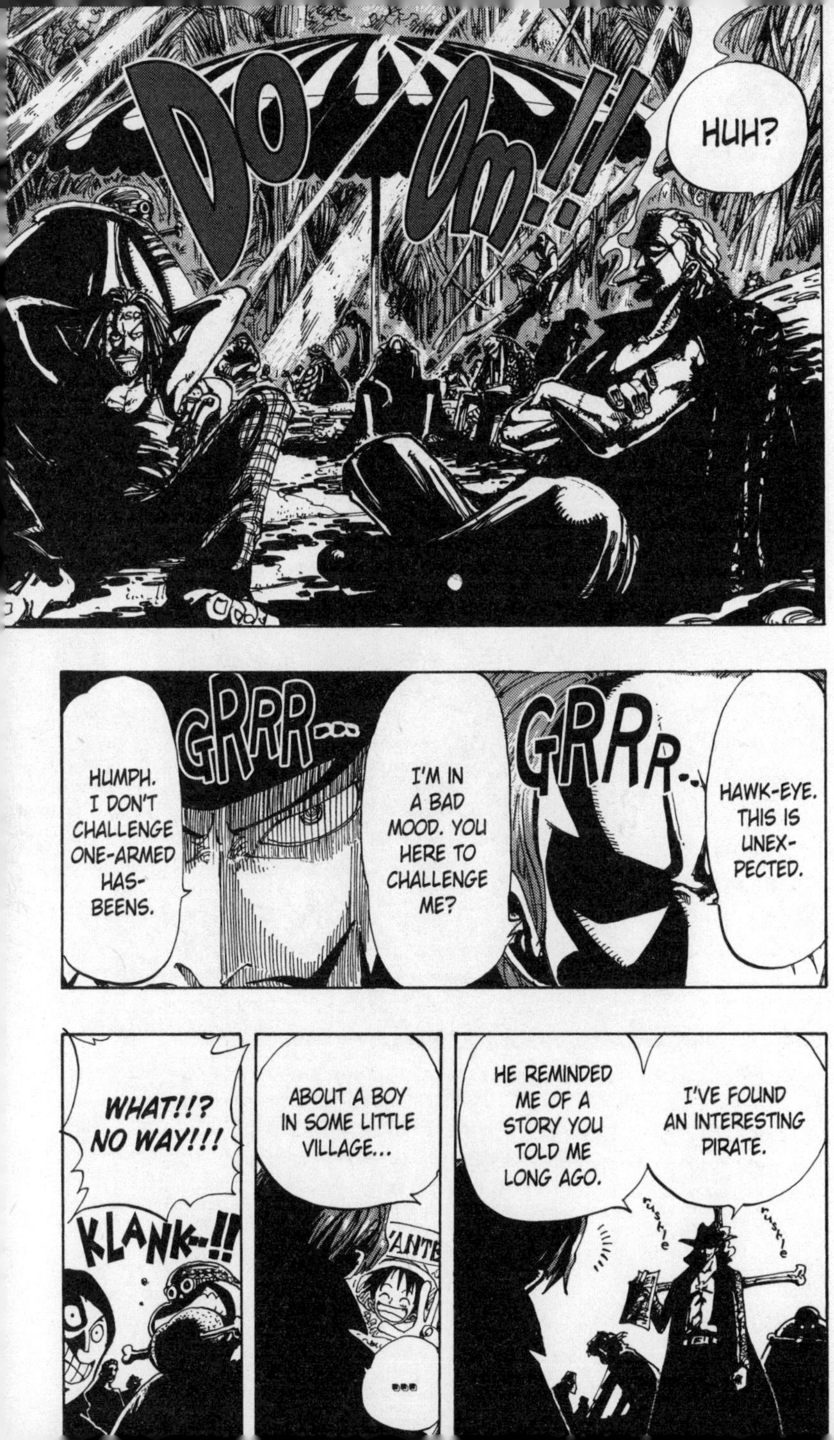
HUH?
DO-OM!!
HAWK-EYE. THIS IS UNEXPECTED.
GRRR..
I'M IN A BAD MOOD. YOU HERE TO CHALLENGE ME?
GRRR...
HUMPH. I DON'T CHALLENGE ONE-ARMED HAS-BEENS.
I'VE FOUND AN INTERESTING PIRATE.
HE REMINDED ME OF A STORY YOU TOLD ME LONG AGO.
rustle
rustle
ABOUT A BOY IN SOME LITTLE VILLAGE...
...
WHAT!!? NO WAY!!!
KLANK--!!

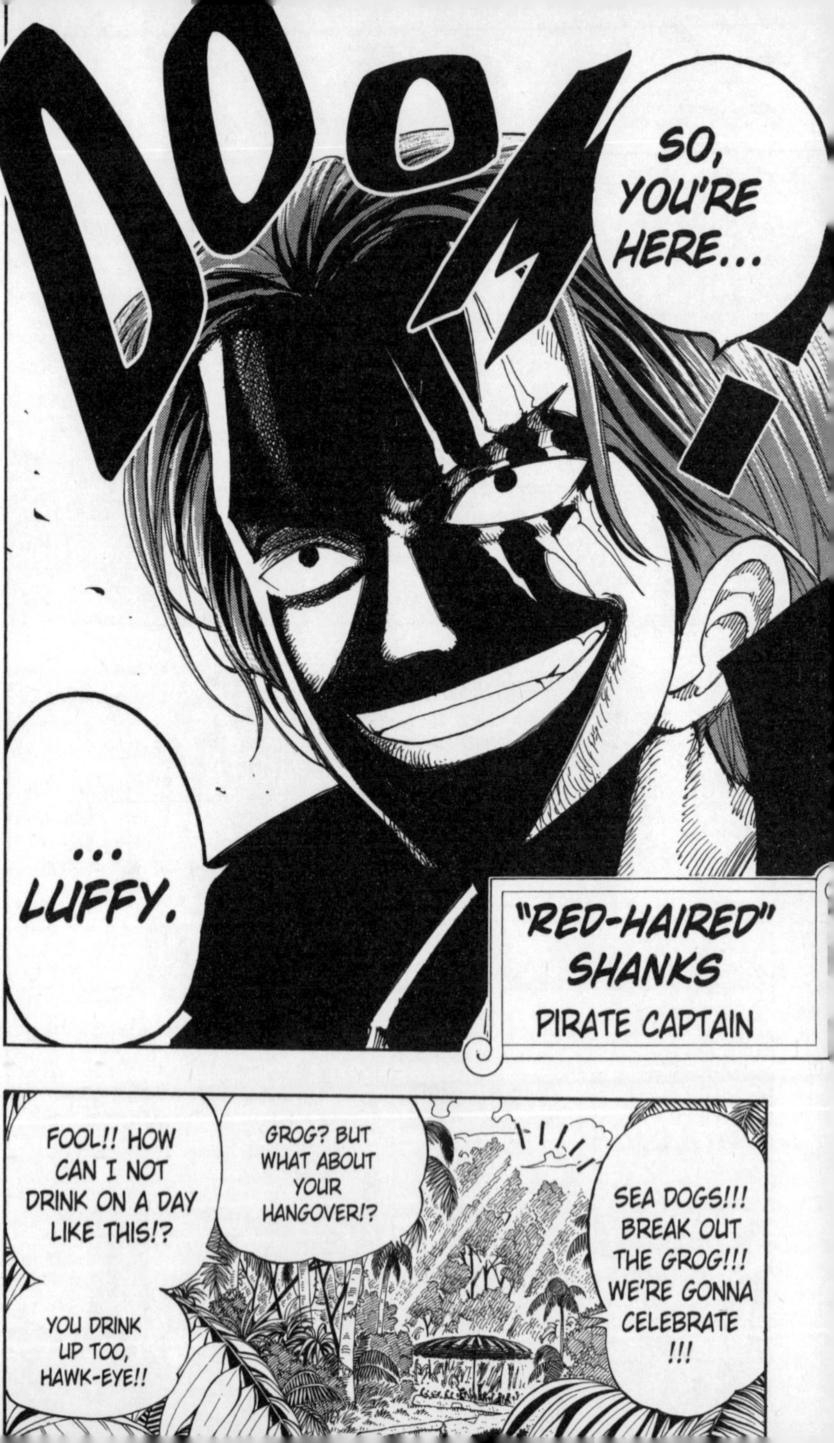
DOOM
SO, YOU'RE HERE...
... LUFFY.
"RED-HAIRED" SHANKS
PIRATE CAPTAIN
SEA DOGS!!! BREAK OUT THE GROG!!! WE'RE GONNA CELEBRATE !!!
GROG? BUT WHAT ABOUT YOUR HANGOVER!?
FOOL!! HOW CAN I NOT DRINK ON A DAY LIKE THIS!?
YOU DRINK UP TOO, HAWK-EYE!!

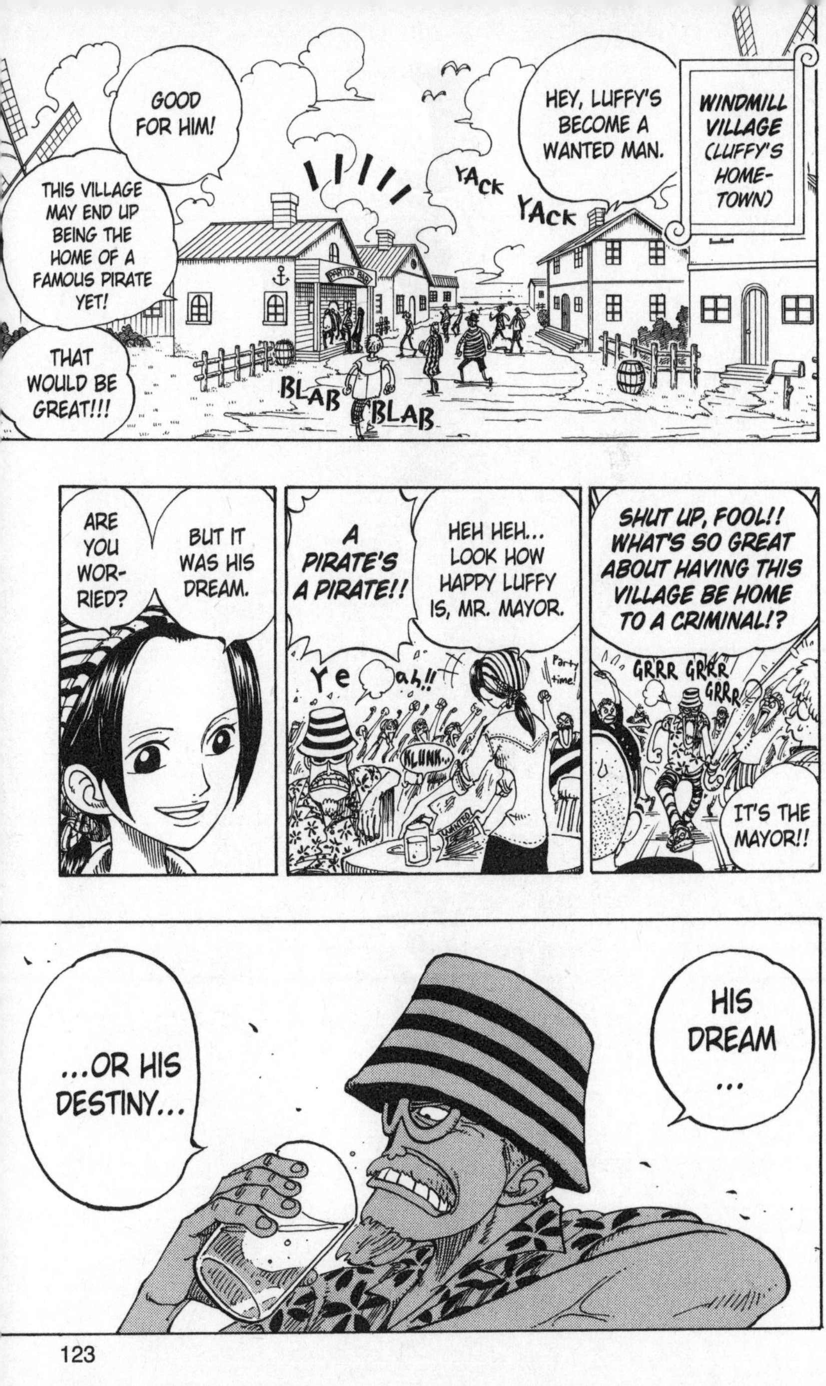
WINDMILL VILLAGE (LUFFY'S HOME-TOWN)
HEY, LUFFY'S BECOME A WANTED MAN.
YACK YACK
GOOD FOR HIM!
THIS VILLAGE MAY END UP BEING THE HOME OF A FAMOUS PIRATE YET!
THAT WOULD BE GREAT!!!
BLAB BLAB
SHUT UP, FOOL!! WHAT'S SO GREAT ABOUT HAVING THIS VILLAGE BE HOME TO A CRIMINAL!?
GRRR GRRR GRRR
IT'S THE MAYOR!!
HEH HEH... LOOK HOW HAPPY LUFFY IS, MR. MAYOR.
A PIRATE'S A PIRATE!!
Party time!
KLUNK..
BUT IT WAS HIS DREAM.
ARE YOU WOR-RIED?
HIS DREAM ...
...OR HIS DESTINY...

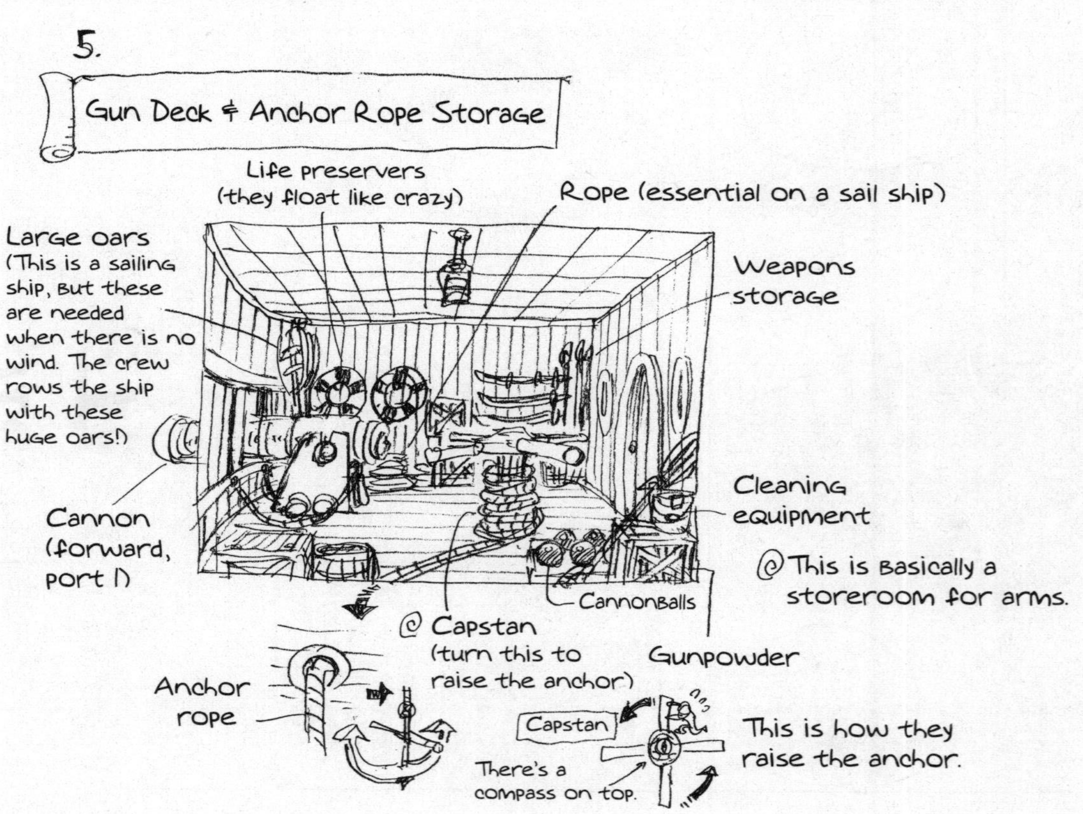
5.
Gun Deck & Anchor Rope Storage
Life preservers (they float like crazy)
Rope (essential on a sail ship)
Large oars (This is a sailing ship, But these are needed when there is no wind. The crew rows the ship with these huge oars!)
Weapons storage
Cleaning equipment
Cannon (forward, port!)
@ This is Basically a storeroom for arms.
CannonBalls
@ Capstan (turn this to raise the anchor)
Gunpowder
Anchor rope
Capstan
This is how they raise the anchor.
There's a compass on top.

Chapter 97: KITETSU III

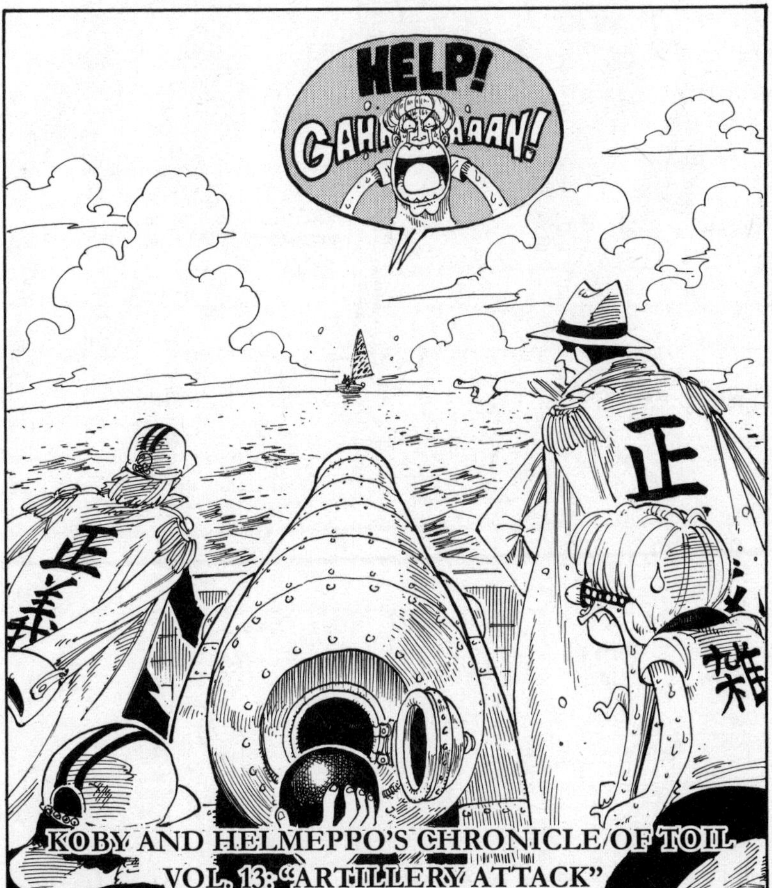
HELP!
GAHHAAAAN!

KOBY AND HELMEPPO'S CHRONICLE OF TOIL
VOL. 13: "ARTILLERY ATTACK"

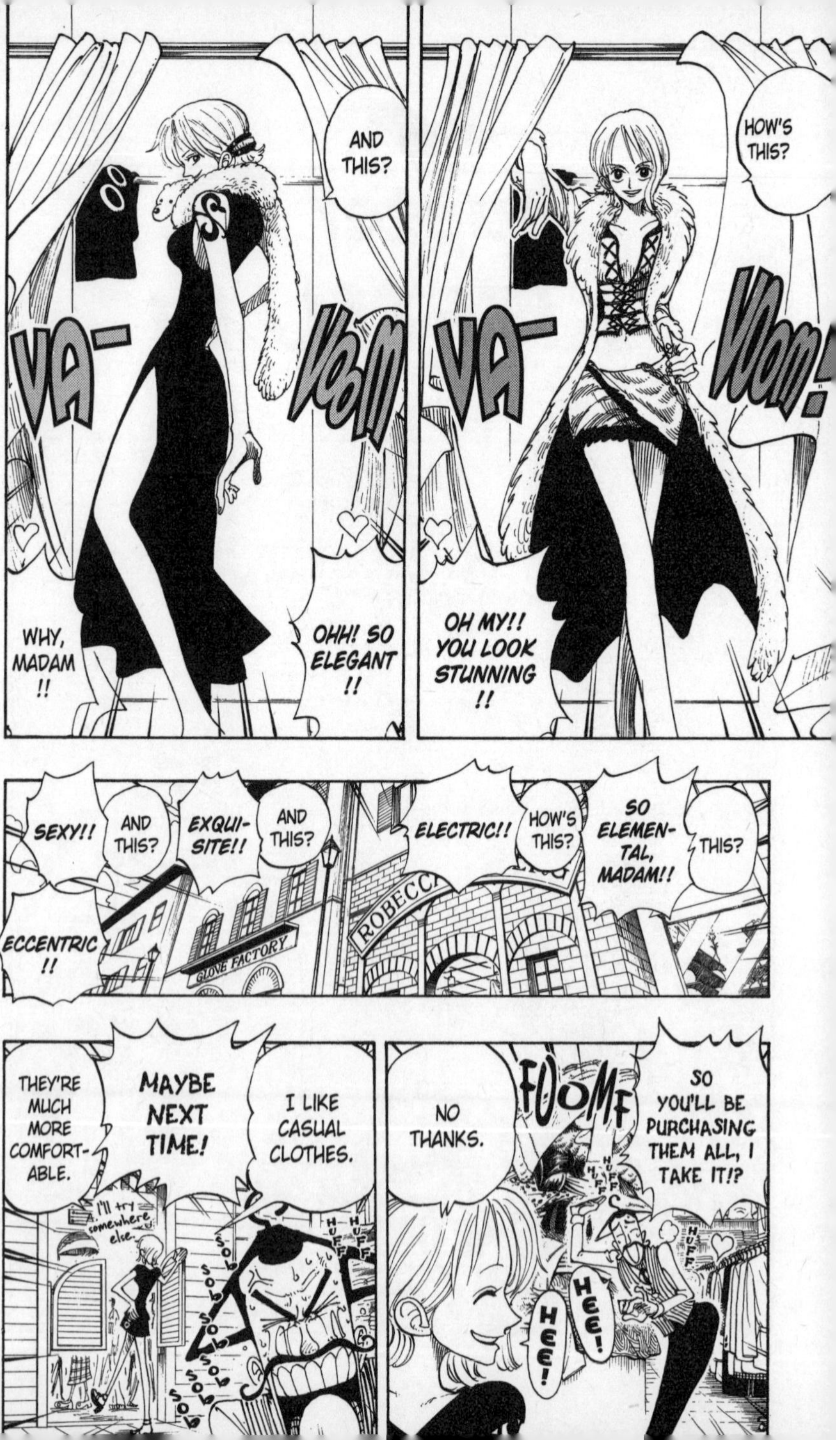
HOW'S THIS?
VA-VOOM!
OH MY!! YOU LOOK STUNNING !!
AND THIS?
VA-VOOM
OHH! SO ELEGANT !!
WHY, MADAM !!
THIS?
SO ELEMENTAL, MADAM!!
HOW'S THIS?
ELECTRIC!!
AND THIS?
EXQUISITE!!
AND THIS?
SEXY!!
ECCENTRIC !!
ROBECC
GLOVE FACTORY
SO YOU'LL BE PURCHASING THEM ALL, I TAKE IT!?
FOOMF
HUFF HUFF
HUFF
NO THANKS.
HEE!
HEE!
I LIKE CASUAL CLOTHES.
MAYBE NEXT TIME!
THEY'RE MUCH MORE COMFORT-ABLE.
I'll try somewhere else.
HUFF HUFF
sob sob sob sob sob sob

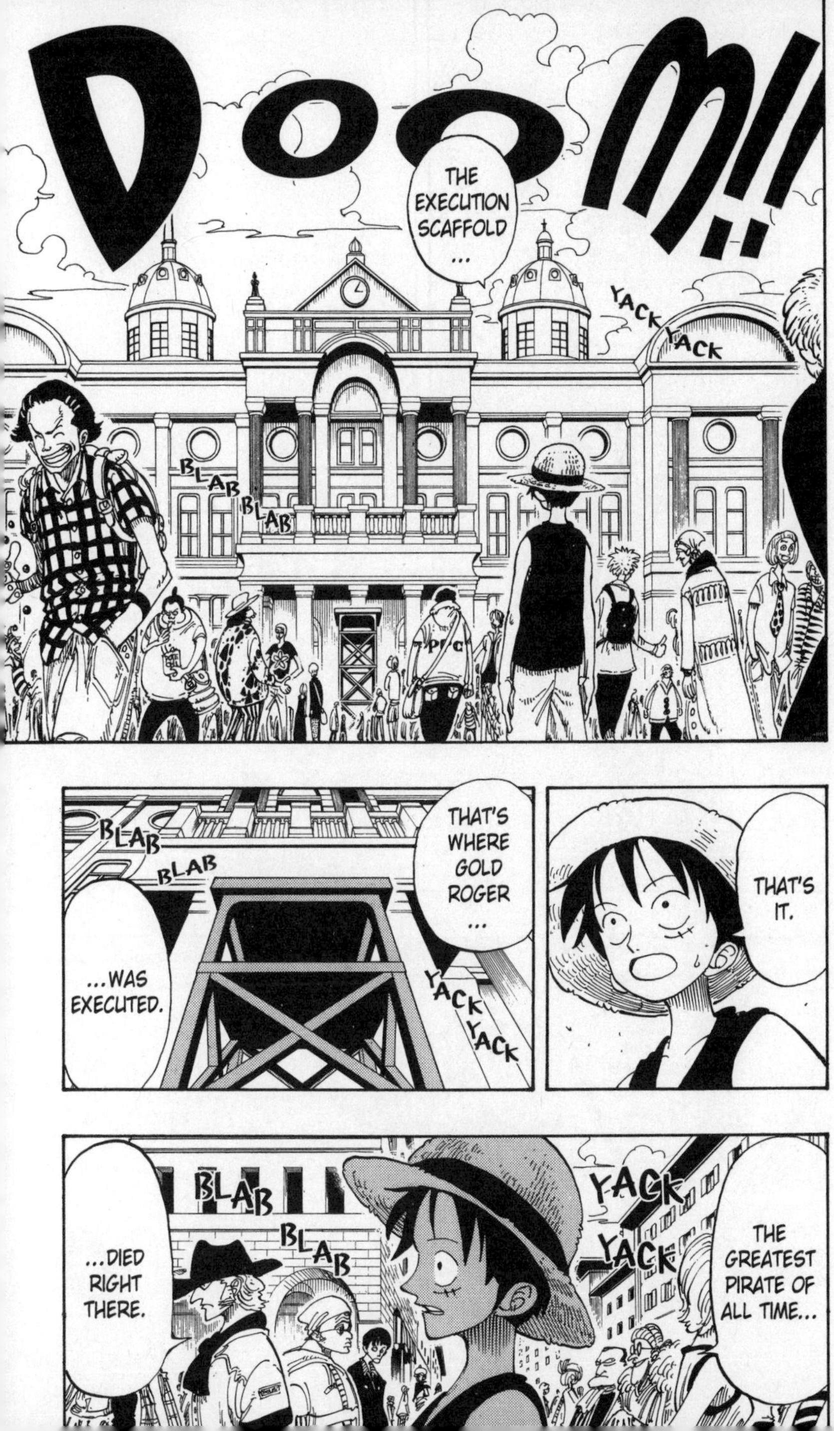
DOOM!!
THE EXECUTION SCAFFOLD ...
YACK YACK
BLAB BLAB
THAT'S IT.
THAT'S WHERE GOLD ROGER ...
YACK YACK
BLAB BLAB
...WAS EXECUTED.
THE GREATEST PIRATE OF ALL TIME...
YACK YACK
BLAB BLAB
...DIED RIGHT THERE.

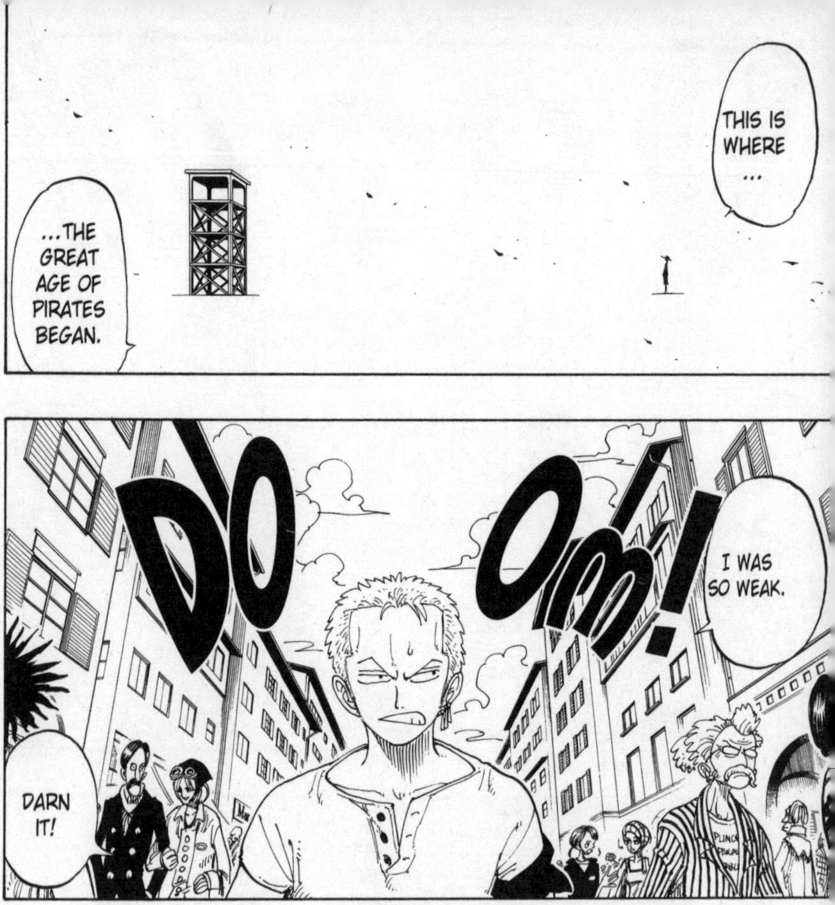
THIS IS WHERE ...
...THE GREAT AGE OF PIRATES BEGAN.
I WAS SO WEAK.
DOOM!
DARN IT!
STILL...
I-I'M SORRY.
IT'S UNCANNY HOW MUCH SHE LOOKS LIKE KUINA.
Like two peas in a pod.
AND SHE'S EVEN A SWORDSMAN!
YACK YACK
I GUESS FEMALE SWORDSMEN DO EXIST.
I DOUBT I'LL SEE HER AGAIN, THOUGH.
BLAB BLAB
STILL, I WAS WEAK.

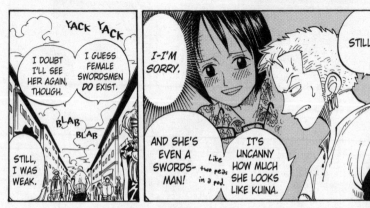

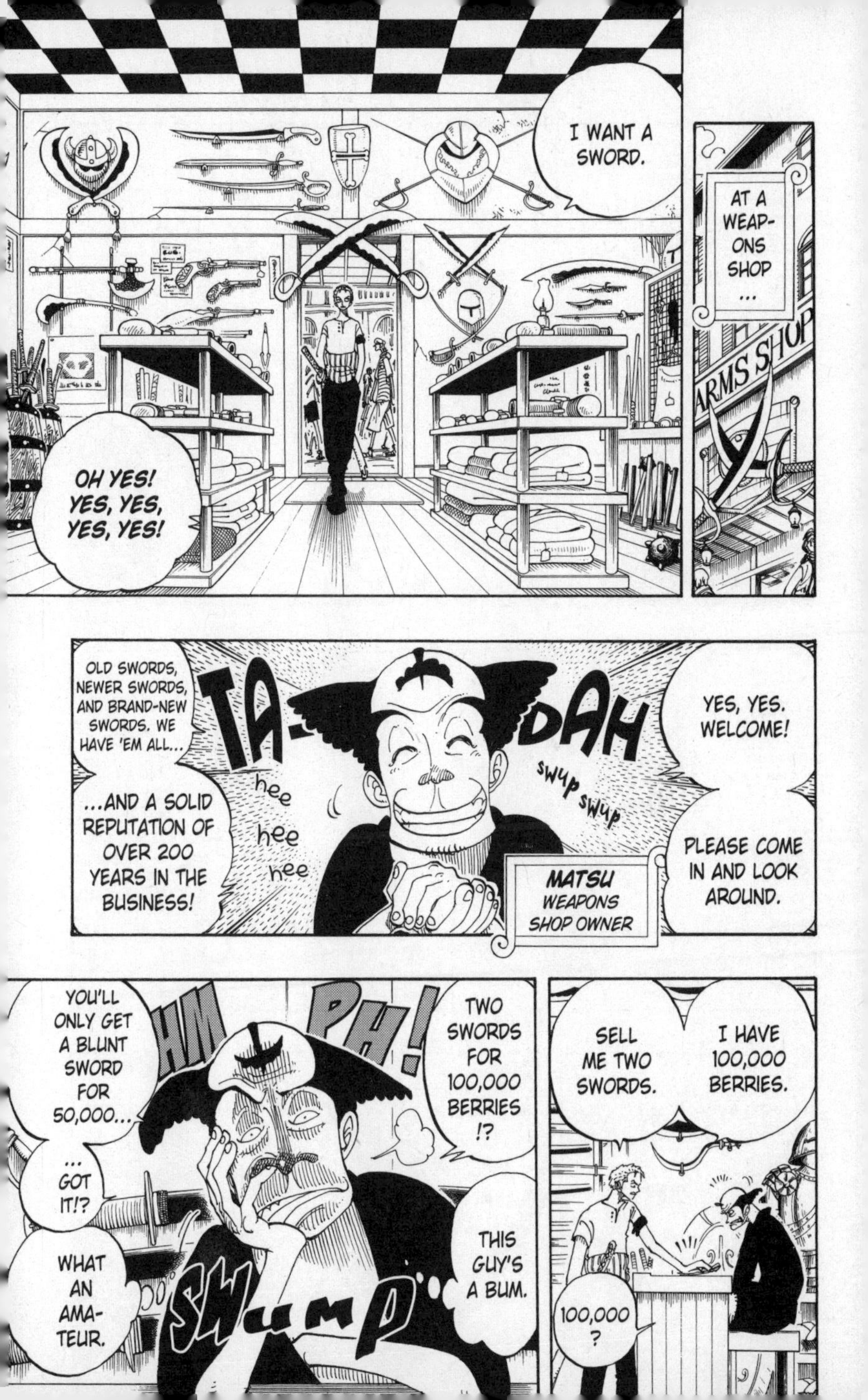
AT A WEAPONS SHOP ...
ARMS SHOP
I WANT A SWORD.
OH YES! YES, YES, YES, YES!
YES, YES. WELCOME!
PLEASE COME IN AND LOOK AROUND.
TA-DAH
swup swup
MATSU WEAPONS SHOP OWNER
OLD SWORDS, NEWER SWORDS, AND BRAND-NEW SWORDS. WE HAVE 'EM ALL...
hee hee hee
...AND A SOLID REPUTATION OF OVER 200 YEARS IN THE BUSINESS!
I HAVE 100,000 BERRIES.
SELL ME TWO SWORDS.
100,000 ?
HMPH!
TWO SWORDS FOR 100,000 BERRIES !?
YOU'LL ONLY GET A BLUNT SWORD FOR 50,000...
... GOT IT!?
THIS GUY'S A BUM.
WHAT AN AMATEUR.
SHUMP

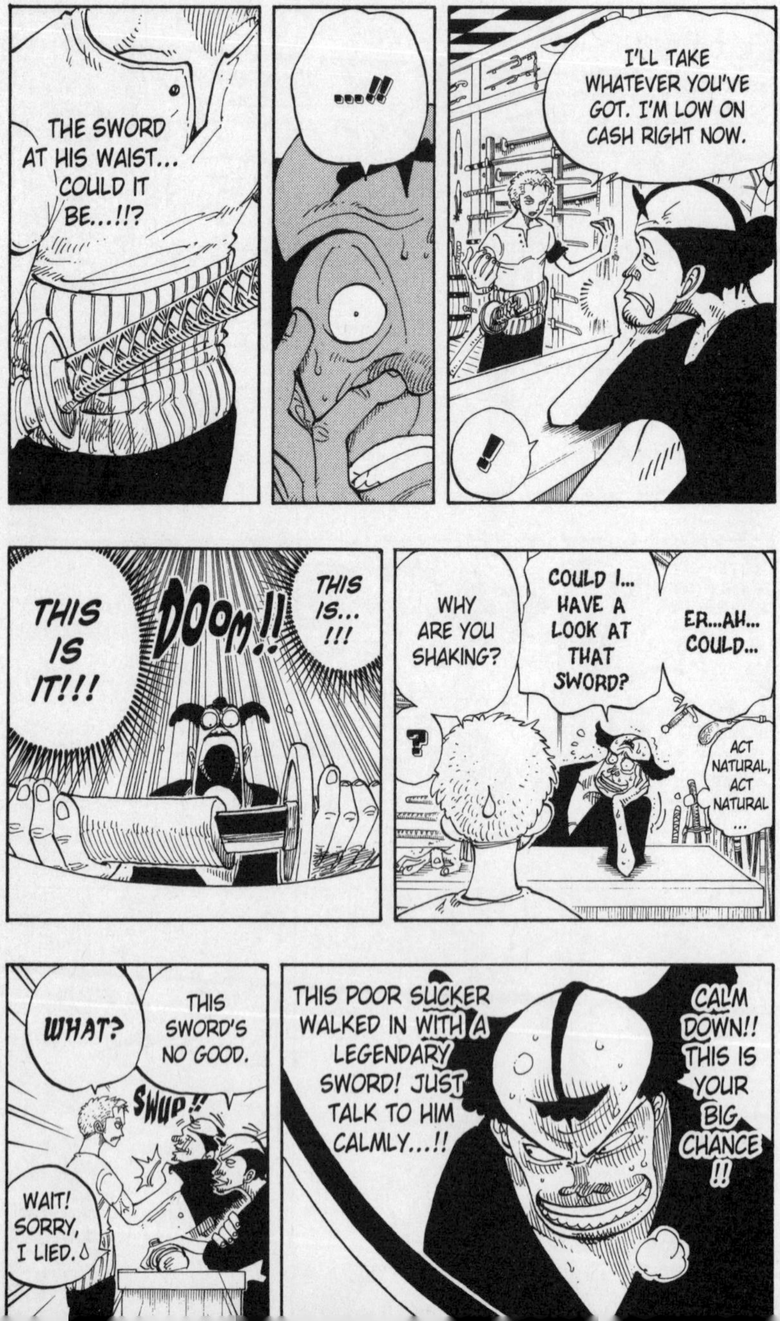
I'LL TAKE WHATEVER YOU'VE GOT. I'M LOW ON CASH RIGHT NOW.
!
...!!
THE SWORD AT HIS WAIST... COULD IT BE...!!?
ER...AH... COULD...
COULD I... HAVE A LOOK AT THAT SWORD?
WHY ARE YOU SHAKING?
ACT NATURAL, ACT NATURAL ...
?
THIS IS... !!!
DOOM!!
THIS IS IT!!!
CALM DOWN!! THIS IS YOUR BIG CHANCE!!
THIS POOR SUCKER WALKED IN WITH A LEGENDARY SWORD! JUST TALK TO HIM CALMLY...!!
THIS SWORD'S NO GOOD.
WHAT?
SWUP!!
WAIT! SORRY, I LIED.

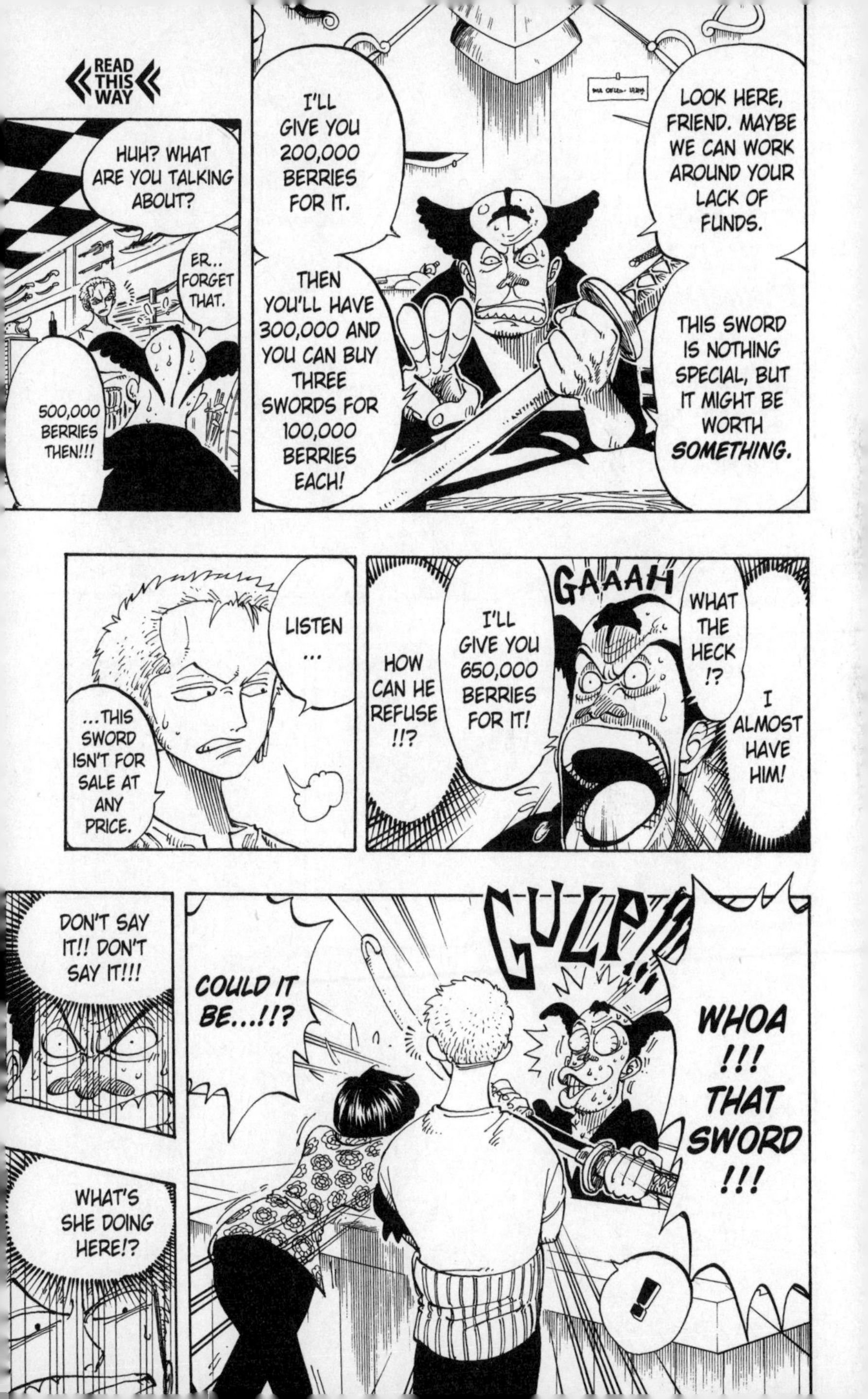
READ THIS WAY
LOOK HERE, FRIEND. MAYBE WE CAN WORK AROUND YOUR LACK OF FUNDS.
THIS SWORD IS NOTHING SPECIAL, BUT IT MIGHT BE WORTH SOMETHING.
I'LL GIVE YOU 200,000 BERRIES FOR IT.
THEN YOU'LL HAVE 300,000 AND YOU CAN BUY THREE SWORDS FOR 100,000 BERRIES EACH!
HUH? WHAT ARE YOU TALKING ABOUT?
ER... FORGET THAT.
500,000 BERRIES THEN!!!
GAAAH
WHAT THE HECK!?
I ALMOST HAVE HIM!
I'LL GIVE YOU 650,000 BERRIES FOR IT!
HOW CAN HE REFUSE!!?
LISTEN...
...THIS SWORD ISN'T FOR SALE AT ANY PRICE.
GULP!!
WHOA!!! THAT SWORD!!!
COULD IT BE...!!?
!
DON'T SAY IT!! DON'T SAY IT!!!
WHAT'S SHE DOING HERE!?

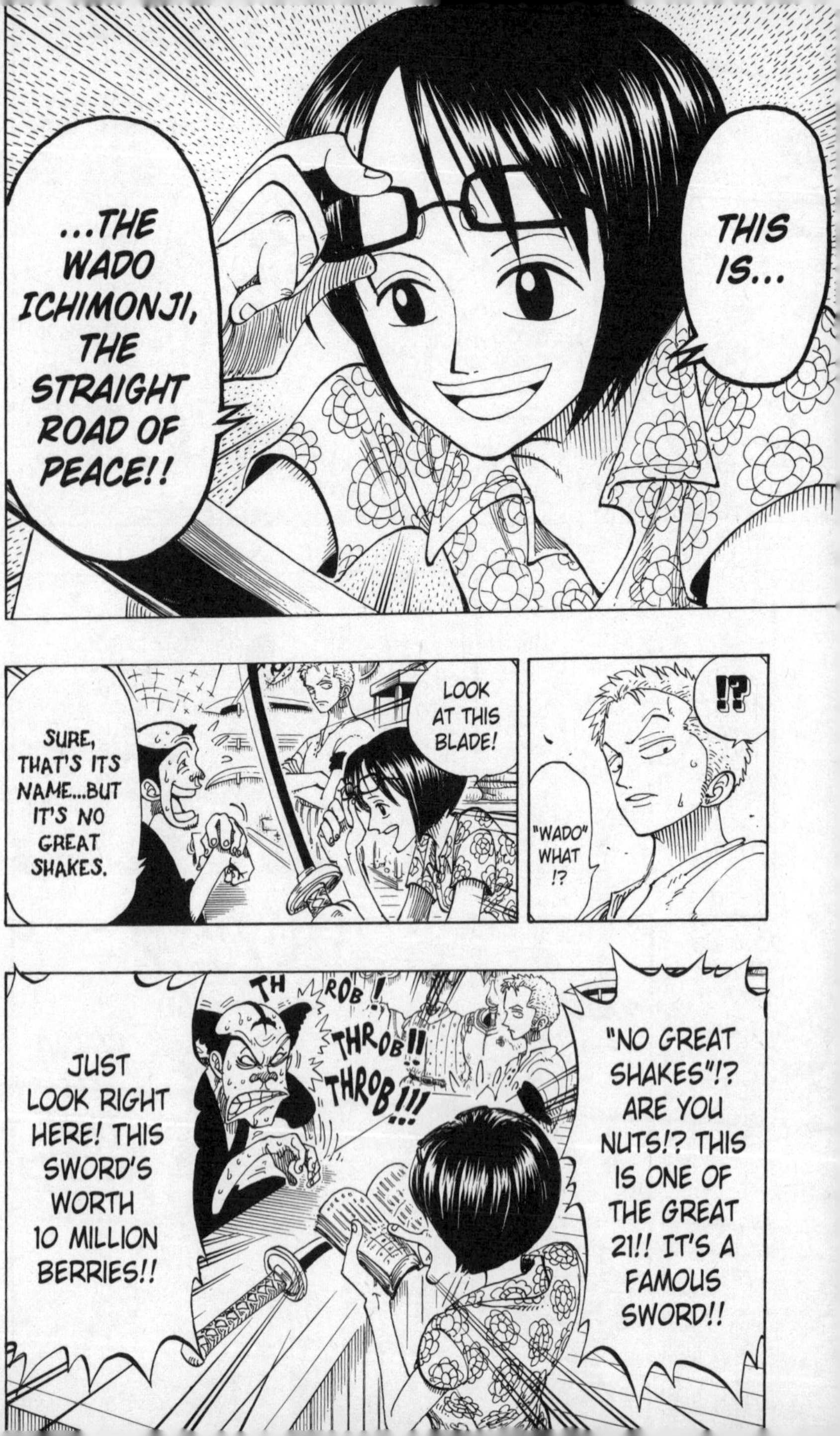
THIS IS...
...THE WADO ICHIMONJI, THE STRAIGHT ROAD OF PEACE!!
!?
"WADO" WHAT !?
LOOK AT THIS BLADE!
SURE, THAT'S ITS NAME...BUT IT'S NO GREAT SHAKES.
"NO GREAT SHAKES"!? ARE YOU NUTS!? THIS IS ONE OF THE GREAT 21!! IT'S A FAMOUS SWORD!!
THROB! THROB!! THROB!!!
JUST LOOK RIGHT HERE! THIS SWORD'S WORTH 10 MILLION BERRIES!!

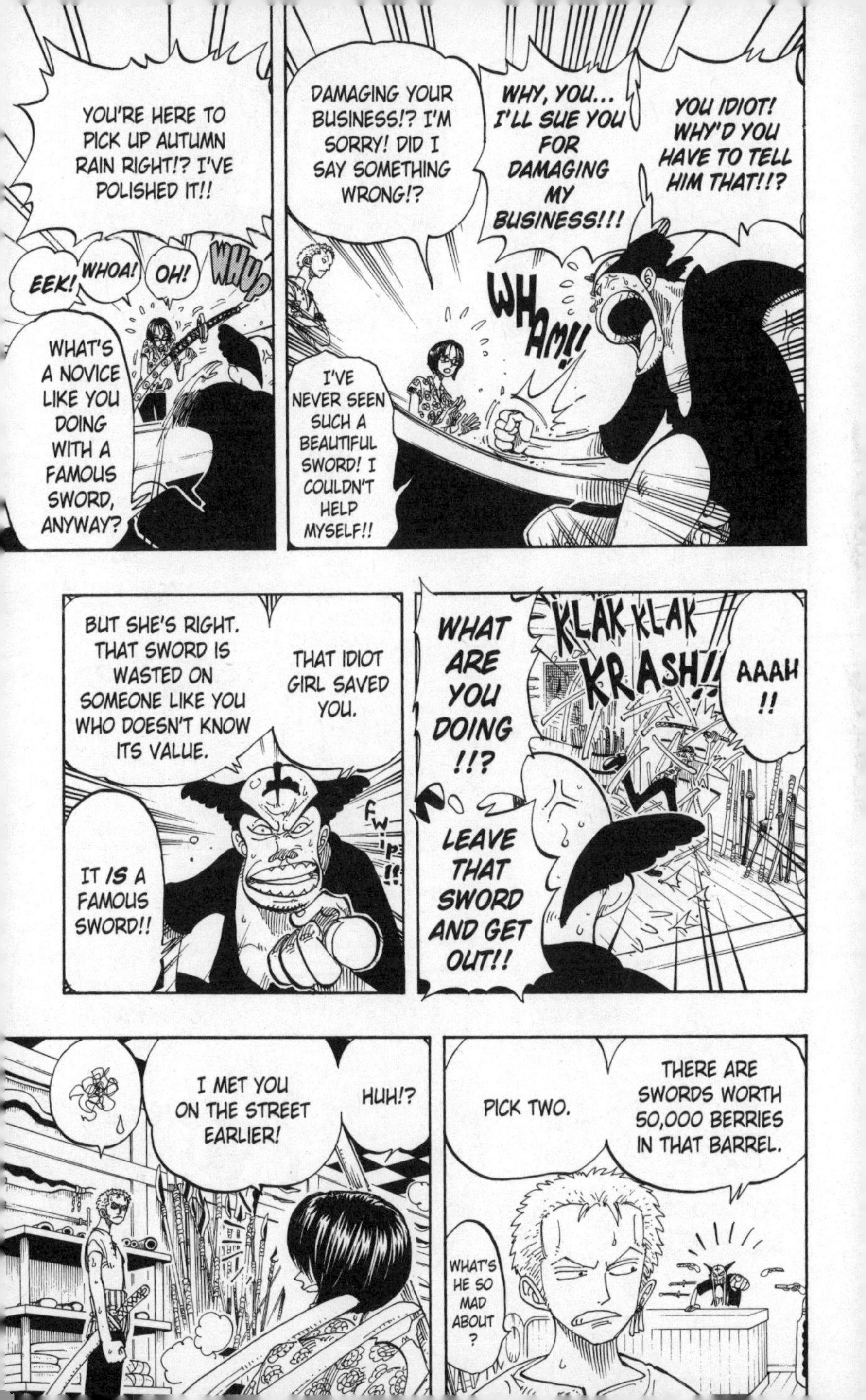
YOU IDIOT! WHY'D YOU HAVE TO TELL HIM THAT!!?
WHY, YOU... I'LL SUE YOU FOR DAMAGING MY BUSINESS!!!
DAMAGING YOUR BUSINESS!? I'M SORRY! DID I SAY SOMETHING WRONG!?
WHAM!!
I'VE NEVER SEEN SUCH A BEAUTIFUL SWORD! I COULDN'T HELP MYSELF!!
YOU'RE HERE TO PICK UP AUTUMN RAIN RIGHT!? I'VE POLISHED IT!!
WHUP
OH!
WHOA!
EEK!
WHAT'S A NOVICE LIKE YOU DOING WITH A FAMOUS SWORD, ANYWAY?
AAAH!!
KLAK KLAK
KRASH!!
WHAT ARE YOU DOING!!?
LEAVE THAT SWORD AND GET OUT!!
THAT IDIOT GIRL SAVED YOU.
BUT SHE'S RIGHT. THAT SWORD IS WASTED ON SOMEONE LIKE YOU WHO DOESN'T KNOW ITS VALUE.
FWIP!!
IT *IS* A FAMOUS SWORD!!
THERE ARE SWORDS WORTH 50,000 BERRIES IN THAT BARREL.
PICK TWO.
WHAT'S HE SO MAD ABOUT?
HUH!?
I MET YOU ON THE STREET EARLIER!

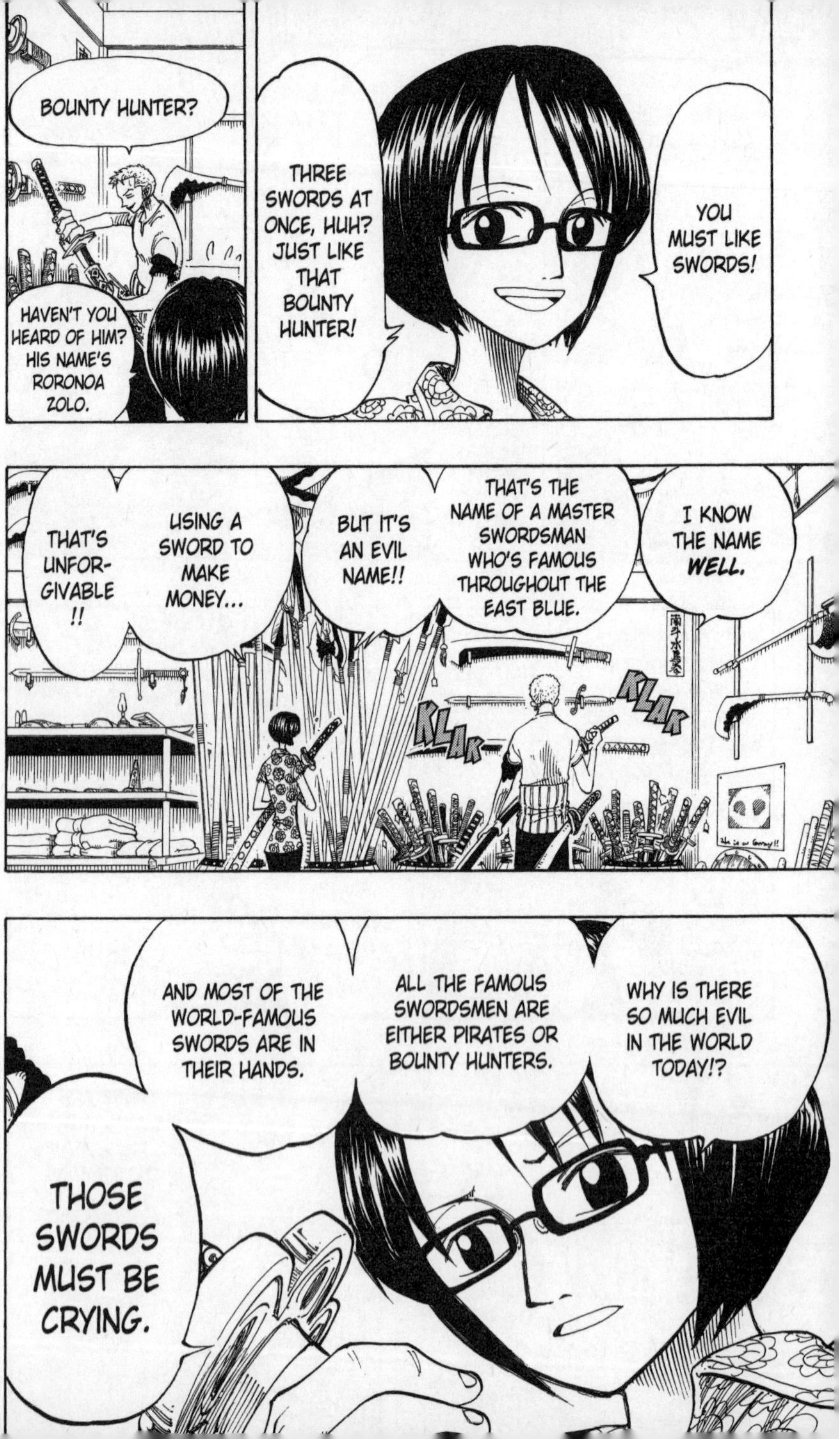
YOU MUST LIKE SWORDS!
THREE SWORDS AT ONCE, HUH? JUST LIKE THAT BOUNTY HUNTER!
BOUNTY HUNTER?
HAVEN'T YOU HEARD OF HIM? HIS NAME'S RORONOA ZOLO.
I KNOW THE NAME *WELL.*
THAT'S THE NAME OF A MASTER SWORDSMAN WHO'S FAMOUS THROUGHOUT THE EAST BLUE.
BUT IT'S AN EVIL NAME!!
USING A SWORD TO MAKE MONEY...
THAT'S UNFORGIVABLE!!
KLAK
KLAK
WHY IS THERE SO MUCH EVIL IN THE WORLD TODAY!?
ALL THE FAMOUS SWORDSMEN ARE EITHER PIRATES OR BOUNTY HUNTERS.
AND MOST OF THE WORLD-FAMOUS SWORDS ARE IN THEIR HANDS.
THOSE SWORDS MUST BE CRYING.

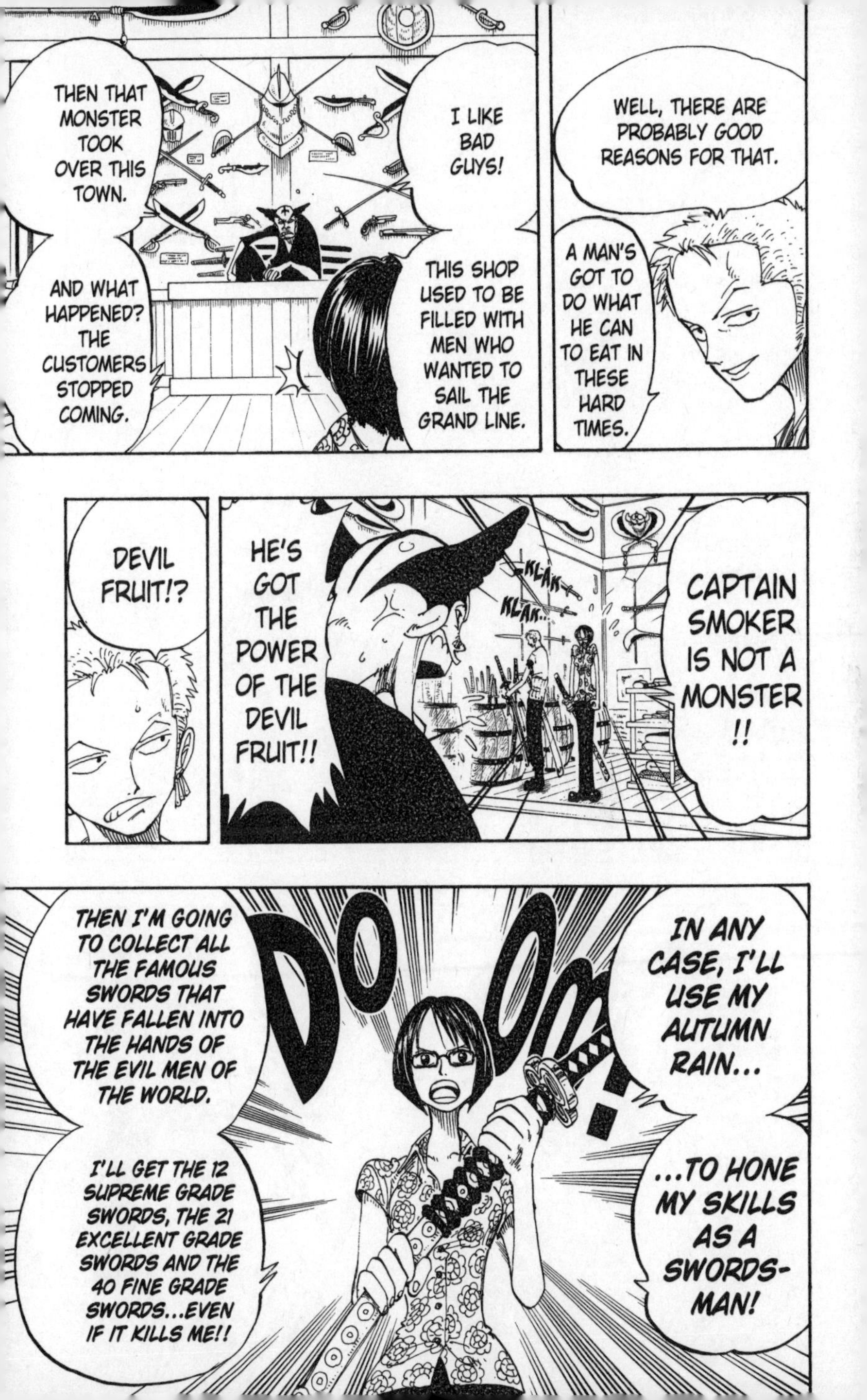
WELL, THERE ARE PROBABLY GOOD REASONS FOR THAT.
A MAN'S GOT TO DO WHAT HE CAN TO EAT IN THESE HARD TIMES.
I LIKE BAD GUYS!
THIS SHOP USED TO BE FILLED WITH MEN WHO WANTED TO SAIL THE GRAND LINE.
THEN THAT MONSTER TOOK OVER THIS TOWN.
AND WHAT HAPPENED? THE CUSTOMERS STOPPED COMING.
CAPTAIN SMOKER IS NOT A MONSTER!!
KLAK
KLAK...
HE'S GOT THE POWER OF THE DEVIL FRUIT!!
DEVIL FRUIT!?
IN ANY CASE, I'LL USE MY AUTUMN RAIN...
...TO HONE MY SKILLS AS A SWORDS-MAN!
DOOM!
THEN I'M GOING TO COLLECT ALL THE FAMOUS SWORDS THAT HAVE FALLEN INTO THE HANDS OF THE EVIL MEN OF THE WORLD.
I'LL GET THE 12 SUPREME GRADE SWORDS, THE 21 EXCELLENT GRADE SWORDS AND THE 40 FINE GRADE SWORDS...EVEN IF IT KILLS ME!!

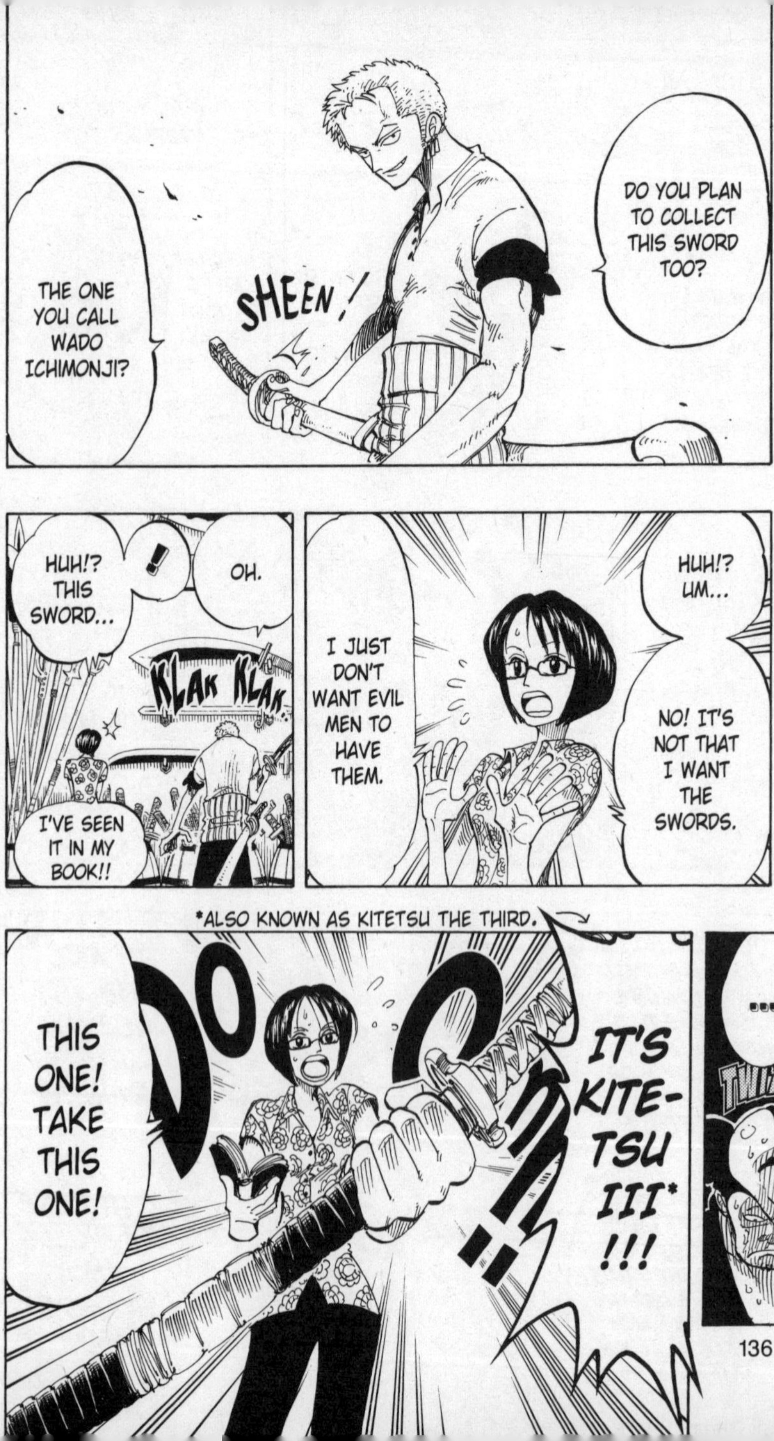
DO YOU PLAN TO COLLECT THIS SWORD TOO?
SHEEN
THE ONE YOU CALL WADO ICHIMONJI?
HUH!? UM...
NO! IT'S NOT THAT I WANT THE SWORDS.
I JUST DON'T WANT EVIL MEN TO HAVE THEM.
OH.
!
HUH!? THIS SWORD...
KLAK KLAK
I'VE SEEN IT IN MY BOOK!!
*ALSO KNOWN AS KITETSU THE THIRD.
...!
TWITCH...
IT'S KITE-TSU III*!!!
DO
THIS ONE! TAKE THIS ONE!

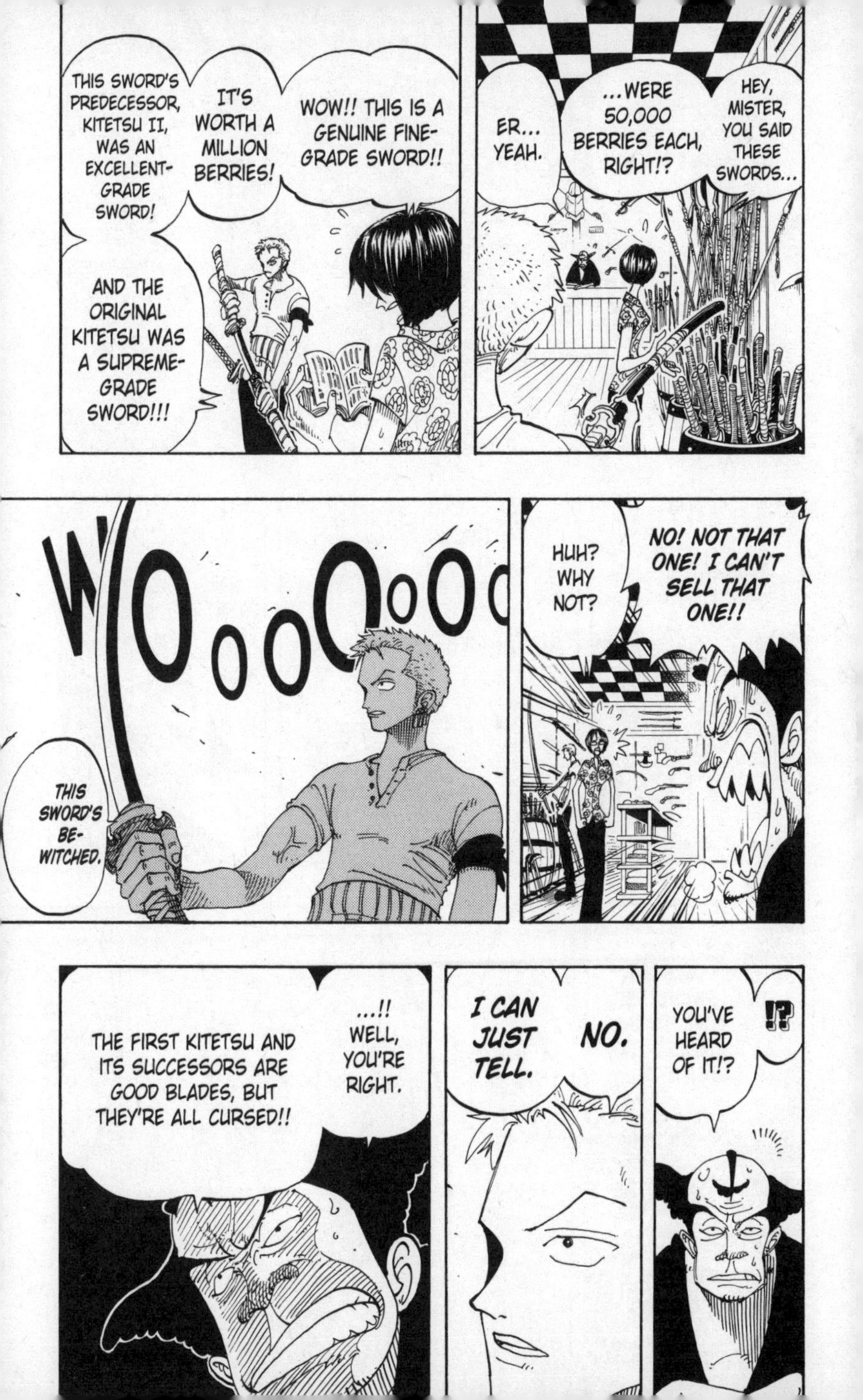
HEY, MISTER, YOU SAID THESE SWORDS...
...WERE 50,000 BERRIES EACH, RIGHT!?
ER... YEAH.
WOW!! THIS IS A GENUINE FINE-GRADE SWORD!!
IT'S WORTH A MILLION BERRIES!
THIS SWORD'S PREDECESSOR, KITETSU II, WAS AN EXCELLENT-GRADE SWORD!
AND THE ORIGINAL KITETSU WAS A SUPREME-GRADE SWORD!!!
NO! NOT THAT ONE! I CAN'T SELL THAT ONE!!
HUH? WHY NOT?
WOOOOOOO
THIS SWORD'S BE-WITCHED.
!?
YOU'VE HEARD OF IT!?
NO.
I CAN JUST TELL.
...!! WELL, YOU'RE RIGHT.
THE FIRST KITETSU AND ITS SUCCESSORS ARE GOOD BLADES, BUT THEY'RE ALL CURSED!!

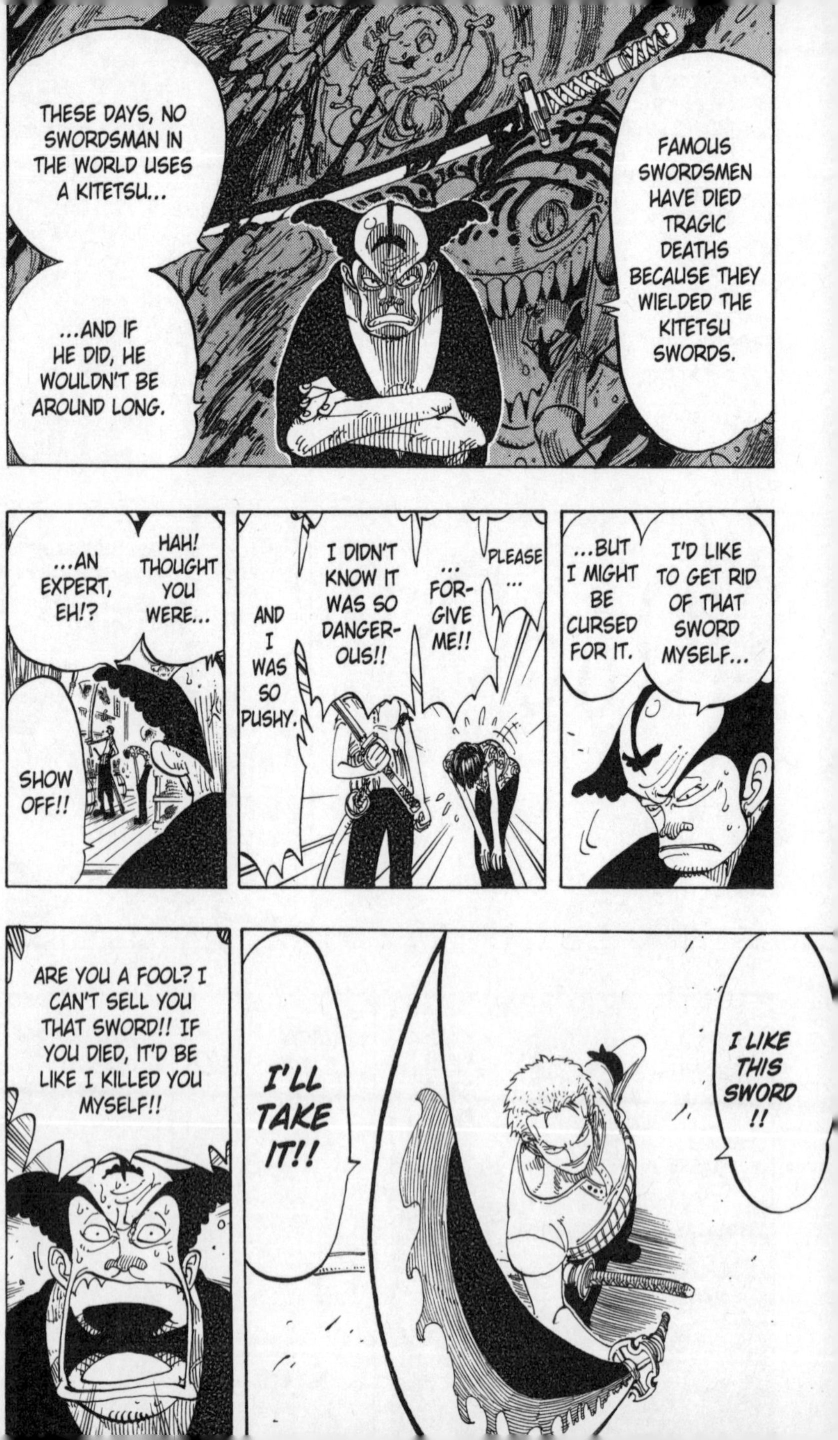
FAMOUS SWORDSMEN HAVE DIED TRAGIC DEATHS BECAUSE THEY WIELDED THE KITETSU SWORDS.
THESE DAYS, NO SWORDSMAN IN THE WORLD USES A KITETSU...
...AND IF HE DID, HE WOULDN'T BE AROUND LONG.
I'D LIKE TO GET RID OF THAT SWORD MYSELF...
...BUT I MIGHT BE CURSED FOR IT.
PLEASE...
...FOR-GIVE ME!!
I DIDN'T KNOW IT WAS SO DANGER-OUS!!
AND I WAS SO PUSHY.
HAH! THOUGHT YOU WERE...
...AN EXPERT, EH!?
SHOW OFF!!
I LIKE THIS SWORD!!
I'LL TAKE IT!!
ARE YOU A FOOL? I CAN'T SELL YOU THAT SWORD!! IF YOU DIED, IT'D BE LIKE I KILLED YOU MYSELF!!

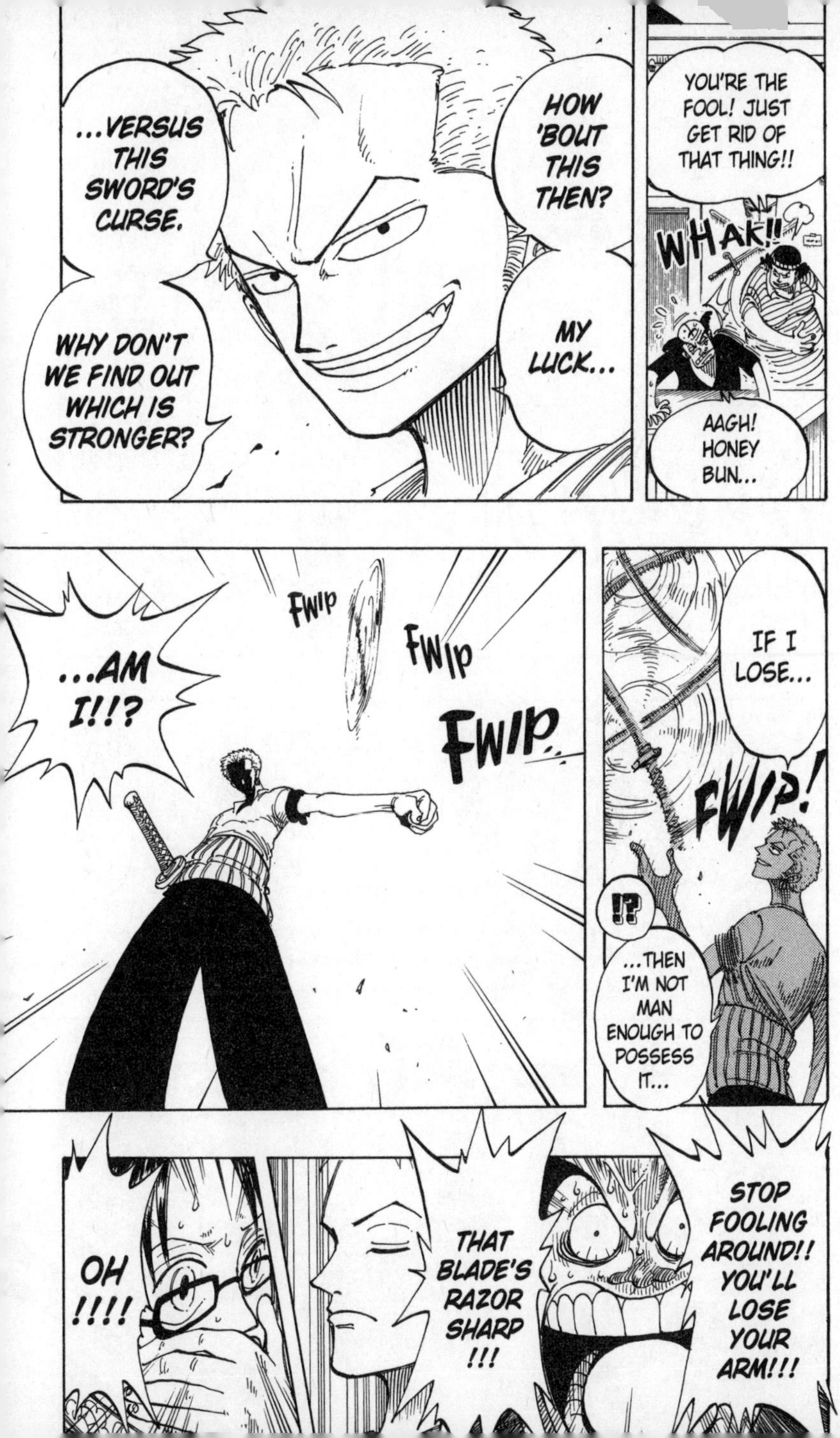
YOU'RE THE FOOL! JUST GET RID OF THAT THING!!
WHAK!!
AAGH! HONEY BUN...
HOW 'BOUT THIS THEN?
MY LUCK...
...VERSUS THIS SWORD'S CURSE.
WHY DON'T WE FIND OUT WHICH IS STRONGER?
IF I LOSE...
FWIP!
!?
...THEN I'M NOT MAN ENOUGH TO POSSESS IT...
FWIP
FWIP
FWIP
...AM I!!?
STOP FOOLING AROUND!! YOU'LL LOSE YOUR ARM!!!
THAT BLADE'S RAZOR SHARP!!!
OH!!!!

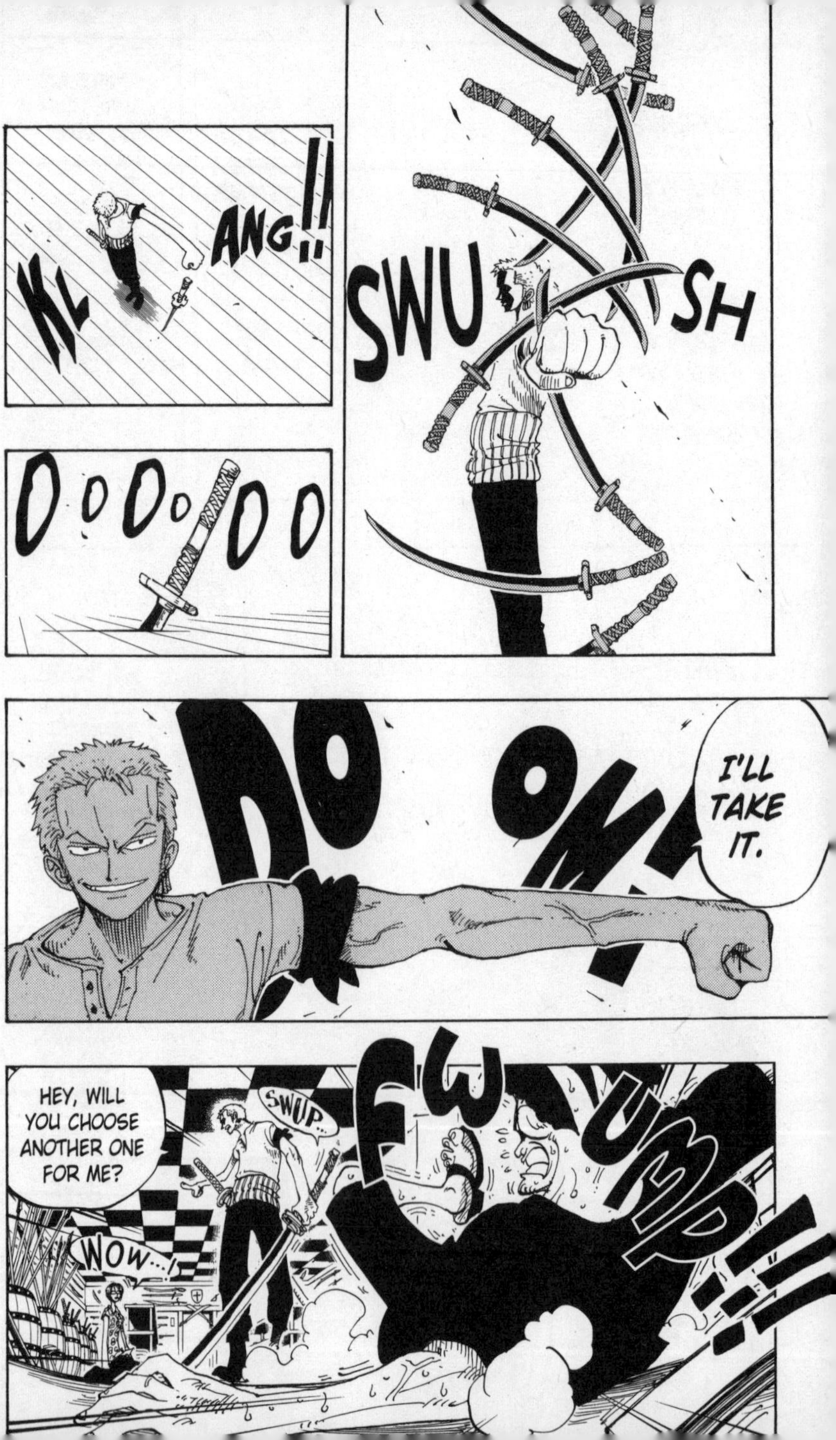
SWUSH
KLANG!!
DOOM
I'LL TAKE IT.
FWUMP!!!
SWUP...
HEY, WILL YOU CHOOSE ANOTHER ONE FOR ME?
WOW...!

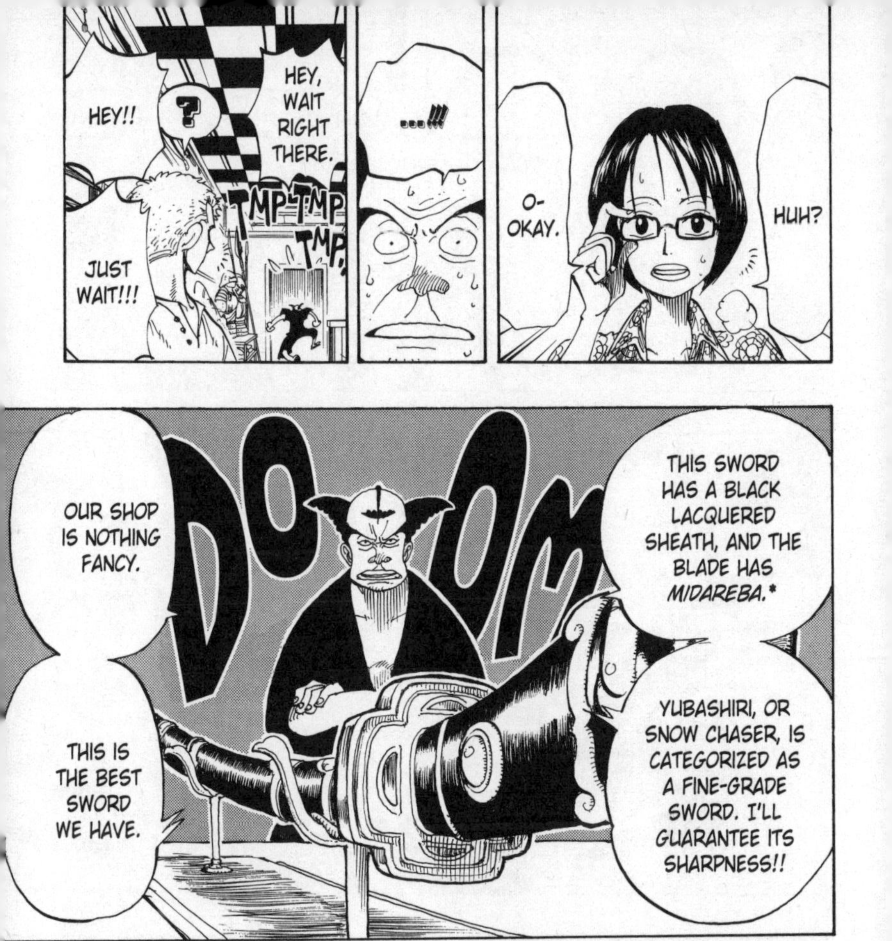
HUH?
O-OKAY.
...!!!
HEY, WAIT RIGHT THERE.
HEY!!
?
TMP TMP TMP
JUST WAIT!!!
THIS SWORD HAS A BLACK LACQUERED SHEATH, AND THE BLADE HAS *MIDAREBA.**
DOOM
OUR SHOP IS NOTHING FANCY.
YUBASHIRI, OR SNOW CHASER, IS CATEGORIZED AS A FINE-GRADE SWORD. I'LL GUARANTEE ITS SHARPNESS!!
THIS IS THE BEST SWORD WE HAVE.

*A SWORD TERM FOR AN IRREGULAR PATTERN.

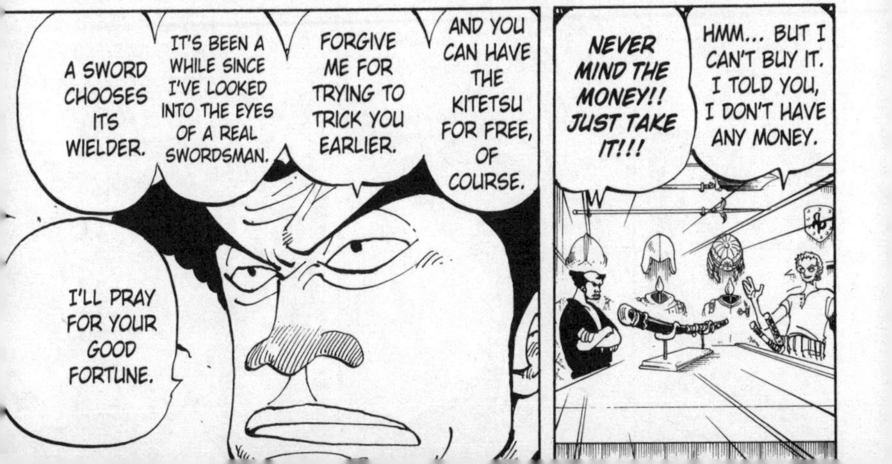
HMM... BUT I CAN'T BUY IT. I TOLD YOU, I DON'T HAVE ANY MONEY.
NEVER MIND THE MONEY!! JUST TAKE IT!!!
AND YOU CAN HAVE THE KITETSU FOR FREE, OF COURSE.
FORGIVE ME FOR TRYING TO TRICK YOU EARLIER.
IT'S BEEN A WHILE SINCE I'VE LOOKED INTO THE EYES OF A REAL SWORDSMAN.
A SWORD CHOOSES ITS WIELDER.
I'LL PRAY FOR YOUR GOOD FORTUNE.

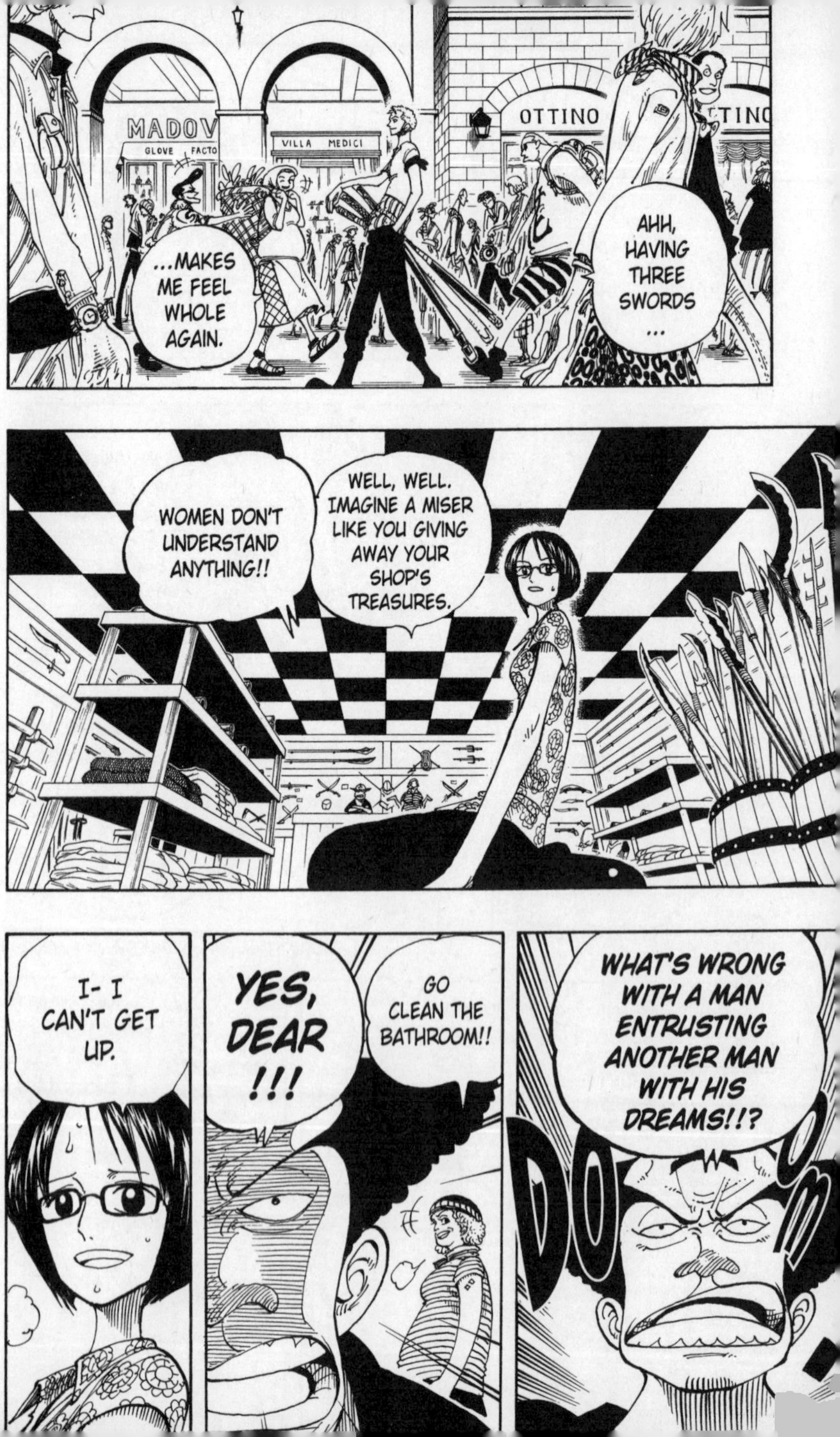
OTTINO
AHH, HAVING THREE SWORDS ...
VILLA MEDICI
MADOV
GLOVE FACTO
...MAKES ME FEEL WHOLE AGAIN.
WELL, WELL. IMAGINE A MISER LIKE YOU GIVING AWAY YOUR SHOP'S TREASURES.
WOMEN DON'T UNDERSTAND ANYTHING!!
WHAT'S WRONG WITH A MAN ENTRUSTING ANOTHER MAN WITH HIS DREAMS!!?
GO CLEAN THE BATHROOM!!
YES, DEAR!!!
I- I CAN'T GET UP.

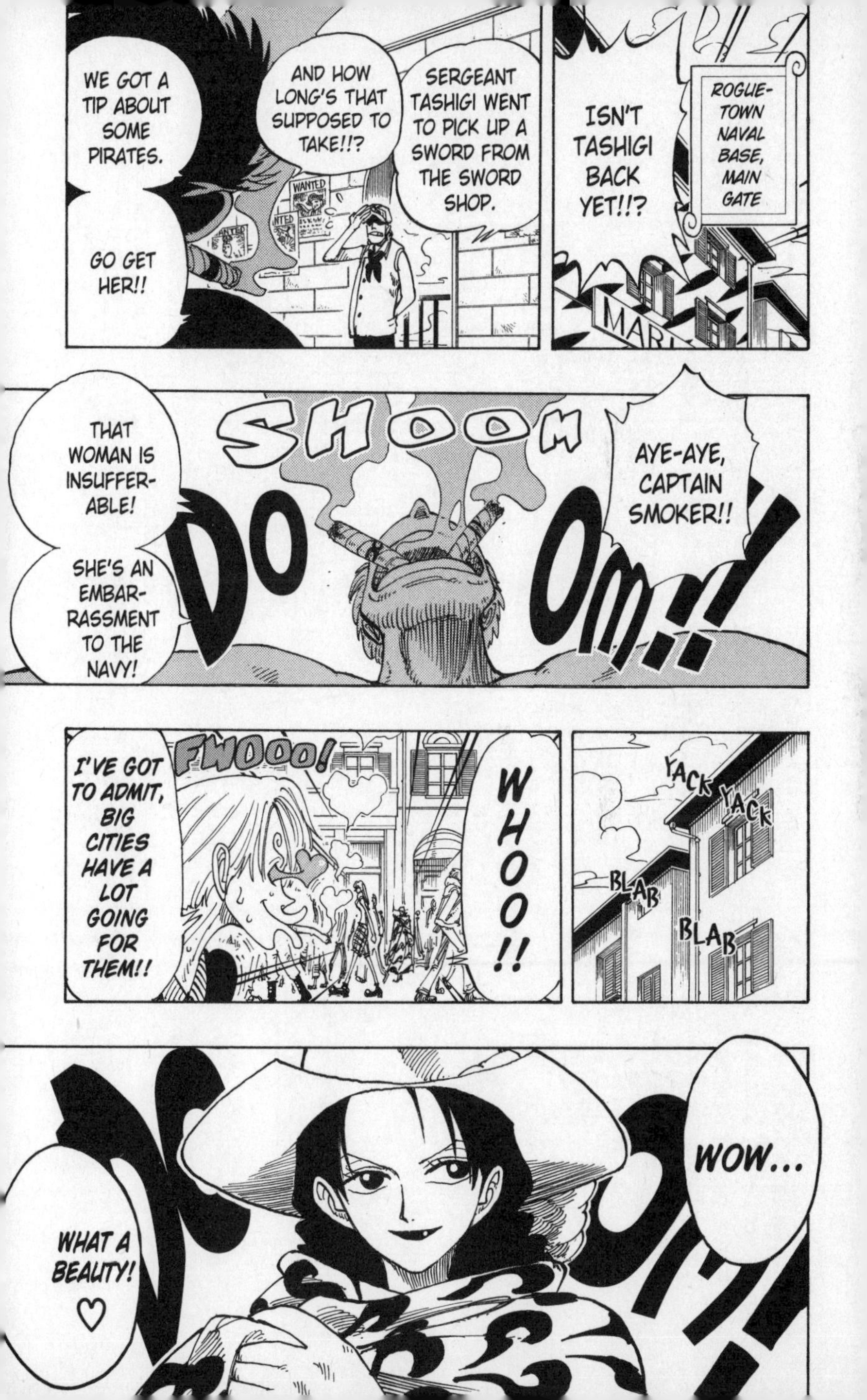
ROGUE-TOWN NAVAL BASE, MAIN GATE
ISN'T TASHIGI BACK YET!!?
SERGEANT TASHIGI WENT TO PICK UP A SWORD FROM THE SWORD SHOP.
AND HOW LONG'S THAT SUPPOSED TO TAKE!!?
WE GOT A TIP ABOUT SOME PIRATES.
GO GET HER!!
WANTED
AYE-AYE, CAPTAIN SMOKER!!
SHOOM
DOOM!!
THAT WOMAN IS INSUFFER-ABLE!
SHE'S AN EMBAR-RASSMENT TO THE NAVY!
YACK YACK
BLAB
BLAB
WHOOO!!
FWOOO!
I'VE GOT TO ADMIT, BIG CITIES HAVE A LOT GOING FOR THEM!!
WOW...
WHAT A BEAUTY! ♡

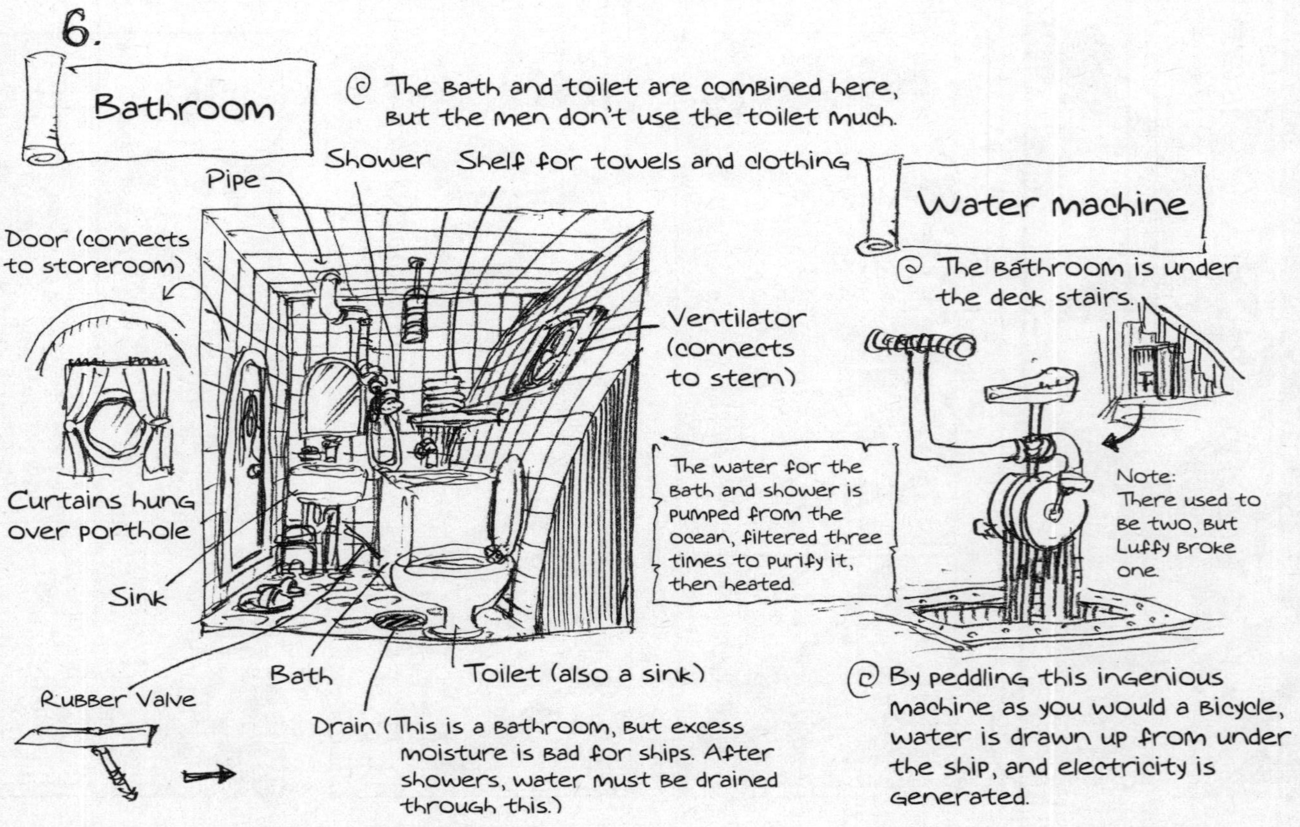
6.
Bathroom
The bath and toilet are combined here, but the men don't use the toilet much.
Shower
Shelf for towels and clothing
Pipe
Door (connects to storeroom)
Ventilator (connects to stern)
Curtains hung over porthole
Sink
The water for the bath and shower is pumped from the ocean, filtered three times to purify it, then heated.
Bath
Toilet (also a sink)
Rubber Valve
Drain (This is a bathroom, but excess moisture is bad for ships. After showers, water must be drained through this.)
Water machine
The bathroom is under the deck stairs.
Note: There used to be two, but Luffy broke one.
By peddling this ingenious machine as you would a bicycle, water is drawn up from under the ship, and electricity is generated.

Chapter 98: DARK CLOUDS

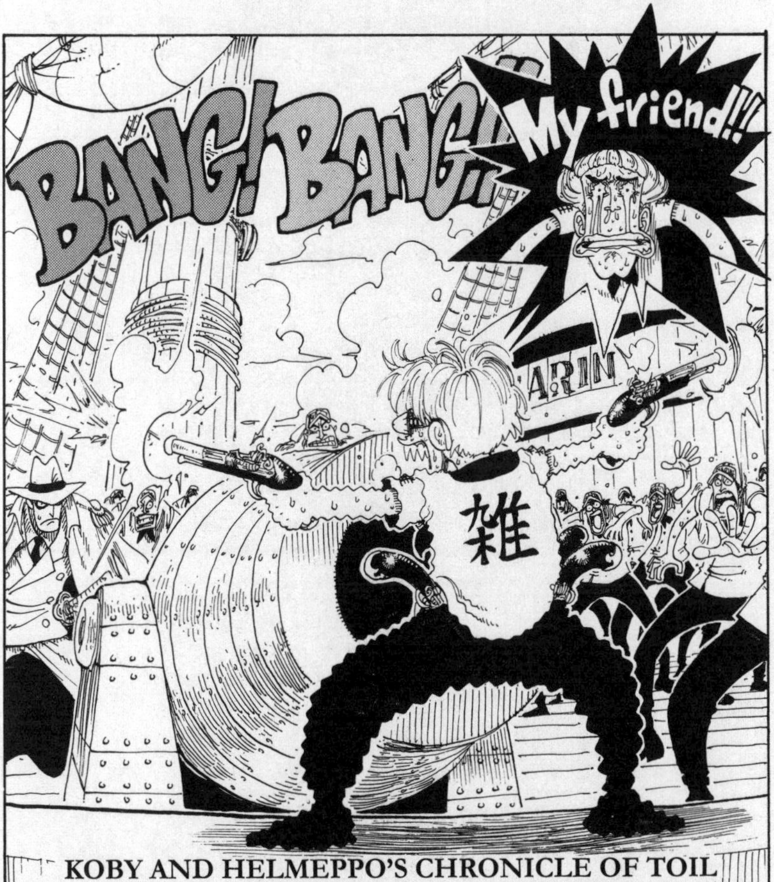
My friend!!!
BANG! BANG!!
雑

KOBY AND HELMEPPO'S CHRONICLE OF TOIL
VOL. 14: "A HINDRANCE TO THE ARTILLERY ATTACK"

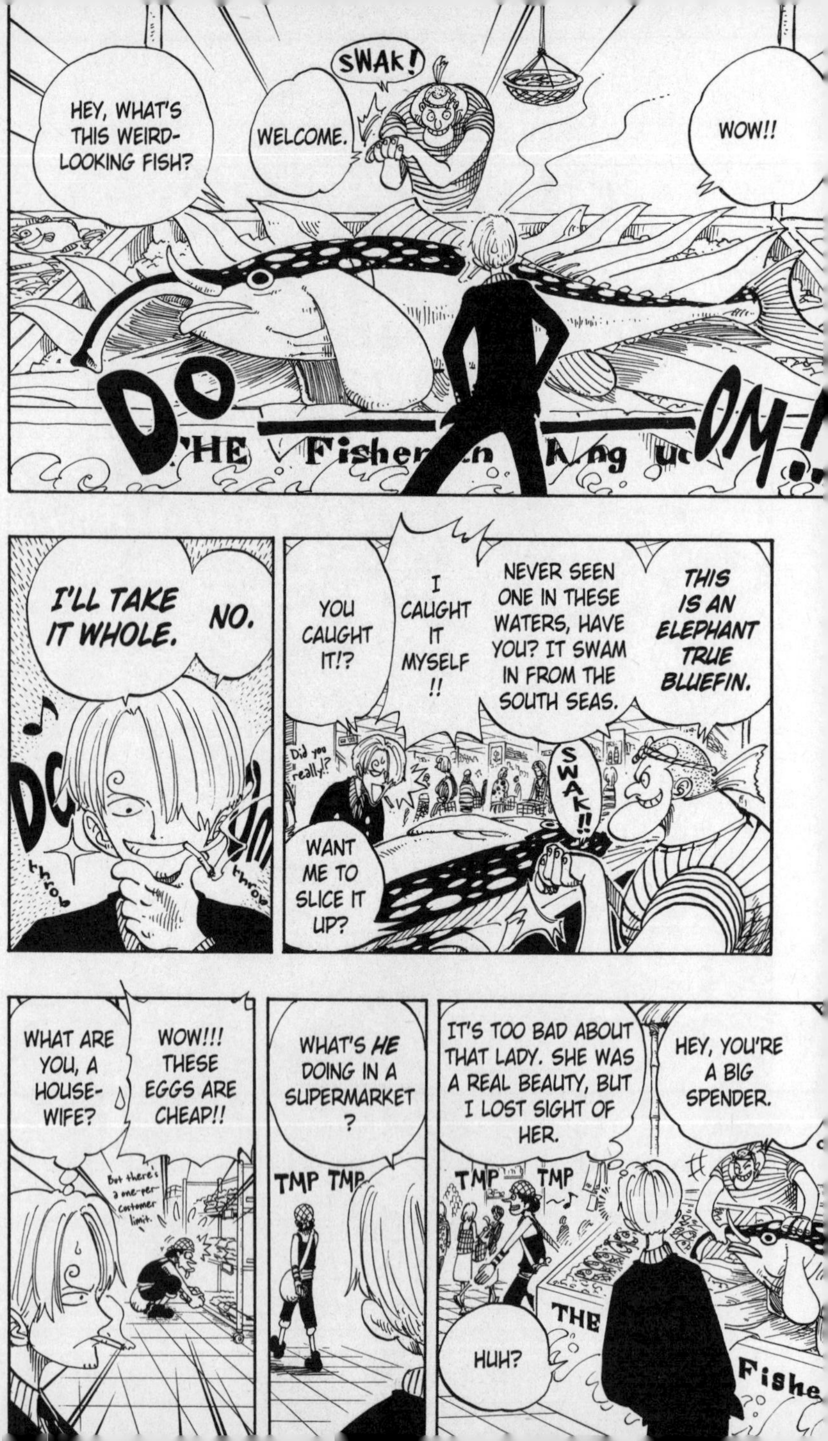
WOW!!
SWAK!
WELCOME.
HEY, WHAT'S THIS WEIRD-LOOKING FISH?
DO—OM!!
THIS IS AN ELEPHANT TRUE BLUEFIN.
NEVER SEEN ONE IN THESE WATERS, HAVE YOU? IT SWAM IN FROM THE SOUTH SEAS.
I CAUGHT IT MYSELF!!
YOU CAUGHT IT!?
Did you really!?
SWAK!!
WANT ME TO SLICE IT UP?
NO.
I'LL TAKE IT WHOLE.
throb throb
HEY, YOU'RE A BIG SPENDER.
IT'S TOO BAD ABOUT THAT LADY. SHE WAS A REAL BEAUTY, BUT I LOST SIGHT OF HER.
TMP TMP
HUH?
WHAT'S HE DOING IN A SUPERMARKET?
TMP TMP
WOW!!! THESE EGGS ARE CHEAP!!
WHAT ARE YOU, A HOUSE-WIFE?
But there's a one-per-customer limit.

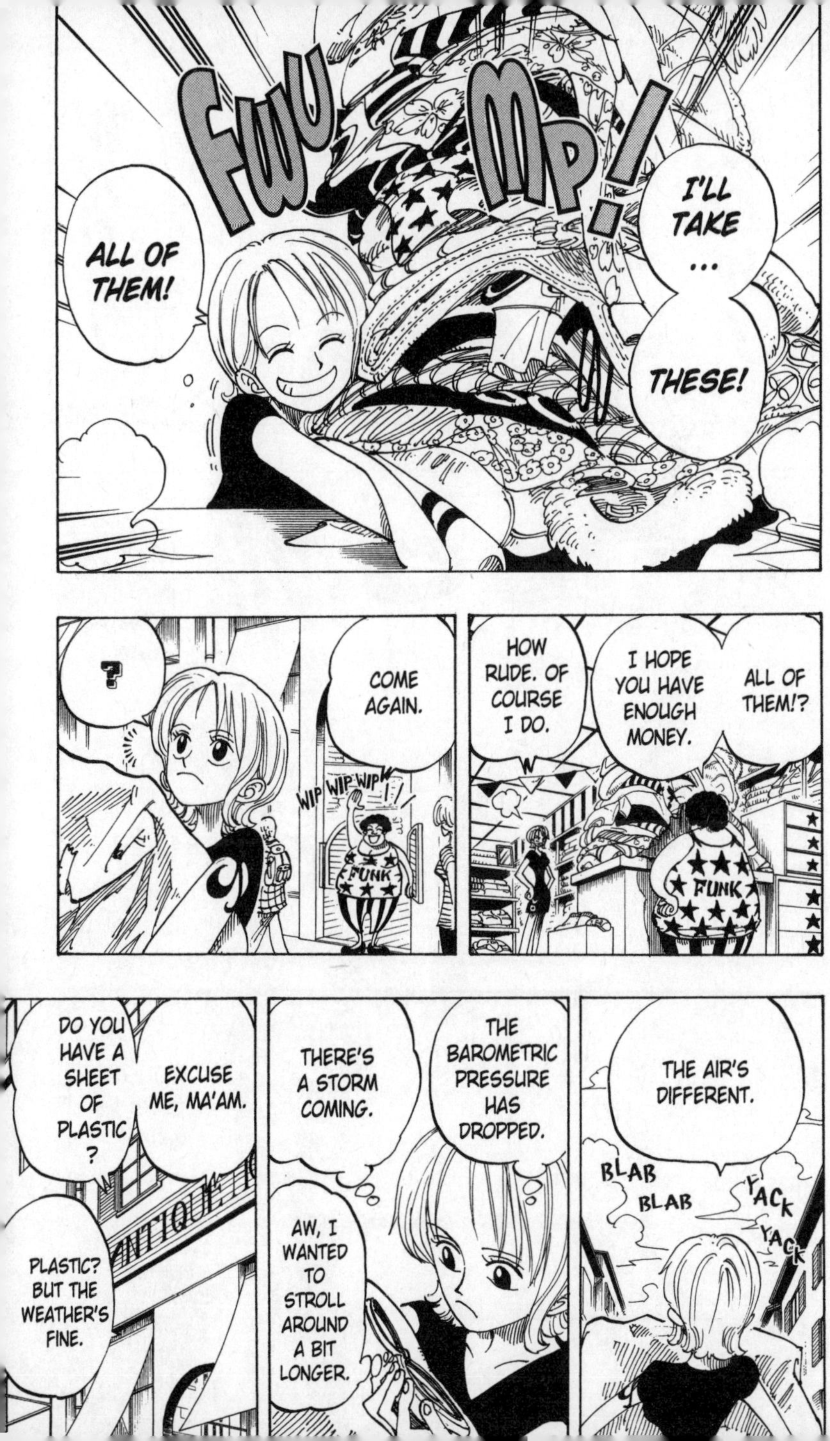
I'LL TAKE ... THESE!
FWUUMP!
ALL OF THEM!
ALL OF THEM!?
I HOPE YOU HAVE ENOUGH MONEY.
HOW RUDE. OF COURSE I DO.
COME AGAIN.
WIP WIP WIP
FUNK
?
FUNK
THE AIR'S DIFFERENT.
YACK YACK
BLAB BLAB
THE BAROMETRIC PRESSURE HAS DROPPED.
THERE'S A STORM COMING.
AW, I WANTED TO STROLL AROUND A BIT LONGER.
EXCUSE ME, MA'AM.
DO YOU HAVE A SHEET OF PLASTIC?
PLASTIC? BUT THE WEATHER'S FINE.

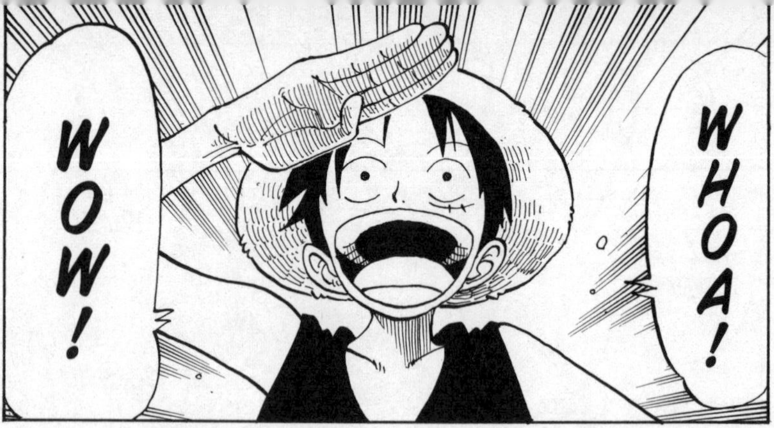
WHOA!
WOW!

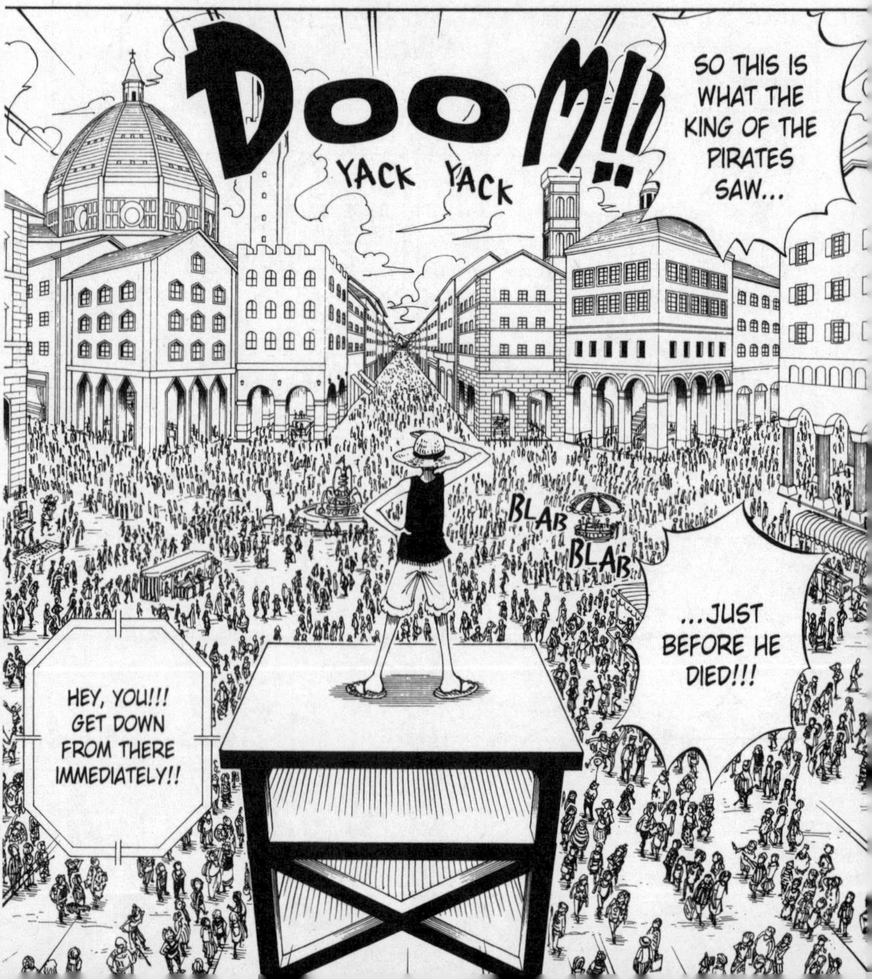
SO THIS IS WHAT THE KING OF THE PIRATES SAW...
DOOM!!
YACK YACK
BLAB BLAB
...JUST BEFORE HE DIED!!!
HEY, YOU!!! GET DOWN FROM THERE IMMEDIATELY!!

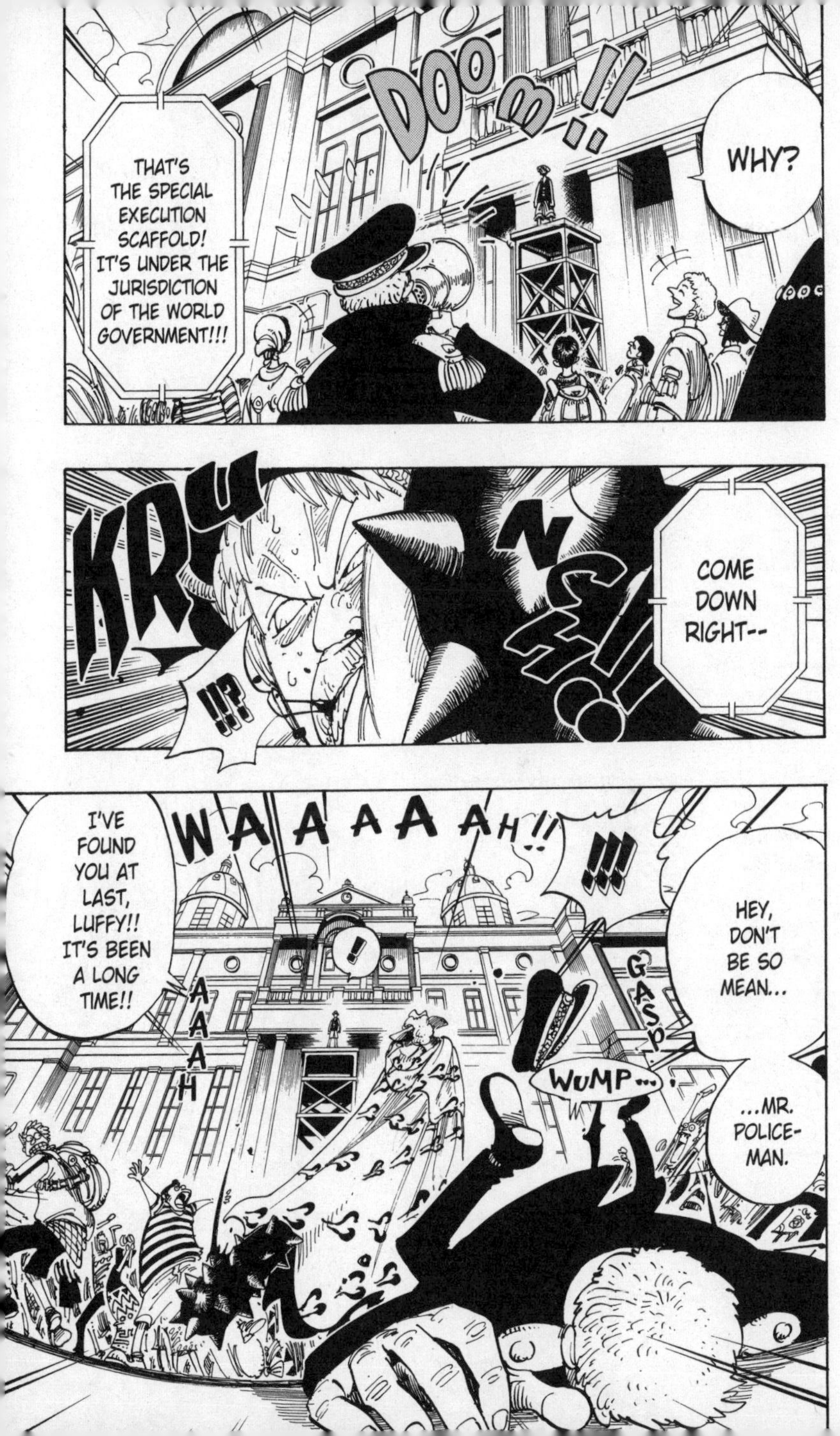
WHY?
DOOM!!
THAT'S THE SPECIAL EXECUTION SCAFFOLD! IT'S UNDER THE JURISDICTION OF THE WORLD GOVERNMENT!!!
COME DOWN RIGHT--
KRUNCH!!
!!?
HEY, DON'T BE SO MEAN...
...MR. POLICE-MAN.
GASP
WUMP...
!!!
WAAAAAH!!
!
AAAAH
I'VE FOUND YOU AT LAST, LUFFY!! IT'S BEEN A LONG TIME!!

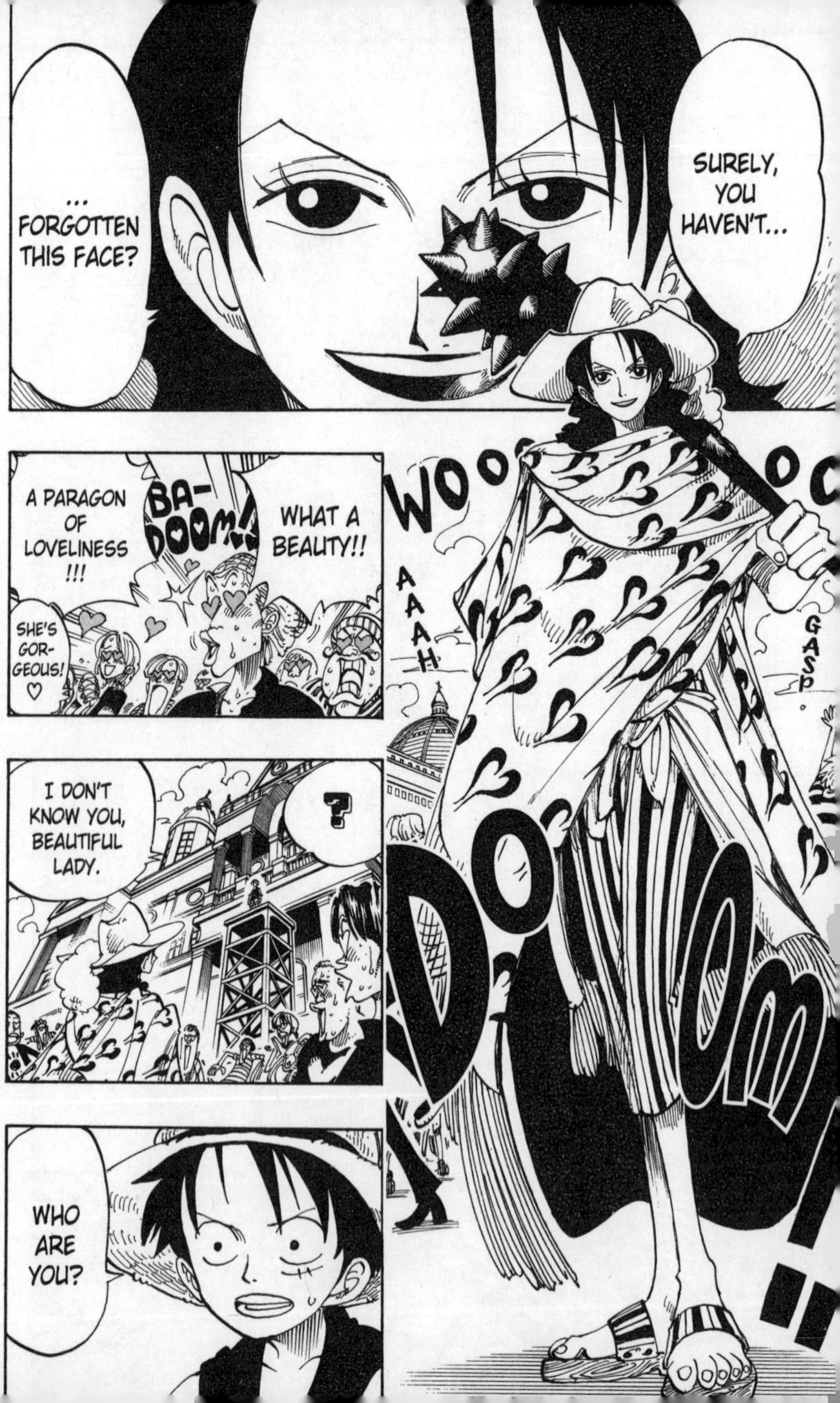
SURELY, YOU HAVEN'T...
... FORGOTTEN THIS FACE?
WOO
OO
GASP.
AAAH
DOOOM!!
WHAT A BEAUTY!!
BA-DOOM!!
A PARAGON OF LOVELINESS !!!
SHE'S GORGEOUS! ♡
?
I DON'T KNOW YOU, BEAUTIFUL LADY.
WHO ARE YOU?

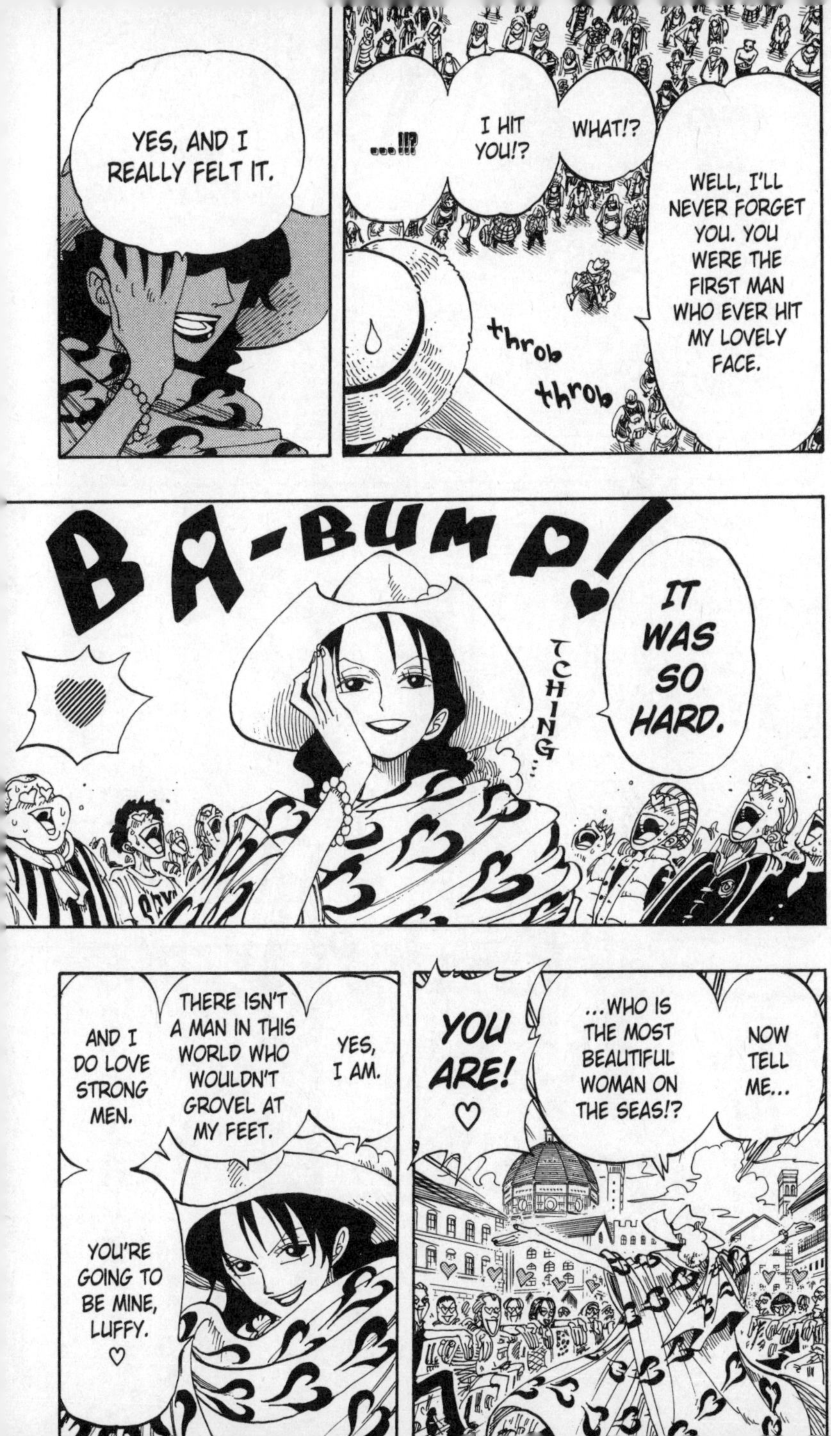
WELL, I'LL NEVER FORGET YOU. YOU WERE THE FIRST MAN WHO EVER HIT MY LOVELY FACE.
WHAT!?
I HIT YOU!?
...!!?
throb
throb
YES, AND I REALLY FELT IT.
BA-BUMP!
IT WAS SO HARD.
TCHING...
NOW TELL ME...
...WHO IS THE MOST BEAUTIFUL WOMAN ON THE SEAS!?
YOU ARE! ♡
YES, I AM.
THERE ISN'T A MAN IN THIS WORLD WHO WOULDN'T GROVEL AT MY FEET.
AND I DO LOVE STRONG MEN.
YOU'RE GOING TO BE MINE, LUFFY. ♡

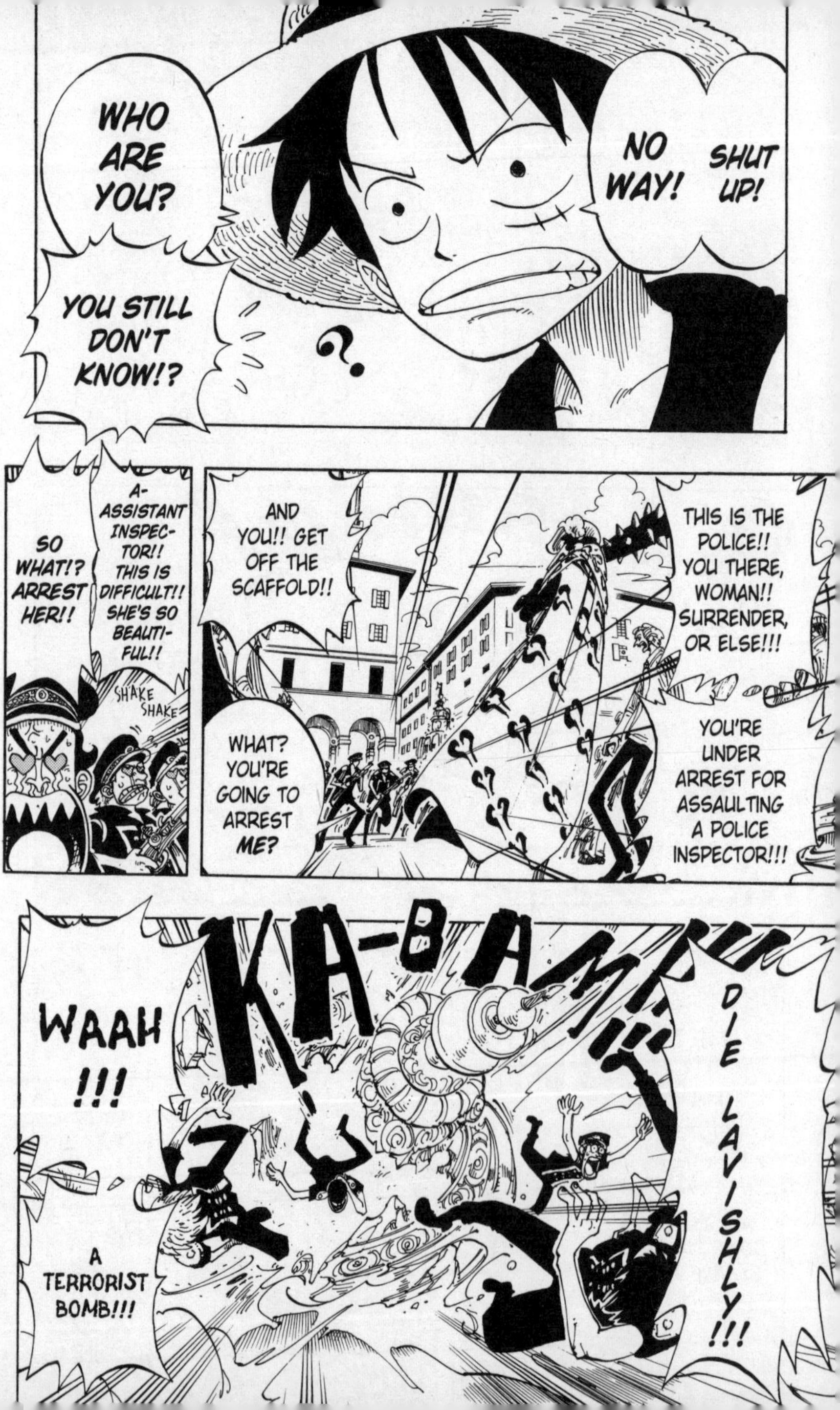
NO WAY! SHUT UP!
WHO ARE YOU?
YOU STILL DON'T KNOW!?
THIS IS THE POLICE!! YOU THERE, WOMAN!! SURRENDER, OR ELSE!!!
YOU'RE UNDER ARREST FOR ASSAULTING A POLICE INSPECTOR!!!
AND YOU!! GET OFF THE SCAFFOLD!!
WHAT? YOU'RE GOING TO ARREST ME?
A- ASSISTANT INSPECTOR!! THIS IS DIFFICULT!! SHE'S SO BEAUTIFUL!!
SHAKE SHAKE
SO WHAT!? ARREST HER!!
KA-BAM!!!
DIE LAVISHLY!!!
WAAH!!!
A TERRORIST BOMB!!!

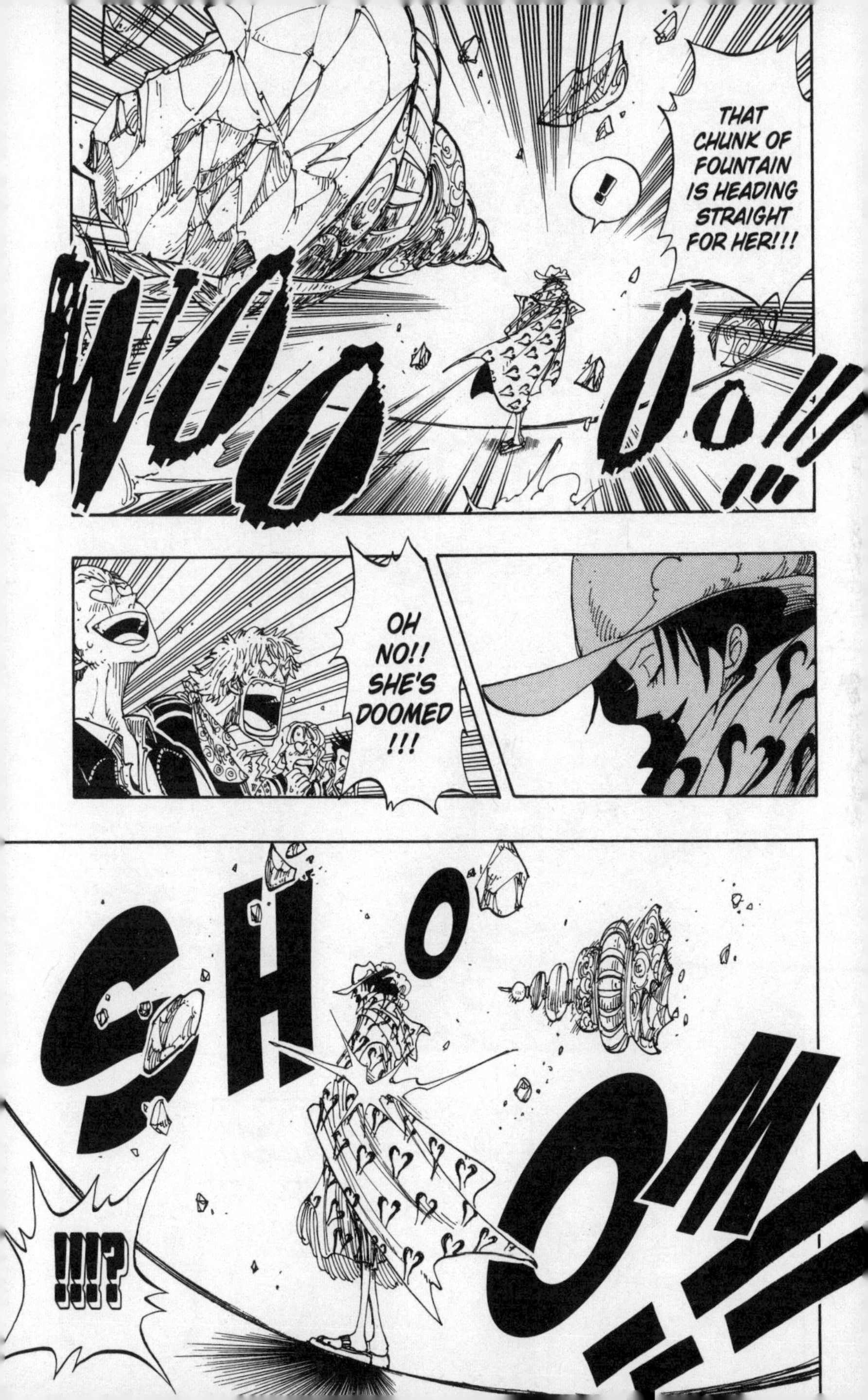!
THAT CHUNK OF FOUNTAIN IS HEADING STRAIGHT FOR HER!!!
WOOOOO!!!
OH NO!! SHE'S DOOMED!!!
CHOOM!!
!!!?

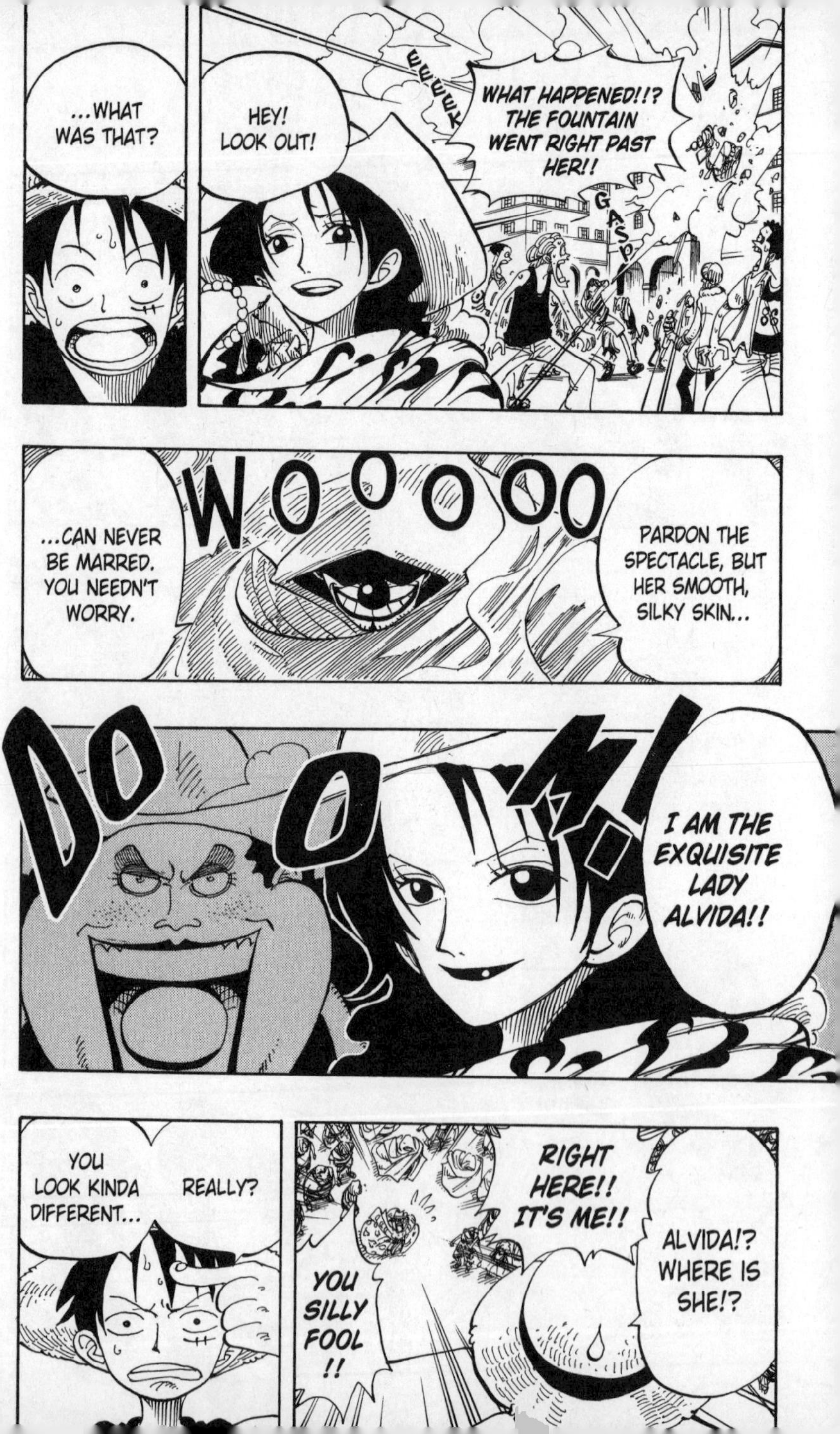
WHAT HAPPENED!!? THE FOUNTAIN WENT RIGHT PAST HER!!
WEEEEK
HEY! LOOK OUT!
GASP
...WHAT WAS THAT?
PARDON THE SPECTACLE, BUT HER SMOOTH, SILKY SKIN...
WOOOOO
...CAN NEVER BE MARRED. YOU NEEDN'T WORRY.
I AM THE EXQUISITE LADY ALVIDA!!
DOOM!
ALVIDA!? WHERE IS SHE!?
RIGHT HERE!! IT'S ME!!
YOU SILLY FOOL!!
REALLY?
YOU LOOK KINDA DIFFERENT...

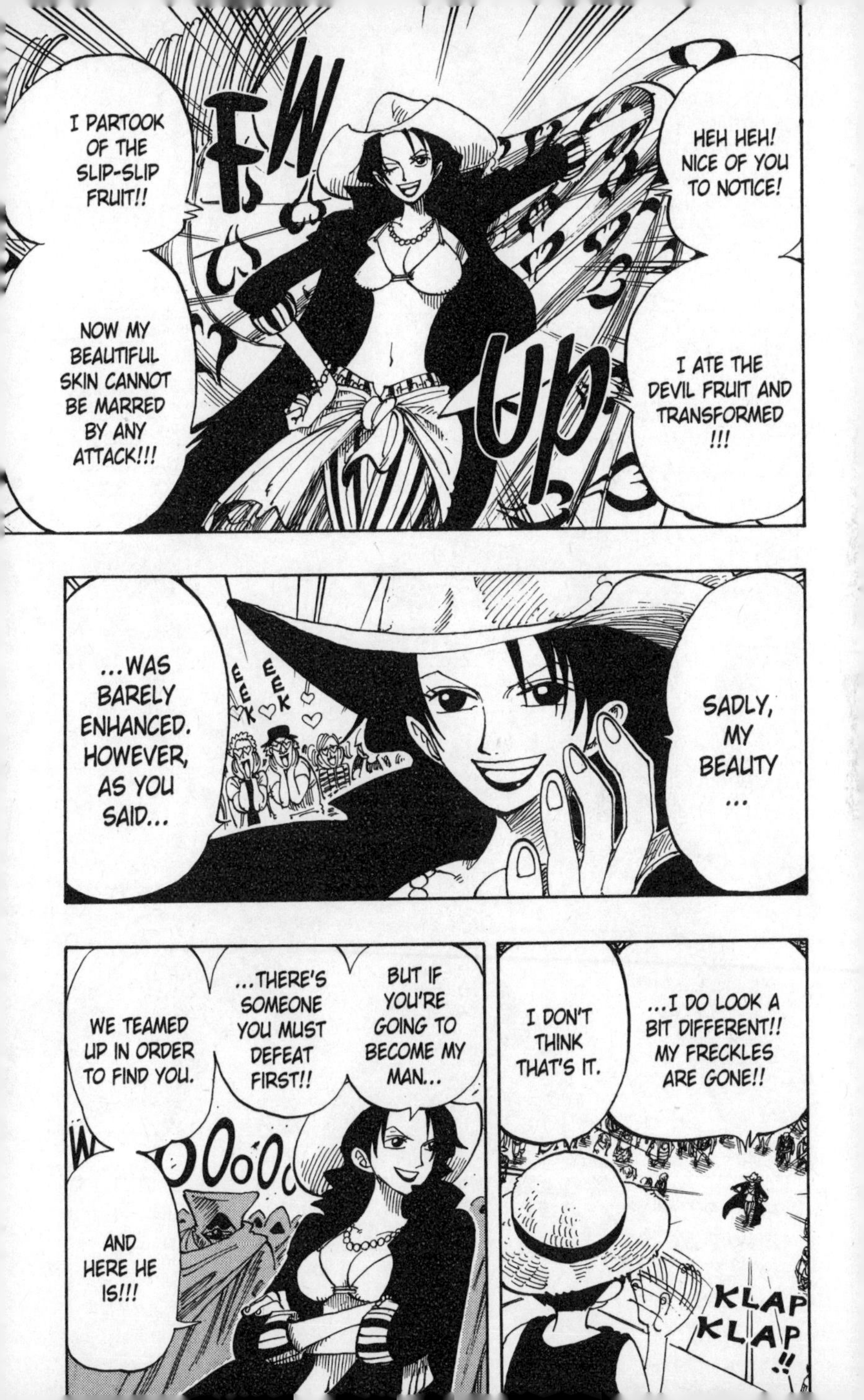
HEH HEH! NICE OF YOU TO NOTICE!
I ATE THE DEVIL FRUIT AND TRANSFORMED!!!
I PARTOOK OF THE SLIP-SLIP FRUIT!!
NOW MY BEAUTIFUL SKIN CANNOT BE MARRED BY ANY ATTACK!!!
FWUP
SADLY, MY BEAUTY...
...WAS BARELY ENHANCED. HOWEVER, AS YOU SAID...
EEEK
EEEK
...I DO LOOK A BIT DIFFERENT!! MY FRECKLES ARE GONE!!
I DON'T THINK THAT'S IT.
KLAP KLAP!!
BUT IF YOU'RE GOING TO BECOME MY MAN...
...THERE'S SOMEONE YOU MUST DEFEAT FIRST!!
WE TEAMED UP IN ORDER TO FIND YOU.
AND HERE HE IS!!!

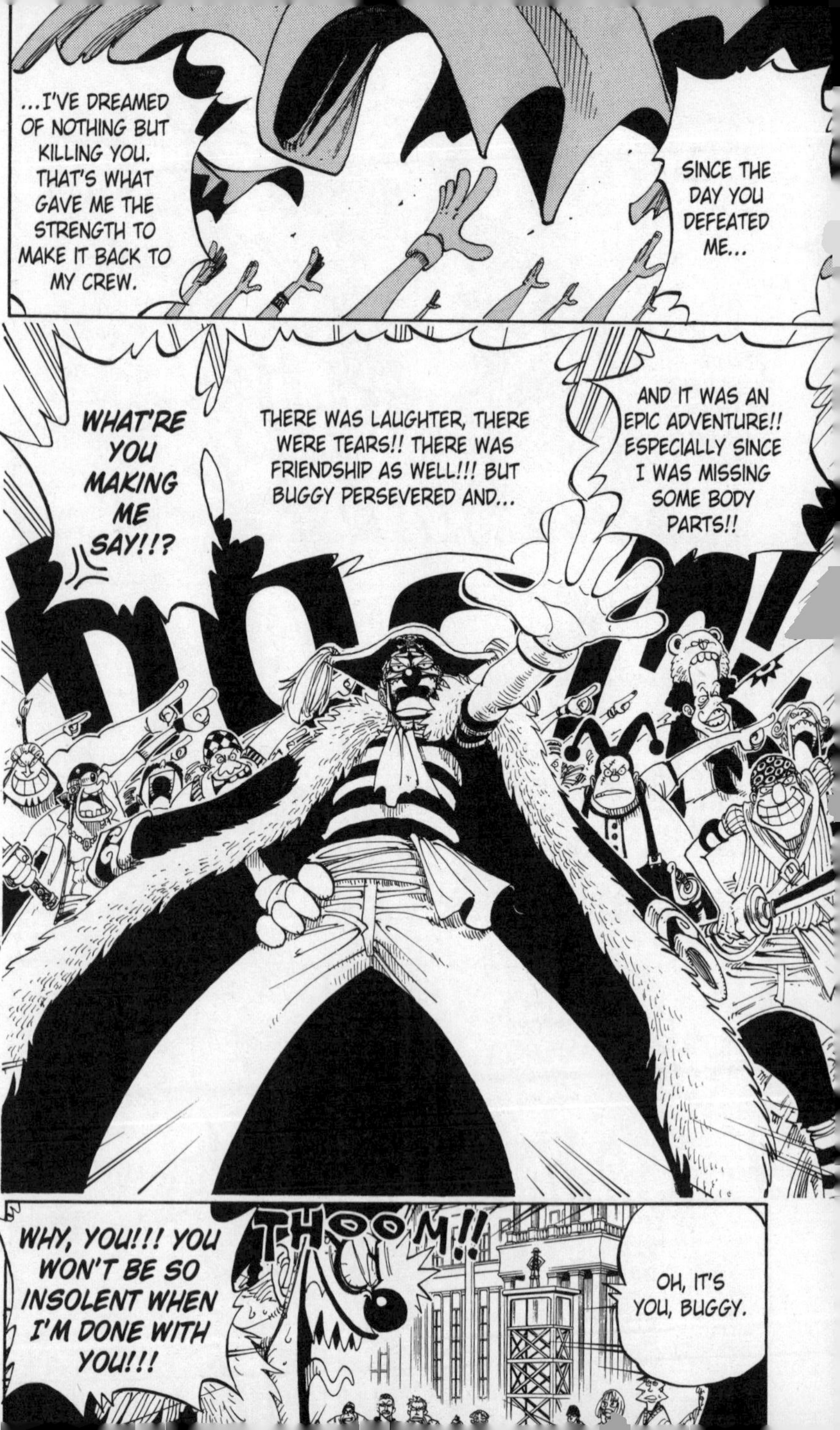
SINCE THE DAY YOU DEFEATED ME...
...I'VE DREAMED OF NOTHING BUT KILLING YOU. THAT'S WHAT GAVE ME THE STRENGTH TO MAKE IT BACK TO MY CREW.
AND IT WAS AN EPIC ADVENTURE!! ESPECIALLY SINCE I WAS MISSING SOME BODY PARTS!!
THERE WAS LAUGHTER, THERE WERE TEARS!! THERE WAS FRIENDSHIP AS WELL!!! BUT BUGGY PERSEVERED AND...
WHAT'RE YOU MAKING ME SAY!!?
OH, IT'S YOU, BUGGY.
THOOM!!
WHY, YOU!!! YOU WON'T BE SO INSOLENT WHEN I'M DONE WITH YOU!!!

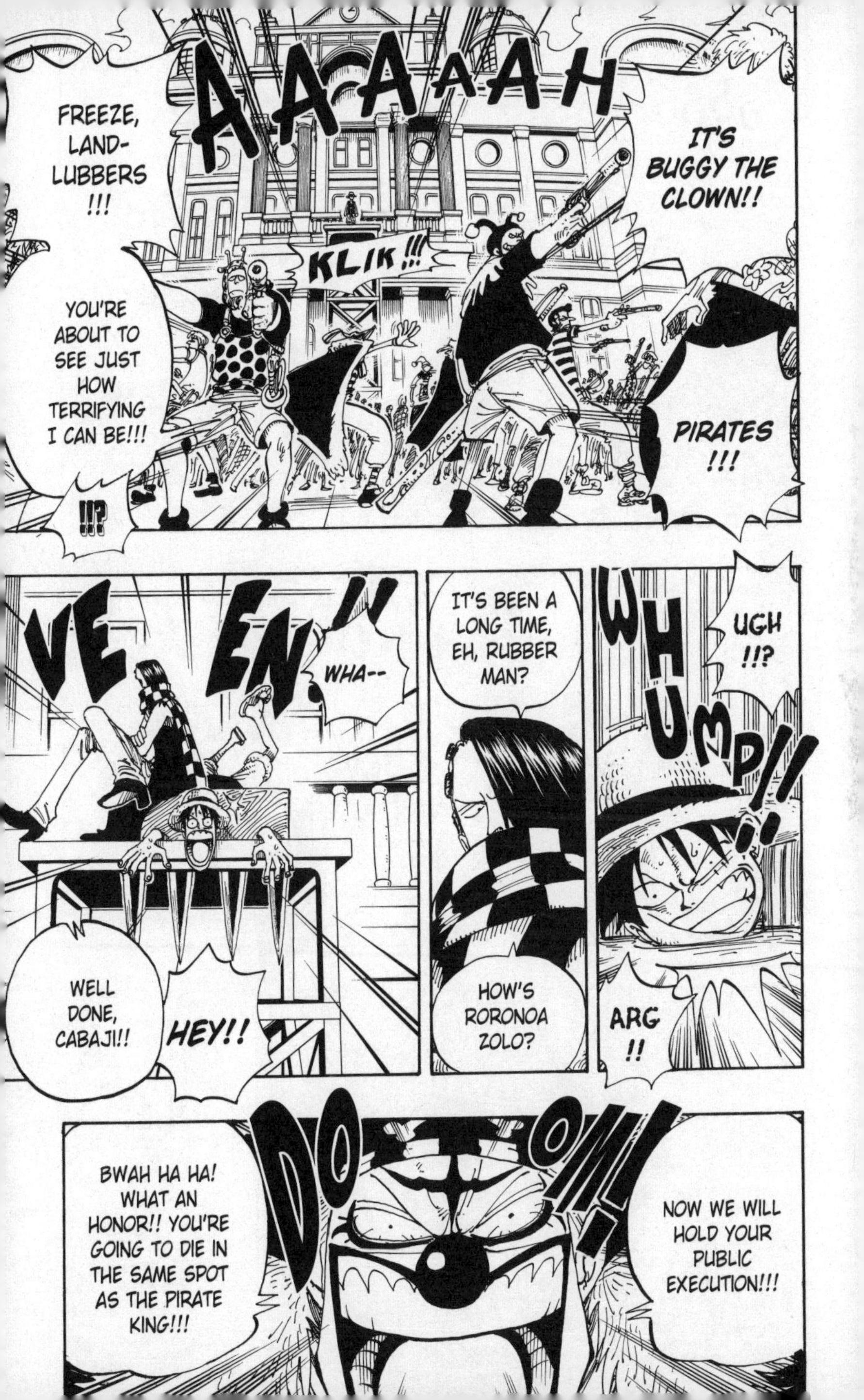
IT'S BUGGY THE CLOWN!!
AAAAAH
PIRATES!!!
KLIK!!!
FREEZE, LAND-LUBBERS!!!
YOU'RE ABOUT TO SEE JUST HOW TERRIFYING I CAN BE!!!
!!?
UGH!!?
WHUMP!!
ARG!!
IT'S BEEN A LONG TIME, EH, RUBBER MAN?
HOW'S RORONOA ZOLO?
VE EN!!
WHA--
HEY!!
WELL DONE, CABAJI!!
NOW WE WILL HOLD YOUR PUBLIC EXECUTION!!!
DO OM!!
BWAH HA HA! WHAT AN HONOR!! YOU'RE GOING TO DIE IN THE SAME SPOT AS THE PIRATE KING!!!

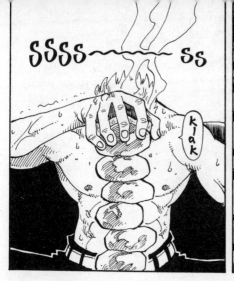

SSSS ~~~~~ ss

krak

CAPTAIN SMOKER!! TERRIBLE NEWS!!!

MARINE

KLUNK

KRAK!!

KLUNK KLUNK!!

PIRATES ARE CAUSING A DISTURBANCE AT THE EXECUTION SCAFFOLD!!!

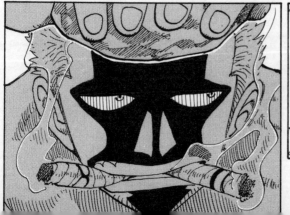

UH...

THE PIRATES ARE--!!

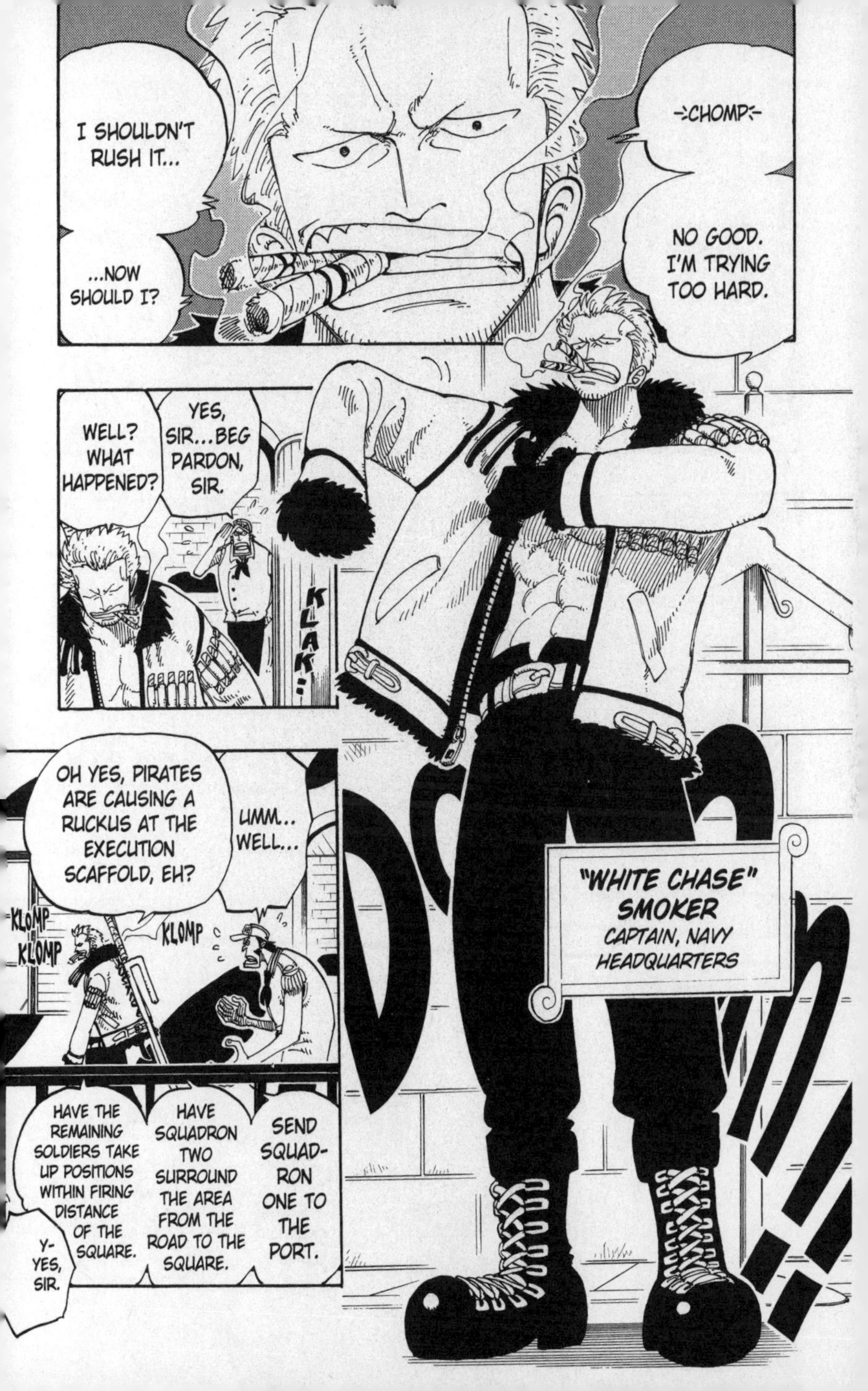
-CHOMP-
NO GOOD. I'M TRYING TOO HARD.
I SHOULDN'T RUSH IT...
...NOW SHOULD I?
"WHITE CHASE" SMOKER
CAPTAIN, NAVY HEADQUARTERS
KLAK!!
YES, SIR...BEG PARDON, SIR.
WELL? WHAT HAPPENED?
UMM... WELL...
OH YES, PIRATES ARE CAUSING A RUCKUS AT THE EXECUTION SCAFFOLD, EH?
KLOMP
KLOMP
KLOMP
SEND SQUAD-RON ONE TO THE PORT.
HAVE SQUADRON TWO SURROUND THE AREA FROM THE ROAD TO THE SQUARE.
HAVE THE REMAINING SOLDIERS TAKE UP POSITIONS WITHIN FIRING DISTANCE OF THE SQUARE.
Y-YES, SIR.

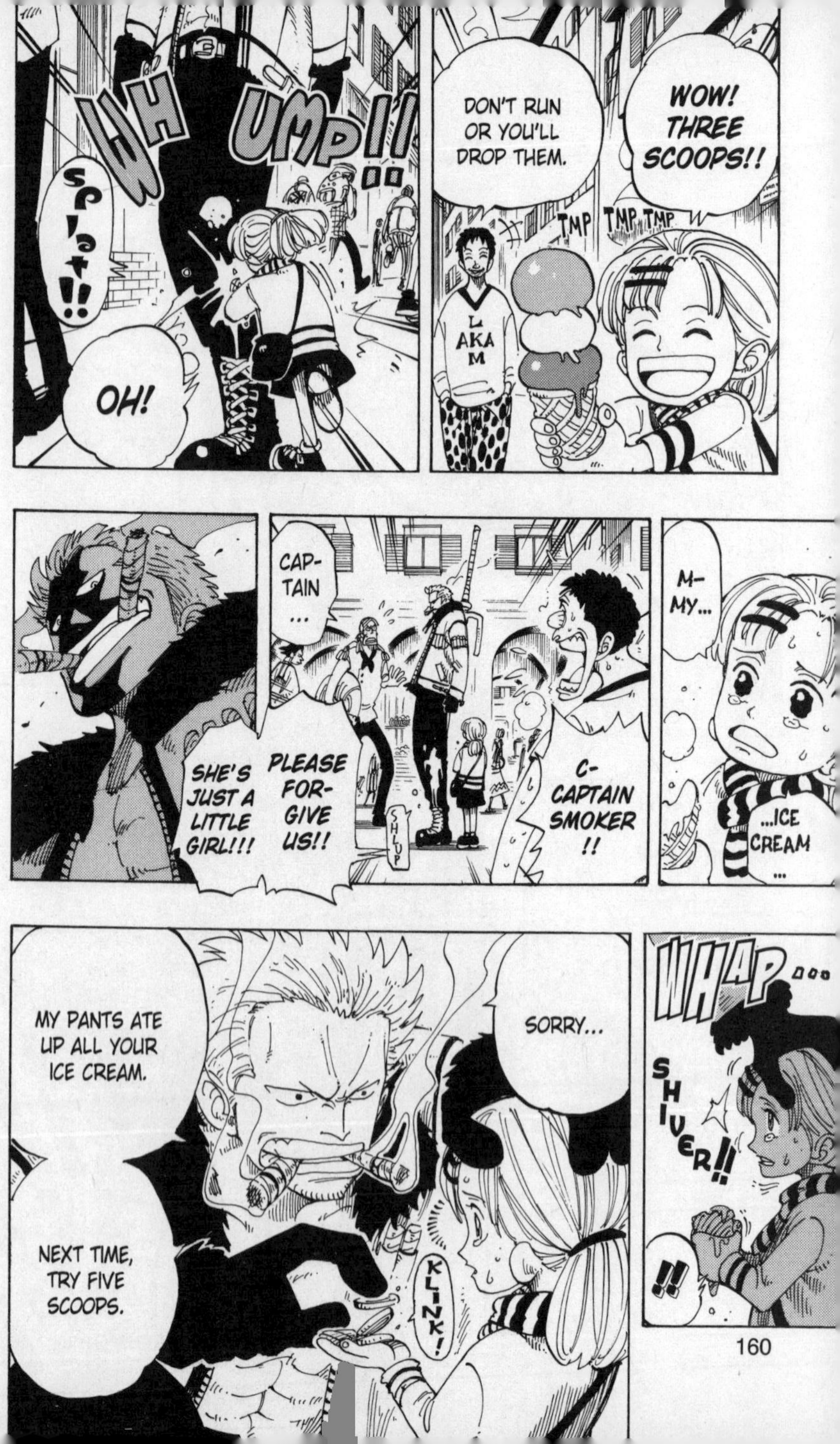
WOW! THREE SCOOPS!!
DON'T RUN OR YOU'LL DROP THEM.
TMP TMP TMP
WHUMP!!
splat!!
OH!
M-MY...
...ICE CREAM...
CAPTAIN...
C-CAPTAIN SMOKER!!
SHLUP
PLEASE FORGIVE US!!
SHE'S JUST A LITTLE GIRL!!!
WHAP...
SHIVER!!
!!
SORRY...
MY PANTS ATE UP ALL YOUR ICE CREAM.
KLINK!
NEXT TIME, TRY FIVE SCOOPS.

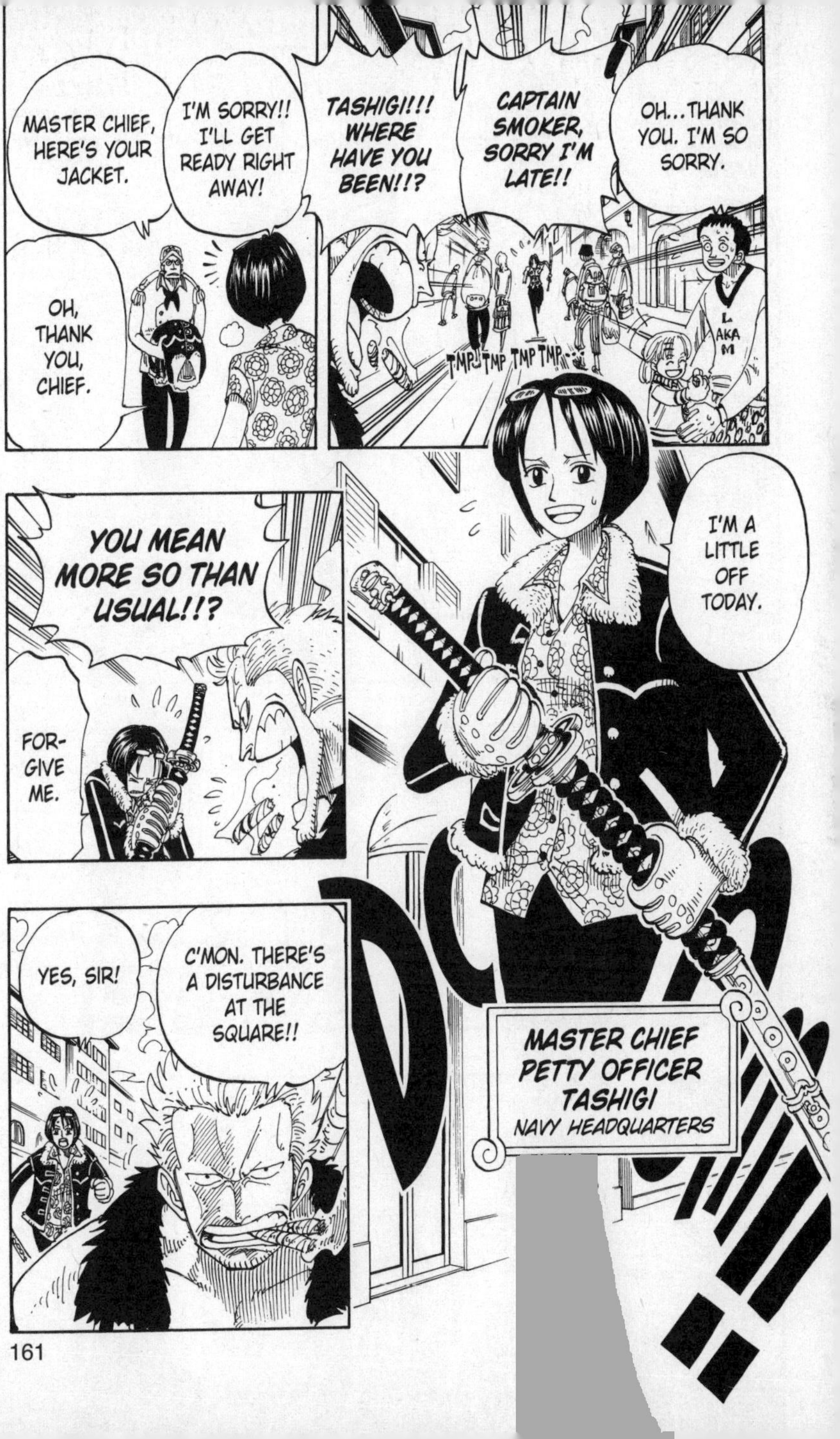
OH...THANK YOU. I'M SO SORRY.
CAPTAIN SMOKER, SORRY I'M LATE!!
TASHIGI!!!! WHERE HAVE YOU BEEN!!?
TMP TMP TMP TMP
I'M SORRY!! I'LL GET READY RIGHT AWAY!
MASTER CHIEF, HERE'S YOUR JACKET.
OH, THANK YOU, CHIEF.
I'M A LITTLE OFF TODAY.
MASTER CHIEF PETTY OFFICER TASHIGI
NAVY HEADQUARTERS
YOU MEAN MORE SO THAN USUAL!!?
FOR-GIVE ME.
C'MON. THERE'S A DISTURBANCE AT THE SQUARE!!
YES, SIR!

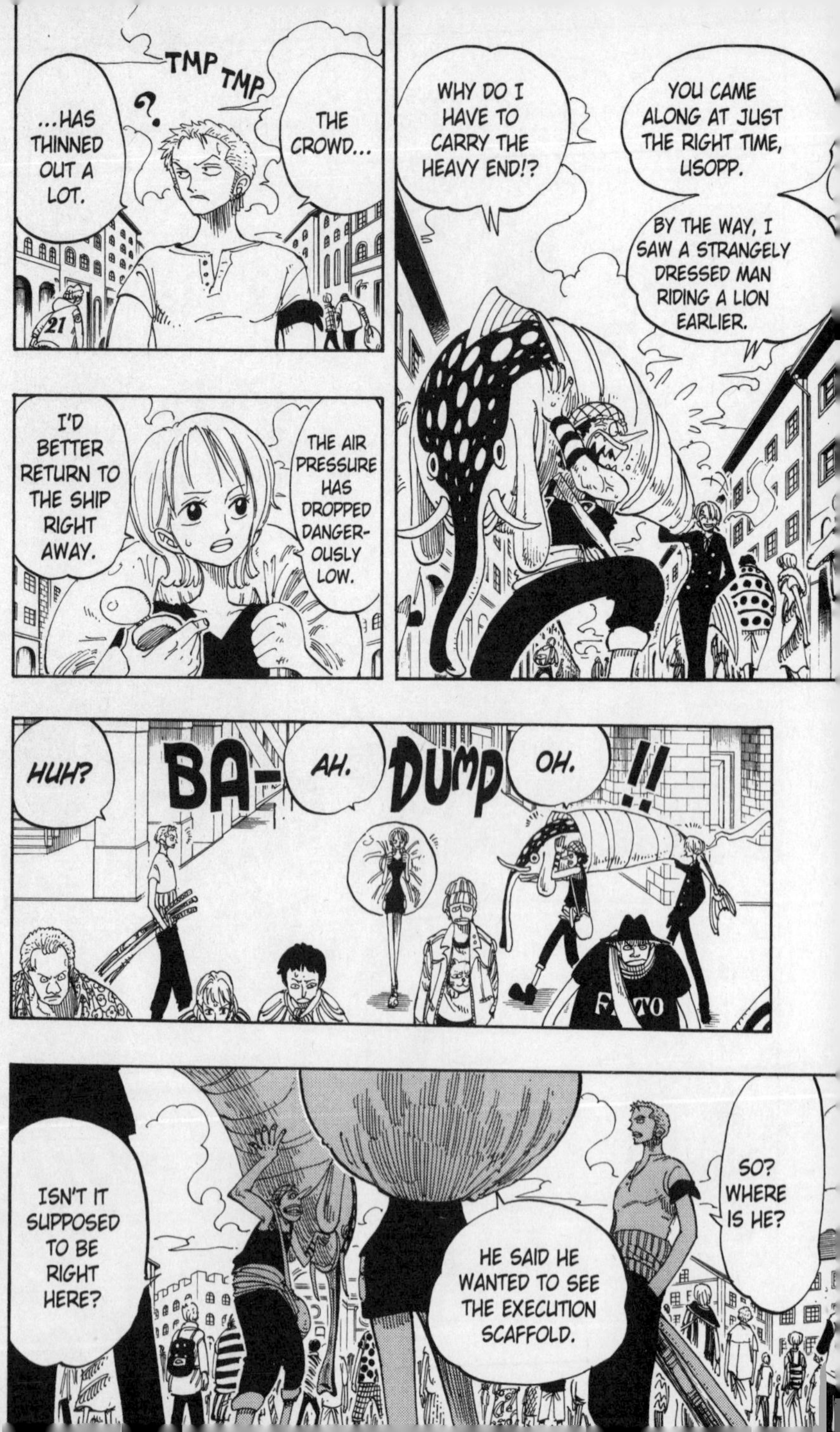
YOU CAME ALONG AT JUST THE RIGHT TIME, USOPP.
WHY DO I HAVE TO CARRY THE HEAVY END!?
BY THE WAY, I SAW A STRANGELY DRESSED MAN RIDING A LION EARLIER.
TMP TMP
THE CROWD...
...HAS THINNED OUT A LOT.
THE AIR PRESSURE HAS DROPPED DANGEROUSLY LOW.
I'D BETTER RETURN TO THE SHIP RIGHT AWAY.
!!
OH.
AH.
HUH?
BA-DUMP
SO? WHERE IS HE?
HE SAID HE WANTED TO SEE THE EXECUTION SCAFFOLD.
ISN'T IT SUPPOSED TO BE RIGHT HERE?

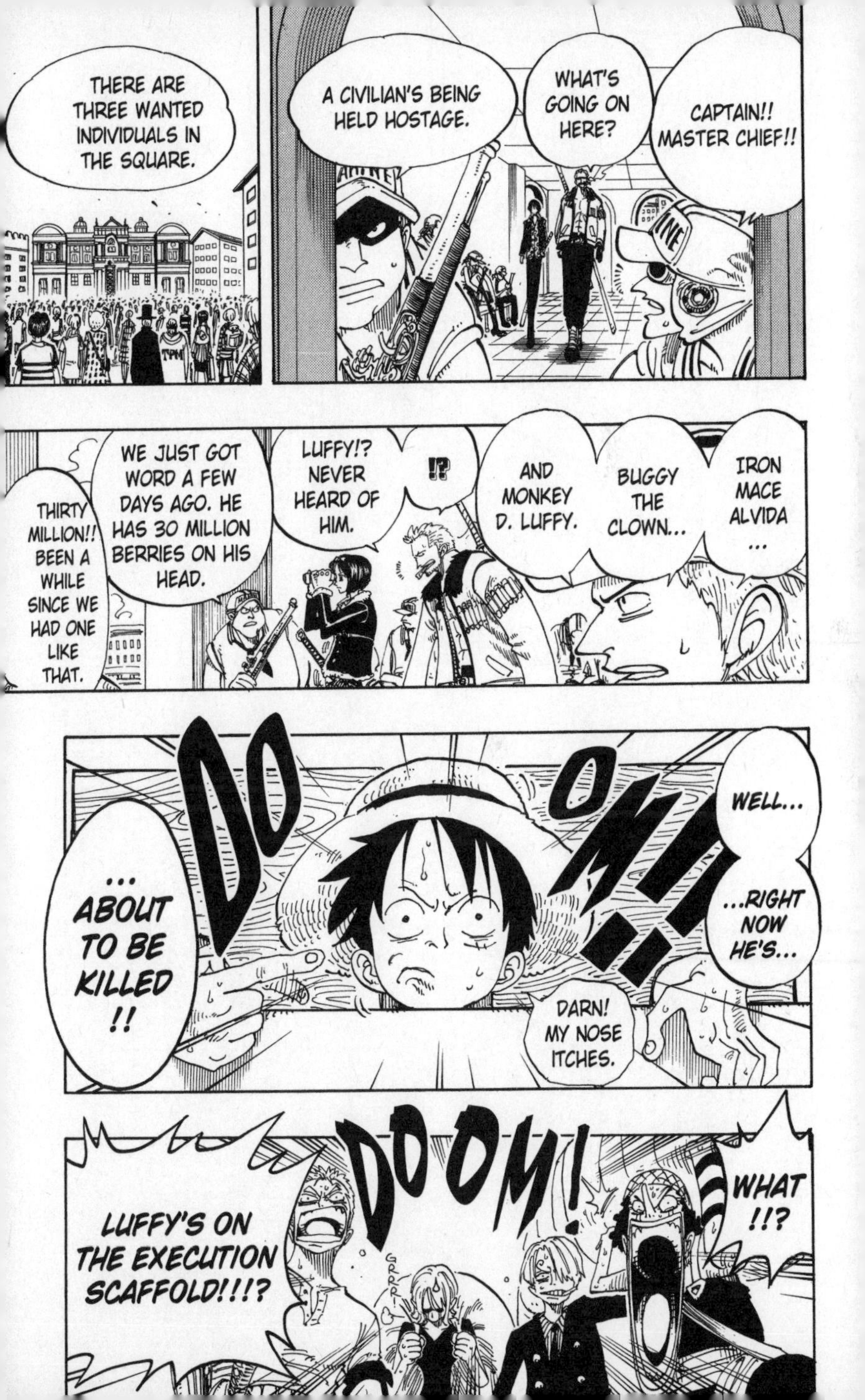
CAPTAIN!! MASTER CHIEF!!
WHAT'S GOING ON HERE?
A CIVILIAN'S BEING HELD HOSTAGE.
THERE ARE THREE WANTED INDIVIDUALS IN THE SQUARE.
IRON MACE ALVIDA ...
BUGGY THE CLOWN...
AND MONKEY D. LUFFY.
!?
LUFFY!? NEVER HEARD OF HIM.
WE JUST GOT WORD A FEW DAYS AGO. HE HAS 30 MILLION BERRIES ON HIS HEAD.
THIRTY MILLION!! BEEN A WHILE SINCE WE HAD ONE LIKE THAT.
WELL...
...RIGHT NOW HE'S...
DOOM!!
... ABOUT TO BE KILLED !!
DARN! MY NOSE ITCHES.
WHAT !!?
DOOM!
GRRR!
LUFFY'S ON THE EXECUTION SCAFFOLD!!!?

7.

Luffy's Special Seat

- Captain's chair

- Luffy seems to like this chair. He's always sitting in it.

- He can't swim, so why would he sit in a spot like this? Who knows? But he seems happy, so what's wrong with that?

Nami's Tangerine Grove

- When Nami left Coco Village, she took three of Belle-Mère's tangerine trees with her.

- Nami tends this little orchard.

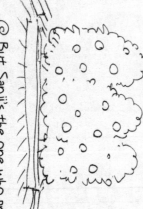

- But Sanji's the one who protects the trees from tangerine snatchers (like Luffy).

- The tangerines are supposed to be very sweet.

Chapter 99:
LUFFY DIED

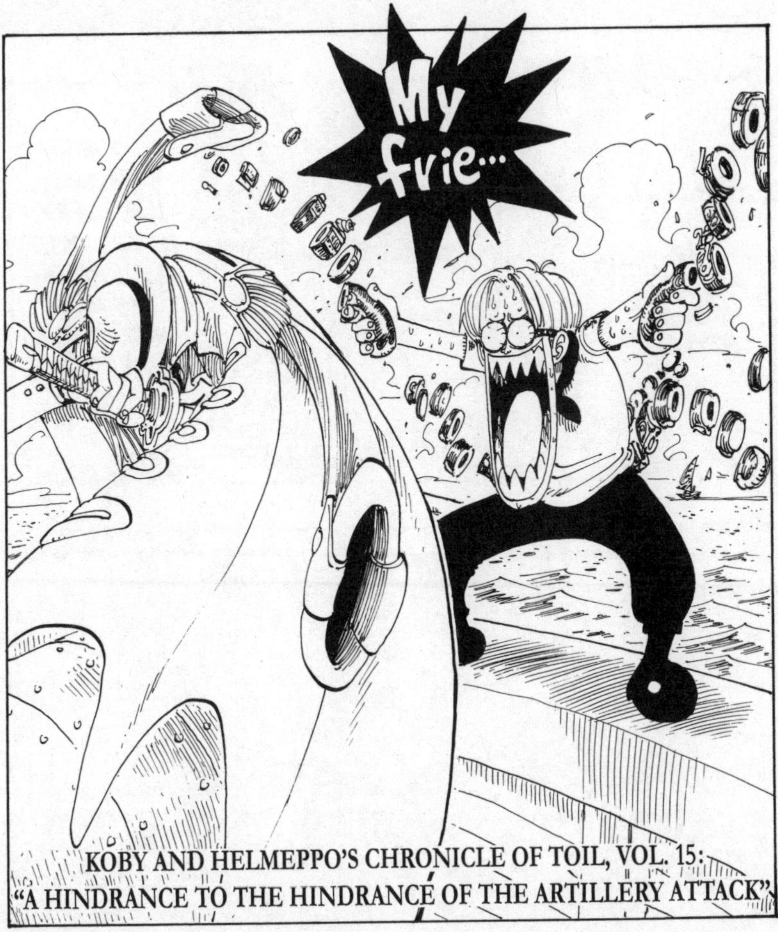
My frie...
KOBY AND HELMEPPO'S CHRONICLE OF TOIL, VOL. 15:
"A HINDRANCE TO THE HINDRANCE OF THE ARTILLERY ATTACK"

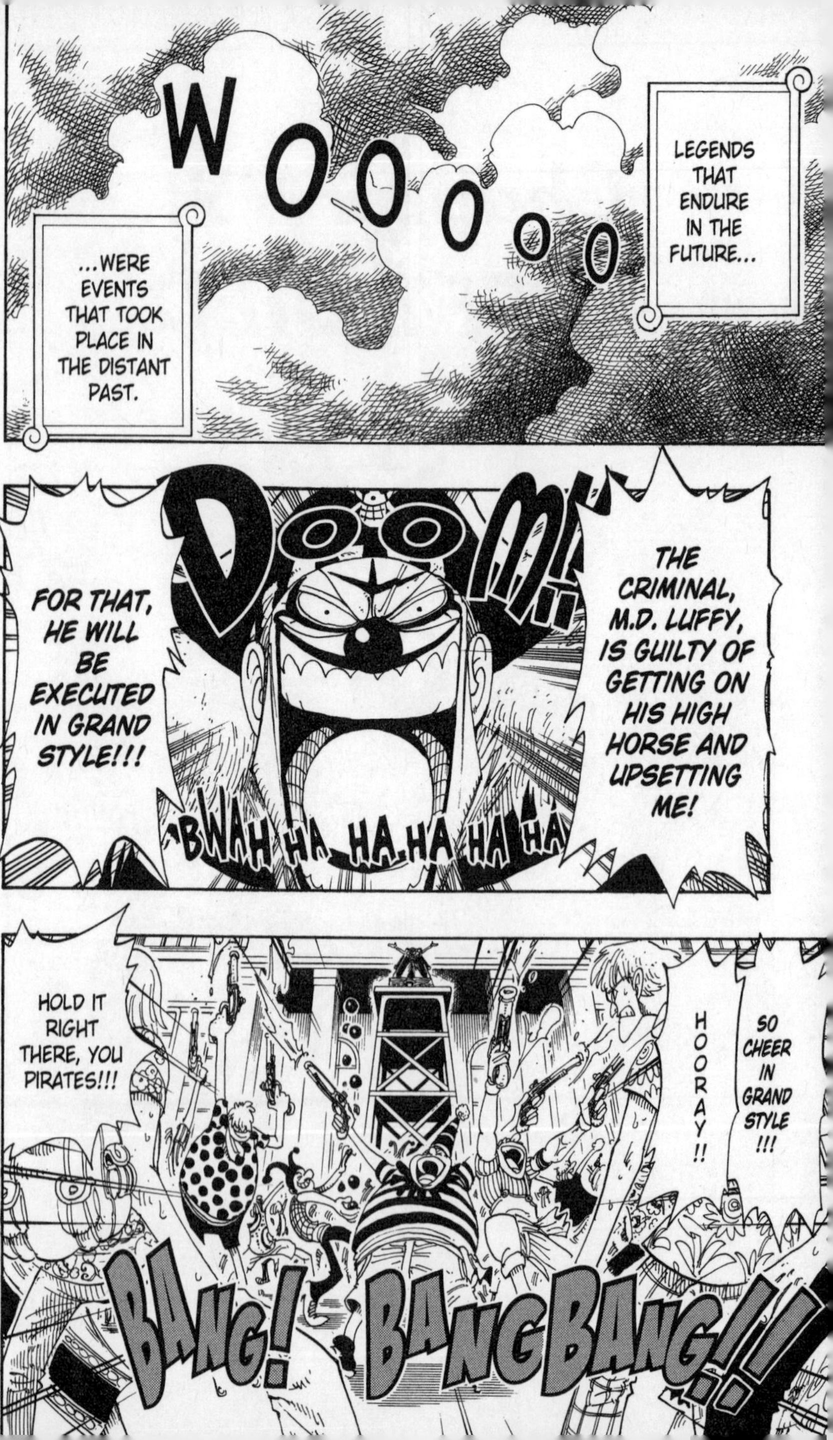
LEGENDS THAT ENDURE IN THE FUTURE...
WOOOOOO
...WERE EVENTS THAT TOOK PLACE IN THE DISTANT PAST.
THE CRIMINAL, M.D. LUFFY, IS GUILTY OF GETTING ON HIS HIGH HORSE AND UPSETTING ME!
DOOM!!
FOR THAT, HE WILL BE EXECUTED IN GRAND STYLE!!!
BWAH HA HA HA HA HA
SO CHEER IN GRAND STYLE!!!
HOORAY!!
HOLD IT RIGHT THERE, YOU PIRATES!!!
BANG! BANGBANG!!

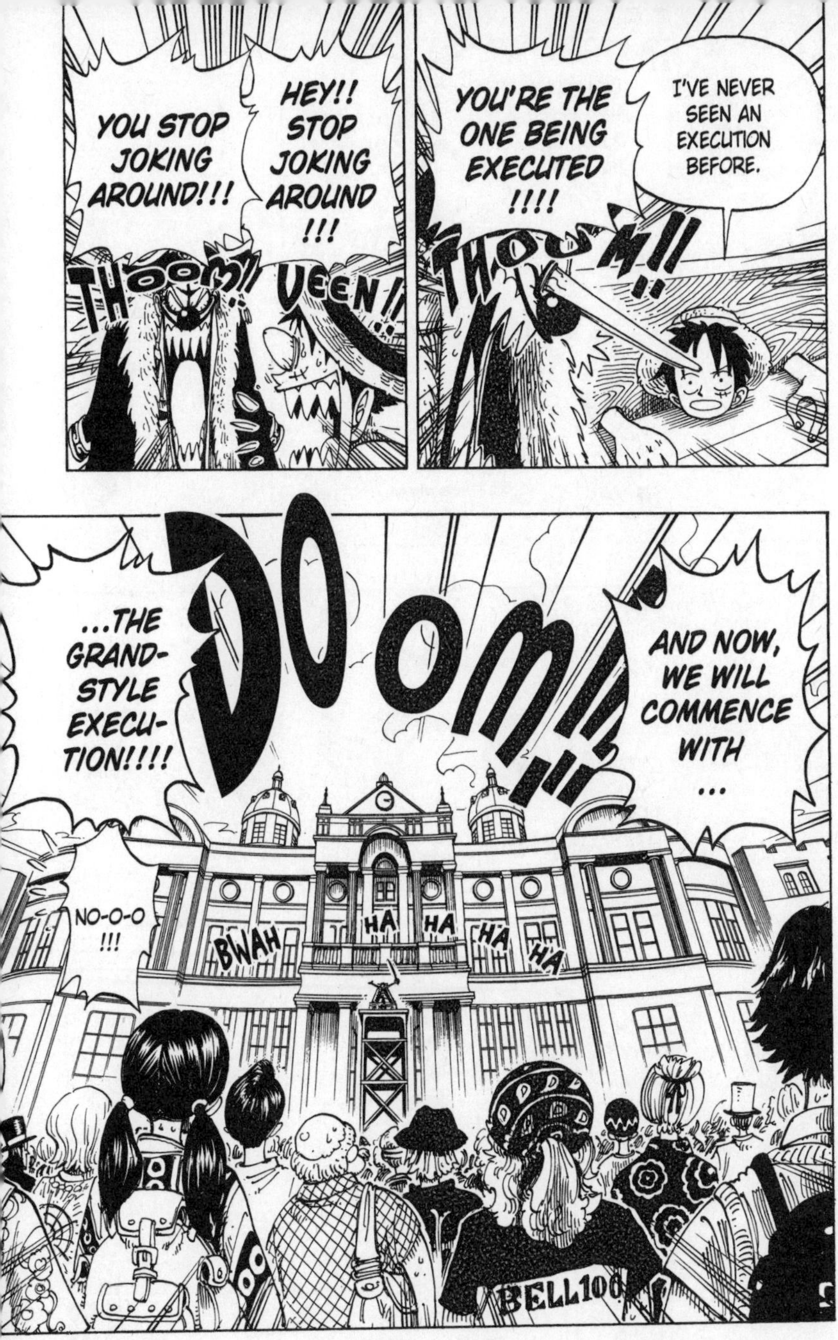
I'VE NEVER SEEN AN EXECUTION BEFORE.
YOU'RE THE ONE BEING EXECUTED!!!!
THOOM!!
HEY!! STOP JOKING AROUND!!!
YOU STOP JOKING AROUND!!!
VEEN!!
THOOM!!
AND NOW, WE WILL COMMENCE WITH ...
DOOM!!!
...THE GRAND-STYLE EXECUTION!!!!
NO-O-O !!!
BWAH HA HA HA HA
BELL100

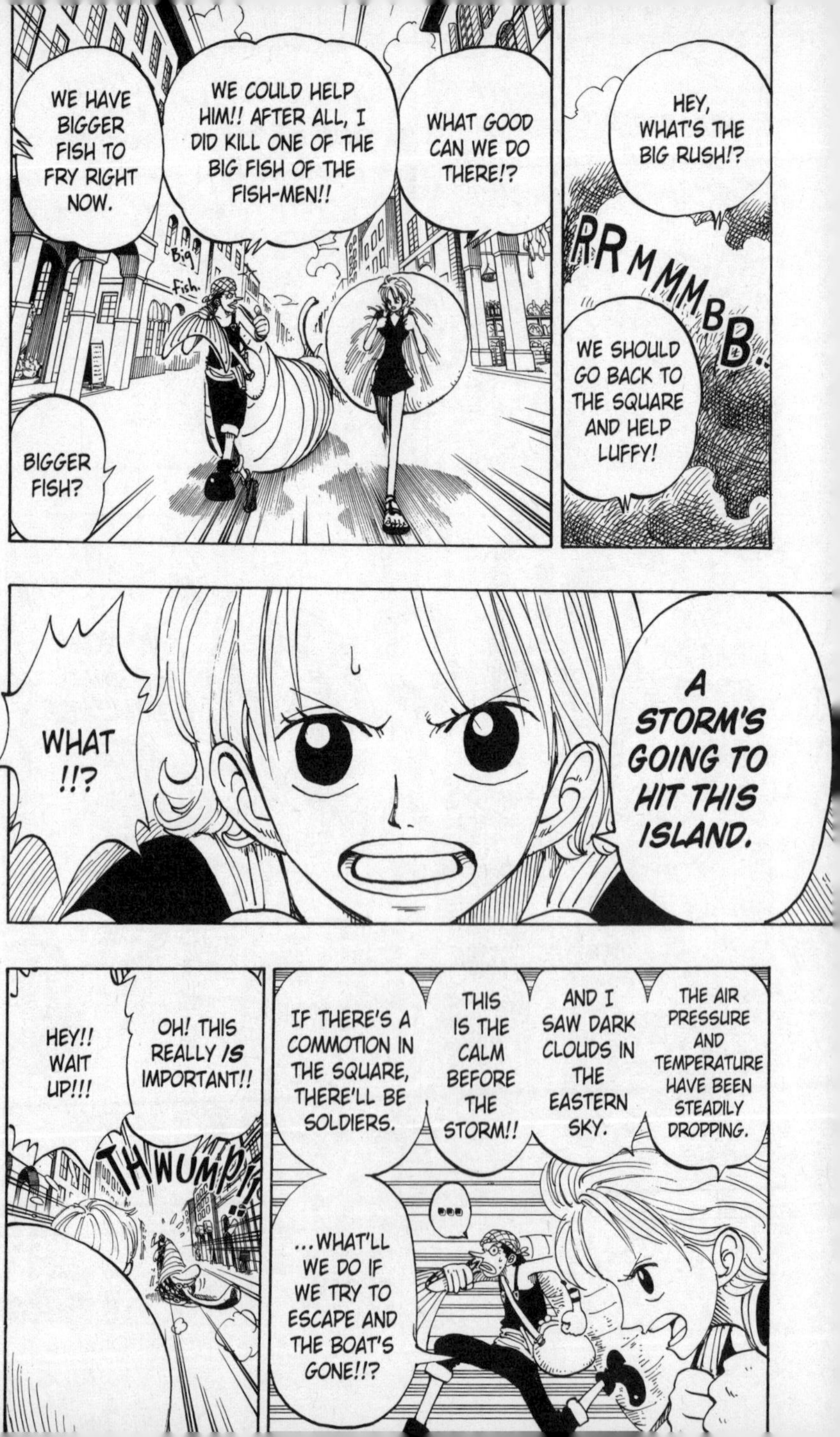
HEY, WHAT'S THE BIG RUSH!?
RRMMMBB..
WE SHOULD GO BACK TO THE SQUARE AND HELP LUFFY!
WHAT GOOD CAN WE DO THERE!?
WE COULD HELP HIM!! AFTER ALL, I DID KILL ONE OF THE BIG FISH OF THE FISH-MEN!!
WE HAVE BIGGER FISH TO FRY RIGHT NOW.
Big Fish.
BIGGER FISH?
A STORM'S GOING TO HIT THIS ISLAND.
WHAT !!?
THE AIR PRESSURE AND TEMPERATURE HAVE BEEN STEADILY DROPPING.
AND I SAW DARK CLOUDS IN THE EASTERN SKY.
THIS IS THE CALM BEFORE THE STORM!!
IF THERE'S A COMMOTION IN THE SQUARE, THERE'LL BE SOLDIERS.
...
...WHAT'LL WE DO IF WE TRY TO ESCAPE AND THE BOAT'S GONE!!?
OH! THIS REALLY *IS* IMPORTANT!!
HEY!! WAIT UP!!!
THWUMP!!

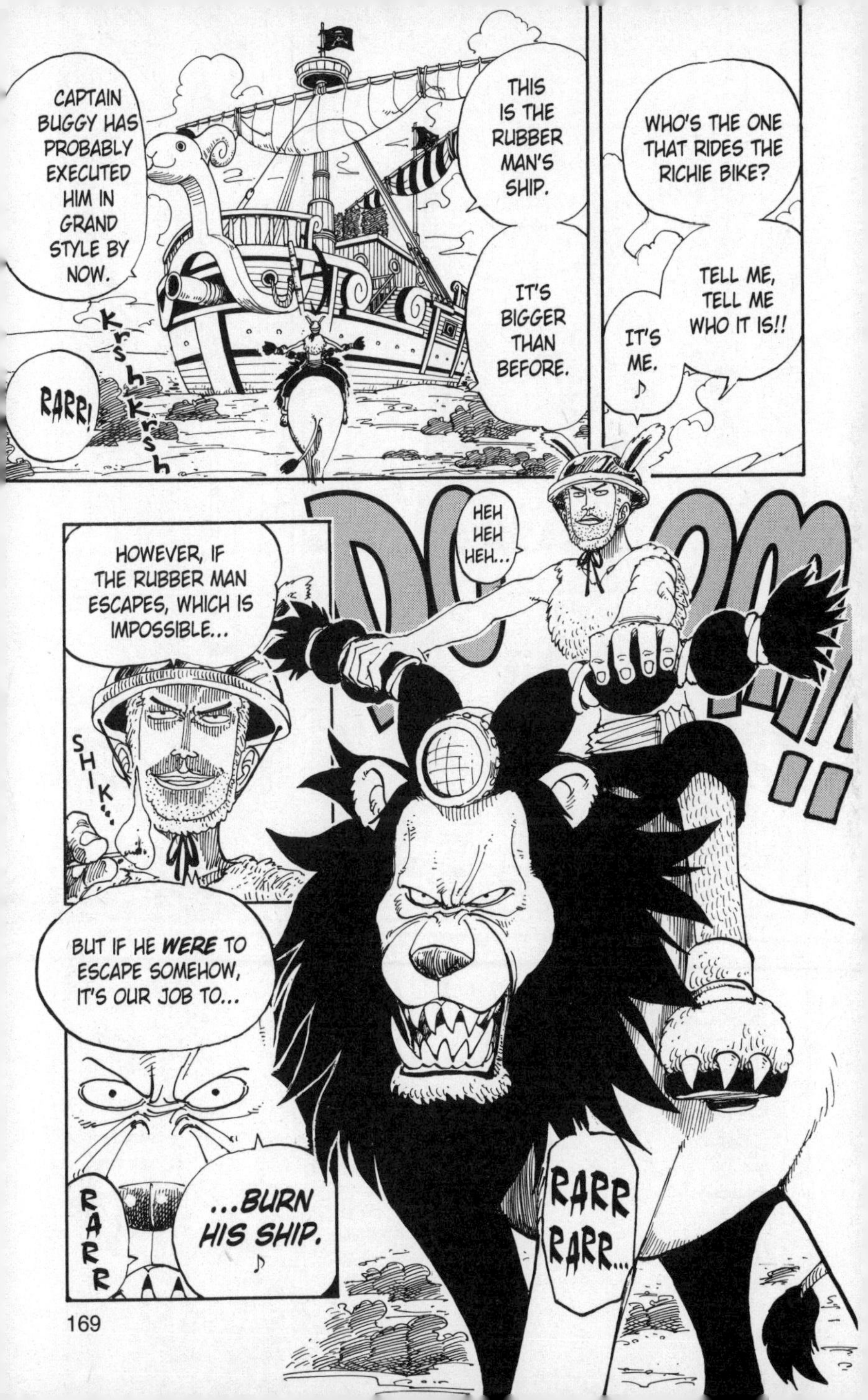
WHO'S THE ONE THAT RIDES THE RICHIE BIKE?
TELL ME, TELL ME WHO IT IS!!
IT'S ME. ♪
THIS IS THE RUBBER MAN'S SHIP.
IT'S BIGGER THAN BEFORE.
CAPTAIN BUGGY HAS PROBABLY EXECUTED HIM IN GRAND STYLE BY NOW.
Krshkrsh
RARR!
DOOOM!!
HEH HEH HEH...
RARR RARR...
HOWEVER, IF THE RUBBER MAN ESCAPES, WHICH IS IMPOSSIBLE...
SHIK...
BUT IF HE *WERE* TO ESCAPE SOMEHOW, IT'S OUR JOB TO...
...BURN HIS SHIP. ♪
RARR

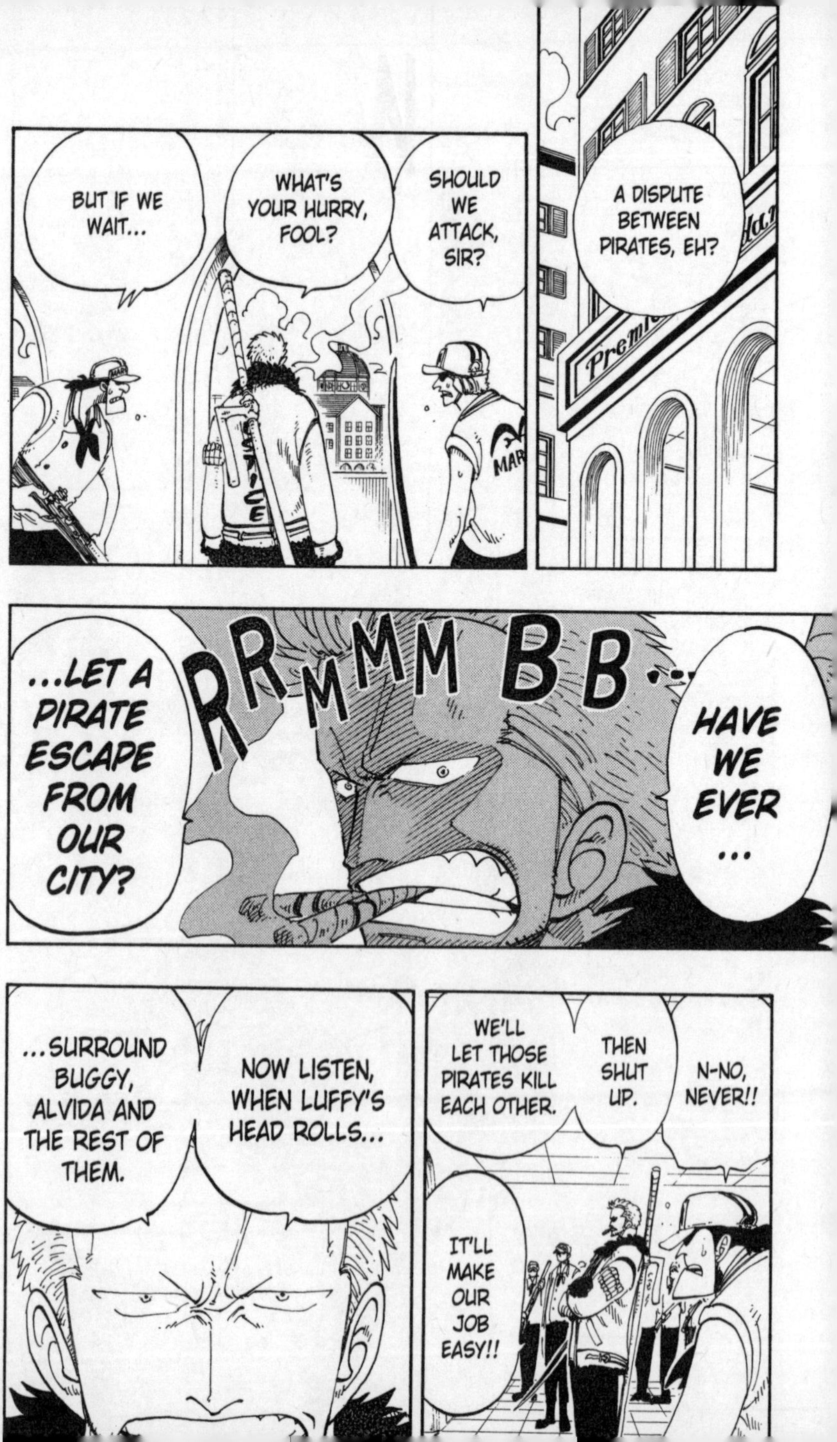
A DISPUTE BETWEEN PIRATES, EH?
SHOULD WE ATTACK, SIR?
WHAT'S YOUR HURRY, FOOL?
BUT IF WE WAIT...
HAVE WE EVER ...
RRMMMBB...
...LET A PIRATE ESCAPE FROM OUR CITY?
N-NO, NEVER!!
THEN SHUT UP.
WE'LL LET THOSE PIRATES KILL EACH OTHER.
IT'LL MAKE OUR JOB EASY!!
NOW LISTEN, WHEN LUFFY'S HEAD ROLLS...
...SURROUND BUGGY, ALVIDA AND THE REST OF THEM.

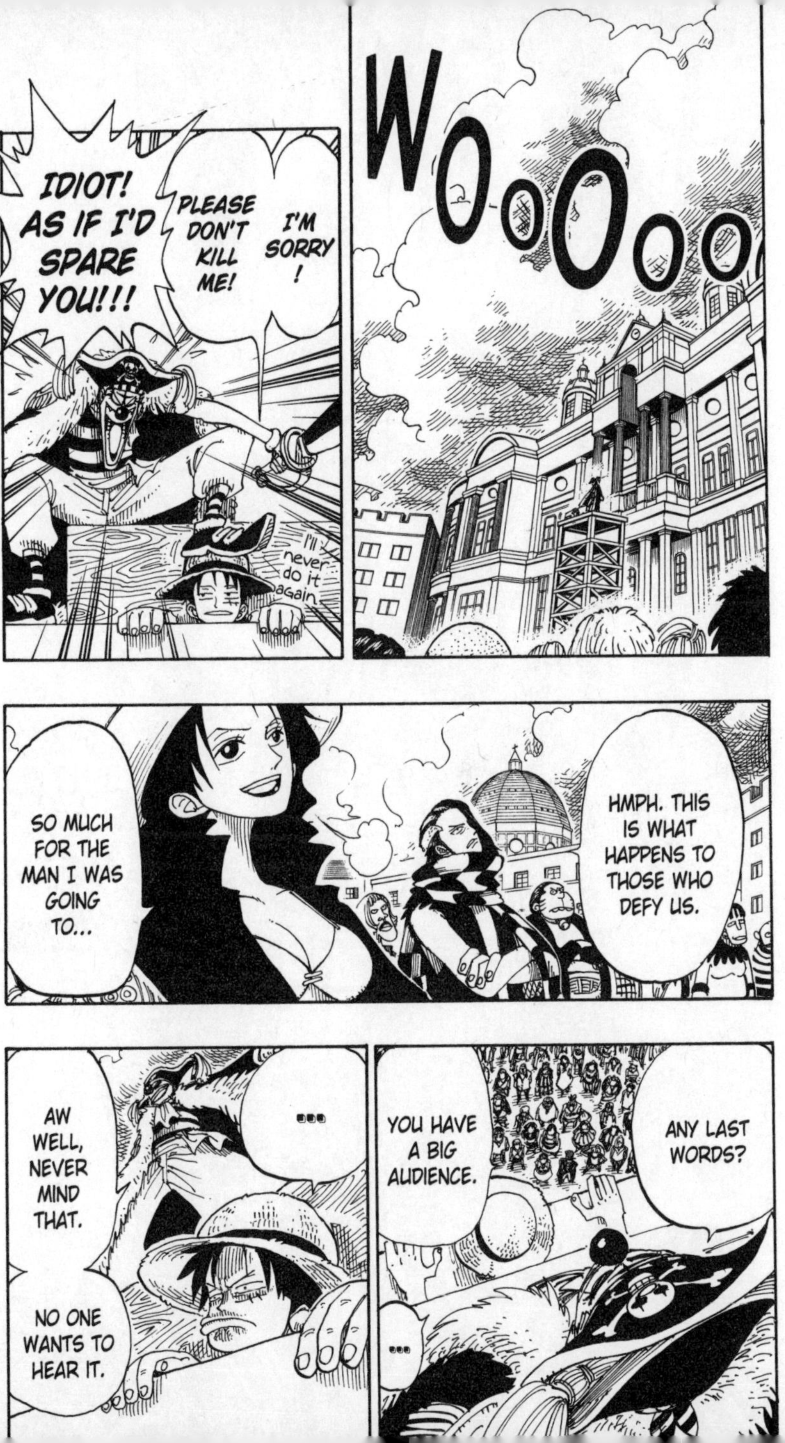
WOOOOOO
I'M SORRY!
PLEASE DON'T KILL ME!
IDIOT! AS IF I'D SPARE YOU!!!
I'll never do it again
HMPH. THIS IS WHAT HAPPENS TO THOSE WHO DEFY US.
SO MUCH FOR THE MAN I WAS GOING TO...
ANY LAST WORDS?
YOU HAVE A BIG AUDIENCE.
...
...
AW WELL, NEVER MIND THAT.
NO ONE WANTS TO HEAR IT.

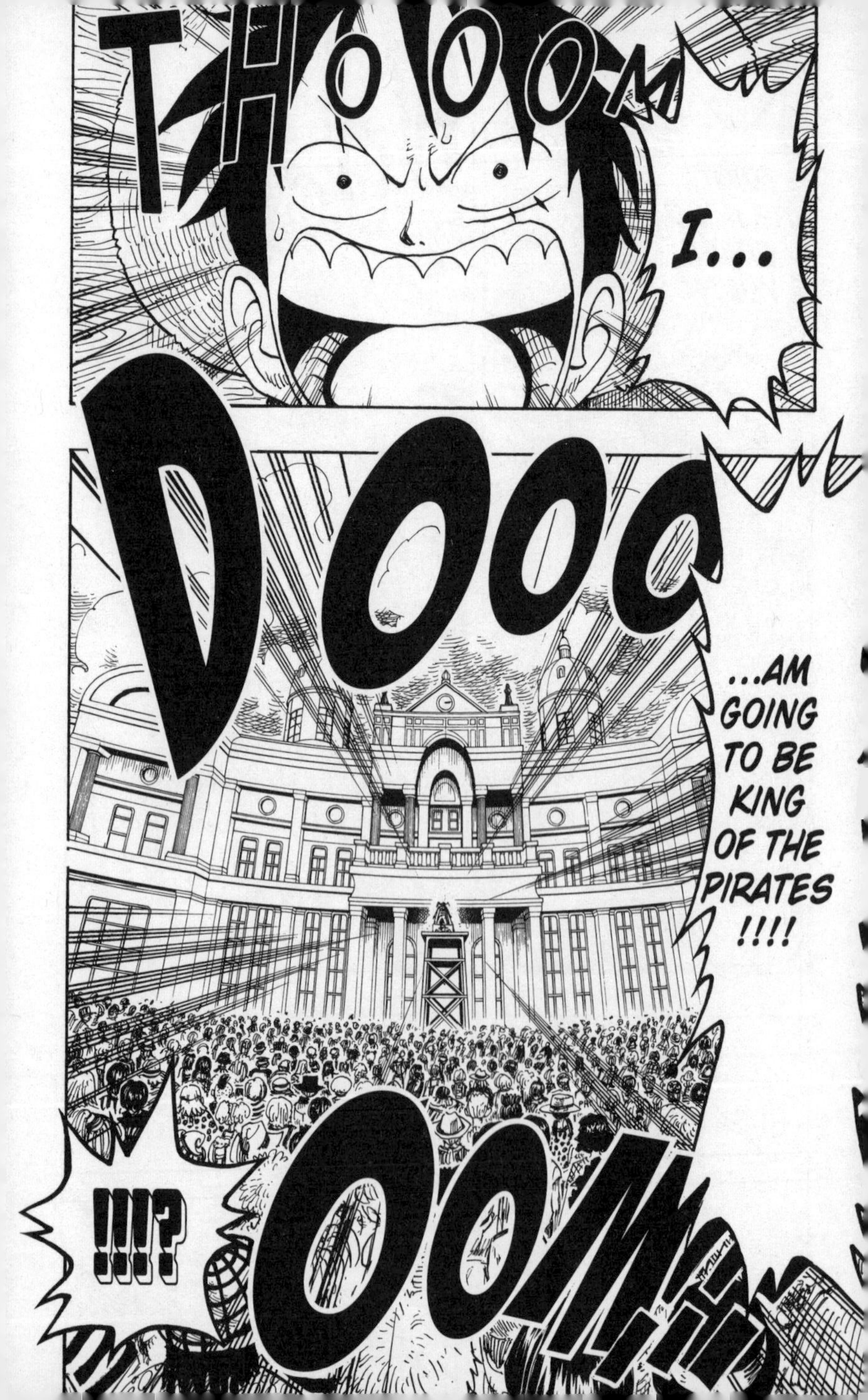

THOOOM
I...
...AM GOING TO BE KING OF THE PIRATES !!!!
DOOOOOM
!!!?

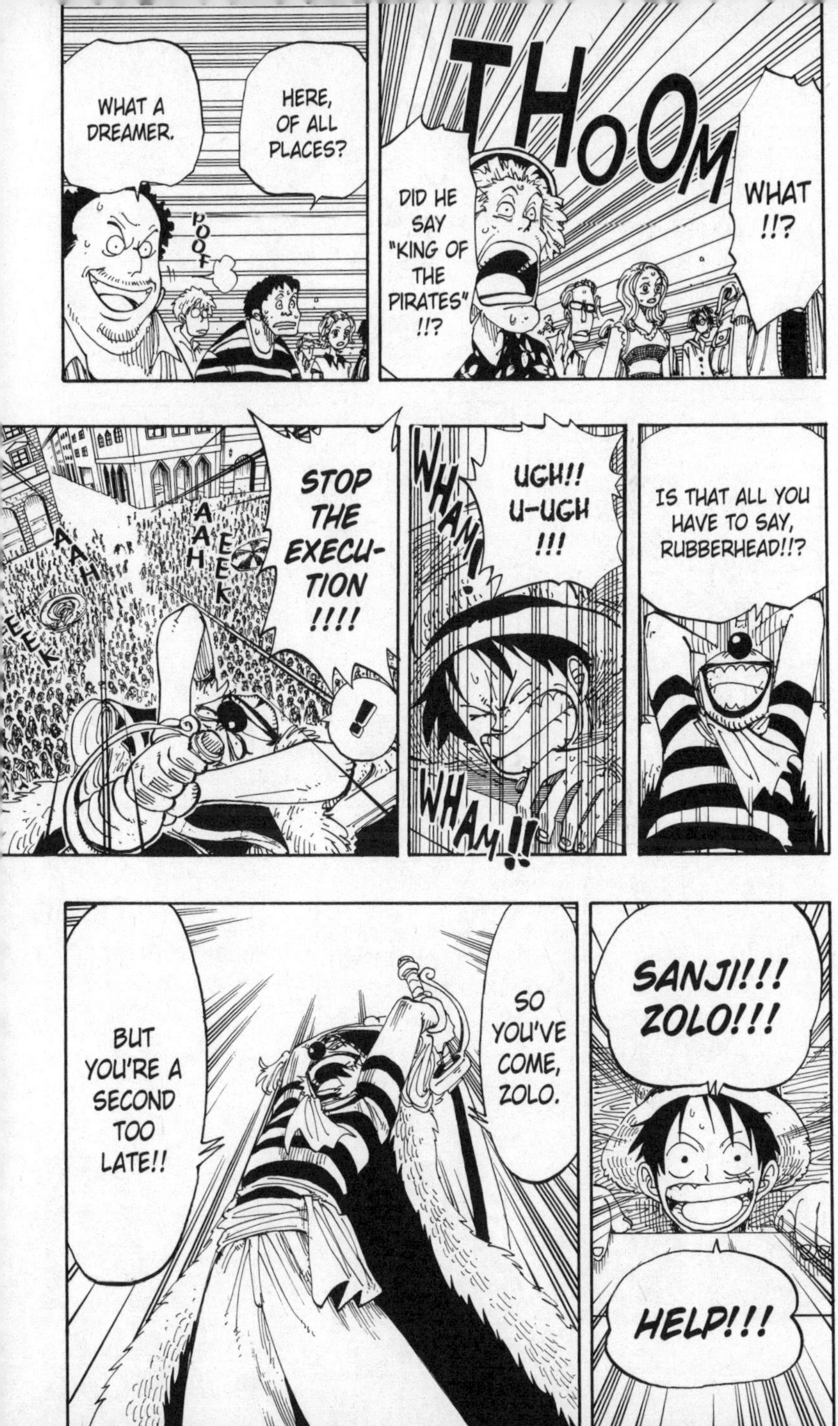
THOOM
WHAT!!?
DID HE SAY "KING OF THE PIRATES"!!?
HERE, OF ALL PLACES?
WHAT A DREAMER.
POOF
IS THAT ALL YOU HAVE TO SAY, RUBBERHEAD!!?
WHAM!
UGH!! U-UGH!!!
WHAM!!
STOP THE EXECUTION!!!!
AAH
EEK
AAH
EEK
!
SANJI!!! ZOLO!!!
HELP!!!
SO YOU'VE COME, ZOLO.
BUT YOU'RE A SECOND TOO LATE!!

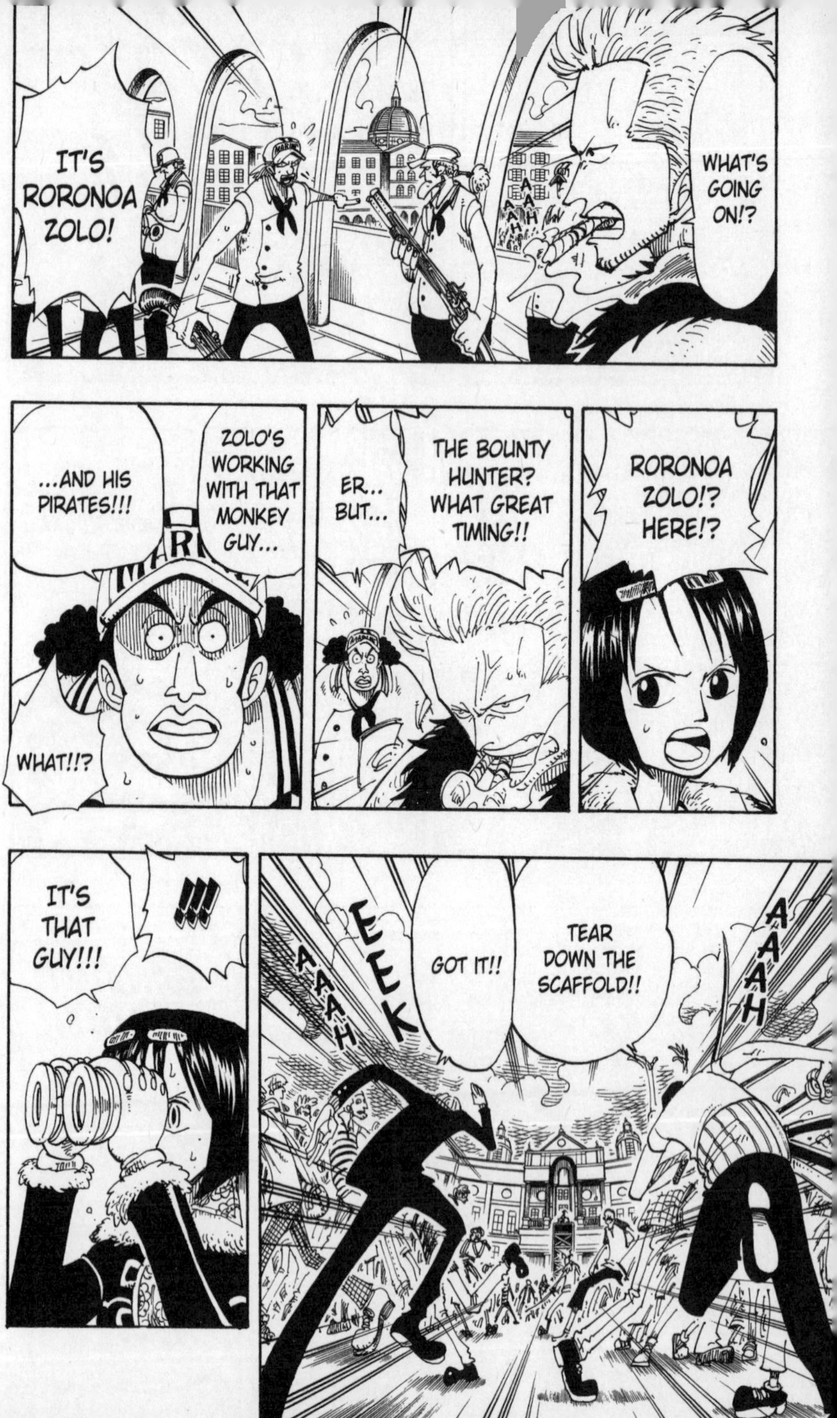
WHAT'S GOING ON!?
AAAH
IT'S RORONOA ZOLO!
RORONOA ZOLO!? HERE!?
THE BOUNTY HUNTER? WHAT GREAT TIMING!!
ER... BUT...
ZOLO'S WORKING WITH THAT MONKEY GUY...
...AND HIS PIRATES!!!
WHAT!!?
AAAH
TEAR DOWN THE SCAFFOLD!!
GOT IT!!
EEEK
AAAH
!!!
IT'S THAT GUY!!!

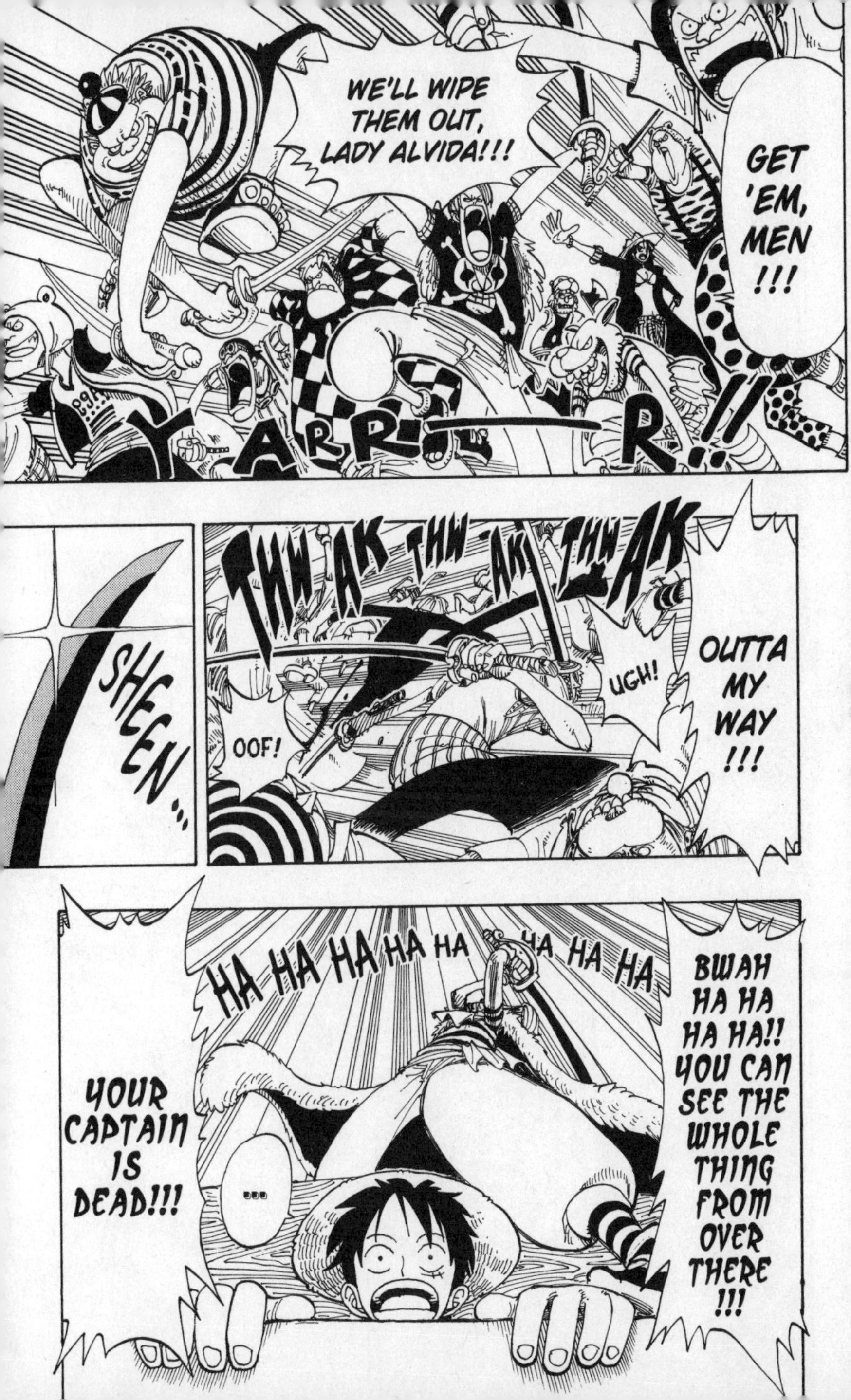
GET 'EM, MEN!!!
WE'LL WIPE THEM OUT, LADY ALVIDA!!!
YARRR——R!!
THWAK THWAK THWAK
OUTTA MY WAY!!!
UGH!
OOF!
SHEEN...
BWAH HA HA HA HA!! YOU CAN SEE THE WHOLE THING FROM OVER THERE!!!
HA HA HA HA HA HA HA HA
...
YOUR CAPTAIN IS DEAD!!!

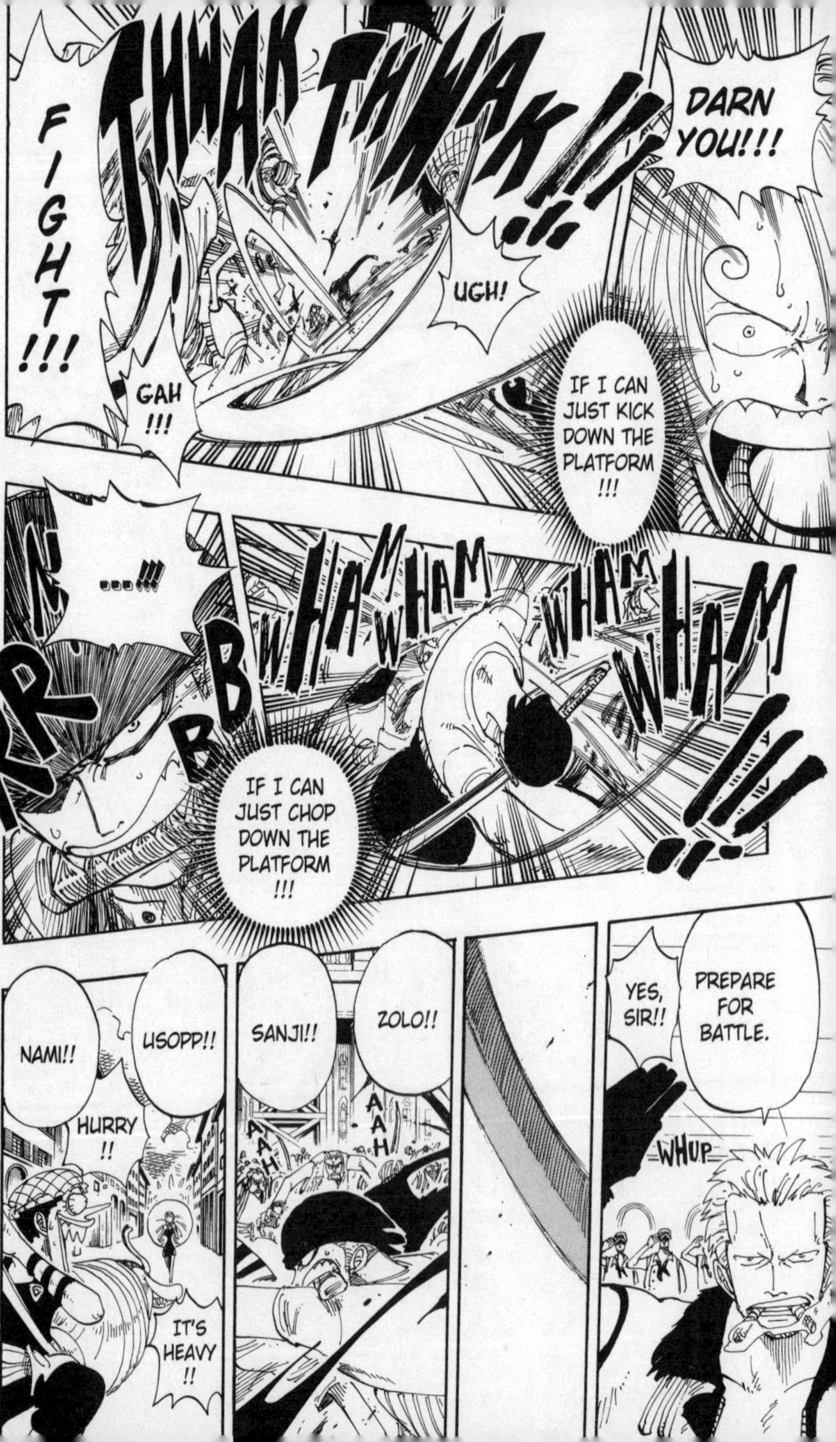

DARN YOU!!!
THWAK THWAK!!!
UGH!
IF I CAN JUST KICK DOWN THE PLATFORM !!!
FIGHT!!!
GAH !!!
WHAM WHAM WHAM WHAM!!!
IF I CAN JUST CHOP DOWN THE PLATFORM !!!
...!!!
PREPARE FOR BATTLE.
YES, SIR!!
WHUP
ZOLO!!
SANJI!!
AAAH
AAAH
USOPP!!
NAMI!!
HURRY !!
IT'S HEAVY !!

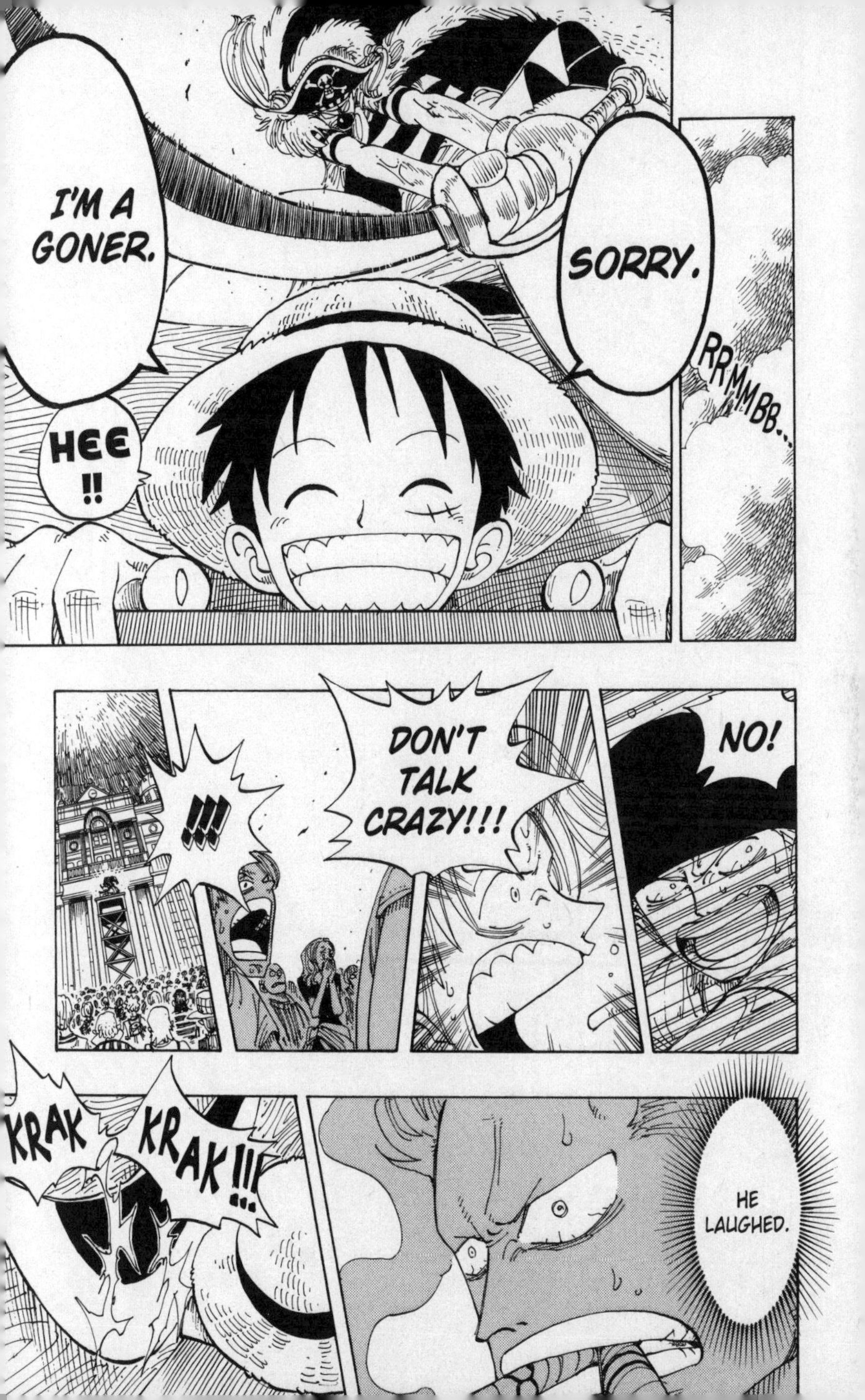
RRMMBB...
SORRY.
I'M A GONER.
HEE !!
NO!
DON'T TALK CRAZY!!!
!!!
HE LAUGHED.
KRAK KRAK!!!

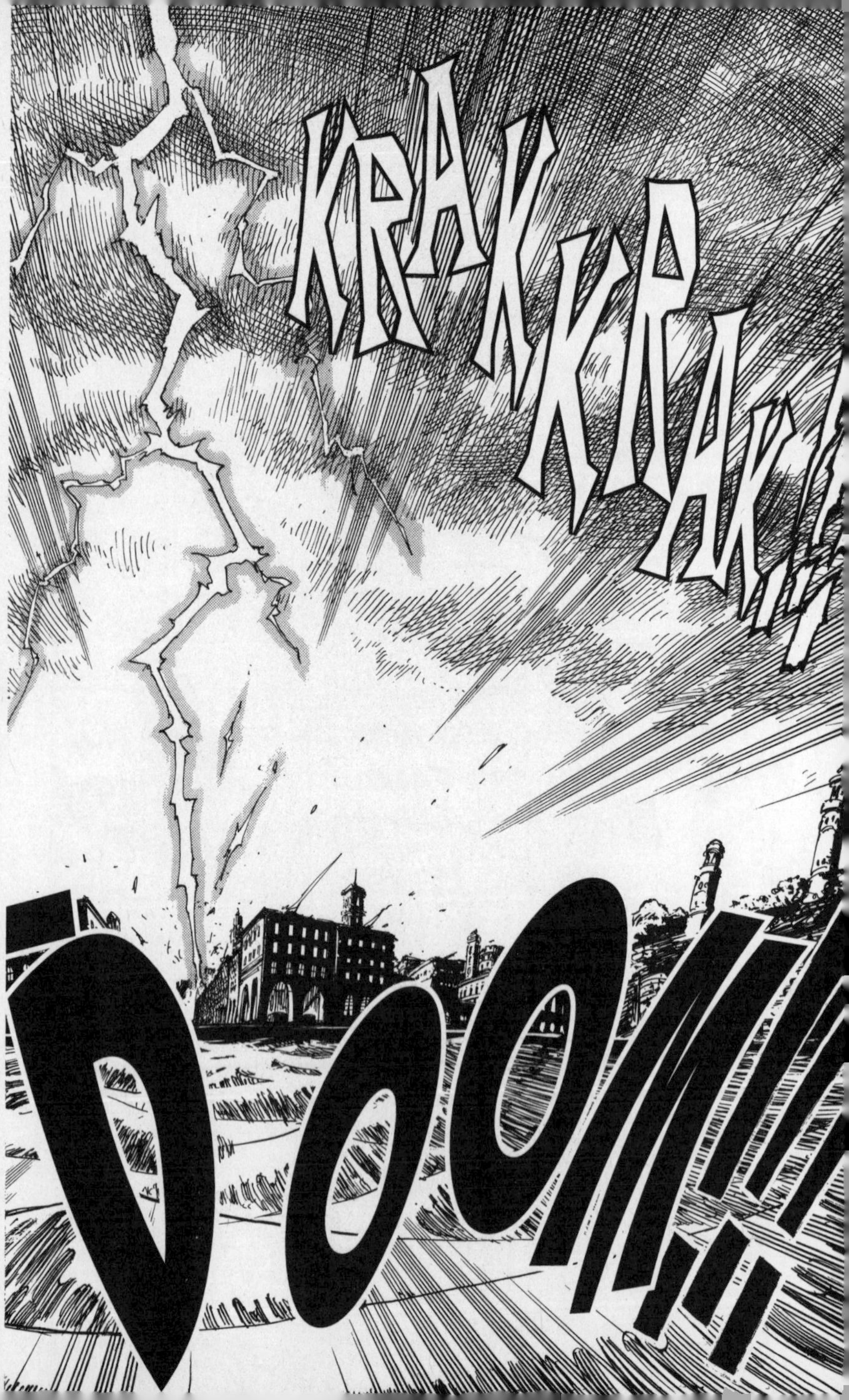
KRAK KRAK!!
DOOM!!

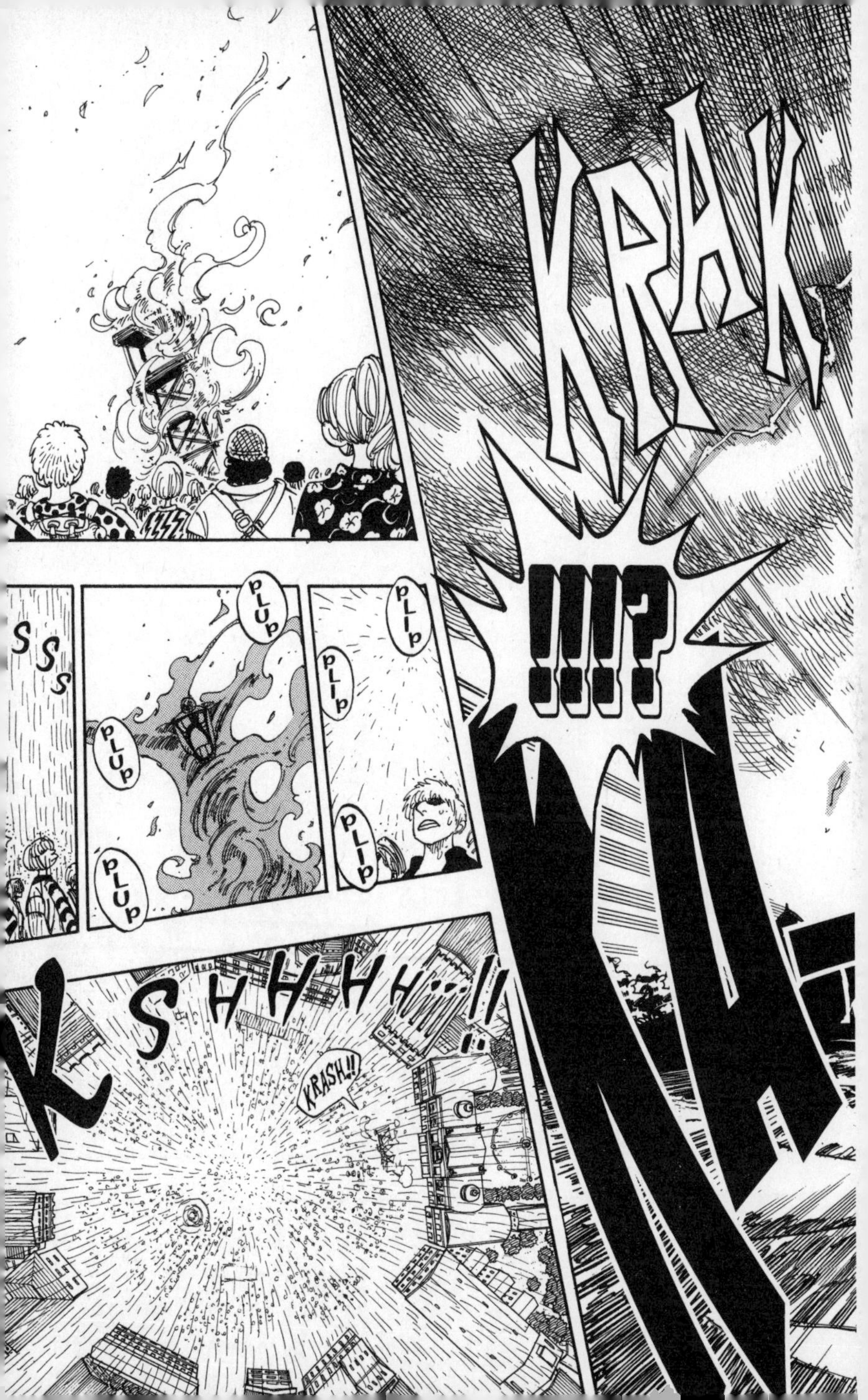
KRAK
!!!?
pLip
pLip
pLip
pLUp
pLUp
pLUp
SSS
KSHHHH...!!
KRASH!!

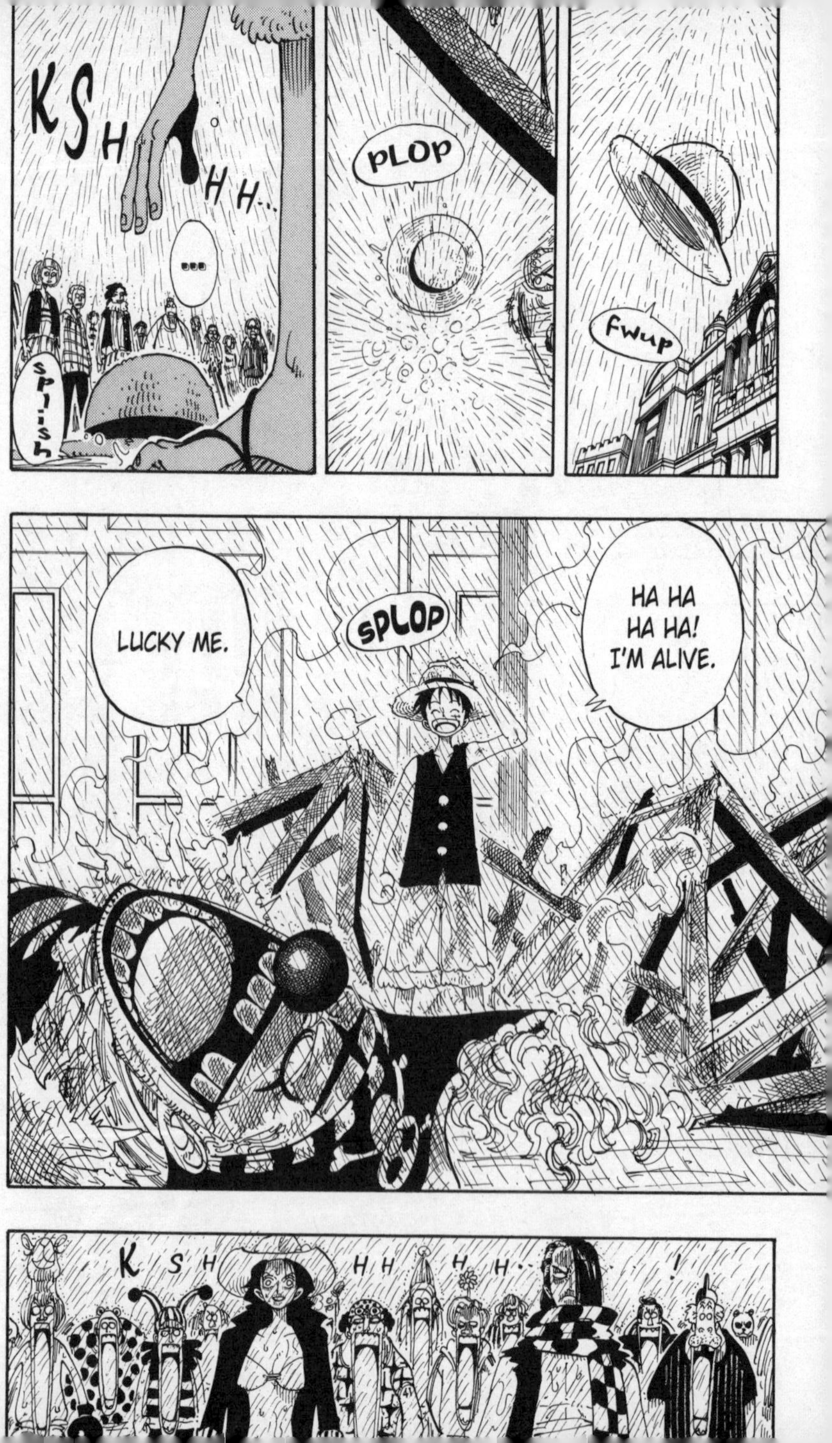
fwup
PLOP
KSHHH...
...
splish
HA HA HA HA! I'M ALIVE.
SPLOP
LUCKY ME.
KSHHHHH...!

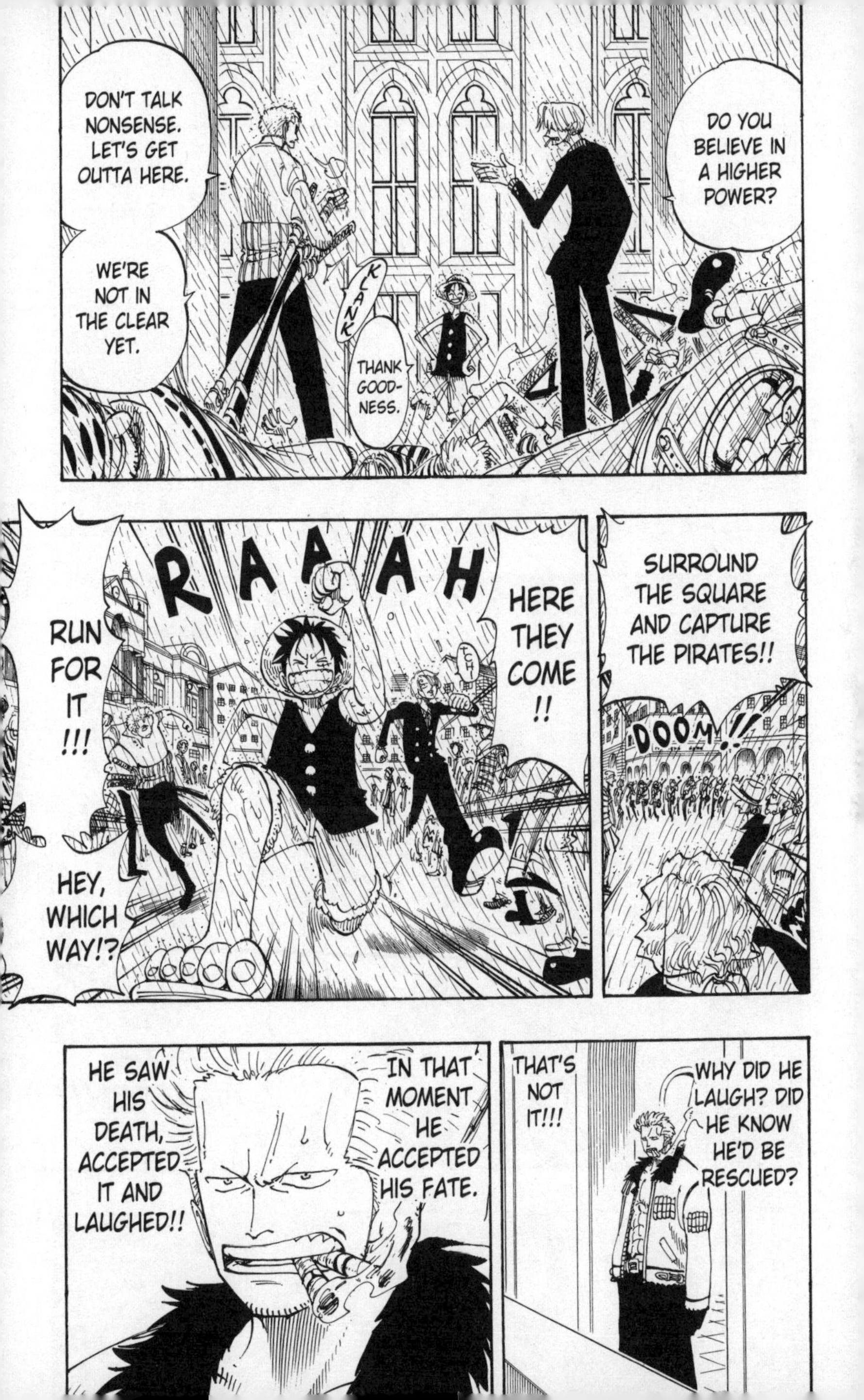
DO YOU BELIEVE IN A HIGHER POWER?
DON'T TALK NONSENSE. LET'S GET OUTTA HERE.
KLANK
THANK GOODNESS.
WE'RE NOT IN THE CLEAR YET.
SURROUND THE SQUARE AND CAPTURE THE PIRATES!!
DOOM!!
HERE THEY COME!!
RAAAH
RUN FOR IT!!!
HEY, WHICH WAY!?
WHY DID HE LAUGH? DID HE KNOW HE'D BE RESCUED?
THAT'S NOT IT!!!
IN THAT MOMENT HE ACCEPTED HIS FATE.
HE SAW HIS DEATH, ACCEPTED IT AND LAUGHED!!

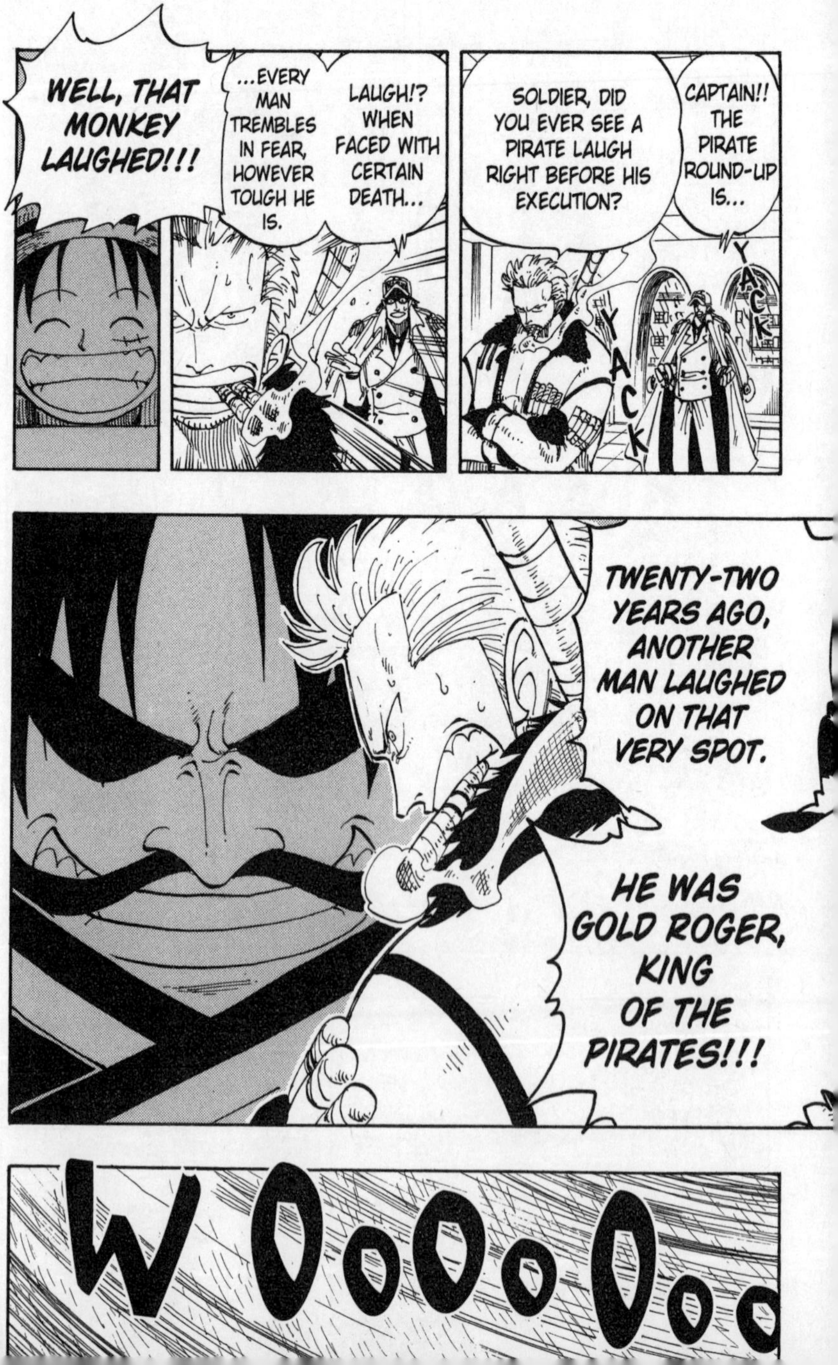
CAPTAIN!! THE PIRATE ROUND-UP IS...
YACK
SOLDIER, DID YOU EVER SEE A PIRATE LAUGH RIGHT BEFORE HIS EXECUTION?
YACK
LAUGH!? WHEN FACED WITH CERTAIN DEATH...
...EVERY MAN TREMBLES IN FEAR, HOWEVER TOUGH HE IS.
WELL, THAT MONKEY LAUGHED!!!
TWENTY-TWO YEARS AGO, ANOTHER MAN LAUGHED ON THAT VERY SPOT.
HE WAS GOLD ROGER, KING OF THE PIRATES!!!
WOOOOOOO

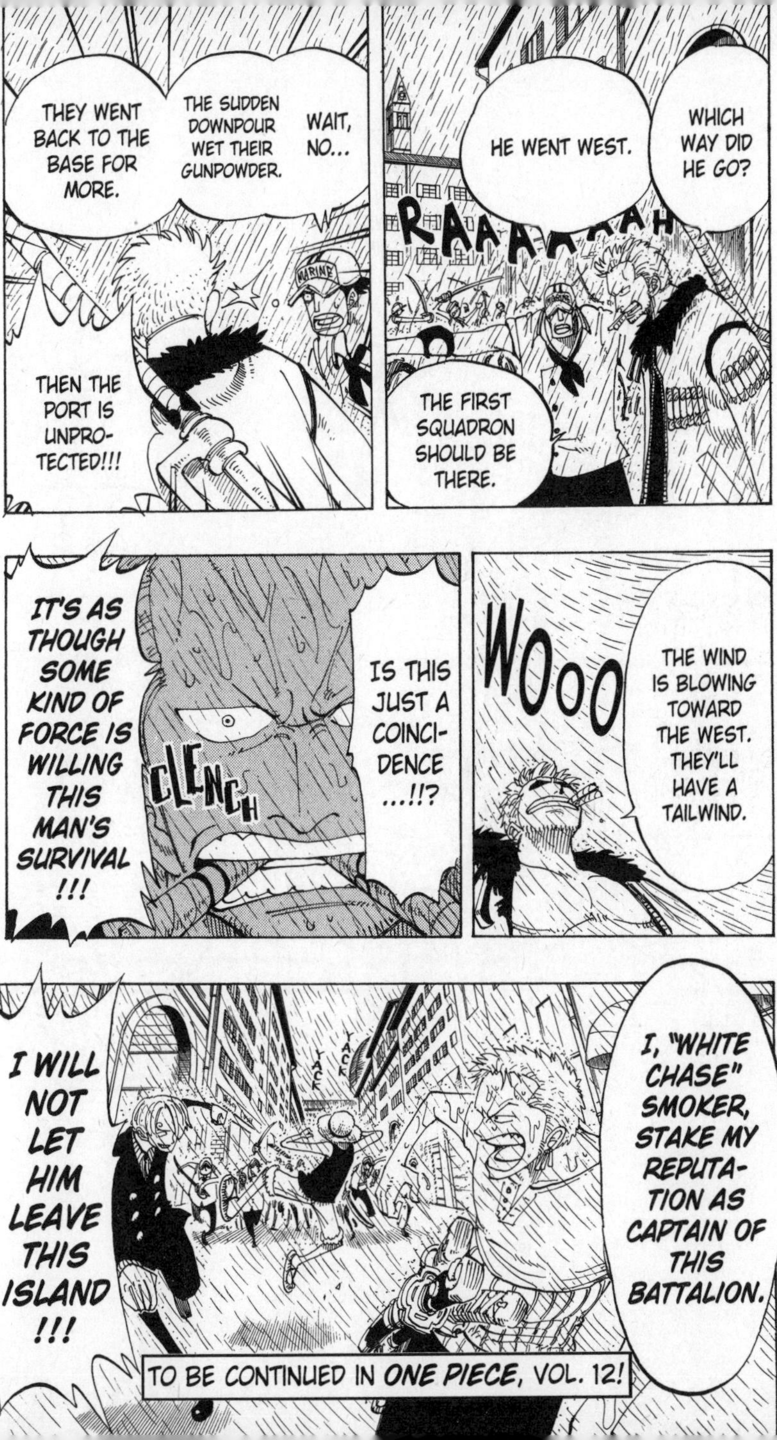
WHICH WAY DID HE GO?
HE WENT WEST.
RAAAAAAAH
THE FIRST SQUADRON SHOULD BE THERE.
WAIT, NO...
THE SUDDEN DOWNPOUR WET THEIR GUNPOWDER.
THEY WENT BACK TO THE BASE FOR MORE.
THEN THE PORT IS UNPROTECTED!!!
WOOO
THE WIND IS BLOWING TOWARD THE WEST. THEY'LL HAVE A TAILWIND.
IS THIS JUST A COINCIDENCE ...!!?
CLENCH
IT'S AS THOUGH SOME KIND OF FORCE IS WILLING THIS MAN'S SURVIVAL !!!
I, "WHITE CHASE" SMOKER, STAKE MY REPUTATION AS CAPTAIN OF THIS BATTALION.
YACK
YACK
I WILL NOT LET HIM LEAVE THIS ISLAND !!!
TO BE CONTINUED IN ONE PIECE, VOL. 12!

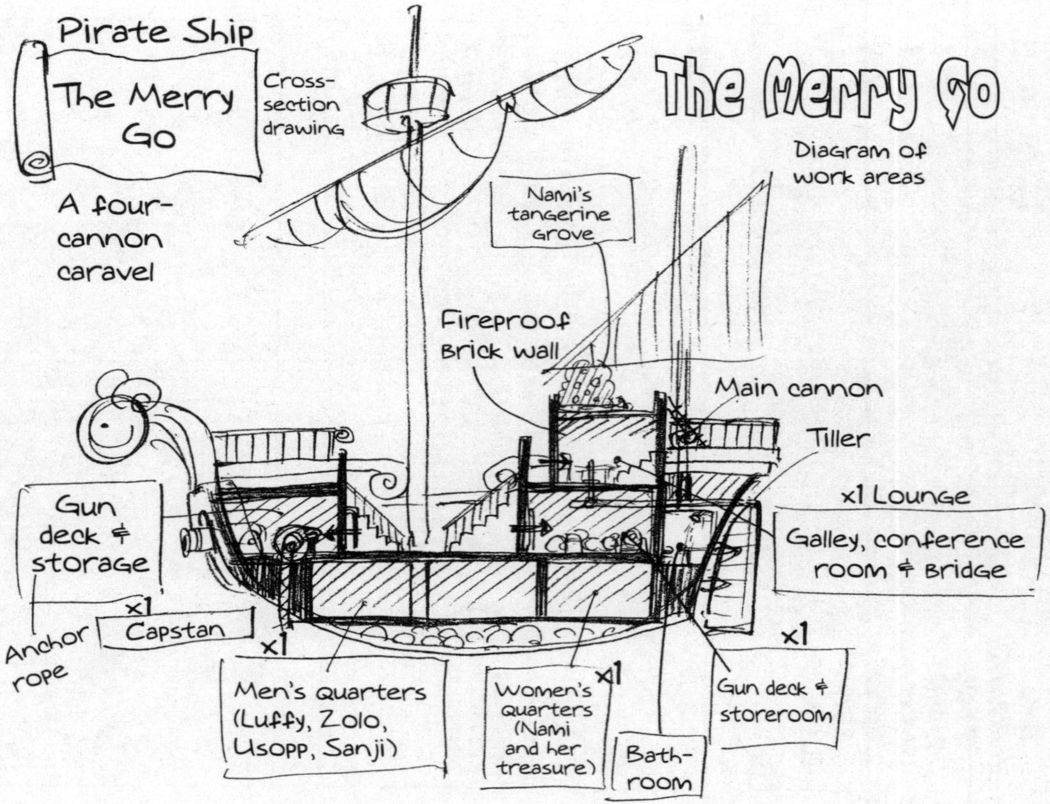
The Merry Go
Diagram of work areas
Pirate Ship
The Merry Go
Cross-section drawing
A four-cannon caravel
Nami's tangerine grove
Fireproof Brick wall
Main cannon
Tiller
x1 Lounge
Galley, conference room & Bridge
Gun deck & storage
x1
Capstan
Anchor rope
x1
Men's quarters (Luffy, Zolo, Usopp, Sanji)
x1
Women's quarters (Nami and her treasure)
Bath-room
x1
Gun deck & storeroom

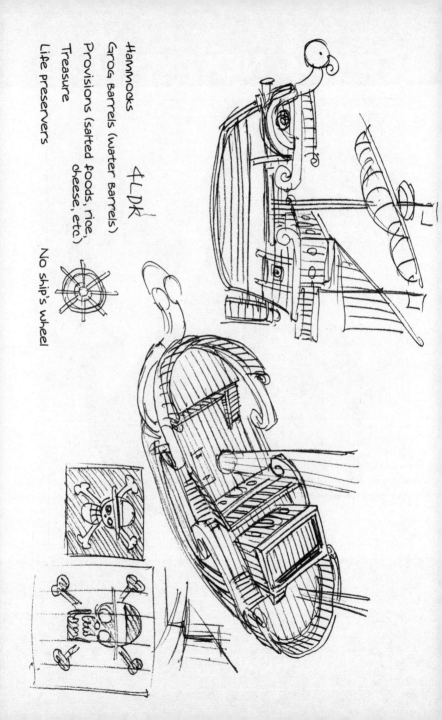

Hammocks
Grog Barrels (water barrels)
Provisions (salted foods, rice, cheese, etc.)
Treasure
Life preservers

4LDK

No ship's wheel

COMING NEXT VOLUME:

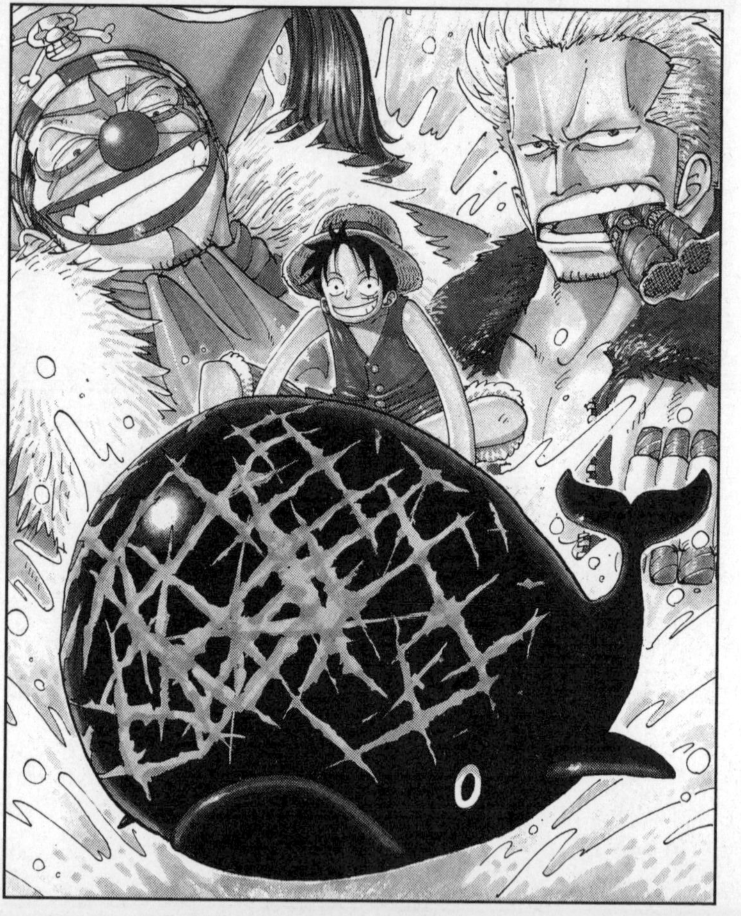

Luffy and his crew are bound for the Grand Line at last, with both newfound enemies and old ones in hot pursuit. Braving a terrible storm, the Straw Hat Pirates make their way toward what they believe is the entrance to the famed sea. But Nami's map is pointing straight up the side of a mountain!

ON SALE NOW!

Story and Art by
KOYOHARU GOTOUGE

In Taisho-era Japan, kindhearted Tanjiro Kamado makes a living selling charcoal. But his peaceful life is shattered when a demon slaughters his entire family. His little sister Nezuko is the only survivor, but she has been transformed into a demon herself! Tanjiro sets out on a dangerous journey to find a way to return his sister to normal and destroy the demon who ruined his life.

KIMETSU NO YAIBA © 2016 by Koyoharu Gotouge/SHUEISHA Inc.

THE ACTION-PACKED SUPERHERO COMEDY ABOUT ONE MAN'S AMBITION TO BE A HERO FOR FUN!

ONE-PUNCH MAN

STORY BY
ONE | ART BY
YUSUKE MURATA

Nothing about Saitama passes the eyeball test when it comes to superheroes, from his lifeless expression to his bald head to his unimpressive physique. However, this average-looking guy has a not-so-average problem—he just can't seem to find an opponent strong enough to take on!

Can he finally find an opponent who can go toe-to-toe with him and give his life some meaning? Or is he doomed to a life of superpowered boredom?

ONE-PUNCH MAN © 2012 by ONE, Yusuke Murata/SHUEISHA Inc.

  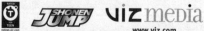

www.viz.com

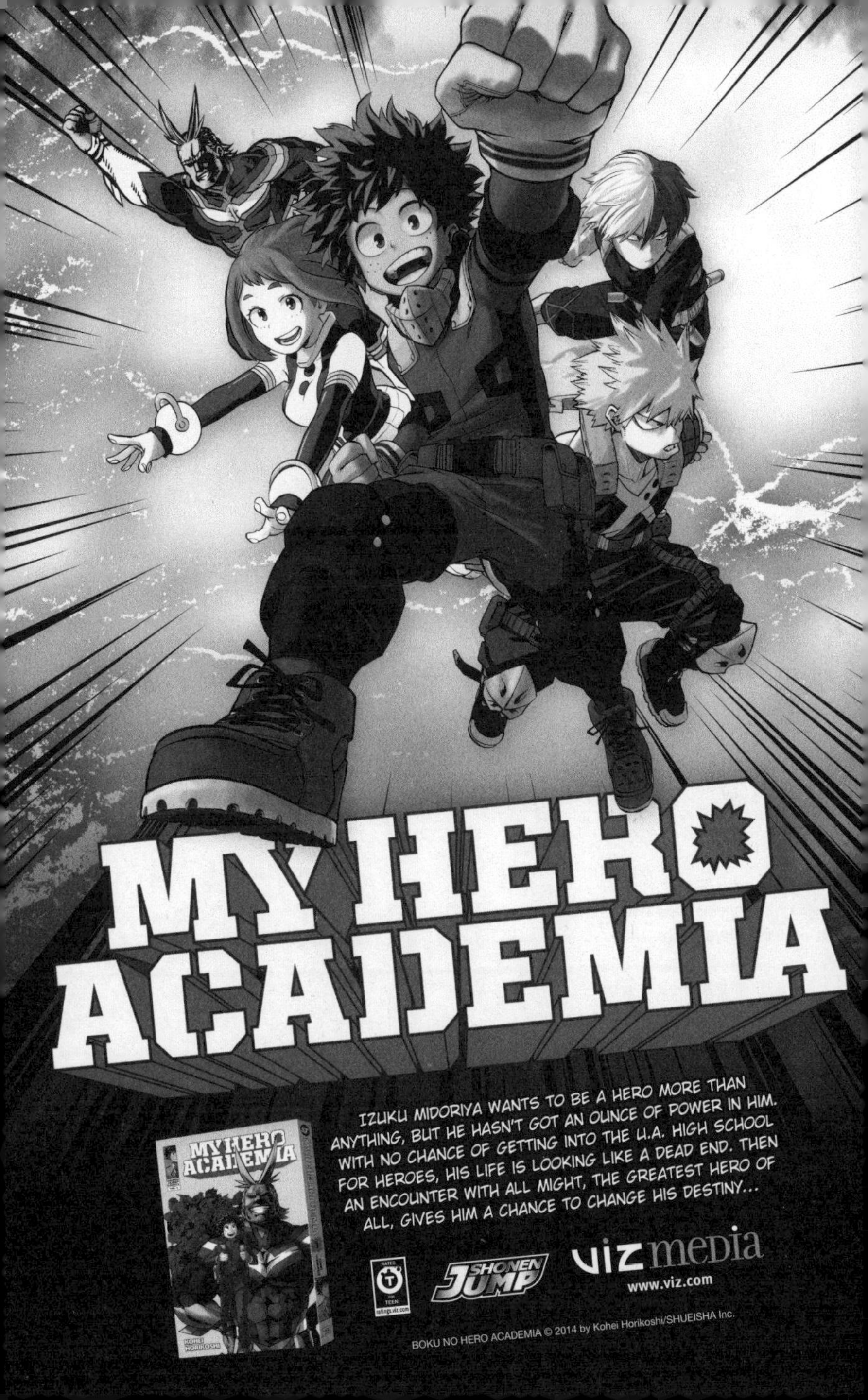
MY HERO ACADEMIA
IZUKU MIDORIYA WANTS TO BE A HERO MORE THAN ANYTHING, BUT HE HASN'T GOT AN OUNCE OF POWER IN HIM. WITH NO CHANCE OF GETTING INTO THE U.A. HIGH SCHOOL FOR HEROES, HIS LIFE IS LOOKING LIKE A DEAD END. THEN AN ENCOUNTER WITH ALL MIGHT, THE GREATEST HERO OF ALL, GIVES HIM A CHANCE TO CHANGE HIS DESTINY…
MY HERO ACADEMIA
KOHEI HORIKOSHI
RATED T TEEN ratings.viz.com
SHONEN JUMP
viz media
www.viz.com
BOKU NO HERO ACADEMIA © 2014 by Kohei Horikoshi/SHUEISHA Inc.

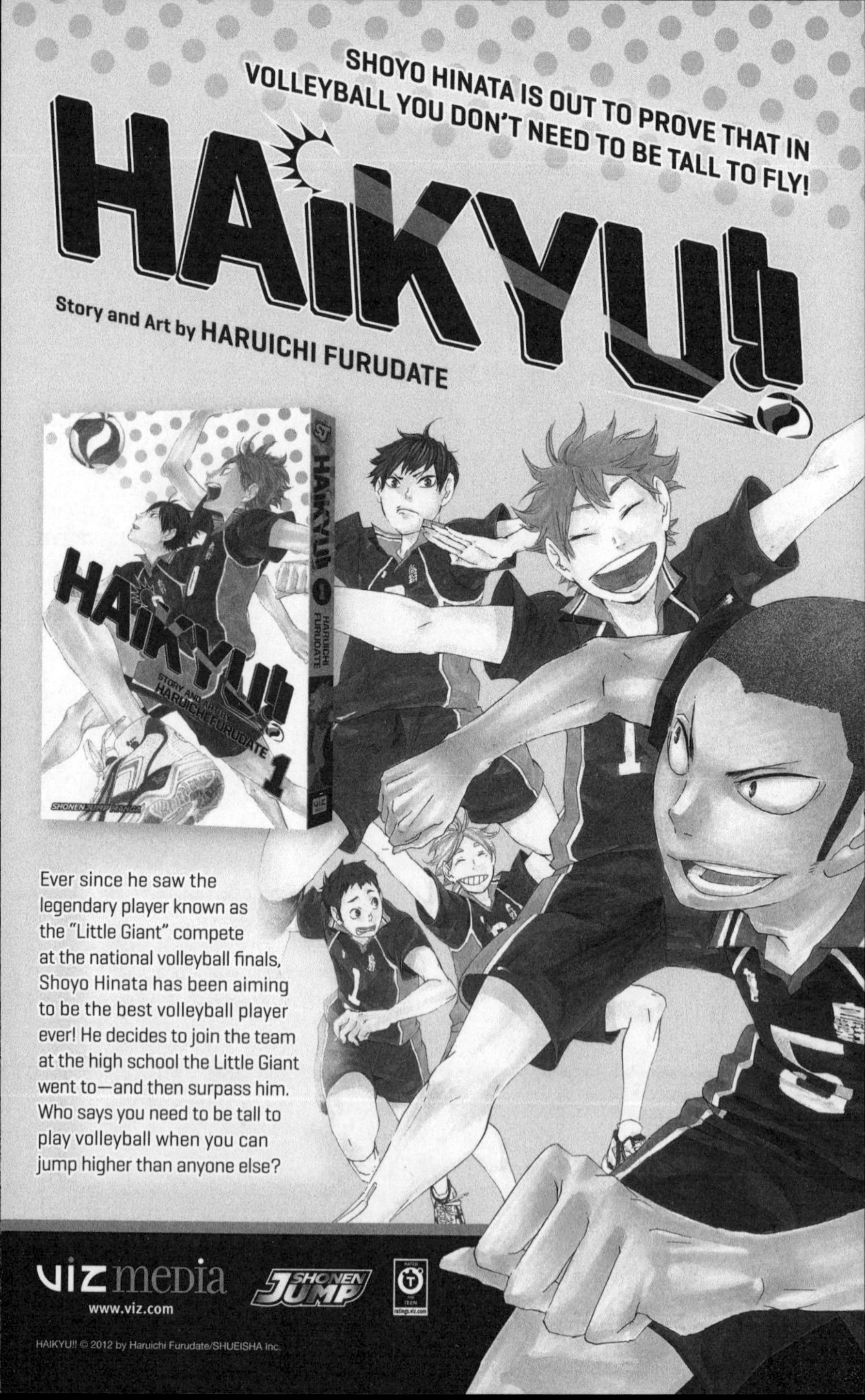
SHOYO HINATA IS OUT TO PROVE THAT IN VOLLEYBALL YOU DON'T NEED TO BE TALL TO FLY!
HAIKYU!!
Story and Art by HARUICHI FURUDATE
HAIKYU!! 1
STORY AND ART BY HARUICHI FURUDATE
SHONEN JUMP MANGA
Ever since he saw the legendary player known as the "Little Giant" compete at the national volleyball finals, Shoyo Hinata has been aiming to be the best volleyball player ever! He decides to join the team at the high school the Little Giant went to—and then surpass him. Who says you need to be tall to play volleyball when you can jump higher than anyone else?
viz media
www.viz.com
SHONEN JUMP
RATED T FOR TEEN ratings.viz.com
HAIKYU!! © 2012 by Haruichi Furudate/SHUEISHA Inc.

Kuroko's BASKETBALL

TADATOSHI FUJIMAKI

When incoming first-year student Taiga Kagami joins the Seirin High basketball team, he meets Tetsuya Kuroko, a mysterious boy who's plain beyond words. But Kagami's in for the shock of his life when he learns that the practically invisible Kuroko was once a member of "the Miracle Generation"—the undefeated legendary team—and he wants Kagami's help taking down each of his old teammates!

THE HIT SPORTS MANGA FROM _SHONEN JUMP_ IN A 2-IN-1 EDITION!

www.viz.com

KUROKO NO BASUKE © 2008 by Tadatoshi Fujimaki/SHUEISHA Inc.

You're Reading in the Wrong Direction!!

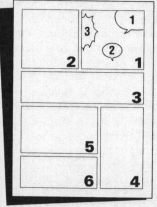

Whoops! Guess what? You're starting at the wrong end of the comic!

...It's true! In keeping with the original Japanese format, **One Piece** is meant to be read from right to left, starting in the upper-right corner.

Unlike English, which is read from left to right, Japanese is read from right to left, meaning that action, sound effects and word-balloon order are completely reversed... something which can make readers unfamiliar with Japanese feel pretty backwards themselves. For this reason, manga or Japanese comics published in the U.S. in English have sometimes been published "flopped"– that is, printed in exact reverse order, as though seen from the other side of a mirror.

By flopping pages, U.S. publishers can avoid confusing readers, but the compromise is not without its downside. For one thing, a character in a flopped manga series who once wore in the original Japanese version a T-shirt emblazoned with "M A Y" (as in "the merry month of") now wears one which reads "Y A M"! Additionally, many manga creators in Japan are themselves unhappy with the process, as some feel the mirror-imaging of their art skews their original intentions.

We are proud to bring you Eiichiro Oda's **One Piece** in the original unflopped format. For now, though, turn to the other side of the book and let the journey begin...!

–Editor